C000243688

EARLY MODERN GERMAN SHAKESPEARE VOLUME 2

Other titles

Early Modern German Shakespeare Volume 1
Hamlet and *Romeo and Juliet: Der Bestrafte Brudermord* and
Romio und Julieta in Translation

https://www.unige.ch/emgs

EARLY MODERN GERMAN SHAKESPEARE: *TITUS ANDRONICUS* AND *THE TAMING OF THE SHREW*

William Shakespeare
Tito Andronico and *Kunst über alle Künste,*
ein bös Weib gut zu machen in Translation

Edited by
LUKAS ERNE, FLORENCE HAZRAT AND MARIA SHMYGOL
Advisory Editor: Professor Tiffany Stern,
the Shakespeare Institute, University of Birmingham, UK

THE ARDEN SHAKESPEARE
LONDON • NEW YORK • OXFORD • NEW DELHI • SYDNEY

THE ARDEN SHAKESPEARE
Bloomsbury Publishing Plc
50 Bedford Square, London, WC1B 3DP, UK
1385 Broadway, New York, NY 10018, USA
29 Earlsfort Terrace, Dublin 2, Ireland

BLOOMSBURY, THE ARDEN SHAKESPEARE and the Arden Shakespeare logo are
trademarks of Bloomsbury Publishing Plc

First published in Great Britain 2022
This paperback edition published in 2023

Cover design: Charlotte Daniels
Cover image: *Singing Boy with a Flute*, between 1623 and 1625,
Frans Hals. (© Alamy Stock Photo)

A catalogue record for this book is available from the British Library.

A catalog record for this book is available from the Library of Congress.

ISBN: HB: 978-1-3500-9475-8
        PB: 978-1-3502-6243-0
        ePDF: 978-1-3500-9477-2
        eBook: 978-1-3500-9476-5

Typeset by RefineCatch Limited, Bungay, Suffolk

To find out more about our authors and books visit www.bloomsbury.com
and sign up for our newsletters.

The Editors

Lukas Erne is Professor of English Literature at the University of Geneva. He is the author of *Shakespeare as Literary Dramatist* (2003; 2nd edn 2013) and *Shakespeare and the Book Trade* (2013). He gave the Lyell Lectures at the University of Oxford in 2012.

Florence Hazrat is a Leverhulme Early Career Fellow at the University of Sheffield. She is author of *Standing on Points: The History and Culture of Punctuation* (forthcoming) and *Refrains in Early Modern Literature* (forthcoming).

Maria Shmygol is a Research Fellow on the 'Complete Works of John Marston' project at the University of Leeds. She is the editor of William Percy's *The Aphrodysial* (1602) in the Malone Society Reprints series (forthcoming 2022).

For Anthony Mortimer

CONTENTS

LIST OF
ILLUSTRATIONS

LIST OF TABLES

ACKNOWLEDGEMENTS

The Swiss National Science Foundation (SNSF) generously funded research towards this edition and subsidized the digital as well as the pre-print stage of the bibliographic versions of the present publication. For their assistance, we wish to thank Christine Etienne, Regula Graf, Maude Joye and Katharine Weder. At the University of Geneva, where the research project was undertaken, we received help from Nadège Berdoz, Philippe Coet, Anne-Lise Farquet Severi, Delphine Goldschmidt-Clermont, Frédéric Goubier, Isabelle Kronegg, Angela Simondetta, Clare Tierque, Roxana Vicovanu and Hélène Vincent. We also wish to acknowledge the generous assistance and advice we have received from many librarians, notably at the Beinecke Rare Book & Manuscript Library, the Bibliothèque de Genève, the Bibliothèque de l'Université de Genève, the Folger Shakespeare Library, the Herzog August Bibliothek Wolfenbüttel, the Herzogin Anna Amalia Bibliothek Weimar, the Kislak Center at the University of Pennsylvania, the Österreichische Nationalbibliothek, the Staatsbibliothek Bamberg, the Staatsbibliothek zu Berlin, the Staats- und Universitätsbibliothek Dresden, the Universitäts- und Landesbibliothek Sachsen-Anhalt, the Universitätsbibliothek Kassel, the LMU Universitätsbibliothek München, the University of Chicago Library, the Uppsala Universitetsbibliotek, the Wienbibliothek im Rathaus, and the Württembergische Landesbibliothek Stuttgart. Special thanks to Christoph Boveland and Andreas Herz at the Herzog August Bibliothek Wolfenbüttel for assistance well beyond the call of duty.

The present book is the second of two 'Early Modern German Shakespeare' volumes published by the Arden Shakespeare, following *Hamlet and Romeo and Juliet: Der Bestrafte Brudermord and Romio und Julieta in Translation*, edited by Lukas Erne and Kareen Seidler (2020). As co-editor of the companion volume, Kareen has had an impact on the present volume in manifold ways. The two volumes belong to the same editorial project, and our editorial principles have been applied to each of the four plays published in the two volumes. The 'Note on the commentary and collation' and the 'Note on the translations' partly draw on the corresponding notes in the *Brudermord* and *Romio und Julieta* volume.

A word about the nature of the collaboration among the three editors that has led to the present volume over the last six years. Lukas initiated the project, secured the funding and first elaborated the principles informing the translation and editing, many of which were later adjusted and refined thanks to input by Florence and Maria. Maria worked with Lukas on *Tito Andronico*, and Florence and Lukas on *Kunst über alle Künste*. Maria and Florence produced a conservative German text (see below, p. xvii), with textual notes, and drafted the translation, commentary, collation and large parts of the introduction. Lukas checked and provided feedback on all these components, from where the work developed in conversation. Late in the process, Lukas revised and added to the introductions and the commentaries, and, later still, we shared the labour of seeing this volume into print. Our collaboration also benefited from countless conversations among the three of us during our joint time in Geneva. It has been an exhilarating and stimulating process that has allowed each of us to benefit greatly from the other two.

While our editorial work was in progress, we had the pleasure of organizing staged readings of *Tito Andronico* and *Kunst über alle Künste*, in our English translations, at the University of Geneva in June and November 2017. We thank all those who participated in those memorable and insightful events, in particular Aleida Auld, Amy Brown, Emma Depledge, Valerie Fehlbaum, Jeanne Gressot, Lexie Intrator, Elizabeth Kukorelly, Vincent Laughery, Jia Liu, Roberta Marangi, Giuseppe Samo, Kilian Schindler, Anne Schutt-West, Devani Singh and Bryn

Skibo-Birney. We further wish to acknowledge the kind help we have received from René Wetzel on early modern German, Damien Nelis on Latin, and Paul Schubert on ancient Greek. Other colleagues who have generously discussed with us aspects of our editions and provided assistance of various kinds include Guillemette Bolens, Emma Depledge, Tobias Döring, Neil Forsyth, Indira Ghose, Ton Hoenselaars, Zachary Lesser, Noémie Ndiaye, Scott Newstok, June Schlueter, Kareen Seidler, Tiffany Stern, Michael Suarez, Anna Swärdh, Bart van Es and Richard Waswo. Our heartfelt thanks to them all.

The Doctoral Workshop in Medieval and Early Modern English Studies at the University of Geneva offered a friendly and inspiring venue in which to present our work in progress. A seminar devoted to 'Shakespearean Drama and the Early Modern European Stage' at the conference of the European Shakespeare Research Association (ESRA) in Gdansk in July 2017 allowed us to discuss some of our ideas as they were taking shape and to receive incisive feedback from colleagues. Special thanks to Ton Hoenselaars, who co-led the seminar and provided helpful advice about our edition during the conference. In the context of the Geneva–Exeter Renaissance Exchange (GEREx), undertaken by members of the English departments of the Universities of Geneva and Exeter and generously subsidized by the two universities, we have initiated a stimulating conversation with Pascale Aebischer, Freyja Cox Jensen and Harry McCarthy about innovative ways of exploring early modern German Shakespeare adaptations which we now plan to develop. Maria's work on *Tito* has benefited from participation in Curtis Perry and Marissa Nicosia's seminar on 'Shakespearean Distortions of Early Modern Drama' at the Shakespeare Association (SAA) Annual Meeting in 2017, and Karen Newman's seminar on 'Continental Shakespeare' at SAA 2018; she is grateful to the hosts and seminar participants, particularly Anston Bosman, Ton Hoenseelars, M. A. Katritzky and Noémie Ndiaye, who provided detailed feedback on her papers. Maria is likewise grateful to the Folger Shakespeare Library for supporting her work through a short-term fellowship.

At the Arden Shakespeare, Margaret Bartley has provided untiring support, and we are grateful to her anonymous external readers for incisive input. Our advisory editor, Tiffany Stern, provided immensely helpful feedback to a draft of the complete typescript. When this book was in production, we benefited from the labours of Lara Bateman, Meredith Benson, Ian Buck, Ronnie Hanna and Merv Honeywood.

We have been very fortunate to benefit from Anthony Mortimer's help and expertise over the years. He has read and helpfully commented on every part of this volume (and its companion volume), has much improved our prose translation and has translated the verse passages and poems in *Kunst* based on our prose renderings. He has truly been a model of generosity. In gratitude for all his kind help and encouragement this book is dedicated to him.

Finally, on a more personal note, we wish to thank those whose love and support have been the rock on which this book was built: Katrin, Rebecca, Raphael and Miriam; Habibi and Juro; and Anatoliy, Svitlana and Douglas.

Lukas Erne
Florence Hazrat
Maria Shmygol

PREFACE

The present is the second of two 'Early Modern German Shakespeare' volumes published by the Arden Shakespeare. Volume 1 (2020), edited by Lukas Erne and Kareen Seidler, contains *Der Bestrafte Brudermord* (in English *Fratricide Punished*), a version of *Hamlet*, and *Romio und Julieta* (*Romeo and Juliet*). Volume 2 adds *Tito Andronico* (*Titus Andronicus*) and *Kunst über alle Künste, ein bös Weib gut zu machen*, in English *An Art beyond All Arts, to Make a Bad Wife Good* (*The Taming of the Shrew*). Jointly, the two volumes make available in English translation the best versions of Shakespeare's plays as they existed in seventeenth-century Germany.

The aim of Arden's 'Early Modern German Shakespeare' edition is to make these versions join the conversation about Shakespeare's texts. As scholars have come to realize, many of Shakespeare's English texts embed within themselves the contributions of actors, revisers and adapters. They are socialized products, in keeping with the eminently socialized art form that is theatre. We have been used to thinking of Shakespeare's socialized early modern texts as purely English, but such monolingualism imposes upon them a restriction that simply does not square with the international traffic of early modern theatre companies and their plays. From the late sixteenth century, plays that were performed in commercial theatres in London also had an existence elsewhere, not only in the provinces but also on the Continent, and in particular its German-speaking parts. At a time when the United Kingdom has recently left the European Union, it seems a good moment to remember that Shakespeare's plays have always also been European, and that we have much to gain from recovering the life they led on the Continent.

We acknowledge that the German-English language barrier may be a greater obstacle in the modern world of scholarship than it was in the early modern world of the theatre. German is no longer the language of learning that it was in the nineteenth century, and the language of international Shakespeare scholarship is now emphatically English. Editing Shakespeare's early modern German plays in German therefore means cutting them off from the attention of most Shakespeareans. That is the reason why the present volume and its companion volume make the plays available in English translation. We have also prepared editions of the original German texts, with short introductions and textual notes, and they are available online and for download on the University of Geneva's institutional repository, 'Archive ouverte UNIGE', at https://doi. org/10.13097/archive-ouverte/unige:150834 (*Tito Andronico*) and https://doi.org/10.13097/archive-ouverte/unige:150835 (*Kunst über alle Künste*).

The preface to the first volume of our 'Early Modern German Shakespeare' edition provides short introductions to the presence of English actors on the Continent from the late sixteenth century and to Shakespeare's contributions to the repertoires of early modern German theatre companies. It also supplies an illustration of the impact a passage in an early modern German version can have on our editorial and critical reception of a Shakespeare play. These prefatory materials, which are relevant to both volumes, are not repeated here (see Erne and Seidler, xiv–xxi).

Tito Andronico and *Kunst über alle Künste* have the distinction of being, respectively, the earliest and the best of the extant early modern German Shakespeare versions. *Tito Andronico* was published in a dramatic collection that appeared in 1620. The earliest dramatic collection containing a Shakespeare play was thus not the First Folio, published in London in 1623, but the *Engelische Comedien vnd Tragedien* (*English Comedies and Tragedies*) published in octavo in Leipzig, Germany, and in German. Its early date means that it is closely connected to and can throw light on several Titus documents, not only Shakespeare's play but also the Peacham Drawing and the chapbook prose history of Titus Andronicus. As our edition aims to show, it is a key witness to the early history of Shakespeare's play.[1]

Published in two duodecimo editions dated 1672, *Kunst über alle Künste* bears witness to the sophistication German drama had acquired in the half-century since *Tito*. While it essentially preserves the *dramatis personae* and plot outline of *The Taming of the Shrew* (except for the Induction), and at times follows the original speech by speech and almost word for word, it also confidently reworks and elaborates on it. It constitutes a shrewd engagement with Shakespeare's play, keenly alert to its dramatic potential and attuned to its gender and social issues while not afraid of positioning itself differently vis-à-vis those points.

Shakespeare's has long become the epitome of dramatic authorship, but his seventeenth-century German translators and adaptors remain shrouded in mystery. *Der Bestrafte Brudermord* was probably revised for performance by the company of Carl Andreas Paulsen in the 1660s and *Romio und Julieta* for performance by Eggenberg's Comedians at the court theatre of Český Krumlov (Bohemian Krumlov) in 1688, but who undertook the revisions is now beyond recovery (Erne and Seidler, 28–31, 90–100). Contrary to what might be expected, the earliest of the four plays, *Tito Andronico*, is the only one for which we can name a writer who was almost certainly involved in the adaptation: Friedrich Menius, a colourful figure who was prosecuted and condemned for both bigamy and heresy. Yet the exact form that Menius's involvement took is far from clear (see below, pp. 64–74). *Kunst über alle Künste* is the work of an adaptor who is identified as a 'Teutsche[r] Edelman', a German gentleman, on the title page; he writes an address to

---

[1]   For the co-authorship of *Titus Andronicus*, see below, p. 2, n. 1.

the reader in a distinctive voice but chooses to remain anonymous. To paraphrase the characteristically poignant formulation with which he explains his anonymity, it does not matter what a kitten is called, provided it catches mice (see below, pp. 140–3). While little is known about the identity of Shakespeare's early modern German translators and adaptors, the plays published in this and its companion volume bear witness to the ingenuity of their dramatic engagement with Shakespeare's drama.

INTRODUCTION TO
TITO ANDRONICO
(*TITUS ANDRONICUS*)

Until not so long ago, *Titus Andronicus*, first published in London in 1594, was considered a barbarous and savage play. Generations of critics were repulsed by what they saw as its excessive violence, and passed it off as a piece of Shakespeare's juvenilia or denied that he wrote it at all.[1] Yet it was that very violence which made the story of Titus Andronicus immensely popular in its own day, both in England and on the Continent. When English travelling actors performed plays in their native tongue in the Netherlands and in Germany, the audience's lack of linguistic comprehension was compensated for by physical action and, in the case of versions of *Titus*, by displays of spectacular violence: bloodshed, torture, rape and mutilation. That the Titus material was popular in Germany from at least the early seventeenth century is suggested by a German collection of *Engelische Comedien vnd Tragedien* (*English Comedies and Tragedies*, Leipzig, 1620) which contains *Eine sehr klägliche Tragœdia von Tito Andronico vnd der hoffertigen Käyserin* (*A Very Lamentable Tragedy of Tito Andronico and the Haughty Empress*). The play's action largely corresponds to what we find in *Titus*, although *Tito* is much shorter, written entirely in prose, and differs from the English play in intriguing ways. Since the nineteenth century, *Tito Andronico* has sporadically attracted the interest of scholars, but, prior to the present edition, it has never received the attention it deserves.[2] It is a play that has much to teach us and is an important witness to the early history of Titus plays on the English stage.

---

[1] See Metz, *Studies*, 17–43.
[2] The most comprehensive studies of *Tito* are Fuller and Braekman.

The German play is only 1,154 lines long, whereas *Titus*, now commonly believed to have been co-authored by Shakespeare and George Peele, comes in at approximately 2,500 lines.[1] Unlike the early quarto texts of *Titus*, which have no formal act or scene divisions, *Tito* is divided into eight acts.[2] While the plot is similar to that of *Titus*, the action in *Tito* is more streamlined and some elements are absent, including the classical references: no mention is made of Philomel and Tereus (2.2.43; 2.3.38–43; 4.1.47–53; 5.2.194), and no copy of Ovid's *Metamorphoses* appears on the stage (4.1.42). The language of *Tito* is simpler than that of *Titus*, but it is not without moments of rhetorical force, particularly in Tito's outrage at Aetiopissa (4.3.8–20) and his moving response to the futile loss of his hand (4.3.21–7), as well as his lamentations over his dead sons (4.3.28–33) and his defiled daughter (4.3.60–76). Throughout the play, there are parallels with the language and imagery of *Titus*, a number of which are discussed below, and many more in the commentary.

The number of roles in *Tito* is significantly smaller than in *Titus*. The German play omits Mutius, Young Lucius, Publius, Sempronius, Caius, Valentine, Emillius and Alarbus; all that remains of Quintus and Martius are their heads: those of two unnamed sons of Tito are brought on stage in Act 4, Scene 3.

---

[1] Hart counts 2,522 lines (21), which includes the Folio-only 'Fly Scene' (3.2), of which *Tito* shows no trace, so the quarto text of *Titus* has approximately 2,435 lines. For Shakespeare and Peele's co-authorship of *Titus*, see Vickers, 148–243, and Taylor and Loughnane, 490–3.

[2] Quarto editions of *Titus Andronicus* appeared in 1594, 1600 and 1611. The First Folio collection of Shakespeare's dramatic works, which divides the play into five acts, was published in 1623, three years after the first edition of *Tito*. Four plays in the 1620 volume are divided into five acts (and one of them, *Sidonia und Theagene*, is further divided into scenes). *Julio und Hyppolita* is in four Acts, while two plays in the collection, *Von dem verlornen Sohn* (*The Prodigal Son*) and *Von eines Königes Sohne auß Engellandt vnd des Königes Tochter aus Schottlandt* (*A King's Son of England and a King's Daughter of Scotland*), have six acts. It is most unusual for early modern plays in Germany or England to be divided into eight acts, and we know of no other instance.

2

Yet all the major characters are present, although with the exception of Tito their names are entirely different: Vespasianus (Lucius), Victoriades (Marcus), Andronica (Lavinia), Aetiopissa (Tamora), Helicates (Demetrius), Saphonus (Chiron) and Morian (Aaron).[1] *Tito*'s equivalent of Saturninus has no name but is simply referred to as the Roman Emperor. As we will see below, the characterization of Morian and Aetiopissa differs substantially from that of Aaron and Tamora, and there are other, subtler differences that impact the other characters, notably Tito, Andronica and Vespasianus.

Despite these differences, *Tito Andronico* can shed much light on the English play, and recent editors of *Titus Andronicus* have shown some awareness of this. Jonathan Bate's Arden edition bases a crucial stage direction on *Tito*. In Act 3, Scene 1, Titus is tricked by Aaron into cutting off his hand in the hope of saving the life of his sons Quintus and Martius. But they are executed nonetheless, and their heads are sent to Titus along with his hand, as recorded in a startling stage direction, '*Enter a* Messenger *with two heads and a hand*' (3.1.234 SD). The remaining Andronici, Titus, Marcus, Lucius and the mutilated Lavinia, are aghast. Commenting on an unscripted stage action, Marcus says, 'Alas, poor heart, that kiss is comfortless / As frozen water to a starved snake' (3.1.251–2).[2] No early edition clarifies what action prompts Marcus' words, leading editors to speculate about various possibilities: 'Lavinia kisses [Marcus]', 'Lavinia kisses Lucius' or 'Lavinia kisses Titus' (Ard[3] *TA*, 47). Yet the stage direction in the German version states that Lavinia '*goes to the heads and kisses them*' (4.3.80 SD), which Bate adopts and slightly adapts: '*Lavinia kisses the heads*' (3.1.250 SD). Arrestingly, the 'tongueless woman', Lavinia, thus 'kisses the severed heads of her

---

[1] For the names of the characters in *Tito*, see below, pp. 168–70. *Tito* can be performed by a minimum of ten actors as opposed to the much larger number needed for *Titus* (see the Appendix).

[2] All references are from Ard[3] *TA* unless indicated otherwise.

brothers', Quintus and Martius (Ard³ *TA*, 47). Close attention to the German version here leads to the insertion of poignant stage business into an authoritative edition of Shakespeare's play.

Gary Taylor and his fellow editors of *The New Oxford Shakespeare* have similarly given prominence to *Tito*. Like Bate, they draw on the German play to make Lavinia kiss her brothers' severed heads, and, unlike Bate, they quote directly from a translation of *Tito* when doing so (5.248 SD). Later in the scene, when Titus invites Lucius, Marcus and Lavinia to swear an oath with him, the editors of *The New Oxford Shakespeare* use evidence from *Titus*, namely the protagonist's 'You heavy people, circle me about' (5.275), as the basis for their inserted stage direction: '*They form a circle and make a vow*' (5.277 SD). The equivalent stage direction in *Tito* does not call for a circle and is somewhat different in how it handles the swearing of the oath, yet the editors of the *New Oxford Shakespeare* demonstrate the value of the German play as an early witness of theatrical practice by reproducing the corresponding stage direction in the margin (see *Tito*, 5.1.61 SD) in one of the edition's 'Performance Notes', whose purpose it is 'to call attention to more complex staging possibilities' (47) than those embedded in the stage directions of the main text.

Despite this incipient awareness of *Tito*'s importance, the German play remains a vastly underused resource in the study of *Titus Andronicus*. For while recent editors of *Titus* incorporate one or two of its stage directions, they take no account of many others that are no less important. For instance, in the opening scene of both plays, the Moor character, Morian in *Tito* and Aaron in *Titus*, is silent during the succession crisis but remains on stage when all the other characters leave and speaks a soliloquy. In *Tito*, the play's opening stage direction points out that Morian '*has a humble cloak pulled over his magnificent clothes*' (1.1.0 SD), and when the other characters have left, another stage direction informs us that '*He pulls off the old cloak*' (1.1.83 SD) to reveal his magnificent clothes. There is no equivalent stage direction in *Titus*, but Aaron's words are suggestive: 'Away with slavish weeds and servile thoughts! / I will be bright, and shine in pearl and gold' (1.1.517–18). Does Aaron remove his 'slavish weeds' at the same time as he mentions them? At the very least, Morian enacts a version of what Aaron says, and it is not impossible that Aaron's words were accompanied by a similar costume change.

There are other moments in the play when a stage direction in *Tito* may reflect how *Titus* was performed. When Aaron arrives to announce that the Emperor will spare Titus' sons in exchange for a chopped-off hand, Marcus and Lucius plead with Titus to let one of them undergo the ordeal. When Titus declines the offer, they keep pleading (3.1.151–83). At the equivalent point, Tito's brother and son '*fall on their knees before him*' (*Tito*, 4.1.32 SD) as a way of intensifying their pleas. A stage direction close to the end of *Tito* similarly conveys how a moment of emotional crisis was staged. When Aetiopissa, as *Tito*'s Empress is called, has been informed by Tito that the pie from which she has been eating contains her sons' remains, she '*shakes and trembles violently in fright*' (8.2.51 SD). Neither stage direction has an equivalent in *Titus*, but the action they designate is perfectly compatible with the English play and may reflect what happened in early performances.

Similarly, after Tamora has given birth, the Nurse enters to Aaron, Demetrius and Chiron with the '*blackamoor child*' (4.2.51 SD). Tamora's sons are dismayed and want to 'dispatch' (4.2.88) the baby. The conflict comes to a head when Demetrius demands, 'Nurse, give it me' (4.2.88), yet the baby is rescued by Aaron. There is no stage direction in the early editions of the English play to indicate how the moment was staged. The English dramatist Edward Ravenscroft, who produced an adaptation of *Titus Andronicus* in 1678 (published 1687), inserted a stage direction, '*Aron takes the child from the Woman*' (Ard[3] *TA*, 265), and Hughes comments that 'Aaron probably takes the child from the Nurse' (126). The stage action in *Tito* is different, however, and arguably more dramatic: Saphonus *'takes the child from the midwife, draws his sword and is about to kill the child'* (6.1.47 SD) when it is snatched from him by Morian. Here and elsewhere, *Tito* provides the best evidence we have of how the English play may have been performed, and the stage action is different from and arguably more complex and more interesting than that mediated to us through modern editions of *Titus*.

Other stage directions in *Tito* that may reflect the early performance history of *Titus* concern the character of Andronica (*Tito*'s Lavinia). When Andronica and her husband enter in the scene that will lead to the former's rape and the latter's murder, they do so *'hand in hand'* (3.3.0 SD). The equivalent stage direction in *Titus* ('*Enter* BASSIANUS *and* LAVINIA', 2.2.50 SD) does not convey this detail, although physical intimacy between Lavinia and her husband is suggested in the allusion to the newlyweds' consummation of their marriage (2.1.14–17). When the husband is murdered, *Titus* has no stage direction that tells us what she does, but *Tito* informs us that *'She goes to sit on the ground with the corpse'* (3.3.69 SD). After Lavinia/ Andronica has been raped, she reappears on stage with the rapists who have mutilated her, and now make cruel fun of the fact (*Titus*, 2.3.1–10; *Tito*, 4.2.1–9). When the brothers have left, she remains on stage alone, and a stage direction in *Tito*, with no equivalent in *Titus*, informs us that she is *'sighing and looking wretchedly up to heaven'* (4.2.9 SD2). When the mutilated Lavinia has been found by her uncle and brought by him before her father and her brother, Lucius responds verbally to the sight of his sister – 'Ay me, this object kills me' (3.1.65) – and the following line, spoken by Titus, implies that he has responded physically, too, for Titus asks him to 'arise and look upon her' (3.1.66). According to an editorially added stage direction in the Arden edition, Lucius *'fall[s] to his knees'* (3.1.64 SD), whereas the editors of the *New Oxford Shakespeare* comment that 'Lucius must have sat, fallen, or knelt, or perhaps fainted at the sight of Lavinia's injuries' (215). Neither edition mentions that *Tito* supports this last possibility, for a stage direction spells out that Vespasianus, as the Lucius character is called in *Tito*, '*falls to the ground in a swoon*' (4.3.59 SD).

If, with Bate and the editors of the *New Oxford Shakespeare*, we assume that, in some instances, *Tito*'s stage directions reflect how *Titus* was performed, then we have reason to suppose that they may do so in other instances too. *Tito* thus has much to offer to editors, critics and actors who want to come to a fuller understanding of *Titus Andronicus*, of how it may be staged now and of how it may have been staged in Shakespeare's time.

THE RELATIONSHIP OF *TITO ANDRONICO* TO *TITUS ANDRONICUS*

Other early modern German plays edited for Arden Shakespeare – *Der Bestrafte Brudermord, Romio und Julieta* and *Kunst über alle Künste* – are adaptations of Shakespeare's plays. *Tito* is special insofar as it may be based not on the surviving *Titus Andronicus* at all, but an earlier version of the play or a common source play (see below, pp. 36–40). Nonetheless, the relationship between *Tito* and *Titus* is close, and the aim of this section is to explore it.

In *Tito*'s first scene, eight of the nine principal characters are onstage (only Victoriades is not), and the only extras called for are unspecified 'Romans'.[1] The first scene of *Titus*, by contrast, calls not only for fourteen named characters to be onstage (Saturninus, Bassianus, Titus, his brother, his four sons and his daughter, Tamora, her three sons and Aaron) but also for a

---

[1] Victoriades may be absent from the opening scene because the actor who plays his role later in the play is needed in this scene as one of the unnamed 'Romans' (see Appendix, pp. 417–19).

series of unnamed characters: Tribunes, Senators, Soldiers, Goths and a Captain. The opening scene of *Tito* is short compared to that of *Titus*. It focuses on a single issue, the selection of the new emperor, before concluding with Morian's soliloquy. Vespasianus identifies Tito as the most deserving candidate for the imperial crown, to which the future Emperor (who is given no proper name) angrily objects, prompting Tito to recuse himself; as a result, the Emperor is crowned and Tito's prisoners are presented to him. The action of the first scene thus ends harmoniously, without any physical confrontations or deaths, and the only indication of future complications is the Emperor's volatile hot-headedness and the suggestion that he has a romantic interest in Aetiopissa despite his betrothal to Andronica (1.1.51–3). The English play, by contrast, dramatizes many issues: the contest for the imperial crown (1.1.1–66); Titus' arrival in Rome and the sacrifice of Alarbus (1.1.66–171); Titus' candidacy for the crown and his promotion of Saturninus (1.1.172–237); the fray following the disagreement over Lavinia (1.1.238–342); the burial of Mutius (1.1.343–95); Tamora's deceitful peace-making between the Andronici and Saturninus (1.1.404–99); Aaron's soliloquy (1.1.500–24); and Chiron and Demetrius' quarrel about Lavinia (1.1.525–635).[1] Two important episodes in *Titus* have no equivalent in *Tito*, namely the sacrificial murder of Alarbus and the disagreement about Lavinia, which leads to Titus' murder of his own son, Mutius. The opening scene of *Tito* is thus considerably more streamlined than the complex action found in *Titus*.

In *Titus*, Saturninus rejects Lavinia in favour of Tamora because of the altercation with Bassianus and the Andronici (1.1.280–325), but the Emperor in *Tito* does not have the same motivation for rejecting Andronica. He simply states that he loves Aetiopissa far more than Andronica. He then crowns his

---

[1] The Folio introduces an act division after 1.1.499, so that Aaron's soliloquy and the quarrel between the two brothers form the opening of the second act.

new consort onstage, whereas Saturninus only expresses his intention to make Tamora his consort (1.1.320–5). *Tito* thus dramatizes what *Titus* verbalizes.

Although *Tito* is much shorter than *Titus*, there is one element of the opening scene that is more substantial in the German play: the Moor's soliloquy. In *Titus*, Aaron's soliloquy reveals his tendencies for villainy and ill will in general terms (1.1.500–24), whereas Morian's longer speech (1.1.81–130) provides an account of the speaker's background and history. Morian's presentation is also more dramatic than Aaron's; he throws off the old cloak that covers his fine clothing before sharing his hopes for Aetiopissa's seduction of the Emperor. He reveals that he had cuckolded the King of Ethiopia, whom Aetiopissa poisoned with a cup of wine, boasts of his villainies (such as secret murders at the Ethiopian court) and military prowess (noting that he was known as the 'Thunder and Lightning of Ethiopia', 1.1.111–12), and recounts Tito's invasion of his homeland, his engagement with Tito in combat and the Romans' devastation of Ethiopia. Whereas *Titus* introduces Aaron as the stock type of the black villain, *Tito* thus provides a fuller sense of who Morian is.

The action that follows corresponds more closely to *Titus*: Helicates and Saphonus declare their love for Andronica and quarrel over who shall have her (2.1.38–66) in much the same way as Chiron and Demetrius do (1.1.525–44). Both plays highlight the problem that the object of the brothers' desire is already married, and in both plays the Moor is instrumental in devising the rape plot. A hunt is called for, and the apparent pleasantness of the new day is offset by a foreboding dream (*Tito*, 3.2.1–5; *Titus*, 2.1.1–2, 9–10). This is followed by the rape and mutilation of Andronica/Lavinia and the imprisonment of two Andronici sons. Whereas in *Titus* significance is placed on Aaron's plot to frame Titus' sons for Bassianus' murder by means of a pit, a forged letter and a bag of gold (2.2.1–50), in *Tito* the focus is exclusively on the attack on Andronica.

9

In *Tito* there is no reason for Morian and Aetiopissa to cross paths before meeting Andronica and her husband as there is in *Titus* (2.2.1–50), which means that the couple do not witness the Empress' dalliance with the Moor, and therefore have no cause to berate them. In *Tito* 3.3, Aetiopissa enters to Andronica and, without any provocation, mocks her for not having a large retinue of servants. Andronica responds by commenting on the Empress' 'haughty spirit' (3.3.28), which causes Aetiopissa to fly into a rage. In *Titus* the equivalent exchange takes a different course: Lavinia and Bassianus mock Tamora after seeing her dalliance with Aaron (2.2.51–88), and it is this that enrages her. Aetiopissa's attack on Andronica and her subsequent vow for revenge (3.3.41–6) thus lack Tamora's justification. The two versions of the confrontation between Andronica/Lavinia and the Empress reveal how the characters differ in the two plays. Tamora's amorous dalliance with the Moor, which is absent from *Tito*, arises from her sexual licentiousness. The emphasis in the German play is on Aetiopissa's arrogance, as the title's reference to the 'haughty Empress' suggests.

After the murder of Bassianus and Lavinia's rape, Titus' younger sons are lured into a pit containing Bassianus' corpse, and the evidence which seemingly corroborates their guilt (actually forged by Aaron) seals their fate (2.2.192–306). This episode is not in *Tito*, where Andronica's husband is never mentioned again, and it is thus unclear what happens with his body.

In fact, no sons other than Vespasianus are mentioned in *Tito* until the beginning of Act 4, when we learn that two unnamed sons have, in fact, been imprisoned, not for murder but on the charge of having insulted Aetiopissa with 'mockery and libels' (4.1.7).[1] Their imprisonment not only leads to their beheading,

---

[1]   Aetiopissa's reference to 'brothers' (3.3.75) is the first indication in the play that Tito has more than one son.

which is necessary for the plot, but also draws further attention to Aetiopissa's pride and cunning. Her responsibility for the sons' imprisonment logically follows her threat to Andronica in the previous scene, where she vows to 'murder your entire kin, including your parents and brothers' (3.3.74–5). The difference between *Tito* and *Titus* thus highlights the status of the Empress as the chief villain in the German play.

In both plays, Tito/Titus is tricked into cutting off his hand on the promise of his sons' liberty, only to have it returned to him with their heads. This happens in close proximity to the protagonist's discovery of his ravished daughter, but the order of events is different in the two versions. In *Titus*, Marcus discovers Lavinia and delivers a long speech (2.3.11–57); after Titus attempts to plead with the Tribunes for his sons' lives (3.1.1–58), Marcus presents the ravished Lavinia, who is lamented over and comforted by her brother and father (3.1.59–150); Aaron arrives bearing a message from the Emperor, and Titus sends his brother and son to cast lots, while the Moor helps him to cut off his hand onstage before taking it away (3.1.151–206). Later in the same scene, a messenger brings back the heads and hand (3.1.235–41), which precipitates the Andronici's oath for revenge. In *Tito* 4.1, Morian arrives to deliver the Empress' offer to pardon the sons if Tito sacrifices his hand (16–20), and Tito severs his hand offstage after he tricks Vespasianus and Victoriades into drawing lots for the sacrifice (33–41). The next scene shifts to Andronica, who is left in the forest by her attackers and is discovered by her uncle. Act 4, Scene 3 returns to Tito, who receives his severed hand and sons' heads from Morian. His grief is compounded when Victoriades presents him with the ravished Andronica (4.3.55–76). The order of events in *Titus* means that after the protagonist pleads in vain for his sons' lives and is confronted with his ravished daughter, there is a glimmer of hope: Aaron arrives with his message. The hopes are then dashed with the revelation that Titus and his kin have been tricked, which leads them to

11

swear an oath of revenge. In *Tito*, the hopefulness that accompanies the severing of his hand is dashed by Morian's return with the hand and severed heads, and Tito's grief and outrage are compounded by the revelation that his daughter has been raped and maimed.

Differences between the two plays in the Moor's delivery of his message have a significant effect on his character. In *Titus*, where he is the principal villain, the Moor tells Titus that Saturninus proposes to let his sons live in exchange for a hand (3.1.151–7), but his comments to Lucius later in the play suggest that Saturninus had no knowledge of Aaron's proposition (5.1.111–20). Thus, Aaron not only tricks Titus, but also usurps Saturninus' authority. Furthermore, the fact that it is Aaron who physically severs Titus' hand cements the fact that he is the play's chief villain. In *Tito*, Aetiopissa is the principal antagonist, and she rather than Morian is responsible for tricking Tito. Morian delivers the message on Aetiopissa's orders (4.1.16–20), which he confirms later when confessing to Vespasianus (7.1.84–9).[1] Morian does not express anything akin to Aaron's ghoulish glee at seeing Tito realize that he has been deceived. On the contrary, Morian twice expresses sympathy for Tito: when Tito exits to cut off his hand, he says, 'even though I have a pitiless heart, I pity you, old Tito Andronico' (4.1.45–6); when he returns the body parts he adds, 'I pity you, for you have been tricked out of your noble and valiant hand' (4.3.1–2). While that last could on its own be thought feigned pity, Morian's first expression of sympathy for Tito, made when alone, suggests that it is genuine. Morian thus does not share Aaron's motivations and boundless maliciousness, and the play's villainous agency is firmly centred on Aetiopissa.

In *Titus*, the return of Titus' hand and his sons' heads leads to the first of two oaths sworn by the Andronici. The first oath

---

[1] Aetiopissa's responsibility for the trick is corroborated by the Emperor, who congratulates her on her ingenious plan in 5.2.1–6.

12

(3.1.276–80) follows the gruesome delivery of the severed heads (which arrive after the raped Lavinia has been discovered and presented to her father), and the second oath is sworn once the identity of Lavinia's attackers has been revealed (following 4.1.78). In *Tito*, there are not two oaths but one: Act 4 ends with Victoriades' proposal to 'consider how we can find out who has abused her thus' (4.3.83–4), and Act 5 opens with the Andronici's re-entry and Andronica's revelation of her attackers' identities, which prompt the Andronici to swear an oath.[1] This means that the main catalyst for Titus' first oath is a desire to revenge his sons' deaths rather than his daughter's attackers. By contrast, it is Andronica's revelation that is the call to arms in *Tito*.[2] *Tito*'s plot construction is thus such that it arguably gives greater importance to the protagonist's daughter than does *Titus*.

Although the means by which Andronica and Lavinia reveal the names of their attackers are almost identical, the circumstances surrounding the disclosure are different. In *Titus*, Lucius is not present on account of his banishment, and it is his son, Young Lucius, who enters running from Lavinia, who chases him and attempts to seize the book that he clutches: a copy of Ovid's *Metamorphoses* (4.1.1–43). When she points to the tale of Philomel, Marcus invites Lavinia to take his staff in her mouth and write the names of the perpetrators on a 'sandy plot' (4.1.69). It is seventy-eight lines into the scene before the names are finally written. The circumstances leading up to the

---

[1]   It is possible that in performance there was a break between Acts 4 and 5, given that this is the midway point of the play, which would explain the immediate re-entry. Victoriades' comment and Tito's response, 'Let us go in and have no rest until we have found them out' (4.3.85–6), may anticipate the passage of stage time spent during the interval.

[2]   In fact, she provides only one name in writing: 'There is "Helicates" and also "hunt"' (5.1.28–9). Tito infers that Saphonus was also involved and that the Empress was likewise to blame. While the dialogue in *Titus* implies that Lavinia makes arm gestures to indicate that there was more than one attacker (4.1.37–9), there is no such indication in *Tito*.

revelation of the names in *Tito* 5.1 are more direct, and the initiative to communicate them does not come from the female victim but from her brother. The scene opens with Tito lamenting and attempting to comfort Andronica, and Vespasianus enters with a basket of sand and a stick, stating that his sister should attempt to write the names by this means (5.1.18–20).[1] Tito places the stick between Andronica's stumps and she immediately succeeds in writing with it (5.1.21–7). *Tito* is thus less elaborate than *Titus*, and the two plays differ substantially in terms of the agency ascribed to the ravished daughter. Whereas Lavinia actively seeks to reveal her ordeal to her relatives, Andronica is prompted to do so by them.

A possible reason why *Tito* foregrounds Vespasianus' agency at this important moment is that it reinforces his status as a worthy successor to the Roman crown. After the oath of revenge is sworn, Tito entrusts his son with the weighty task of taking the 'vast store of my treasury' (5.1.65) in order to raise an army. Vespasianus rises to the task and proclaims, 'by the god Mars that I shall not cease my rage and fury until pale Death has triumphed over my heart' (5.1.69–71). Tito's faith in his son is reiterated in his recollection of their recent military exploits:

> [I]n the recent battle with the Moors I saw him fight like a fierce tiger. In you I place all my hope, and if I must end my old life here, I know that you will take vengeance on our enemies.
>
> (5.1.79–82)

In *Titus*, Lucius is not present in the equivalent scene, and though Marcus has his other family members swear to 'prosecute by good advice / Mortal revenge upon these traitorous Goths' (4.1.92–3), no military plan is made at this point. Conversely, in *Tito*, Andronica's revelation leads directly

---

[1] An advantage of bringing a basket of sand that is then poured onto the floor is that it makes the action easier for the audience to follow.

to a call to arms, and Vespasianus is called upon to raise an army with which to destroy Rome.

The events at the end of Act 5, Scene 1 and in Act 5, Scene 2 loosely correspond to *Titus* 4.3.76–120 and 4.4.39–67, where Titus meets the Clown, who is on his way to the court with a basket of pigeons. Titus bids him deliver a letter with a knife enfolded within it to Saturninus. Saturninus does not read the letter aloud, but has a strong reaction to it, presumably prompted by the knife, and orders the Clown to be executed. *Tito* devotes more attention to the message intended for the Emperor. Tito dictates a message that he wants delivered orally to the Emperor, and further asks the messenger to deliver a 'letter together with its contents' (5.1.96) and a sword. At court, the messenger recounts Tito's words and offers the sword to the Emperor. When the Emperor opens the letter he finds in it the 'naked blade' (5.2.52–3) and immediately orders that the messenger be turned over to the hangman. The presentation of the sword may be the result of a conflation of the Messenger's letter with a different episode from the source play, preserved in *Titus* 4.2.1–16, where Young Lucius provocatively presents swords to Chiron and Demetrius. *Titus* thus has two kinds of objects (knife and sword) in two passages which *Tito* dramatizes in one.

Following Tito's declaration of war at the end of Act 5, Act 6 shifts to the domestic concerns of the Empress, namely the birth of the mixed-race child. The action is similar to *Titus* 4.2.52–148, where the Nurse enters to Aaron, Chiron and Demetrius, and presents them with the child, telling Aaron that Tamora has ordered him to kill it; Aaron refuses and instead kills the Nurse. In *Tito*, the Midwife enters with the infant, noting that Aetiopissa wishes Morian to 'secretly put it out of the way' (6.1.2–3). Yet after Saphonus and Helicates discover the Midwife and question her about her ward, we learn that the child's mother has ordered her to take the child to Morian 'so that he can have it brought up in secret to make sure that no-one knows about it' (6.1.28–9). Just as the outraged brothers are about to kill the child, Morian

15

enters and dismisses them, and the Midwife is able to deliver Aetiopissa's message in full, bidding him 'take it in secret to Mount Thaurin, where your father lives, so that he can raise it; no-one must know that it was born of the Empress' (6.1.85–8).[1] Thus, the respective plans of Tamora and Aetiopissa for dealing with the child are starkly different: where the former proposes death, the latter plans for future life.

Morian's attempt to deliver the infant to his father is cut short when he is captured on Mount Thaurin (7.1.16–18). Although *Titus* has a similar moment where Aaron and his son are apprehended (5.1.20–39), the Moor's reaction to his capture is different. Whereas Aaron refuses to answer Lucius' questions until his infant is threatened with hanging (5.1.47–60), Morian immediately begins to bargain for his own life, promising not only to reveal the Empress' crimes, but also to serve Vespasianus and help him to overthrow the Emperor (7.1.30–5). Morian's lengthy summary of earlier events reveals that Aetiopissa bade him keep watch on Andronica's husband and 'kill him, so that [Saphonus and Helicates] could satisfy their lust on her' (7.1.57–8), but that he was unable to find a suitable opportunity for doing so. No equivalent of Morian's blame of his paramour is found in *Titus*, where Aaron confesses his villainies and boasts of his ingenuity in devising them (5.1.89–144). The dramatization of Morian's capture thus contributes to making the Empress rather than the Moor the play's chief villain.

The following scene, Act 7, Scene 2, shifts to Rome, where the Emperor expresses his alarm at Vespasianus' military success. The Emperor divulges Aetiopissa's plan to disguise herself and her sons in order to 'weaken [Tito] with cunning and treachery' (7.2.17). In the scene that follows, Aetiopissa further clarifies her intentions when she orders her sons to stay with Tito and '[l]end careful attention to the cunning stratagems he

---

[1] For Mount Thaurin, which has no equivalent in *Titus*, see below, p. 220.

will use in battle' and murder him if the bloodshed does not cease (7.3.3–5, 6–9). Tamora's plan, on the other hand, is to trick Titus into persuading Lucius to a parley with Saturninus (4.4.88–98, 107–11); she does not originally intend to leave her sons with Titus until he demands it. In the English play, Titus' feigned madness gives Tamora hope that the disguise plot will succeed, and in a substantial exchange between the two, Tamora attempts to persuade Titus that she is Revenge, accompanied by Murder and Rapine, while Titus' asides alert the audience to the fact that he is not fooled (5.2.9–120). Ultimately, Tamora departs because she thinks that her plan has succeeded. In the German play, Tito does not pretend madness when Aetiopissa presents herself and her sons: they are accepted by Tito seemingly without question, as being 'ordained by the gods to help . . . with good counsel in these wars' (7.3.18–19). The brevity of the scene in *Tito* quickens the pace of the action that leads up to the climax of the scene, where the brothers are executed.

Having been tricked into thinking that he has fallen for the disguises, Aetiopissa leaves her sons with Tito, who slaughters them and states his intention to bake their heads into a pie. The murder is dramatized similarly in the two plays: the brothers are bound, their mouths gagged, their throats slit, and their blood collected into a receptacle (*Tito* 7.3.40 SD–45 SD; *Titus* 5.2.164–5, 196–203). A difference with profound implications, however, is that whereas in *Titus*, Lavinia is present and collects the brothers' blood, in *Tito*, Andronica is absent. Instead, Tito is assisted by two unnamed soldiers, one of whom holds a vessel to collect the blood. Andronica's absence undermines the gruesome sense of justice that Lavinia can be said to receive in *Titus*. On the other hand, her absence may result from a desire not to taint her character by association with such a violent murder.

The ending of *Tito* is more streamlined than that of *Titus*. Tito calls a conciliatory banquet, whereas it is the disguised Tamora who suggests a feast in the English play (5.2.111–19).

Since peace has already been proclaimed in *Tito*, the banquet commences without incident. Tito serves the pies, is questioned about his melancholy by the Emperor, kills Andronica, proclaims that Aetiopissa is to blame, reveals that the pies are made of her sons' flesh, kills Aetiopissa and is in turn killed by the Emperor. Vespasianus takes revenge on the Emperor, and Victoriades asks Vespasianus to take the crown; he initially protests but then agrees to do so. The pace of the ending in *Tito* is fast, and there is not much action that follows the spectacular deaths that occur onstage.

Titus has a much longer conclusion. Once Lavinia, Tamora, Titus and the Emperor have been killed, Aaron is brought back to be punished (5.3.175–89). In *Tito*, Morian is not mentioned again after Vespasianus orders him to be hanged at the end of Act 7, Scene 1, and, given that Aetiopissa is the principal antagonist, he is not brought back in the last act. Lucius' promotion to emperor receives more attention in *Titus* than that of Vespasianus in *Tito* and is rooted in a public bid for his candidacy (5.3.145). This differs from the hasty promotion of Vespasianus in *Tito*, in which no address is given to the populace. The initial reluctance to take the crown is not in *Titus*. It may underscore Vespasianus' humility, echoing Tito's lack of political ambition at the beginning of the play. It also contrasts with Aetiopissa's pride: now that the haughty Empress is dead, a humble Emperor ascends the throne.

In sum, *Tito* and *Titus* essentially provide different dramatizations of the same basic plot. The German play is substantially shorter than the English and is more fast-paced at critical moments in the action. The plot of *Tito* is not as complex as that of *Titus*, which includes episodes such as the competition over Lavinia, the sacrifice of Alarbus, Aaron's plot to frame Titus' younger sons for the murder of Bassianus, and the 'arrow-shooting' scene. *Tito*'s streamlined plot goes together with the fact that it uses fewer characters than *Titus*. The German play also frequently provides a different interpretation

18

of the prompts for characters' interactions. *Tito* thus constitutes a fascinating alternative version of *Titus*.

ISSUES OF RACE IN *TITO ANDRONICO*

Titus figures prominently in scholarly discussions of early modern theatrical representations of blackness and racial difference.[1] Aaron, whose soul is apparently as black as his face, in many ways conforms to the stock type of the malevolent black villain found elsewhere in early modern drama (as, for instance, in Peele's *The Battle of Alcazar*). But while he remains an unrepentant villain until the end, Aaron is more than a simple stereotype: his display of paternal tenderness and affection towards his child humanizes him, and he draws attention to his skin colour in ways that engage meaningfully with early modern theories of racial difference. *Tito* engages with issues of race in different but no less interesting ways, and the play has much to contribute to the study of race in the early modern period.

A major difference between *Tito* and *Titus* is the fact that the non-Roman characters in the former are not Goths but Africans, hailing from 'Mohrenlandt' (literally, 'Land of the Moors') or 'Aethiopia'.[2] This difference has significant implications for the black villain's position in the play, and indeed for the enemy faction as a whole. Jonathan Bate and Sonia Massai have commented on the difference between the Goths in *Titus* and the Ethiopians in *Tito*:

[1]   For example, see Hall; Jones; Barthelemy; de Sousa; Bartels, 'Making'; and Vaughan and Vaughan.
[2]   'Mohrenland' is defined by Grimm as 'a land where Moors live, notably Mauritania and Ethiopia' (*n. land worin die mohren wohnen; vornehmlich Mauritanien und Aethiopien*).

19

In the Renaissance Goths were synonymous with Germans; if you are an English company touring in Germany, you would be ill advised to have a barbarous Gothic/German queen and her rapist sons, and, therefore, you turn them into more distant barbarians, namely Ethiopians (this also means that you avoid the scandal of miscegenation between the empress and the Moor, a change that is in accordance with a certain moral cleansing of the text appropriate to Luther's Germany . . .).[1]

There are yet more points to be made about the complexity of race in *Tito*. Even if we suppose that the transformation of 'Germanic' Goths to 'more distant barbarians' was simply an act of problem-solving by the travelling players, it raises its own new problems which need to be addressed. That 'the scandal of miscegenation' is avoided does not hold because a mixed-race infant appears in the play. Aetiopissa's sons are outraged when they discover that she is the mother of the dark-skinned child that the Midwife holds in her arms at the beginning of Act 6. It is clear from their exchange with the Midwife that Aetiopissa and Morian do not belong to the same racial category. Saphonus asks, 'Who is this child's mother? I see that he is the father, so with whom has our Morian slept?' (6.1.14–15), drawing attention to Morian's racial singularity. This is confirmed by the Midwife's report of Aetiopissa's reaction following the child's birth: 'when she saw that the child was black she was very frightened' (6.1.26–7). The child's pigmentation is starkly different from Aetiopissa's and provides visual proof of its parentage.

So Bate and Massai's suggestion conflates ethnicity and race. A shared ethnic or national origin (Ethiopia) does not

---

[1]   Bate and Massai, 140. The long-standing assumption that Goths are synonymous with Germans has recently been challenged by Ndiaye, 'Aaron's Roots'.

necessarily mean that Aetiopissa and Morian belong to the same racial category, as the anxiety about their son's appearance makes clear, and the issue of miscegenation is by no means 'cleansed' from the play. Even before the birth of the child, a contrast between Morian and Aetiopissa's skin colour is firmly established. The opening stage direction insists as much on Aetiopissa's whiteness as it does on Morian's blackness: '*Also enter* AETIOPISSA, *the Queen of Ethiopia, who is lovely and white, . . . and* MORIAN, *who is black*' (1.1.0 SD). Although the term 'Ethiopian' was typically associated with very dark skin, the plot requires a white queen.[1] Her whiteness, evident in performance, is here spelled out for the reader to avoid confusion. In Act 1 the speech prefixes are variously 'Königin auß Mohrenlandt' ('Queen of Africa') and 'Ætiopis.', but after she is crowned in Act 2 she is largely 'Käyserin', which removes any reminders of her African origins. In Morian's case, the reader is invited to visualize a black body, and the speech prefix ('Morian' from the German word for Moor) reiterates his racial difference throughout.[2] As the text insists on Morian's blackness, it seems likely that the travelling players capitalized on the sensational nature of this 'black devil' ('schwartzer Teufel', 7.1.22) by performing him in blackface.

But what is one to make of a white Ethiopian queen? The depiction of Aetiopissa's skin-colour might seem unexpected –

---

[1] 'Ethiopia' cannot be read as applying exclusively to the Ethiopian empire; in light of common usage it is reasonable to assume that Ethiopia here refers to sub-Saharan Africa more generally, which was often associated with black Africans. See Vaughan and Vaughan, Hall and Bartels.

[2] Vaughan (9–15) discusses various strategies for performing blackness, including blackface make-up, masks, stockings and gloves. As Vaughan demonstrates, blackface was commonly used to represent Moors on the early modern English stage, so it is reasonable to assume that the travelling players would have replicated the technique in *Tito*. It seems more likely that the white actor who played Morian pigmented his face than that he hid it behind a mask. He has a substantial speaking part, and it might have been impeded by a face-covering, but see Smith for uses of sartorial blackface.

perhaps an oversight or a lapse in logic on the play's part, arising from a hasty and arbitrary switch from Goths to Ethiopians. Yet there is a literary and visual tradition concerning white Ethiopian princesses, among them the mythical princess Andromeda, Chariclea (from Heliodorus' *Aethiopica*, an ancient Greek prose romance) and Clorinda (from Torquato Tasso's *Jerusalem Delivered*).[1] Chariclea in particular had a vibrant afterlife: Heliodorus' *Aethiopica* underwent an impressive number of translations across early modern Europe, which in turn gave rise to a range of stage adaptations.[2] Thomas Underdowne's English translation of the *Aethiopica* was published in 1569, and it probably influenced the lost play, *Chariclea* (1572).[3] Further evidence of white Ethiopian princesses on the stage is found in the titles of other lost plays such as *Perseus and Andromeda* (1574) and *The Queen of Ethiopia* (1578), which may have been another adaptation of Heliodorus' romance.[4] Although the whiteness of the African female characters in these narratives was anomalous, dramatizations such as these established a theatrical precedent for the staging of white Ethiopian royal women.

That does not mean that Aetiopissa's whiteness is straightforward, and it is possible that the term 'white' is applied to her in a relative way, given the complex and often contradictory early modern European conceptions of sub-Saharan Africans. In the seventeenth century, terms such as 'Ethiope' and 'Moor' are by no means stable or clear-cut, and in *Tito* they are especially difficult to pin down. It is possible to

---

[1] See Spicer and Iyengar.

[2] See Ricquier, 15–22. On European stage adaptations, see Ndiaye, 'Everyone'.

[3] Prior to Underdowne's translation, material from the *Aethiopica* was available in John Sanford's *The Amorous and Tragicall Tales of Plutarch Wherevnto is Annexed the Hystorie of Cariclea & Theagenes* (London, 1567, STC 20072). On the lost play, see Wiggins, 2.91–2.

[4] See Wiggins, 2.109–10 and 2.183.

envisage Aetiopissa as a 'tawny' African, since distinctions were sometimes drawn between people from different parts of Africa and the degree of their 'blackness' in early modern literature.[1] A claim could even be made about Ethiopia as a Christian stronghold, which would make it imaginatively 'easier' to identify Aetiopissa and her sons as set apart from Morian, whose name carried Muslim connotations.[2] However, the play makes no allusions to religious difference and presents Aetiopissa as Queen of Ethiopia and 'Mohrenlandt' interchangeably, which makes claims about such fine differences problematic. Francesca T. Royster has argued that in *Titus* the trajectory of Moor, Goth, and Roman encapsulates a 'denaturalization of whiteness . . . and its construction along an unstable continuum of racial identities' (432). The German play, while not as explicitly interested in drawing attention to the polarized nature of black and white as *Titus*, nonetheless problematizes whiteness through the presence of a white African queen.

The continuum of racial identities is complicated further through the character of Morian. Virginia Mason Vaughan has demonstrated that Aaron conforms to many of the stereotypes of the black villain figure and echoes the associations between sin and blackness found in medieval drama.[3] To some extent, Morian, in his capacity as 'black devil' (7.1.22), performs the same function as Aaron, but he bears a rather different relationship to both his fellow captives and his homeland. Unlike *Titus*, the play does not contain *invading* Goths, some of whom were captured, kept alive and brought to Rome. Instead, we have *invaded* Ethiopians, whose country was attacked and

---

[1] The slipperiness of terms used to describe northern and sub-Saharan Africans are addressed in Vaughan and Vaughan, 19–29; Loomba, 44–59; Barthelemy, 6–10; and Bartels, 'Making', 433–4.

[2] For a discussion of Christianity in Ethiopia, see Salvadore, and Lowe, 'Representing'.

[3] Vaughan, 2, 43–50.

ravaged by the Romans. Aaron, whether as a slave or as a free man serving the Goth queen, is an outsider.[1] Morian, on the other hand, is his mistress's countryman and has a powerful set of connections to their homeland.[2]

Morian's lengthy speech at the end of the first act provides an account of his affair with Aetiopissa, which implies that he had privileged access to the Ethiopian court (1.1.89–91). In the first part of this long speech, Morian shares details of his affair (including how Aetiopissa poisoned her husband in order to be with Morian), noting that he killed those who looked unfavourably on them, and that he has 'committed thousands and thousands of villainies and robberies' (1.1.102–3). Morian thus conforms to stereotypical associations of blackness with lasciviousness and villainy before his speech takes a different turn. He boasts of his martial prowess and establishes his background as a soldier: 'In battles and perilous wars I fought like a formidable lion – not like a man but like a very devil' (1.1.107–9). Morian tells us that his skills as a soldier became known throughout the world and earned him the title of the 'Thunder and Lightning of Ethiopia' (1.1.111–12). In fact, the reason why the Romans invaded Ethiopia, according to Morian, is because '[m]y fame finally reached the Romans, who armed themselves mightily and came for us in Ethiopia, devastating and destroying the land with unheard-of cruelty' (1.1.112–15).

Morian's narration of his encounter with Tito and the Roman army on the Ethiopian battlefields implies that he was acting in the capacity of general: 'I went out against them with *my* army' (1.1.115–16, emphasis added). The fact that the Romans invaded Ethiopia gives Morian and Aetiopissa reason enough to be revenged on Tito, who played a key role in the attack. More importantly, Morian's speech establishes a clear rivalry

---

[1] For a discussion of Aaron and his skin-colour, see Fiedler.

[2] The play does not specify whether Morian was born in Ethiopia, but it is clear that he identifies powerfully with his erstwhile homeland.

between him and Tito: 'Before long, old Tito rushed at me and – something that no man had ever done before – struck me off my horse with his lance so fiercely that I didn't know whether I were dead or alive' (1.1.123–7). Although Morian emerges as a powerful military figure, his account makes clear that he was finally overcome and humiliated by the superior skills of the Roman warrior.[1]

The play's representation of Morian as a military champion calls to mind popular cultural associations of black Africans with martial skills and expert horsemanship.[2] However, the most immediate means of situating Morian within a familiar framework is achieved visually through his wearing of luxurious attire. The opening stage direction tells the reader that Morian wears 'magnificent clothes' under his cloak, which he dramatically casts aside as 'old rags' (1.1.81). His splendid attire stresses his former supremacy in Ethiopia, but also places him in a visual tradition in which black bodies are shown sumptuously dressed in order to heighten the contrast between black and white, juxtaposing the supposed dullness of the dark skin with the shimmering sartorial finery.[3] Interestingly, this kind of contrast can be seen in the Peacham drawing (see below, p. 29), which is generally thought to be an illustration of *Titus*. In the drawing, the blackness of the Moor's body and hair is sharply offset by the clothes and headband that he wears (see Fig. 1). This sort of contrast can be found in paintings, coats of

---

[1] See below (pp. 43–4) for a discussion of how this encounter echoes material in the chapbook. In Jan Vos' Dutch adaptation, *Aran en Titus* (*Aran and Titus*, 1641), the Moor publicly declares himself to be a supreme warrior (Buitendijk, ll. 176–9), and the List of Roles identifies him as the 'Veldheer der Gotten', which places him on an equal military footing with Titus, who is 'Veldtheer der Romeinen' (Buitendijk, l. 114).

[2] See Lowe, 'Stereotyping', 32–3.

[3] This visual tradition is discussed by Korhonen. Examples of this type of contrast are found in Bindman and Gates, vol. 3, part 1.

arms, impresas and decorative objects such as Christoph Jamnitzer's 'Moor's Head' cup.[1] As Anu Korhonen suggests:

> In [European] popular culture, blackness was fictionalised into a highly abstract but simply observable bodily category. Proverbs, sayings, biblical quotations and many passing remarks in Renaissance texts all come together to construct blackness as an absolute, without differences or degrees, juxtaposed with a whiteness similarly simplified and categorized. Black skin was perceived as a spectacle produced by this opposition, particularly when it was coupled with something white, be it white skin or white clothes, or with something precious and beautiful, such as gold, silver or jewels. Creating the dichotomy between black and white was essential to judging black as black, the conceptual and 'racial' black, not just a darker hue.
>
> (99)

In *Titus*, Aaron invokes this sort of contrast when he imagines himself rising to a position where he will cast off his 'slavish weeds and servile thoughts' and instead be 'bright, and shine in pearl and gold' (1.1.517–18). In *Tito* this image is literalized when Morian reveals the finery hidden under his cloak, setting up precisely the kind of contrast that Korhonen describes, given Morian's probable blackface.[2]

---

[1] See Seelig, 183.

[2] Another play in the Leipzig volume, *Eine schöne lustig triumphirende Comœdia von eines Königes Sohne auß Engellandt vnd des Königes Tochter auß Schottlandt* (*A Pleasant, Merry, Triumphant Comedy of the King of England's Son and the King of Scotland's Daughter*), sees the King of England's son temporarily disguise himself as a Moor in order to gain access to the King of Scotland's daughter. While the character wears the disguise, his speech heading changes from 'Sohn' to 'Morian', but this disguise does not involve the use of make-up. A stage direction tells us that he dons a long black garment ('ein schwartzen Rock', sig. U7v) and covers his face with a type of veil ('bindet einen Flor vor Angesichte', sig. U7v). He then introduces himself to the King as a true-born Moor ('ein geborner Aetiopis',

Unlike Aaron, Morian is presented as a character with a powerful sense of the past through a personal narrative that makes clear his former importance in Ethiopia. The speech he delivers is filled with anecdotal specificity, unlike the general and unspecific glimpses of Aaron's past and background as a perpetrator of villainies not rooted in any particular time or place. More importantly, the narrative delivered by Morian at the end of Act 1 offers a rival construction of his character as his country's champion that is quite distinct from Vespasianus' later identification of him as a 'black devil'. Morian's identity as the 'Thunder and Lightning of Ethiopia' is predicated on ferocity in battle and the honourable defence of his country, and the audience is made aware of this early on in the play. By contrast, in *Titus*, 'nothing but the blackness of his skin seems to link Aaron to a place of origin ... Aaron displays no sense of a cultural past and seems to possess no memories' (de Sousa, 104). As Emily C. Bartels points out, in appearing without a past, without a distinct culture, and being left to shape his identity from the quality of blackness, 'the "raven-coloured" Moor appears to be a self-contained, self-incriminating sign system – a darkness that seems undeniably visible' (*Speaking*, 80). Morian, however, renders such a sign system more complex, because his identity is shaped by more than the colour of his skin.

The vision of racial difference in *Tito* is complex. Morian's status as the black villain is complicated by the fact that he is a celebrated warrior. *Tito* treats the issue of miscegenation in a

sig. U8v) who has sailed from Ethiopia to trade jewels. With this disguise he manages to fool the King's daughter until he removes the veil from his face ('Ziehet den Flor vom Gesicht', sig. X2r). Although in both cases 'Morian' hails from Ethiopia, it is clear that in this play, where the disguise needs to be put on and removed with speed, the Moor's race is figured sartorially by means of a veil rather than through cosmetic blackface. See Wiggins, *British Drama*, 4.21–2, and the Lost Plays Database entry on *The King of England's Son and the King of Scotland's Daughter* (*c.* 1598). Wiggins suggests that the disguise in the English play would have entailed 'presumably dark skin' (22), but in light of the German play, this seems unlikely (but see Smith on the use of vizors for blackface).

27

different way from *Titus* and the chapbook prose history (see below, pp. 44–5). Whereas Tamora is eager to eradicate the child born of her amorous indiscretion, Aetiopissa hopes to preserve her son's life by sending him to live with his paternal grandfather, who may be imagined to be a sub-Saharan black African like Morian. The baby is not an aberration that needs to be killed off as in *Titus*. Rather, the infant can be integrated into a vision of the Roman Empire that hosts a diasporic community represented by an African patriarchal figure. This may suggest that the source play on which *Titus* is based (see below, pp. 36–40) had a more hopeful and inclusive vision of racial difference than it did after being reworked by Peele and Shakespeare.

THE SOURCE OF *TITO ANDRONICO*

The relationship between *Tito* and *Titus* has been examined in this introduction. The main action of the two plays is similar, and many echoes between the English play and *Tito* are detailed in the Commentary, but there is reason to believe that *Tito* was not directly based on the English play as we know it. Some scholars have been keen to identify *Tito* as an adaptation of *Titus*, including Creizenach (5) and Fuller (12). Yet from Albert Cohn in his 1865 edition of *Tito* onwards, other scholars have voiced serious doubt about a direct line of descent. Most importantly, Jonathan Bate, in his revised Arden edition of *Titus Andronicus* (2018), has changed his earlier view that *Tito* is 'a translation of Shakespeare's play into plain German prose, with heavy cutting and a reduction of the cast to twelve parts' (Ard[3] *TA*, 43). Instead, he now suggests that *Tito* may be based on an earlier version of the English play called *Titus and Vespasian* (Ard[3] *TA*, 138–9). In what follows, we discuss this possibility in relation to several pieces of interrelated evidence, in particular the Peacham drawing, early references to *Titus and Vespasian*, and the chapbook prose history and ballad of Titus Andronicus.

The Peacham drawing

There is a single-leaf manuscript in the library of the Marquess of Bath at Longleat House (Wiltshire, Great Britain) commonly referred to as 'the Peacham drawing'.[1] The manuscript is of importance to scholars of early modern drama because it is a rare early modern document that may provide insights into Elizabethan costuming and theatrical practice. The leaf contains a pen and ink illustration (see Fig. 1) that depicts, from left to right, two male figures in military attire, a male figure in Roman

1 The Peacham drawing (Longleat House, Warminster, Wiltshire, Great Britain).

---

[1]   The document is among the Harley Papers (Harley Papers I, fol. 159v). An overview of the provenance of these papers is provided by Schlueter, 'Rereading', 171, and Waith, 26–7.

dress wearing a laurel wreath and holding a standard or staff while what appears to be a sceptre lies on the ground, a crowned, kneeling female figure in an apparent show of supplication, two kneeling men with their hands bound, and a black male figure gesturing with his right hand at the sword that he holds in his left hand.[1] The illustration is separated by a horizontal line from a stage direction, '*Enter Tamora pleadinge for her sonnes going to execution*' (not in Shakespeare's play), followed by a speech by Tamora that largely corresponds to *Titus* 1.1.107–23, and a reply from Titus that combines lines 124 and 128 from the same scene, with an additional two invented lines directed at Aaron that warn him to prepare for his death. Then follows a speech by Aaron that corresponds to *Titus* 5.1.124–44, where he boasts of his villainies, and, following Aaron's speech, there is a speech prefix for Alarbus (who never speaks in *Titus*). Near the bottom left of the leaf is a signature, 'Henricus Peacham', with a date rendered in roman numerals, which has generally been identified as 1594 or 1595.[2] An annotation opposite the drawing

---

[1] Metz, in agreement with Wilson (21), suggests that the staff may be 'a spear or a Roman *hasta*, a ceremonial staff' (*Studies*, 233). For a discussion of the military attire and armour depicted in the drawing, see Holmes, 150–3.

[2] Chambers interpreted the date as either 1594 or 1595 (Metz, *Studies*, 234), as did Adams (33), given that the terminal 'qt°' could be read as *quinto* or *quarto*. Foakes (*Illustrations*, 48) interprets the date more firmly as 1595, following Wilson (19), and Waith (23), who provides the most detailed interpretation. Metz (*Studies*, 235) notes that 1595 is 'probably correct'. Bate (Ard³ *TA*, 39) does not overrule the 1595 interpretation but offers an alternative set of dates as possibilities (1604, 1614, 1615). The date was reinterpreted as 1594 by Berry (5–6). The signature has generally been associated with Henry Peacham (b. 1578), author of *The Complete Gentleman* (1622), who would have been sixteen or seventeen in 1595. Peacham's abilities as a draughtsman are attested in his collections of emblems, among them *Minerva Britanna* (London, 1612, STC 19511). Waith (24) draws comparisons between the Peacham drawing and some of Peacham's emblem drawings that survive in manuscript (three were based on the 1603 edition of James I's *Basilikon Doron* and were carried out between 1603 and 1619: Bodleian Library MS Rawlinson Poetry 146; British Library MS Harleian 6855, art. 13, and MS Royal 12 A lxvi; a later collection from *c.* 1621 is at the Folger Shakespeare Library: MS V.b.45).

reading 'Henrye Peachams Hande 1595' was probably made by the nineteenth-century scholar and forger John Payne Collier and therefore cannot be trusted (Waith, 23; Ard³ *TA*, 39).

The fact that the drawing does not appear to depict any one given moment from *Titus* has given rise to a number of interpretations that attempt to make sense of the drawing and the circumstances of its composition. For instance, R. A. Foakes supposes that the 'drawing does not fit any point in the action, and was probably not drawn from life' (50), whereas Eugene Waith (25) conjectures that Henry Peacham may have been present at a performance of *Titus* at Burley-on-the-Hill in January 1596 and based the drawing on that performance. John Dover Wilson suggests that the drawing depicts a performance that the artist saw first-hand (20), and G. Harold Metz (*Studies*, 243) concurs, arguing that the drawing is a representation of a performance, either at Burley or one of the commercial theatres in London. A particular difficulty is the relationship of the image and the text underneath it. Although the interpolated stage direction and the lines from *Titus* that are found under the drawing make it tempting to assume that the drawing in some way represents the first scene of *Titus*, the discrepancies between text and image are great. Indeed, the text as it appears in the manuscript does not fully agree with any of the quartos or the Folio version of *Titus*.

For this reason, commentators such as Waith (22, 25) argue that the drawing is 'comprehensive' in that it depicts multiple episodes simultaneously, whilst Metz (*Studies*, 243–5) suggests that the image works in an emblematic way.[1] Like Metz, Bate invites us to consider the drawing as a 'composite representation' that offers not just a depiction of several distinct episodes from *Titus* but 'an emblematic reading of the whole play'

---

[1] Waith follows Munro's initial suggestion about the technique of simultaneous representation.

(Ard³ *TA*, 41). Bate proposes that read left to right, the first two figures should be taken as Roman soldiers, 'who represent Titus' victory in war and service to the state' (Ard³ *TA*, 41), and that the third figure is Titus wearing a laurel bough and holding in his left hand a 'ceremonial spear or staff', dressed in a toga and breastplate, which signal his civic dignity and martial prowess (Ard³ *TA*, 41).[1] The figure kneeling before him is Tamora, whose 'flowing dress of the exotic Goth' (Ard³ *TA*, 41) and physical posture sets up a powerful contrast with Titus, while the two kneeling figures behind her are 'emblems of all the play's sons' (Ard³ *TA*, 42). The final figure, Aaron, brandishes a sword 'to indicate the deaths he has instigated' (i.e. of Titus' sons), which may also echo the drawing of his sword to protect his new-born son (Ard³ *TA*, 42), although Metz notes that Aaron here 'personifies the indignation of the Gothic queen and princes' (*Studies*, 244). In his interpretation of the drawing, Bate (Ard³ *TA*, 41) calls attention to the general division of Romans and Goths: the triumphant, virtuous Romans stand to the left, and are visually separated from the cruel, villainous Goths by Titus' upright staff, thus setting up an opposition that sits at the very heart of the play.

Although such an interpretation generally reflects scholarly orthodoxy,[2] it nevertheless remains open to challenge because the emblematic and symbolic approaches do not fully explain the apparent discrepancies between the image and the text, which sit uneasily alongside one another. Part of the problem may be, as Foakes (*Illustrations*, 48) observed, that the drawing

---

[1]   Ard³ *TA* (41) agrees with Wilson (20–1), who identified the figures on the left as soldiers because they, unlike the central figure (Titus), are not wearing Roman costume as one might expect. Wilson (21), in light of the text below the drawing, assumes that Titus' sons are offstage with Alarbus, but this takes for granted that the drawing and the text correspond to one another. In his discussion of armour on the early modern stage, Holmes (150–3) identifies the figures as Titus' sons.

[2]   See Waith, 23–7.

could have been made first and the text added later, perhaps by a different hand. June Schlueter subscribes to Foakes' suggestion and argues that the drawing is a representation of a Titus play that pre-dates *Titus* and is preserved in the German *Tito*, which she claims was based on the lost play, *Titus and Vespasian* ('Rereading'). It is for this reason, she argues, that there is an awkward relationship between the image and the text: 'we must conclude that the Shakespearean lines were added by someone whose assumption about the drawing confused and misled generations of scholars' ('Rereading', 176).

Schlueter states that there is a 'clear correspondence' (176) between the Peacham drawing and Act 1 of *Tito*. Although *Tito* calls for all principal characters except Victoriades to be present at the beginning of the play, Andronica, who ought to be in the drawing by this logic, is not depicted, perhaps, Schlueter argues, on account of her silence in this scene ('Rereading', 174). Schlueter invites us to see the figures, from left to right, as corresponding to Vespasianus, Titus, the Emperor, Aetiopissa, Helicates and Saphonus, and Morian, which would account for the absence of Victoriades (who is absent from Act 1). Schlueter's argument is attractive. The kneeling female figure and the bound men behind her certainly correspond more closely to Aetiopissa and her two sons in *Tito* than to Tamora and her three sons in *Titus*. Furthermore, the sword Morian brandishes may be a visual representation of his former military status, which he describes at the end of Act 1 and which is not in *Titus*.[1]

Schlueter's suggestion that the drawing was based on a lost play that served as the source for *Tito* yields interesting insights into the disagreements between the drawing and the text in the Peacham manuscript. However, despite its insights, Schlueter's reading of the drawing is not without its problems. In particular,

---

[1]   Waith (23) notes the disjunction between Aaron's apparently lacklustre apparel in *Titus* and the magnificent attire of the Moor in the Peacham drawing.

the identification of the central figure as the Emperor rather than Titus is open to question, as Richard Levin has demonstrated ('Longleat', 325–9). Levin challenges the idea that the bearded male figure, who is wearing a laurel bough, could be anyone but Tito, given that the stage directions and the dialogue in Act 1 differentiate between the bough worn by Tito and the imperial crown that is eventually given to the Emperor (327–8). Levin (326) also takes issue with Schlueter's proposition that the drawing is a literal representation of Act 1 of *Tito*. For instance, he draws attention to Morian's sword, which is present in the drawing, although the text says nothing about it at this point, so it must either be read as a symbol of his former military exploits, or as a literal rendering of Morian later in the play. Furthermore, in the text Morian is alone when he delivers his speech on his past villainies, so the presence of other characters in the drawing only makes sense if we assume that the drawing represents different moments from Act 1 simultaneously (Levin, 326).

Where Levin rejects Schlueter's argument in its entirety, we suggest that the Peacham drawing may be a composite representation of the first scene of an early Titus play that served as the basis for *Tito* and was later reworked into *Titus*. Read left to right, the figures may represent Titus' son and brother, Titus wearing his laurel bough, the supplicant captive Queen, who kneels and holds up her hands in an action that is suggestive of her subordinate position and reliance on Titus' mercy, her two sons, also bound to signify their status as prisoners, and the Moor as he appears at the end of the Act, no longer wearing a 'humble' cloak and boasting of his military supremacy. In fact, the Moor's right hand is raised, the index finger pointing in the direction of the Queen (suggestive of their amorous dalliance) and towards Titus (recalling the hand-to-hand encounter the two men have had in *Tito*; see 1.1.123–7). The presence of the Moor's sword is a detail that may be symbolic, but otherwise, the depiction of this figure agrees with what he wears in *Tito*. If we accept that the drawing may be a

34

composite and, given Andronica's absence, also selective representation, it corresponds remarkably well to what comes down to us textually in Act 1 of *Tito*.

Such a reading raises the question of why Titus' brother would be present in the drawing when he is not called for in the opening stage direction of *Tito*. A possible answer is that *Tito* is not a perfect translation of the lost play. Indeed, even if *Tito* correctly records the characters present in the opening scene of the play as it was performed in Germany, there is no guarantee that the equivalent of Victoriades would have been missing from the source play as performed in England, all the more so as the constraints of a travelling company often necessitated a trimming of certain roles on account of doubling.[1]

Given the disagreements between image and text in the Longleat manuscript, Metz proposes that the drawing 'should be studied directly, not through or under the guidance of or influence of the appended verses' (*Studies*, 242). If we follow this invitation to think about the drawing without the impediment of reconciling it with the text that follows, it is easy to imagine that what we have in front of us is a representation of an *Ur-Titus*. Given the other evidence to support a lost *Ur-Titus* presented below, it seems plausible that the drawing is based on a performance of that play.[2] If Foakes and Schlueter are right that the text was added by a different, and perhaps later, hand, this would account for the discrepancy between the opening scene of *Titus* and the illustration. Schlueter's call to reinterpret the Peacham drawing in the light of evidence preserved in *Tito*

---

[1] As noted above (p. 3), *Tito* could be performed with a minimum of ten actors, and if this was the case then it may not have been possible to have Victoriades on stage.

[2] Metz (*Studies*, 241) quotes Foakes on the likelihood that the drawing was done from memory, although there is no reflection on the amount of time that could have elapsed between the performance and the drawing (i.e. it could have been a number of years, in which case the date on the manuscript may reflect the year in which the artist executed the drawing, not the year in which he saw the play).

is thus useful, even though the evidence is too complex to allow for more than a tentative conclusion.[1]

Titus and Vespasian *and the* Ur-Titus

Schlueter's argument that *Titus and Vespasian* is an early Titus Andronicus play revives an old set of assumptions about the content of this lost play and its possible relationship to *Titus* and *Tito*. Cohn proposed that in *Tito* 'the original form of Shakespeare's tragedy ... may still be distinctly seen to glimmer through' (cxii), and that 'original form' he assumed to be the lost *Titus and Vespasian*. Cohn's point was based on the agreement of the characters' names – Vespasian and Vespasianus – and not much else, yet it does not follow that he was necessarily wrong.

The existence of *Titus and Vespasian* is attested by a series of entries in Philip Henslowe's 'diary' that notes performances in the early 1590s. The first entry records a performance of the play by Lord Strange's Men at the Rose theatre: 'ne – Rd at tittus & vespacia the 11 of ap^{r}ell 1591 [i.e. 1592] iij^{li} iiij s' (Foakes, *Diary*, 17). Henslowe's use of 'ne' has generally been taken to refer to a play that was new or possibly newly licensed after revisions (Foakes, *Diary*, xxxiv–xxxv; Knutson, 1–3). Six more entries for the same title (two of them omit the extra 't' from 'tittus') follow between 20 April and 6 June in the same year. After a six-month interval the season was resumed for a further month, and there are three more entries that refer only to 'Titus' without 'Vespasian' between 6 and 25 January 1593

---

[1] Note that Schlueter, in a so far unpublished essay, has recently revisited the Peacham drawing and its relationship to *Tito*. She proposes a new interpretation of the date (in the 1570s, if the third letter in the date is taken as a 'g', or in the 1570s or 1560s if the third letter is taken to be a long 's'), and argues that Henry Peacham senior, not his son, may have been responsible for both drawing and text, which record 'visually and literally, an early scene from *Titus and Vespasian*' ('Longleat', 10). We are grateful to Schlueter for sharing her essay with us.

('titvs', 'tittus', 'titus') (Foakes, *Diary*, 19–20). Under the entries pertaining to the Earl of Sussex's Men for the year 1594, there is found a 'ne' play performed on 23 January: 'titus & ondronicus', two more performances of which are noted ('titus & ondronicus' on 28 January and 'tittus & ondronicus' on 6 February) (Foakes, *Diary*, 21).

Apart from Henslowe's entries and the presence of Vespasianus in the German play, early allusions may point to a connection between the lost play, *Tito*, and *Titus*. *A Knack to Know a Knave* was first entered in Henslowe's diary as 'ne' on 10 June 1592, when it was performed by Lord Strange's Men. The quarto of *Knack*, published in 1594, contains three direct references to Emperor Vespasian[1] and an allusion to Titus that may point to subject matter found in *Titus*:

> My gratious Lord, as welcome shall you be,
> To me, my Daughter, and my sonne in Law,
> As *Titus* vnto the Roman Senators,
> When he had made a conquest on the Goths:
> That in requitall of his seruice done,
> Did offer him the imperiall Diademe:
> As they in *Titus*, we in your Grace still fynd,
> The perfect figure of a Princelie mind.
>
> (*Knack*, sig. F2v)

It is tempting to suppose that this refers to *Titus Andronicus* or an early version thereof. If so, the fact that *Knack* combines references to both Vespasian and Titus may be reason to suspect that *Titus and Vespasian* was indeed an early version of *Titus*, and therefore the version that served as the source for *Tito*.

---

[1] 'Lyke wise *Vaspasian, Romes* rich Emperour' (sig. A2r); 'Or lyke *Vaspasian, Romes* vertuous gouernour, / Who for a blowe his sonne did giue a Swaine, / Did straight commaund that he should loose his hand. / Then vertuous *Edgar*, be *Vaspasian* once,' (sig. B3v).

Henslowe's entries tell us that the play was popular, but they are unable to tell us what the play was about. For Cohn, the name Vespasianus was evidence enough to show that the lost play must have focused on the same material as the German play. For others, such as Eleanor Grace Clark, the link was too tenuous. She argued instead that the lost play was about the historical emperor Vespasian (AD 9–79), and the siege of Jerusalem by his son Titus in AD 70, who was promoted to joint emperor on his return to Rome (Clark, 524). More recently, Martin Wiggins has also identified the lost play with the siege of Jerusalem story, suggesting that the play may have drawn 'on the medieval romance version of the story (*The Destruction of Jerusalem by Titus and Vespasian*, printed c. 1508)'.[1] Yet Bate has argued that *Titus and Vespasian* may have been the *Ur-Titus*. If it was, he suggests (Ard[3] *TA*, 138–9), the conjunction 'and' in the original title may explain why Henslowe misnamed the revised play 'Titus & Ondronicus' when it was performed by the Earl of Sussex's Men on 23 January 1594 (Foakes, *Diary*, 21).[2] Scholarly opinion on the subject matter of the lost *Titus and Vespasian* thus remains divided.[3]

[1] Wiggins, 3.172–3 (172). Thomas Nashe's *Christ's Tears Over Jerusalem* (1593), which discusses the historical Titus and Vespasian and the siege of Jerusalem, contains a number of important parallels with *Titus*, such as the presence of a rival named 'Saturninus', an act of cannibalism where a mother eats her own son, and a hand being cut off (see Tobin, 186, and Streete, 56).

[2] Chambers (*William Shakespeare*, 1.319) notes the 'appearance of a *Titus and Vespasian* in a Revels list of plays about 1619' and suggests that it 'gives some confirmation to the view that the titles are equivalent'. For a discussion of the list and the titles found therein, see Chambers, 'Review'. The fragment that bears the title 'Titus and Vespatian' is digitally reproduced on the Lost Plays Database: https://lostplays.folger.edu/Titus_and_Vespasian.

[3] McCarthy and Schlueter propose that *Titus and Vespasian* was written by Thomas North (1535–1603?) in 1562 in response to Jasper Heywood's *Thyestes* (1560) and Thomas Norton and Thomas Sackville's *Gorboduc* (1561). They argue that this play was later adapted by Shakespeare and Peele into *Titus Andronicus*, and that traces of North's original are preserved therein. Their evidence for this comes from an analysis, using EEBO and the plagiarism software WCopyfind, of 'rare or

If we suppose that Titus' son was called Vespasian in an earlier version of the English play, we need to ask why he would have been a titular character. W. W. Greg pointed out that the title of the German play, *Tito Andronico and the Haughty Empress*, is not the same as that of the lost English play, and argued that the role occupied by Vespasianus therein is subordinate rather than equal to that of Tito.[1] Yet the title of the play may have been changed by the travelling players or when *Tito* was prepared for publication in 1620. Moreover, although Tito is clearly the main protagonist in the German play, his son is not necessarily as 'subordinate' as Greg suggests. The play begins and ends with a powerful visual pairing of Vespasianus and the Roman crown: in Act 1, he holds the crown in his hand and announces his father's candidacy for the honour (1.1.1–13), and at the close of the play, Vespasianus exits with his uncle, who now holds the crown that he will bestow upon his nephew before the populace (8.2.75–7).[2] As demonstrated

exclusive phrases' (90) common to *Titus* and North's earliest surviving work, *The Dial of Princes* (1557). McCarthy and Schlueter also note the agreements between the chapbook prose history and *Tito* against Shakespeare and Peele's *Titus*, proposing that these shared elements refute 'the view that the Titus story in the German play and the prose history comes exclusively from the Shakespeare play' (93–4). They argue that all four extant versions of the Titus Andronicus story (*Titus*, *Tito*, the ballad and the chapbook prose history) have a common source, which they believe was most likely to have been North's *Titus and Vespasian*.

[1] Greg, *Diary*, 2.155.

[2] Braekman argues that the opening speech is wrongly ascribed to Vespasianus, and that Victoriades must have delivered it because it echoes lines spoken by Marcus in *Titus*, where he is a tribune and is thus in a position to act as spokesperson for his brother, whereas 'this is not the case with Vespasianus' (48). This is questionable, given Vespasianus' prominence in the play. If the play was performed with ten actors, perhaps it had to be decided whether it was more important to have Tito's brother or his son onstage at the beginning of the play (see Appendix, pp. 418–19). Having Vespasianus enter holding the crown in the opening scene may serve to foreshadow the play's ending, where Vespasianus exits in order to receive the crown formally.

above (see pp. 14–15), Vespasianus is an important character in *Tito*, perhaps more prominent than his equivalent in *Titus*. It may be significant that the original *dramatis personae* list of *Tito* begins with Vespasianus. The important role played by Vespasianus in *Tito*, together with the fact that *Tito* corresponds to material in the English chapbook prose history that is absent from *Titus*, may indeed be evidence that *Titus and Vespasian* was the *Ur-Titus* that Shakespeare and Peele later reworked.[1]

The chapbook prose history and the ballad

The story of Titus Andronicus exists in three extant English versions: Shakespeare and Peele's play, a widely reprinted ballad, and a prose history. The prose history, entitled *The History of Titus Andronicus, the Renowned Roman General, Newly Translated from the Italian Copy Printed at Rome*, is extant in a mid-eighteenth-century chapbook printed by Cluer

---

[1]   The existence of a lost *Ur-Titus* has important implications for the much-debated question of the date of *Titus* (see Ard³ *TA*, 136–9, and Metz, *Studies*, 190–7). The first performance of *Titus* is recorded by Henslowe's 'ne – Rd at titus & ondronicus the 23 of Jeneway [1594]' (Foakes, *Diary,* 21), when it was played by Sussex's Men. Scholars who take seriously the allusion to Titus in *Knack* (see above, p. 37) maintain that *Titus* must already have been in existence by 1592. Others opt for an even earlier date, in order to reconcile the date of *Titus* with Jonson's comment about audiences' tastes in *Bartholomew Fair* (1614): 'Hee that will sweare, *Ieronimo*, or *Andronicus* are the best playes, yet, shall passe vnexcepted at, heere, as a man whose Iudgement shewes it is constant, and hath stood still, these fiue and twentie, or thirtie yeeres' (sig. A5v). This would date the two plays mentioned between 1584 and 1589, which has led to speculation about *Titus* being a very early play indeed. However, Jonson might have been conflating the *Ur-Titus* with *Titus* in his appraisal of Andronicus' popularity with audiences. It is plausible that Shakespeare's *Titus* as we know it was composed, in the sense of being adapted from an older play, shortly before Henslowe's first recorded performance, which would warrant the description 'ne'.

Dicey.[1] The prose history largely conforms to the main points of the action found in *Titus*, but there are also some substantial departures and episodes that have no equivalents in the play. The narrative printed in the chapbook undoubtedly reproduces, or is otherwise based on, an Elizabethan source, but it is impossible to date this source.

The discovery of the chapbook led to scholarship that tried to identify the prose history as the source for *Titus*.[2] Adams (7–9) and Sargent proposed that the prose history must have been printed together with the ballad, citing John Danter's entrance in the Stationers' Register, dated 6 February 1594, of 'a booke intituled *a Noble Roman Historye of Tytus Andronicus*' and 'the ballad thereof' (Arber, 644).[3] Most recent scholars consider it more likely, however, that Danter entered the play and the ballad at the same time (Waith, 2; Ard[3] *TA*, 82).

The orthodox view today of the relationship between the three iterations of the Titus story is that the prose history was the source for *Titus*, which then served as the source for the ballad (Waith, 28–32; Metz, '*History*' and 'Versions'). Yet there have been notable exceptions. Bate expands upon earlier arguments to propose a different order of composition,

[1] There is no evidence to indicate that this, or its Elizabethan precursor, was a translation of an Italian source. The chapbook was printed by Cluer Dicey sometime between 1736 and 1764 (see Adams, 8). The chapbook is in duodecimo and contains three generic woodcuts (a landscape with armoured figures, an interior scene of a couple at a table, and a bust of a woman), as well as some decorative end-pieces. There is only one extant copy of the chapbook, held at the Folger Shakespeare Library (ESTC N33327, call number PR3291.H685 Cage). We quote from and refer to the more easily accessible reprint in Geoffrey Bullough's *Narrative and Dramatic Sources of Shakespeare*, 6.35–44.

[2] There was some awareness of the prose history's existence in the nineteenth century (see the Malone-Boswell *Variorum*, 21.381, and Halliwell-Phillipps, 71). J. Quincy Adams was the first to remark at length on the significance of the prose narrative in his 1936 edition of *Titus*, which followed the discovery of the chapbook.

[3] The earliest extant version of the ballad is entitled 'Titus Andronicus' Complaint', published by Richard Johnson in *Golden Garland of Princely Pleasures and Delicate Delights* (1620). The ballad is reprinted in Bullough, 6.44–8.

whereby *Titus* served as the basis for the ballad, and the ballad was expanded into the prose history in the eighteenth century (Ard³ *TA*, 82–4). Bate is dismissive of the idea that the chapbook could be the source of *Titus*, but he does add the caveat that 'there is always the possibility that it drew on some other lost prose narrative or that Shakespeare was reworking a lost old play' (Ard³ *TA*, 84). Bate does not address *Tito* in his consideration of the play–ballad–chapbook relationship, yet the German adaptation may shed light on it. There are a number of features on which *Tito* and the chapbook agree against *Titus*, which may imply that the prose history served as the source for a lost Titus play that was taken to the Continent by travelling players and is now preserved in *Tito*.[1] If this early version served as the source for *Titus*, this would explain why particular episodes are altered further, shifted or removed altogether.

Aetiopissa's haughty nature is identified in the play's full title (she is 'der Hoffertigen Käyserin', the haughty Empress) and is repeatedly referenced throughout the play (see note on p. 189). The chapbook likewise describes the Goth Queen, Attava, as 'an imperious Woman, and of a haughty Spirit' (38), and her political ambition is noted in the narrative when she ruthlessly plots to have her sons made heirs to the Emperor (39–40). In *Tito*, Aetiopissa is the driving force behind the outrages perpetrated against the Andronici; Morian claims several times that he was sent by Aetiopissa to trick Tito into cutting off his hand, which is also the case in the chapbook, where Attava 'sent the Moor in the Emperor's Name' to cheat Titus out of his hand (41).[2] Sargent

---

[1] Braekman (9.38–108) discusses the parallels between the chapbook and *Tito*. Two such parallels that are absent from *Titus* are present in the Dutch *Aran en Titus* (1641): the Moor's military status (see 1.1.105–12n) and the fact that his paramour murdered her husband in order to be with him (see Buitendijk, ll. 535–8). Braekman suggests that *Tito* and *Aran en Titus* may be based on an *Ur-Titus* (9.37, 110–17; 10.16–17).

[2] Aaron claims he is sent by the Emperor (3.1.151), although his comments later in the play suggest otherwise (5.1.111–20).

notes that in the prose history 'the Moor never emerges as an independent character; he remains, until his concluding confession, the instrument of the Queen' (176), which is also true for Morian in *Tito*, but not for Aaron in *Titus*. There are two other correspondences. For instance, Tito's plan to sell his property in order to raise an army and be revenged upon the Emperor and Aetiopissa (5.1.62–4) echoes the beginning of the chapbook account, where Titus 'got together Friends, and sold whatever he had of value to hire Soldiers' (36) in order to help Rome defeat the Goth invaders. Andronica's unnamed husband (see p. 169) is likewise unnamed in the chapbook, where he is the Emperor's son rather than brother.[1]

There are likewise a number of transposed echoes between the chapbook and *Tito*.[2] Morian's long speech at the end of the opening scene echoes the fortunes endured by the Goth King in the chapbook. The first chapter of the prose history provides an account of how the Goths laid siege to Rome and Titus came to Rome's rescue. While the Goths are undeniably the aggressors in the chapbook, Titus' attack on them following the siege calls to mind Morian's description of the Roman invasion of Ethiopia

---

[1] In the chapbook narrative (39) and the ballad, Titus' daughter is betrothed to the son of the Emperor, which is also the case in Hieronymus Thomasius' *Titus und Tomyris*, a German adaptation of Vos' Dutch *Titus* play (see below, p. 50). In the chapbook, Attava, her two sons and the Moor invite Lavinia's consort 'to hunt on the Banks of the River Tyber, and there murder him . . . by shooting him thro' the Back with a poysoned Arrow' (40). In the 1699 performance programme of a German adaptation of Vos' play, it is noted that the Goth King was killed by Thamera and Aran (i.e. Tamora and Aaron) by means of a poisoned arrow shot by an assassin, which loosely echoes the murder of Lavinia's consort in the chapbook. Likewise, there may be an echo of this episode in Vos' adaptation (which might have been based directly or indirectly on an early English or German Titus play; see Braekman, 10.11–19). In the chapbook the hunt that heralds the untimely end of Lavinia's consort is held 'in the great Forest, on the Banks of the River Tyber' (40), whilst in *Aran en Titus*, Lucius rushes in to announce that a great boar has been sighted on the banks of the Tiber, and the court then proceeds to the hunt (see Braekman, 10.23).

[2] See Braekman, 9.43–108, and McCarthy and Schlueter, 93–4.

(1.1.112–30). The chapbook narrative notes how Titus' forces 'made such a Slaughter, that the Cry and Confusion were exceeding great' (36), and relates how during this encounter Tottilius 'labour'd to rally his flying Men; but being desperately charged by Andronicus, he was thrown from his Horse and much wounded' (36). When Tottilius escapes, he leaves 'the rich Spoils of his Camp, the Wealth of many plunder'd Nations, to Andronicus and his Soldiers' (36). These details are similar to Morian's description of the Roman invasion of Ethiopia: the Romans 'devastat[ed] and destroy[ed] the land with unheard-of cruelty' (1.1.114–15) and 'took many spoils' (1.1.128). Morian tells us that 'I saw my ranks dissolve, beaten like dogs' (1.1.123), and his demise is similar to that of Tottilius: 'old Tito rushed at me and – something that no man had ever done before – struck me off my horse with his lance so fiercely that I didn't know whether I were dead or alive' (1.1.124–7). The similarities between the fortunes of Tottilius and Morian's account of his former exploits may suggest that the prose history influenced the character of the Moor in the version of the play that eventually served as the basis for *Tito*.

The circumstances pertaining to Morian's banishment from the royal court following the King of Ethiopia's growing suspicions (1.1.90–4) also calls to mind features of the prose history. There, the Moor is first introduced after the Goth Queen has married the Roman Emperor and given birth to a dark-skinned child, which she attempts to explain away by saying it was 'conceived by the Force of Imagination' (39).[1] This rouses the Emperor's anger and leads to the Moor's banishment and Attava's later measures to secure access to her paramour once more, which she does by feigning illness and reporting a supposed vision that called for the Moor's return (39). In *Tito*, according to

---

[1]   The power of the imagination to imprint on the foetus was credited by a number of early modern physicians. For example, Ambroise Paré (sig. 4N3v) considered it a possible cause of unnatural or monstrous offspring.

a passage with no equivalent in *Titus*, the Empress also overcomes the problem of being separated from the Moor, which she does by poisoning her husband (1.1.98–100); this happens before she comes to Rome and becomes pregnant with Morian's child.

There may also be an echo of the chapbook's Roman Emperor raising 'a mighty Army in Greece, Italy, France, Spain, Germany, and England' (35) in the report of Vespasianus travelling across the Roman Empire and raising a diverse army (5.2.37–42). While *Titus* does not specify the number of troops raised by Lucius, *Tito* insists on 'sixty thousand horsemen in full armour' (7.1.3), which may echo the 'threescore thousand' (35) men that the Roman Emperor loses to Tottilius at the beginning of the prose history. There are also instances where the order of the action in *Tito* agrees with that of the chapbook against *Titus*. For example, in the English play, Titus' severed hand and the heads of his sons are returned (3.1.235–301) after Lavinia has been brought to her father (3.1.59–150), whereas *Tito* places the equivalent action before the mutilated daughter is discovered, as does the chapbook.

There is a strong case to be made, then, for rethinking the relationship between the prose history and *Titus* in light of *Tito* and its relationship with the lost Titus play. The similarities between the prose history and *Tito* suggest that an early version of the prose history may have been the source for an earlier English Titus play that was eventually taken to the Continent by travelling players, before it was reworked into Shakespeare and Peele's *Titus*. If we suppose that *Titus* is the play taken to the Continent and then adapted into the version that comes down to us as *Tito*, it would be surprising if *Tito* independently invented material that also happens to be found in the chapbook. It seems just as unlikely that the travelling players would import details of the prose history into their performances after taking the play to the Continent. Indeed, a more plausible way of reconciling the agreements between *Tito* and the chapbook is to suppose that the prose history served as the source for a now lost Titus

45

play that was taken to the Continent by travelling players but also served as the basis for Shakespeare and Peele's *Titus*.

The preceding sections have demonstrated that *Tito* provides valuable insights into the contested relationship between *Titus* and the Peacham drawing, *Titus and Vespasian* and the chapbook prose history. There are suggestive correspondences between the first Act of *Tito* and the Peacham drawing, and a number of parallels between *Tito* and the chapbook prose history, which agree against *Titus*. The evidence from the preceding sections strengthens the possibility that *Tito* does not derive from *Titus* but is based on an earlier version, a lost *Ur-Titus*, which revision turned into Shakespeare and Peele's *Titus Andronicus*.

GERMAN TITUS PLAYS IN THE SEVENTEENTH CENTURY

Titus plays were very popular in Germany, as surviving evidence demonstrates. Understandably, *Tito* is the most well-known early German adaptation of this material, given that it has been available in English translation since the nineteenth century. There are two known seventeenth-century performances of *Tito*, both of which took place in a school in Kronstad, Siebenbürgen (present day Braşov, in the Transylvanian region of Romania). Evidence of these performances comes from the diary of Johannes Stamm, a chronicler of Siebenbürgen (Klein, 233). In February 1677, Stamm mentions the performance of a play about 'Tito Andronico and his son Vespasiano' ('von Tito Andronico und seinem Sohn Vespasiano') (*Quellen*, 201). This play was performed again in 1687, and Stamm provides a longer description:

> These plays are acted, namely the first one about how Abraham wants to sacrifice Isaac at God's command; the other one about Andronico and his son Vespasiano,

46

how they recruit people from foreign lands to fight against the Emperor, and how they finally invite the Emperor and his godless wife (who was an instigator of this homegrown war) to a feast, and how during the feast Andronica, the Empress, Andronicus himself and finally also the Emperor are killed.[1]

The correspondences with *Tito* relating to the recruitment of soldiers in foreign lands and the identification of the Emperor's 'godless wife' as the instigator of domestic strife, as well as the mention of 'Vespasiano' and 'Andronica' make clear that the text used for the performance must have been *Tito*. The school's constitution dictated that two plays be performed every year (and this since 1543; Fassel, 183), so it is reasonable to assume that dramatic texts were collected in the school library, and that they held a copy of the Leipzig volume of *Engelische Comedien vnd Tragedien* (1620; 2nd edn 1624).

Tito might also have been performed in Lüneburg in 1666, under the title *Von Tito Andronico, welches eine schöne Romanische Begebenheit, mit schöner Außbildung* (*Of Tito Andronico, which is a goodly Roman Story, of pleasant Making*, Gstach, 644). The fact that no mention is made of a Goth Moor, as is the case in the records of other performances noted below, makes it at least possible that this performance used *Tito* as its basis.

Based on the available evidence of performances and printed material pertaining to Titus plays, it would seem that it was Jan Vos' Dutch adaptation, *Aran en Titus, of Wraak en Weerwraak: Treurspel* (*Aran and Titus, of Revenge and Counter-revenge: A Tragedy*), written in 1638 and published in 1641, that was most

---

[1] 'Werden diese Comedien agiert, als die erste wie Abraham auf Gottes Geheiss seinen Sohn Jsac opfern will; die ander vom Andronico und seinem Sohn Vespasiano, wie sie wider den Kaiser Volk aus fremden Land aufbringen und zuletzte den Kaiser mit seinem gottlosen Weibe (welche ein Anfängerin ist dieses einheimischen Krieges) zu Gast bekommt, und in dieser Gasterei die Andronica, die Kaiserin, und Andronicus selbst und zuletzt auch der Kaiser umbracht werden' (*Quellen*, 210).

47

popular in seventeenth-century Germany.[1] The popularity of *Aran en Titus* cannot be overstated: the play was frequently performed and went through many editions in its home country. A Latin version was performed at the gymnasium in Tiel in 1658 and survives in a printed edition (the translation was probably made by Caspar van Baerle for the rector, J. van Aelhuisen).[2] German adaptations of Vos' play were popular throughout the second half of the seventeenth century, both commercially and as school performances. It is unclear how Vos' play was first translated into German, but the German dramatist Georg Greflinger promised a translation of a play entitled *Andronicus mit dem Aron* (*Andronicus with Aron*) in the preface to his translation of Pierre Corneille's play, *The Ingenious Tragicomedy called Cid* (*Die Sinnreiche Tragi-Comoedia gennant Cid*, Hamburg, 1650, sig. *2v). It is unclear whether this translation was ever completed or published, but it is evident that Greflinger was referring to Vos' play, particularly since the reference comes in the context of Spanish and Dutch plays.

The earliest evidence of a performance of Vos' play in Germany comes from a school production in Schwäbisch Hall in May 1656, described in a programme entitled *Aran und Titus, Oder Tragödia von Raach und Gegen-Raach* (*Aran and Titus, or a Tragedy of Revenge and Counter-revenge*).[3] The programme was printed by Hans Reinhard Laidigen in a quarto pamphlet of eight pages, which includes a list of roles and the names of the boys who played them, as well as an act-by-act summary. The action as we find it in the summary reflects Vos' play, and the text used by the boys probably came from a troupe

---

[1] Vos might have based his play on Adriaen Van den Bergh's lost 1621 translation. See Braekman, 10.17–19, and Buitendijk, 64–5.

[2] This was entitled *Aran en Titus. Mutua vindicatio, interprete schola Thielana* (*Aran and Titus. Mutual Revenge, Acted by the Thiel School*). See Fuller, 14, and Worp, 53.

[3] This document contains a scene-by-scene summary of the action, a short preamble, an 'epilogue' and a list of roles together with the names of the boys who played them. See Rudin, 'Textbibliothek', for a discussion (79–80) and reproduction of this programme (99–105).

of travelling players, whose presence is noted in Schwäbisch Hall that same year. Bärbel Rudin's research demonstrates that the High German (Hoch Teutschen) comedians sold a Moorish cloak, a sceptre and a crown to the City, and that costs for an unbound book of various comedies ('ein vngebunden Buch von vnderschiedlichen comoedien') were met by the Rector ('Textbibliothek', 79). Some months later, in July 1656, the High German comedians petitioned to perform *Von dem Tapffern Römer Tito Andronico (Of the Brave Roman, Tito Andronico)* at Strasbourg, where a note in the hand of the actor Christoph Blümel describes the play as 'a stately, well-written history, for the first time translated into German, and never seen here before' ('eine statliche, wolgeschriebene Histori, die erst ins teutsche gebracht, und noch nie hier gesehen worden'; Rudin, 'Textbibliothek', 79). Whilst the title in Blümel's petition does not explicitly relate to Vos, the fact that the comedians can be traced to Schwäbisch Hall suggests that they were in possession of a German translation of Vos' play (see below, pp. 51–2). Blümel was an educated man, whose handwriting and name can be identified in a number of extant manuscript playtexts from the *Wanderbühne* (Rudin, 'Textbibliothek', 78–9; see p. 51, n. 2), so he may have been responsible for the translation himself, or used a text prepared by someone else like Greflinger.

There is evidence that the High German comedians performed a translation of *Aran en Titus* at Augsburg around 1658. An extant playbill pamphlet entitled *Rach und Gegen-Rach: oder: Titus undt Aran (Revenge and Counter-revenge, or Titus and Aran)* contains a supplication to the city signed by Johann Ernst Hoffmann, Peter Schwartz and Andreas Hart.[1] They had travelled and performed with Blümel, and would work with him again later. The High German comedians spent the autumn and winter season of 1656–7 at Heidelberg Castle, so it is unsurprising that they attached the title 'Heidlbergische' to their troupe (Rudin,

---

[1] A digital reproduction is available through the Bavarian State Library: https://reader.digitale-sammlungen.de/resolve/display/bsb11206615.html.

49

'Textbibliothek', 81–2). The pamphlet contains a prologue, and choruses for Acts 2, 3, 4 and 5, all of which appear to be free verse translations of their equivalents in Vos' *Aran en Titus*.

The popularity of Vos' *Aran en Titus* in Germany is further evidenced by Hieronymus Thomasius' adaptation, entitled *Titus und Tomyris Oder Traur-Spiel, beygenahmt Die rachbegierige Eyfersucht* (*Titus and Tomyris, or a Tragedy called the Vengeful Jealousy*, Giessen, 1661; reissued 1662). This version retains the alexandrines and classical style of its source, but the choruses are omitted, and there are many local embellishments and additions to the dialogue. There is no evidence that this play was performed.

There are many performances of Titus plays in the second half of the seventeenth century. In 1667, at Nürnberg, Carl Andreas Paulsen's troupe acted *Die Comoedie von Tito Andronico und dem Mohren Aron* (*The Comedy of Tito Andronico and Aron the Moor*),[1] while Johannes Velten's troupe performed *Der Berühmte Römische General Titus Andronicus vnd grausamer Tyrann Aran Gottischer Mohren General* (*The Famous Roman General Titus Andronicus and the Cruel Tyrant Aran, the Goth Moor General*) at Bevern Castle in 1680 (Junkers, 169; Gstach, 617, 679–80, 686). In 1685 there are several accounts and ledger references to a Titus play performed in Český Krumlov (south Bohemia) by the Eggenberg comedians (Záloha, 'Divadelní', 71; Hejnic and Záloha, 51–2). The text that was probably used for this performance is extant in a collection of manuscript *Wanderbühne* plays held at the Vienna Rathaus Library (call number Ia 38589). The undated play is

---

[1] This performance is documented by Birken; he notes that 'the Emperor Saturninus falls for the captive Goth Queen, who had an affair with the Moor' ('Key[ser] Saturninus hängt sich an die gefangene Gothische Königin, die mit dem Mohren buhlte', 300). Birken mentions seeing a revival of this production the following year: 'I saw the comedy of the sold and returned Andronico' ('Die Comoedie vom verk[auften] und wiederbeck[ommenen] Andronico gesehen', 397). See also Gstach, 617.

entitled *Titus und Aran* (*Titus and Aran*) and appears to be a free prose translation of Vos' *Aran en Titus*. The choruses are omitted but the names agree with Vos, except for Titus' daughter, who is called Lavinia instead of Rozelyna. Rudin ('Textbibliothek', 78–81) has convincingly demonstrated the likelihood that Blümel's troupe, who had performed Vos' play in Germany, were responsible for this manuscript version, given that various members of their company formed the Eggenberg troupe, including Hoffman, Schwartz and Blümel himself,[1] whose signature and hand are found in other of the plays in the Vienna Rathaus Library collection.[2] Other plays in the collection can be traced to Český Krumlov by their watermarks or by the fact that their titles are also found in the castle's household records.[3]

There is an extant plot summary of a 1699 performance by the High German comedians in Linz, entitled *Tragoedia genannt Raache gegen Raache. Oder Der Streitbare Römer Titus Andronicus* (*The Tragedy called Revenge against Revenge, or: The Brave Roman, Titus Andronicus*) (Cohn, 'Breslau'). Rudin ('Textbibliothek', 81) argues that the Eggenberg version of the play was performed in this instance. There is another mention of a Titus play in the 'Weimar Index' of plays (Dutchess Anna Amalia Library, call number Fol 421/32), which lists *Der mörderische gotthische Mohr sampt Dessen Fall und End* (*The Murderous Goth Moor and His Demise and End*). Here, as in many of the other titles mentioned above, the reference to a

---

[1]   On the beginnings of the Eggenberg comedians, see Záloha, 'Eggenbergischen', 265–7.

[2]   For a recent edition of *Aran und Titus*, see Hulfeld and Mansky (97–180). The sixth play contained in the Vienna Rathaus Library collection of *Wanderbühne* plays, *Comaedia von der glückseligen Eifersucht zwischen Rodrich und Delmira von Valenza* (*The Comedy of the Blissful Jealousy between Rodrich and Delmira of Valencia*), contains a title page bearing Blümel's name, and Český Krumlov castle records provide evidence of a payment for *Die Eifersucht* in the year 1677 (Záloha, 'Divadelní', 70). Likewise, *Aurora und Stella* (*Aurora and Stella*), which is present in the collection, is also mentioned in the castle records for the year 1688 (see Záloha, 'Divadelní', 71).

[3]   See Schindler.

51

Goth Moor means that this play was not based on *Tito*, where the Moor is not a Goth. These texts and traces of performance suggest that translations of Vos' *Aran en Titus* were more popular than the version that we find preserved in *Tito*, but, unlike *Tito*, they all date from the second half of the seventeenth century, not the first.[1]

TEXTUAL INTRODUCTION

The Engelische Comedien vnd Tragedien *of 1620 and 1624*

Tito Andronico appeared in 1620 in an octavo collection of plays entitled *Engelische Comedien vnd Tragedien* (VD17 39:120191N) (see Fig. 2). Translated into English, the title page reads:

> English Comedies and Tragedies, that is, very pleasant, delightful and select spiritual and worldly comic and tragic plays, with Pickelhering, that on account of their agreeable inventions and entertaining and partly true stories have been performed and set forth by the English in Germany at royal, electoral and princely courts as well as in distinguished maritime and trading towns, and have never been previously printed. Now for all lovers of comedies and tragedies and to please others these are publicly printed in such a fashion that they can be easily prepared for performance and serve for the delight and recreation of the mind. Printed in the year 1620.[2]

---

[1] There are no known modern performances of *Tito Andronico*.

[2] 'Engelische Comedien vnd / Tragedien / Das ist: Sehr Schöne, / herrliche vnd außerlesene, / geist- vnd weltliche Comedi vnd / Tragedi Spiel, / Sampt dem / Pickelhering, / Welche wegen jhrer artigen / *Inventionen*, kurtzweiligen auch theils / warhafftigen Geschicht halber, von den Engelländern / in Deutschland an Königlichen, Chur, vnd Fürst-/lichen Höfen, auch in vornehmen Reichs-See- vnd /

2 Title page of *Engelische Comedien vnd Tragedien* (Leipzig, 1620)
(University Library, LMU Munich, shelfmark: W 8 P.germ. 46).

Handel Städten seynd agiret vnd gehalten / worden, vnd zuvor nie im Druck auß-/
gangen. / An jetzo, / Allen der Comedi vnd Tragedi Lieb-/habern, vnd Andern zu
lieb vnd gefallen, der Gestalt / in offenen Druck gegeben, daß sie gar leicht darauß
/ Spielweiß widerumb angerichtet, vnd zur Ergetzligkeit vnd / Erquickung des
Gemüths gehalten wer-/den können. / Gedruckt im Jahr M.DC.XX.'

The collection contains ten plays (including two Pickelhering plays) and five short interludes or jigs. The plays appear in the following order: 1) *The Comedy of Queen Esther and Haughty Haman* ('COMOEDIA. Von der Königin Esther vnd hoffertigen Haman', sigs A4r–G3v); 2) *The Comedy of the Prodigal Son in which Despair and Hope Are Agreeably Introduced* ('COMOEDIA. Von dem verlornen Sohn in welcher die Verzweiffelung vnd Hoffnung, gar artig introduciret werden', sigs G4r–L1v); 3) *The Comedy of Fortunato and his Purse and Little Wishing Hat* ('COMOEDIA. Von Fortunato vnd seinem Seckel vnd Wünschhütlein', sigs L2r–R6r); 4) *A Pleasant, Merry, Triumphant Comedy of a King's Son of England and a King's Daughter of Scotland* ('Eine schöne lustig triumphirende Comoedia von eines Königes Sohne auß Engellandt vnd des Königes Tochter auß Schottlandt', sigs R6v–Y3v); 5) *An Entertaining Merry Comedy of Sidonia and Theagene* ('Eine kurtzweilige lustige Comoedia von Sidonia vnd Theagene', sigs Y4r–2D3v); 6) *A Pleasant, Merry Comedy of Somebody and Nobody* ('Eine schöne lustige Comoedia, von Jemand vnd Niemandt', sigs 2D4r–2K7r); 7) *The Tragedy of Julio and Hyppolita* ('Tragaedia. Von Julio vnd Hyppolita', sigs 2K7v–2N4r); 8) *A Very Lamentable Tragedy of Tito Andonico and the Haughty Empress* ('Eine sehr klägliche Tragædia von Tito Andronico vnd der hoffertigen Käyserin', sigs 2N4v–2S4r). The two Pickelhering plays are called *A Merry Pickelherring Play of Fair Maria and the Old Adulterer* ('Ein lustig Pickelherings Spiel von der schönen Maria vnnd alter Hanrey', sigs 2S4v–2U8v) and *Another Merry Pickelherring Play in which he Makes Merry Jests with a Stone* ('Ein ander lustig Pickelherings Spiel, darinnen er mit einem Stein gar lustige Possen machet', sigs 2X1r–2Y5v).[1] The collection concludes with dramatic anecdotes in verse, or jigs (sigs 2Y6r–3B7v), with accompanying musical notation. They are preceded by the

---

[1]   For the Pickelherring plays in the 1620 volume, see Hilton, 292–9.

54

advice, 'The following English excerpts may be acted between the comedies' ('Nachfolgende Engelische Auffzüge können nach Beliebung zwischen die Comoedien agiret werden', sig. 2Y6r). Each jig focuses on Pickelhering or a clown figure.[1]

The first two plays deal with popular biblical subjects: the Old Testament story of Queen Esther, and the Gospel narrative of the prodigal son.[2] The third play dramatizes the story of Fortunatus which originated in an early sixteenth-century German chapbook and was later dramatized by Hans Sachs in 1553 in Germany and in two English versions: the lost *First Part of Fortunatus* (mentioned by Henslowe in 1596; Foakes, *Diary*, 34–7) and Thomas Dekker's *Old Fortunatus*, published in 1599. The *Comoedia von eines Königes Sohne auß Engellandt vnd des Königes Tochter auß Schottlandt* may well preserve the contents of a lost English play (see Wiggins, 4.21–2). *Sidonia vnd Theagene*, on the other hand, is clearly based on a German verse play, Gabriel Rollenhagen's *Amantes Amentes*, published in Magdeburg in 1609, although Rollenhagen may himself have been influenced by the plays of the English comedians (Seelmann; Haekel, 125–8). The final comedy in the collection, *Jemand vnd Niemandt*, is based on the anonymous English play *No-body and Some-body*, printed in 1606 but perhaps performed as early as the 1590s (Bosman, 570).[3] The first tragedy in the collection, *Julio vnd Hyppolita*, bears some resemblance to Shakespeare's *Two Gentlemen of Verona*,[4] and is followed by *Tito Andronico*, the Pickelhering plays and the jigs. The order of the plays may

[1] For the jigs in the 1620 collection, see Cohn, cviii–cix; Braekman, 9.13; Hilton, 299–302; and Baskerville, 515–49. For early modern English jigs more generally, see Clegg and Sheaping, and Baskerville.

[2] The first play might be related to the lost 'heaster & asheweros' mentioned in Henslowe's diary on 3 June 1594 (Foakes, *Diary*, 21), although Haekel (205–12) considers it likely that it derives from German sources.

[3] A German manuscript of 1608 with a different version of this play is also extant; see below, p. 77.

[4] For *Julio vnd Hyppolita*, see Cohn, cxi, 113–56.

55

reflect a conscious decision to start with the biblical pieces, before progressing to less respectable matter and genres.[1]

Between the title page and the plays, the volume contains a four-page, unsigned prefatory epistle (sigs A2r–A3v), which makes a case for the importance of drama by commenting upon the dignity of actors in ancient Rome. As Fredén has shown, almost the whole preface is copied or closely adapted from a passage in *La Piazza universale di tutte le professioni del mondo*, by Tommaso Garzoni, which had first been published in Venice in 1585 (Fredén, *Friedrich*, 9–15). In fact, Garzoni's encyclopedic work had appeared in a German translation, by Matthäus Merian, in Frankfurt in 1619: *Piazza Universale, das ist: Allgemeiner Schauwplatz* (VD17 12:109736B). The *Piazza universale*, a massive folio of over 700 pages, consists of 153 'discorsi', or 'Discurs' in Merian's translation, of which the 103rd is entitled 'Von Comicis, vnd Tragoedis, beydes denen, so sie beschreiben, vnd denen, so sie spielen' ('Of comedies and tragedies, both they who write and they who act them'; sig. 3B4v). It takes up four pages, and the preface is essentially derived from the first of them (sig. 3B4v).[2] Since the preface in the 1620 collection is unsigned, it is unclear who wrote it (but see below, p. 73). What seems clear, however, is that it must have been added not long before the collection was printed.

The 1620 volume is entirely anonymous: it mentions no author, translator, adapter, theatre company, publisher,

---

[1] For the plays in the 1620 volume, see also Schlueter, 'Across'; Haekel, 120–31; 165–80; Noe; and Cohn, cvii–cix.

[2] For an example of the close correspondence between the two texts, compare the following two excerpts: 'So ist hingegen gewiß vnd auß allen Historien bekandt, daß auch etlichen *particularen* beydes vmb ihrer Kunst vnd dann vmb ihrer Tugendt willen grosse Ehre, vnd solches auch öffentlich ist erzeiget worden' (*Engelische Comedien vnd Tragedien*, sig. A2v); 'so ist doch gewiß vnnd auß allen Historien bekandt, daß auch etlichen *particularen* beydes vmb ihrer Kunst, vnnd dann vmb ihrer Tugendt willen grosse Ehre, vnd solches auch offentlich ist erzeiget worden' (Garzoni, *Piazza Universale*, sig. 3B4v).

bookseller, printer or even place of publication. Yet quite a lot can be inferred about the genesis of the collection from other sources. In 1921, the Swedish scholar Johan Nordström published a handwritten list by the German-born academic Friedrich Menius (1593/4–1659) of works he had written (see below, pp. 58, 66–8), which includes 'English Comedies, 2 parts. Altenburg, published by Gottfried Grosse, bookseller in Leipzig, 1620, in octavo' ('Englische Comoedien 2 Theil. Altenburg in Verlegung Gottfried Großen Buchhändlers zu Leipzig. a:o 1620. in 8:vo'.) (Nordström, 'Friedrich', 86–91, 87). The information in the Menius manuscript (Uppsala, University Library, MS Nordin 1997; see Fig. 3, number 2) is also in a printed list of publications appended to Menius' *Syntagma de origine Livonorum* (Dorpat, 1632 (1635), sigs G2r–G3v), a book about the origins of the Livonians, who lived in what is now northern Latvia and southern Estonia.[1] Much of the information Menius provides about the title and size of the collection of plays is confirmed by the Leipzig book fair catalogue of spring 1620, *Catalogus Universalis* (VD17 1:066359V), published by Gottfried Grosse and Abraham Lamberg, which mentions 'English Comedies and Tragedies together with the Pickelhering, Leipzig, at Gottfried Gross', 8°, 1620' ('Engelische Comoedien vnd Tragoedien sampt den Pickelhaering, Leipzig bey Godfrid Großen, in 8', sig. F3v). The same information appears in an entry in Georg Draud's *Bibliotheca librorum germanicorum classica*, published in Frankfurt in 1625 (VD17 12:154632L), a massive 800-page bibliography of German books. In a list of 'Comedies of various worldly stories, including virtues and vices' ('Comedien von

---

[1] 'Catalogus Lucubrationum Friderici Menii', in *Syntagma de Origine Livonor*[*vm*] (Dorpat: [Jacob Becker], 1632 (1635), sigs G2r–G8v). The information in the printed list is almost identical with that in the manuscript; it reads, 'Engelische Comoedien 2. Theil. Altenburg in Verlegung Gottfried Großen Buchhändlers zu Leipzig. a:o 1620. in 8:vo' (sig. G2r).

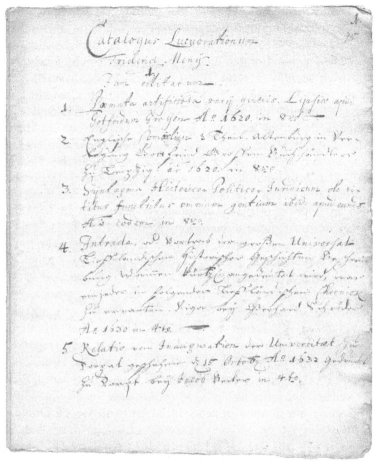

3 Friedrich Menius, 'Catalogus Lucubrationum Friderici Menij' (Uppsala Universitetsbibliotek, shelfmark: Nordin 1997).

allerhand Weltlichen Geschichten, auch Tugenden vnd Lastern', sig. 4A3r) is a reference to 'English Comedies and Tragedies together with the Pickelhering, Leipzig, at Gottfried Gross', 8°, 1620'.[1] The information provided by Menius about the publisher and the place of publication is thus confirmed by independent sources.

Gottfried Grosse (1591–1637) was a bookseller and a publisher, but he was not a printer, and Menius' list tells us that the book was printed in 'Altenburg', a town about thirty miles south of Leipzig.[2] A printer in Altenburg who is known to have produced books that were published in Leipzig is Johann Meuschke (also spelled 'Meuschken'). In 1618, for instance, Meuschke printed Adam Cramer's *Kurtzer Aber doch außführlicher Extract auß denen Böhemischen Stad-Rechten und Lands-Ordnung* (VD17 7:707597S) and three sermons (*Drey FestPredigten*) by Heinrich Eckhard (VD17 12:207509N), both published by Henning Grosse, the younger, Gottfried's brother, in Leipzig. In 1623, Meuschke printed another of Cramer's sermons, *Regenten Ehrenpreiss* (VD17 39:103550G), published by Caspar Kloseman in Leipzig. He has been identified as probably the first printer in Altenburg, active from at least 1610 to 1633 (Hauthal, 22). Other Altenburg printers, Johann Bernhard Bauernfinck, Johann Michael, Otto Michael, Gottfried Richter, Johann Ludwig Richter and George Konrad Rüger, are known to have been active later in the seventeenth century (Bürger, 150–1). It seems very likely, then, that Meuschke printed the 1620 *Engelische Comedien vnd Tragedien*.

Gottfried Grosse was from a family of Leipzig booksellers and publishers. His father, Henning Grosse (1553–1621), is known to have published at least 938 titles in the period from

---

[1] 'Engelische Comedien vnd Tragedien sampt dem Pickelhäring, Leipzig bey Gottfried Gross 8 1620' (sig. 4A3r).

[2] Benzing (1149) notes that Grosse in fact owned a printing house but leased it to a fellow Leipzig stationer, Johann Albrecht Mintzel.

1580 to 1621; he played an important role in moving a significant part of the German book trade from Frankfurt to Leipzig (see Brauer). Gottfried became a partner in his father's business in 1618 and took it over from him after his death, publishing at least 549 titles in the period from 1618 to 1637. He became an alderman of the City of Leipzig in 1623. Gottfried's older brother Friedrich (1580–1602) had set up his own bookshop quite a bit earlier, which another brother, Henning the Younger (1582–1622), took over after his early death (Brauer).

Gottfried Grosse's publications, like his father's, were mostly theological and religious in nature, notably sermons (like Johannes Andreae's *Vier Geist- und Trostreiche Evangelische Predigten*, 1619, VD17 14:017557D, and Johann Meelführer's *Postilla Davidica*, 1619–20, VD17 14:666249W); theological tracts, in Latin, like the *Decas Quaestionum* (1621, VD17 14:028545Q), by Erhart Lauterbach and Tobias Schubart, and in German, like Balthasar Marschner's pamphlet against purgatory, *Päpstischer Irrwisch* (1630, VD17 23:649084E); prayer books like the *Andächtige Christliche Gebet* (1624, VD17 14:681366B); and Luther's hymns, entitled *Geistliche Lieder* (1621, VD17 7:684853N). Grosse also took over from his father the publication of the important Leipzig book fair catalogue, as well as the *Continuatio* (e.g., VD17 39:124315U), a precursor of the newspaper, which regularly appeared in time for the Leipzig book fair and contained political and military news that had accumulated since the previous fair. Grosse also occasionally published books of other kinds, like a Hebrew language manual by Wilhelm Schickard (*Der Hebraische Trichter*, 1629, VD17 23:293103G), or a Latin collection of orations, letters and religious poems by the French humanist Marc-Antoine Muret (1619–20, VD17 28:730179B). Grosse published few literary titles, and those he did seem to have been mostly in Latin, like Ovid's elegies (*P. Ovidii Nasonis De Ponto Libri IV*, 1627, VD17 1:060931C) and a collection of six comedies by Terence, *P. Terentii Afri Comoediae Sex superstites*

(1632, VD17 1:043285K). An exception to this rule was Zacharias Lund's collection of poems, *Allerhand artige Deutsche Gedichte* (1636, VD17 23:293764M). Apart from the *Engelische Comedien vnd Tragedien* (the 1620 and the 1630 volumes; see below, pp. 71–4), Grosse appears not to have been involved in the dissemination of plays in the vernacular.

A second edition of the *Engelische Comedien vnd Tragedien*, also in octavo, appeared in 1624. The title page replicates that of the first, save for an additional line that announces that the collection is a corrected reprint ('Zum Andern mal gedruckt vnd *corrigirt*').[1] Although some of the printer's errors in the first edition were indeed corrected, new ones were introduced. The second edition was clearly set from the first, but type shortage seems to have led to the use of a mixture of differently sized typefaces, including in the portion that contains *Tito* (see Figs 4 and 5).[2] The frequent changes in font size, which give the volume an unusual, unprofessional appearance, suggest that Grosse was not involved in its publication. Indeed, there is no trace of it in the relevant Leipzig book fair catalogues where one would have expected it to be mentioned, that is, those of autumn 1623, spring 1624 and autumn 1624.[3]

---

[1]   One copy of the second edition has survived with a title page of the first edition, and another copy with a facsimile title page of the first edition (see below, p. 80), which has led to scholarly confusion. Creizenach's comments about the collection, for instance, clearly indicate that he mistook the second edition for the first (lxxiv), and Brennecke based his translation on a copy of the second edition (17).

[2]   The replacement of the first edition's roman type by fraktur (a German black-letter typeface) in many gatherings may imply that a Latin text was concurrently printed, which led to a shortage of roman type.

[3]   In 1670, the Frankfurt publisher Johann Georg Schiele issued three octavo volumes entitled *Schau-Bühnen Englischer und Frantzösischer Comödianten* (*Theatre of English and French Comedians*) of which the second (VD17 35:725477W) contains three plays previously published in the 1620 collection (*Fortunato, Sidonia and Theagene*, and *Another Merry Pickelherring Play*) and the third (VD17 35:725483X) two such plays (*Queen Esther and Haughty Haman* and *Prodigal Son*). See Noe, 3. The third volume also contains three plays of the 1630 collection (Noe, 51). *Tito Andronico* was not reprinted until the nineteenth century.

Diener nim jhn alßbald von hinnen/ vnd vber-
antworte dem Hencker / daß er jhn von Stunden an weg henge.

Bote.

Gnädiger Herr Käyser / ich hoffe nicht/daß
mir hie wird Gewalt wiederfahren / vnnd den
Hencker vberantwortet werden / dann solches
were wieder allen Kriegsgebruch / ich habe ja
nichtes mehr gethan / sondern die Botschafft
meines Herrn also außgerichtet/wie er sie mir
befohlen hat.

Keyser.

Es hilffet nichtes dazu/ dein Leben muß dir
genommen werden / hörstu nicht Diener nim
jhn alßfort für meinen Augen weg. etc.

ACTUS SEXTUS.

Jetzt kömpt herauß die weise Muh-
me / hat ein junges schwartzes Kindt im Arm /
welches der Morian mit der Käyserin-
nen.gezeuget.

Weise Mutter.

Ich suche jetzt allenthalben den Morian /
welchem ich dieses Kindt sol vberantworten /

Q v   daß

4 Sample page of *Tito Andronico*, in *Engelische Comedien vnd Tragedien*
(Leipzig, 1620), sig. Qq5r (University Library, LMU Munich, shelfmark:
W 8 P.germ. 46).

Diener nim jhn alßbald von hinnen/
vnd vberantworten dem hencker / daß
er jhn von Stunden an weg henge.

Bote.

Gnädiger Herr Käyser/ich hoffe nit/
daß mir hie wird Gewwalt wiederfah-
ren/ vnd den Hencker vber antwortet
werden/dann solches were wieder allen
Kriegs gebrauch / ich habe ja nichtes
mehr gethan / sondern die Botschafft
meines Herrn also außgerichtet/ wie
er sie mir befohlen hat.

Keyser.

Es hilffet nichtes dazu / dein Leben
muß dir genommen werden / hörstu
nicht Diener nim jhn alßfort für meinen Augen weg etc.

ACTVS SEXTVS.

Jetzt kömpt herauß die weise Wuhme/ hat ein
junges schwartzes Kind im arm, welches der
Morian mit der Keyserinnen gezeuget.

Weise Mutter.

Ich suche jetzt allenthalben den Morian/welchem ich
dieses Kind sol vberantworten/   Qq v   daß

5 Sample page of *Engelische Comedien vnd Tragedien* (n.p., 1624), sig. Qq5r (Württembergische Landesbibliothek Stuttgart, shelfmark: R 17 Come 1).

63

Friedrich Menius and the 1620 Engelische Comedien vnd Tragedien

Before we investigate Menius' involvement in the 1620 *Engelische Comedien vnd Tragedien*, including *Tito Andronico*, it will be useful to clarify who he was and what is known about him. He was born in 1593 or 1594 in the small town of Woldegk in Mecklenburg of which his father, Franz Meyn, was the mayor. He went to school in the neighbouring Friedland, after which he studied at the University of Rostock, probably from 1609 to 1615, and the University of Greifswald, from 1615 to 1617. In 1617, he married and settled in Wolgast as a public notary, referring to himself as 'juratus & immatriculatus Notarius Caesareus' (Fredén, *Friedrich*, 25). Menius moved to Poland in 1621, leaving behind his wife, Sophie, for reasons that are unknown. In 1625, he committed bigamy by marrying the sister of Georg Mancelius, a former colleague at the University in Rostock. Around the same time, he started collecting documents relating to the history of Livonia. In the late 1620s, Menius became acquainted with a number of Swedish dignitaries, including the nobleman Gustav Horn, a member of the Royal Council, who was appointed as a field marshal in 1628. It was through Horn's intercession that Menius was appointed field chaplain for the Swedish troops in Livonia, and when Horn was called to Germany to participate in Gustavus Adolphus's intervention in the Thirty Years' War, he entrusted the management of his estate in Livonia to Menius.

In or around 1630, Menius seems to have briefly served as a pastor near Riga before being offered a post as a history teacher at the gymnasium (grammar school) at Dorpat (now Tartu). When Gustavus Adolphus, in 1632, upgraded the gymnasium to a university, Menius became its first professor of history and antiquities at the newly founded Academia Gustaviana. His quiet, scholarly life in Dorpat seems to have ended in 1637 when a dispute led to the discovery of his bigamy (although his first wife had died in the meantime). He escaped arrest by leaving in a hurry and was outlawed from Dorpat. In the following year we meet him in Ösel (Saaremaa), today an Estonian island but in Menius' time in Danish possession, where he alienated the local governor and other dignitaries. Having moved on to Sweden, he appears to have secured a position as a supervisor in a copper mine in Småland, perhaps through the intercession of his brother, Dietrich Meyn, who was a cook at the royal court in Stockholm. Menius later moved to Stockholm where, in 1644, he published a mystical-occultist work, *Consensus Hermetico-Mosaicus*, which claims to explain the origins of all things visible and invisible. Menius published the book under a pseudonym, Salomon Majus, but this did not prevent him from getting into trouble with the Lutheran authorities. He was arrested, prosecuted and condemned for heresy. Queen Christina seems to have asked for his execution, but he was pardoned after spending a year in prison and making a public recantation. He tried to secure a position as the queen's historiographer, but that understandably came to nothing. His career as a scholar was over, and little more is known about him until his death in 1659.[1]

It is worth noting in the present context that during his time at the University of Dorpat, Menius seems to have been assigned the title of poet laureate. In January 1633, he contributed to a booklet congratulating Petrus Goetschenius on becoming a licentiate in theology, signing as 'Frid: Menius P.L.C. Hist: & Antiq. Prof. Publ.', 'P.L.C.' standing for 'Poeta Laureatus Caesareus' (Flood, 1312–13). This need not imply, however, that Menius was a poet of extraordinary merit, for the title seems to have been an academic honorific.[2] That he wrote some poetry in Latin is known from the title of the now lost

---

[1] This biographical sketch draws on Fredén, *Friedrich*, 17–81; Fredén, 'L'auteur'; Donecker, *Origines*, 125–31; Beyer and Penman; and Åkerman, 87–91.

[2] For laureation in the Holy Roman Empire, see Flood, xlvii–cclv.

collection published in 1620 (see below, pp. 66–7), yet the fact that not a single copy of the collection has survived and that it does not seem to have received any further editions suggests that he remained little known as a poet. What German poetry of his that we have come across is of mediocre quality.[1] The fairly undistinguished and repetitive prose of *Tito* is by no means incompatible with his involvement in the play.

Menius' claim to involvement in the collection of 1620 depends upon the list of his own publications extant in manuscript and printed in 1635. Does the list provide reliable information? The reason why the question is worth asking is that the list of his published books is followed by that of his allegedly forthcoming publications, and the latter raises doubts about Menius' reliability. It consists of forty-six books and is divided into three groups according to format: twenty-one octavos, thirteen quartos and twelve folios. Not only has he decided on format, but he also informs the reader that many of his publications will appear with copperplates and will be in more than one language, typically Latin and German but occasionally also other languages. A history of Scandinavia, for instance, is planned for publication in four folio volumes, in Latin, German and Swedish (*Syntagma*, sigs G7r–v). As it turns out, not a single one of the forty-six books has come down to us, suggesting that most of his planned publications were little more than wishful thinking.[2]

What then of Menius' list of published books? The first three items are all said to have been published in Leipzig in 1620 by

---

[1] An excerpt from an elegy written on the occasion of the death of Gustavus Adolphus, king of Sweden, in 1632, is quoted in Gadebusch (2.251): 'Der, der, der, der ist gestorben, / Der, der, der, der ist verdorben; / Ja die Frommen han verloren / Einen Vater auserkoren; / Ja die Bösen seyn entworden / Den, der ihn'n mit scharfen corden / War zur *disciplin* bereit'. A twelve-line German elegy of his, in alexandrines, is no better (see Klöker, 313).

[2] For Menius' allegedly planned books, see Donecker, 'Arbeiten'.

Gottfried Grosse. The first is a collection of Latin poems, *Poemata artificiosa varij generis*; the second are the *Engelische Comoedien*; and the third is a comparison of funeral rites in different cultures and periods, entitled *Syntagma Historico-Politico-Juridicum de ritibus funebribus omnium gentium*. Of these, only the *Engelische Comoedien* are extant, whereas the other two titles seem to have perished and are not even mentioned in the Leipzig book fair catalogues of 1620 (or 1619).[1] The six other items were all published between 1630 and 1635, one in Riga in 1630 and five in Dorpat between 1632 and 1635. Of the six, four are prolegomena for his major planned work, which never reached print, a chronicle of Livonia ranging from the ancient past to the present: *Intrada und Vortrab der grossen Universal Liefflandischen Historischer Geschichten Beschreibung* (Riga: Gerhard Schröder, 1630) is an announcement and sketch of the great chronicle; *Historischer Prodromus des Lieff-ländischen Rechtes und Regiments von Anfang der Provintz, Erfindunge, als auf I: K: M: von Schweden Gustavi M: Todt* (Dorpat: Jakob Becker, 1633) is about the history of Livonian law; *Diatriba Critica de Maris Balthici nominibus et osijs* (Dorpat: Jakob Becker, 1634) examines various names used to designate the Baltic Sea since ancient times (Donecker, 'Arbeiten', 39); and *Syntagma de origine Livonorum Dorpati* (Dorpat: n.p., 1635) presents materials related to the origins of the Livonians. The other two titles are an account of the opening ceremony of the University of Dorpat, *Relatio von Inauguration der Universität zu Dörpat* (Dorpat: Jakob Becker, 1632), and a tract which counters an interpretation of a recently published sermon by Johannes Döling, according to which the Apocalypse was imminent, *Proba der Letzten Zeit von der großen Verfolgung, Restaurirung*

---

[1] This may suggest that the two lost titles received a small print run, perhaps subsidized by Menius himself.

des Wahren Gottes-dienstes, Vntergang des Pabstuhmbs, und Zukunfft des Jüngsten Tages (Dorpat: Jakob Becker, 1633). These six titles have all survived.[1] In sum, then, seven of the nine titles in Menius' list have come down to us, and the bibliographic information for all of them squares with that provided by Menius. Whereas the list of Menius' forthcoming publications should hardly be trusted, that of his published books seems entirely reliable. We thus have reason to believe that Menius' information about the *Engelische Comedien vnd Tragedien* of 1620 is trustworthy, and that he must indeed have made a significant contribution to the 1620 collection.

Menius included the 1620 volume of 'Englische Comoedien' in the list of his works, but the list as well as the octavo collection do not explain in what way exactly the volume is his. In the absence of clear evidence, scholars have arrived at different conclusions. Fredén ends his long study arguing that Menius deserves to be considered the author ('Verfasser') of the 1620 collection (*Friedrich*, 491). Haekel seems to endorse

---

[1]   Of *Intrada*, a copy is preserved at the University of Tartu Library (shelfmark F 7,s.97). Of *Historischer Prodromus*, two editions are in fact extant, of which one is dated 1633 (VD 17 14:079927K) and the other, also published by Becker according to the imprint, is undated (VD17 39:123077C). (Referring to the end of the preface, VD17 claims that the latter edition is also of 1633, but the date in question, 20 October 1633, dates the original preface, not the edition's year of publication.) We know about only one copy of the first edition, at the Latvian National Library in Riga, whereas quite a number of copies are extant of the second edition, including one at the British Library (shelfmark G.R.C. 1436.b.46). See also Jaanson, items 35 and 36. Of *Syntagma*, at least three copies are extant: at the Latvian National Library in Riga, the Russian National Library in St Petersburg and at the Stiftsbiblioteket in Linköping, Sweden (Donecker, *Origines*, 124; Jaanson, item 89). *Relatio* is extant in various libraries (Jaanson, item 5); of *Proba*, at least two copies have survived: at the Royal Danish Library in Copenhagen and at the University Library of Uppsala (Jaanson, item 37); and of *Diatriba*, two copies are known: at the Tallinn University Academic Library and at the Russian National Library in St Petersburg (Jaanson, item 70). For the contents of these six titles, see also Donecker, 'Arbeiten', 37–43.

Fredén's conclusion (117–18), as does Katritzky, who writes that 'Gustaf Fredén's author attribution is generally accepted' ('Paintings', 213). Braekman (9.22–5) and Bate (Ard[3] *TA*, 43) suggest that Menius 'reported' the plays,[1] and John Alexander writes that Menius 'in all likelihood wrote down the texts from notes and memory' (463). Schlueter, by contrast, contends that 'despite earlier scholars' speculations that these texts were reconstructed from memory, it would appear that the notary, perhaps in his official capacity, had the resident company's playbooks in hand' ('Across', 232–3); accordingly, she holds that the volume was 'Compiled by Menius' ('*Fortunati*', 120). Marti similarly refers to Menius as the volume's 'Herausgeber' (360), i.e. editor.[2] Others have considered Menius as the plays' translator (Williams, 197) or even made of him the first translator of Shakespeare into German ('erster Übersetzer Shakespeares ins Deutsche'; Klöker, 312). While Menius' involvement in the 1620 *Engelische Comedien vnd Tragedien* is generally accepted, there is thus considerable disagreement over the exact form that involvement took.

By far the most sustained analysis has been undertaken by Fredén. He makes a detailed case for the presence of a recognizable hand in much of the volume whose characteristics are compatible with the assumption that it is Menius': a considerable number of Latinisms, usually with correct declensions, and Low-German vocabulary and syntax (*Friedrich*, 119–53); narrative, literary stage directions which often provide information that is also available from the dialogue text, often in the same words (*Friedrich*, 159–70); and stage directions which conceptualize entrances as a coming out ('heraus') and exits as a going in ('hinein'), in contradistinction to the English 'enter'

---

[1]   Bate later refers to a stage direction in *Tito* as 'Menius" (Ard[3] *TA*, 46).

[2]   According to the 'King of England's Son' entry in the *Lost Plays Database*, the 'octavo volume [was] edited by Friedrich Menius'.

69

and 'exit' (*Friedrich*, 170–89).[1] These features are hard to reconcile with the assumption that Menius simply assembled theatrical manuscripts from a touring company and had them published more or less unchanged. That does not mean that Menius necessarily reported plays he had seen in performance. It is equally possible that he had access to theatrical manuscripts but revised them with a view to publication. In particular, he may have expanded and added stage directions.[2] The title page of the 1620 collection, we recall, insists that the plays are 'printed in such wise that they can be easily prepared for performance and serve for the delight and recreation of the mind', a comment that may reflect the particular attention Menius paid to stage directions in preparing the dramatic texts.

One question raised by Menius' involvement in the 1620 collection is how it can be reconciled with the volume's publication in Leipzig. Wolgast, where Menius resided, is on the Baltic Coast, almost 300 miles from Leipzig. So how did the manuscript get from Wolgast, where Menius may have seen plays performed by English players, to Leipzig, where Gottfried Grosse was involved in the book's dissemination? The answer is difficult to recover, although it is just possible that it is bound up with contemporary politics: as the political crisis resulting

[1]   Dahlberg has endorsed Fredén's conclusion that the plays are likely to reflect Menius' involvement, but he suggests that one play, *Sidonia und Theagene*, is of different origins and adopts different conventions (including Latin stage directions) from the others. The differences between *Sidonia und Theagene* and the other plays in the 1620 volume are more likely to be the result of the play's close relationship to Rollenhagen's *Amantes Amentes* (see above, p. 55), of which Dahlberg seems unaware, than of its derivation from the group of plays published in the 1630 collection *Liebeskampff*, for which he argues.

[2]   Dahlberg claims to have identified a linguistic oddity in the 1620 volume that appears in both dialogue text and stage directions, namely the recurrent use of 'hefftig' (severe, intense) as an intensifier ('hefftig gut', 'hefftig gross', etc.), which he takes as evidence that the same writer was responsible for the dialogue text and the stage directions (329). Further analysis of the linguistic make-up of the plays in the 1620 volume might help to strengthen or invalidate Dahlberg's argument.

from the beginnings of the Thirty Years' War was deepening, John George I, Elector of Saxony, convened a Kreistag in Leipzig to take place on 30 January 1620, to which Philip Julius sent delegates from Wolgast and Stettin (see Nicklas, 201–4; Thiede, 2.89). It is not impossible that Menius, as a public notary, was among the delegates, and that he took advantage of his stay in Leipzig to find a publisher for his manuscripts (not only the *Engelische Comedien vnd Tragedien* but also the Latin poems and the tract on funeral rites). Even if Menius did not personally travel to Leipzig, it is possible that he entrusted his manuscripts to someone else who did and who had them published on his behalf.

Menius' list of his own works appended to his *Syntagma de origine Livonorum* mentions 'Englische Comoedien 2. Theil' (sig. G2r), which has understandably puzzled scholars (e.g., Fredén, *Friedrich*, 490–1; Dahlberg). According to today's typographic conventions, '2. Theil' would mean *second part*, but conventions were looser in the seventeenth century than they are today, and, in any case, the manuscript in fact reads '2 Theil' which suggests that Menius meant *two parts*. If so, it may be tempting – but we think mistaken – to believe that the other part Menius had in mind is the collection published ten years after the first, in 1630, with the title 'Love's Fight, or the Other Part of the English Comedies and Tragedies, in which very pleasant, choice Comedies and Tragedies are to be found, never previously printed' ('Liebeskampff Oder Ander Theil Der Engelischen Comoedien vnd Tragoedien, In welchen sehr schöne, außerlesene Comoedien vnd Tragoedien zu befinden, vnd zuvor nie in Druck außgegangen'; VD17 23:285896G). Like the 1620 collection, that of 1630 mentions the year of publication on the title page but no printer, publisher or bookseller. Yet the catalogue of the Leipzig book fair of autumn 1629, *Catalogus Universalis*, published by Gottfried Grosse and Abraham Lamberg (VD17 1:069589P), mentions in a list of 'German books in sundry arts' ('Teutsche Bücher in allerhand

Künsten'), 'English Comedies, the other part, published by the author, Leipzig, to be found at Gottfried Grossen's, 8°' ('Englischer Comaedien Ander theil, in Verlegung des *autoris*, Leipzig bey Gottfried Grossen zu finden. 8.', sig. D4r). The book fair catalogue of the following spring, again co-published by Grosse (VD17 1:069587Y), mentions the collection under its main title, 'Love's Fight, or the other part of the English Comedies and Tragedies, Leipzig, at Gotfriede Grossen's, in 8°' ('Liebes Kampff, oder Ander Theil der Englischen Comoedien vnd Tragoedien. Leipzig bey Gotfriede Grossen, in 8' (sig. E4v). Not only the title, 'Engelischen Comoedien vnd Tragoedien', and the designation of 1630 as 'the other part' ('Ander Theil') connect the 1620 and the 1630 volume. Much of the text on the two title pages is in fact identical (see Brauneck and Noe, 1.vii, 2.3). It should also be noted that the preface to the 1620 volume announces a follow-up volume with further plays if the first one is well received: 'Should it be the case that you enjoy [the plays] and find them pleasant, more of the same kind will follow soon' ('da man nun vermercken wird / daß sie ihnen lieb und angenemb / sollen derselben bald mehr darauff folgen', sig. A3v). Moreover, as has been shown by Richter (9–11), the Preface to the 1630 volume, like that of the 1620, is mostly copied from printed sources, notably chapter 34 of the second part (*Ander Theil. Der guldenen Sendtschreiben*) of Aegidius Albertinus' translation of Antonio de Guevara's *Epistolas familiares* (Munich, 1603, VD17 3:605728D; and reprinted in 1607, 1615, 1618 and 1625), and from a preface to the German translation of the Amadis chivalric romances, which had first appeared in 1569 (*Newe Historia vom Amadis auß Franckreich*, VD16 A 2113) and was frequently reprinted in the early seventeenth century (e.g. in 1617, *Das erste Buch der Historyen vom Amadis auß Franckreich*; VD17 1:631962N).

Given all these connections between the collections of 1620 and 1630, one might be forgiven for relating Menius' reference to '2 Theile' to them. However, Menius unambiguously dates the whole publication 1620, and mentions no additional volume in 1630. Just as importantly, the plays in the 1630 volume are of a very different kind. Unlike the plays that make up the 1620 volume, those in *Liebeskampff* mostly have French and Italian dramatic sources rather than English. The conventions governing their presentation, such as their classical stage directions, are entirely different from those in the 1620 volume. As Price has written, 'Despite its secondary title, the *Liebeskampff* was published quite independently of its predecessor, though it was no doubt suggested by it and though it probably followed its example in some respects . . . The title and the style are Italian rather than English and the author was of Thuringian origin' (22), which is clearly not the case for the 1620 volume. What that means is that Menius' '2 Theile' must somehow relate to the material published in 1620. Perhaps he thought of the full-length prose plays as one part and the jigs, in verse, with accompanying musical notation, as the other. One cannot be sure about the meaning of Menius' '2 Theile', but it makes sense to assume, in keeping with Menius' bibliographic entry, that it refers solely to the 1620 publication, not to the two publications of 1620 and 1630.

A corollary of this argument is that the connections between the paratext of the 1620 and the 1630 collections originate with the publisher, not with Menius. Menius' name is notably absent from the 1620 collection, and this despite the fact that his bibliographic ego was by no means small, as suggested by his long list of his own past and future publications. What this may suggest is that Menius, or someone who acted on Menius' behalf, sold his manuscripts to Grosse, but that Grosse decided on the wording of the title page (with its absence of Menius' name) and contributed the (unsigned) preface. If so, it was Grosse, not Menius, who announced in the preface that another volume of plays would be published if the first one met with approval – an announcement of a commercial spin-off that it makes sense a publisher would make.[1]

The 1620 Engelische Comedien vnd Tragedien *and their theatrical origins*

It has been assumed that Menius probably attended performances of English players at the court of Philip Julius, Duke of Pomerania (1584–1625), in Wolgast (Braekman, 9.9; see also Schlueter, 'Rereading', 179).[2] That may have been the case, although it should be pointed out that the documentary record is too scant to allow for clear conclusions. Evidence about the presence of English players at Julius' court was brought to light by C. F. Meyer, who did extensive research in the royal state archives in Stettin in which the ducal archives of Wolgast were preserved. Meyer shows that Julius hosted English players in 1606, when one Joachim von Wedel complained about the duke's lavish spending: 'recently, many and twenty of the English, musicians, acrobats, dancers and the clown, exercised the *artes voluptarias* [sensual arts], serving no purpose other than guzzling, indulgence and the furthering of disorder and wastefulness'.[3] Later in the same year, the 'Comedianten' performed in nearby Loitz, where the prince's mother had her residence, to which the ducal household seems to have been invited (Meyer, 200). The players set up their stage in the Castle

---

[1] An added complication is that the entry in the 1629 book fair catalogue mentions that the 1630 collection was published by the author ('in Verlegung des *autoris*'). Who this author was and why the collection was published by him and only sold by Grosse now seems impossible to recover. For self-publication in the early modern German book trade, see Meurer.

[2] Nordström speculated that Menius 'was a member of some English troupe of players' ('Editor', 8) but observed that there is no evidence for it.

[3] '[N]eulich etliche und zwantzig Engländer, musicanten, springer, täntzer und der pussenreisser, so die *artes voluptarias* üben und anders nirgends zu nützen, als daß sie fraß, schwalg und ander unordnung und verschwenden befördern' (Meyer, 199).

Church, much to the outrage of the court chaplain, Gregorius Hagius, who vociferously complained in a series of letters to the duke and his mother. In one of his letters, he specifically objects that the plays were written and performed in an 'unknown language' ('Ire Comedien in vnbekannter sprach geschrieben sindt und agirt werden', Meyer, 203), no doubt in English.[1] According to Meyer, we next hear of English players (referred to as 'Musikanten', musicians) at the Wolgast court seventeen years later, in 1623. In a petition to the duke, dated 30 August 1623, prefaced 'Der Musicanten Supplication' and signed by 'Richard Jones', 'Johan Kostreßen' and 'Robert Dulandt', they ask for permission to return to England after a year's employment at the ducal court.[2] A second, unrelated petition, dated 28 May 1624 and signed by 'Musicant Richard Farnaby', mentions an unspecified number of other 'Musicanten' (Meyer, 209) who were also at the Wolgast Court.[3] The third and last petition, dated 10 July 1624, is by Richard Jones (signed 'Richardt Jones / Engelender undt Musikant'; Meyer, 210), who is back in Wolgast and asking for employment after his projects in England had come to nothing (Meyer, 209–10).[4]

---

[1] Julius' interest in English theatre is also documented from the time of his extensive travels in 1602 which led him not only through various parts of Germany, Switzerland, Italy and France, but also to England, where several visits to London theatres are mentioned in the travel account by his secretary and interpreter, Friedrich Gerschow (see von Blow and Powell).

[2] 'Robert Dulandt' is better known as Robert Dowland (*c.* 1591–1641), son of the lutenist and composer John Dowland (1563?–1626). See Greer, and Fredén, *Friedrich*, 111–12.

[3] Richard Farnaby (*c.* 1593–1623), of whom a few musical compositions appear to be extant, is the son of Giles Farnaby (*c.* 1563–1640), the composer and virginalist (see Marlow). See also Fredén, *Friedrich*, 112–16.

[4] For Jones, see Fredén, *Friedrich*, 110–11; and Schrickx, ' "Pickleherring" '. Meyer (207–8) also found a petition by students from the University of Greifswald who asked the duke for financial and logistical support in their staging of a tragedy at the University (whose patron the duke was). The date of this document is corrected by Fredén from 1619, as given by Meyer, to 1614 ('L'auteur', 423–4; *Friedrich*, 95).

The patchy documentary record brought to light by Meyer is thus confined to two periods: 1606 and 1623–24. Fredén seems to have come across additional relevant documents, but, frustratingly, he does not reference them. In 1607, Fredén claims, the duke ordered a small troupe of English 'Musikanten', based in Hamburg, to his court (Fredén, *Friedrich*, 104–6). Four years later, a group of English comedians asked for employment at the duke's court,[1] and in the reply they received, they were asked to accept a previously made offer, or to depart (Fredén, *Friedrich*, 106). Fredén adds that bills dating from 1613 and the following years suggest that considerable amounts were spent on 'Musikanten' (*Friedrich*, 107), although it does not emerge whether these were English or German. All in all, then, what is known about the documentary record does not exclude the possibility that English players were present at the Wolgast court during the years (1617–20) when Menius might have witnessed them, and perhaps received, recorded or adapted their theatrical texts. Nor, however, should theatrical activity at the Wolgast court during the years in question be taken for granted.

More circumstantial evidence may be gathered about the origins of the plays by asking in what company's repertory they may have been. The prominence of the name of 'Pickelherring' on the title page may provide a hint. The name soon became widespread and generic, but it was still recent in 1620 and had previously been associated with the actor George Vincent. In an account book of the court of Wolfenbüttel in Lower Saxony, an entry that can be dated to May 1615 records a payment to 'Georg Vincint alias Pickelhering' (Schrickx, ' "Pickleherring" ', 139), one of a number of English players at that court, including John Green (Schrickx, ' "Pickleherring" ', 141). It emerges from other records that Vincent and Richard Jones who, as explained above,

---

[1]   Fredén points out that in this (unidentified) document, the word 'Komödiant' is
       used as a synonym for 'Musikant' (*Friedrich*, 106).

was at the Wolgast court in 1622 and 1623, were members of the company headed by Green. After their time at the court of Wolfenbüttel, for instance, they seem to have travelled east with other members of the troupe and can be found in Danzig in August 1615 (Schrickx, '"Pickleherring"', 141). Green had started his theatrical career on the Continent around 1603, initially as a member of a company led by Robert Browne, although he seems to have been in charge of his own troupe by summer 1607 (Schrickx, '"Pickleherring"', 137; *Foreign*, 203–7). We know about the repertory of the company led by Green thanks to a letter (commonly known as the 'Theaterbrief') by the Archduchess Maria Magdalena to her brother, the later Emperor Ferdinand II. The letter mentions ten plays performed in Graz from 6 to 19 February 1608, of which three are in the collection published in 1620: 'die Comedi von dem verlorenen sohn' (*The Prodigal Son*), 'fortnatus peitl und Wünschhietel' (*Fortunatus and his Purse and Wishing-cap*) and 'Niemandts und iemandt' (*Nobody and Somebody*) (Schrickx, *Foreign*, 332–3).[1] Of the last of these plays, a manuscript dated 1608 is extant with a dedication by Green to the Archduke Maximilian Ernest of Austria.[2] *Fortunatus*, as pointed out above, is based on Dekker's *Old Fortunatus*, but the version in the 1620 collection has added the character of Pickelhering, which strengthens the connection between Green, Vincent ('alias Pickelhering') and the *Engelische Comedien vnd Tragedien*.

The centre of activity of Green and his fellow players seems to have moved further north by the end of the second decade of the seventeenth century, when they are known to have spent three winters at the Warsaw court (1616–20) and at least part of a summer in Danzig (1619) (Schrickx, '"Pickleherring"', 144–

[1] For an English translation of the 'Theaterbrief', see Schrickx, *Foreign*, 208–12.
[2] For the 1608 manuscript and its relationship to the play printed in 1620, see Chambers, *Elizabethan*, 2.281–2; Flemming; Hay; Brauneck and Noe, 6.28–32; and Bosman.

5). Documents from the Acts of the Privy Council show that Vincent was intermittently back in England in 1617 and 1618, making provision 'of certeyne necessaries for the use of the Prince his master and for the King and Queene of Poland' (Schrickx, '"Pickleherring"', 140) but probably also drafting further players for the troupe led by Green. Vincent, as Schrickx has pointed out, 'was an important intermediary in providing entertainers for the troupe headed by Green' ('"Pickleherring"', 141). In the summer of 1617, Jones was back in England with Vincent, but in the following summer, Jones stayed on the Continent and Vincent returned from England to the Continent with his wife and children as well as with Jones' wife.[1] We know that by 1622, Jones at least was at the Wolgast court, and he and fellow players may of course have been there before. There is thus considerable circumstantial evidence that associates the plays in the 1620 collection with Green, Vincent, Jones and their fellow players.

Given their presence in Danzig on the Baltic coast in 1619, it may be added that Wolgast, also on the Baltic coast and home to a ducal court, may have been an obvious destination for Green and his fellow players. Commenting on the travels of London playing companies, Andrew Gurr has stressed the comparative ease of 'coastal shipping for their travels': 'The sea gave them quick and simple transport to many towns easy of access. Given the loads of expensive costumes and properties they had to carry with them for their plays, carriage by water was probably more secure than by cart or coach and horseback' (63). What is true for travelling around Britain may also apply to travelling on the Continent. Although no records survive that demonstrate the presence of Green's troupe in Wolgast during Menius' presence there (1617–20), it would be compatible with what is known about their whereabouts.

---

[1]   Two letters by Jones and one by his wife, all addressed to Edward Alleyn, have survived (see Greg, *Papers*, 33, 94–5; Schrickx, '"Pickleherring"', 144).

Conclusion

In conclusion, the textual and theatrical origins of *Tito Andronico* are bound up with the plays with which it was published in the collection of 1620, and while some things can be recovered with some confidence about those origins, others remain uncertain. The collection, although published anonymously and without imprint, can be shown to have been published in Leipzig by Gottfried Grosse and printed in Altenburg, probably by Johann Meuschke. Thanks to the survival of a list of his publications, Friedrich Menius, a public notary in Wolgast from 1617 to 1621, is known to have been involved in preparing the plays for publication. Menius may have witnessed the performance of the plays at the Wolgast Court of Philip Julius, Duke of Pomerania, perhaps by the company led by John Green. It is likewise possible that Menius had access to the theatrical manuscripts and revised them with a view to publication. Just how different Menius' play texts are from those that were performed is now impossible to recover. It seems likely that many of the stage directions are essentially his, and it is possible that his contribution to the play texts, including to *Tito*, was substantial.

The 1620/1624 Engelische Comedien vnd Tragedien: *extant copies*

Copies of the 1620 edition are extant in various libraries: the Staatsbibliothek zu Berlin, Unter den Linden (two copies: call numbers Yp 5801 and Libri impr. rari oct. 255); the Universitäts- und Forschungsbibliothek in Erfurt/Gotha (call number Poes 8° 01527/02); the Herzog August Bibliothek in Wolfenbüttel (call number A: 105 Eth. (1)); the Universitätsbibliothek LMU in Munich (call number 0014/W 8 P.germ. 46); the Universitätsbibliothek in Leipzig (call number 94-8-4775); the Gottfried Wilhelm Leibniz Bibliothek in Hannover (call number Lh 3308); the University of Chicago Library (Special Collections, call number PT1264.E57); and the University of Pennsylvania Library (call number V49.163 En3 1620).[1] The copies at the British Library (call number C.95.b.36) and the Folger Shakespeare Library (call number PR1246.G5 E59 Cage) belong in fact to the second edition (1624), although a 1620 title page (or, in the case of the Folger copy, a facsimile title page) has been added to them. Other extant copies of the second edition are at the Herzog August Bibliothek in Wolfenbüttel (call number A: 100.1 Eth. (2)); the Niedersächsische Staats- und Universitätsbibliothek in Göttingen (call number 8 P DRAM III, 30); the Württembergische Landesbibliothek in Stuttgart (call number R 17 Come 1); the Berlin-Brandenburgische Akademie der Wissenschaften (call number B4/DWB); the University of Pennsylvania Library (call number V49.163 En3 1624); and the Beinecke Library, Yale University (call number Zg17 A13 624). A fragmentary copy of the second edition is at the Herzogin Anna Amalia Bibliothek in Weimar (call number Scha BS 4 A 02749).

Editorial history

The first modern edition of the German text was published in Ludwig Tieck's *Deutsches Theater* in 1817. Some decades later, Albert Cohn included the German text alongside an English translation by Moritz Lippner in *Shakespeare in Germany in the Sixteenth and Seventeenth Centuries: An Account of English Actors in Germany and the Netherlands*

---

[1] Our edition of the German text (see above, p. xvii) has been prepared from the Munich copy. Four copies are imperfect and lack certain leaves: the first one at the Staatsbibliothek zu Berlin (Yp 5801) lacks A2, A7, A8, C3 and C6; the one at the Universitätsbibliothek in Leipzig lacks A1–B3; the copy at the University of Pennsylvania Library breaks off at leaf Y5 and lacks the five interludes placed towards the end of the volume; and the title page of the Chicago copy is a photostat facsimile.

and of the Plays Performed by them during the Same Period (1865). The German text was next published in Wilhelm Creizenach's *Die Schauspiele der englischen Kömodianten* in 1889, and, more recently, in Manfred Brauneck and Alfred Noe's *Spieltexte der Wanderbühne* (1970), which conservatively reproduces all the plays contained in *Engelische Comedien vnd Tragedien* (1620) and *Liebeskampff* (1630). These editions contain no or little annotation. The most recent German edition of *Tito*, with a slightly fuller apparatus, appears in an appendix to Markus Marti's German translation of the English play (2008).

There have been two translations of *Tito* into English. Lippner's translation in Cohn's *Shakespeare in Germany* and Ernst Brennecke's in *Shakespeare in Germany 1590–1700* (1964). Brennecke's was unintentionally based on a copy of the second edition (1624): he used the copy at the Folger Shakespeare Library, to which a facsimile of the 1620 title page had been added. Lippner's text is entirely unannotated, and Cohn devotes no more than a page and a half to the play in the introduction (112–13). Brennecke's introduction, at four and a half pages, is longer, but not by much, and his annotation consists of merely three short footnotes. Despite the existence of two retranslations, little has thus been done before the present edition to mediate *Tito Andronico* to an English-speaking readership.

INTRODUCTION TO
KUNST ÜBER ALLE KÜNSTE, EIN BÖS WEIB GUT ZU MACHEN (THE TAMING OF THE SHREW)

Shakespeare's *The Taming of the Shrew* (*c*. 1592) has aroused lively debate right from the start. Shortly after its first recorded performance in 1608, John Fletcher wrote a sequel, *The Woman's Prize, or The Tamer Tamed* (*c*. 1611), featuring the widower Petruccio triumphed over by his new wife Maria. The play continued to have a far-reaching effect throughout the seventeenth century as John Lacy produced another version, called *Sauny the Scot* (1667; printed 1698), which intensifies the violence against the female protagonist. But it was not only at home that Shakespeare's play prompted strong responses. *The Taming of the Shrew* reached the Continent by the middle of the seventeenth century, and a Dutch translation (and partial adaptation), Abraham Sybant's *De Dolle Bruyloft* ('The Mad Wedding'), was published in 1654. A first German version, *Die wunderbare Heurath Petruvio mit der bösen Catharine* ('The wonderful wedding of Petruvio with bad Catharine'), is known to have existed by 1658. *Kunst über alle Künste, ein bös Weib gut zu machen* ('An Art beyond all Arts, To Make a Bad Wife Good'), a five-act prose play published in 1672, is the first extant German version of *The Taming of the Shrew*. It often remains close to the English text, while adapting it intelligently and adjusting it to its new cultural and linguistic context. *Kunst* deeply engages with some of the questions Shakespeare's play raises, including issues of gender, by significantly altering key speeches, adding new passages and inventing a female servant, Sybilla. It also foregrounds social issues by strengthening the prominence of the servants, making them comment on and act as foils for their social betters. The German play is a highly sophisticated early dramatic response to Shakespeare's play. *Kunst* has never been translated into any language, was edited only once, in 1864, by Reinhold Köhler, and has no modern stage history (although it emphatically deserves to have one). The present edition remedies this inaccessibility. Its aims are to provide a detailed examination of the play's engagement with *The Taming of the Shrew* and to assess its role in the reception of Shakespeare abroad.

THE RELATIONSHIP OF *KUNST ÜBER ALLE KÜNSTE* TO *THE TAMING OF THE SHREW*

Kunst über alle Künste is by far the artistically most ambitious and successful of the early modern German Shakespeare adaptations. It is also the only such adaptation that is longer than the original. Whereas *Der Bestrafte Brudermord* and *Tito Andronico* are much shorter than *Hamlet* and *Titus Andronicus*, and *Romio und Julieta* is somewhat shorter than *Romeo and Juliet*, *Kunst* is longer than *The Taming of the Shrew* by about 40 per cent.[1] *Kunst* does not preserve the Sly Induction, but it does feature a brief prologue that introduces the theme of wife-taming and frames the play to come as an exemplary how-to lesson for the audience. The rest of the play is divided into five acts ('Handlungen'), largely mapping onto *The Shrew*'s structure, although with some exceptions (see below, pp. 87–93). This part of the introduction is devoted to an exploration of the relationship between *Kunst* and *The Shrew*, and has four sections. The first establishes the basics by explaining how the

[1]   *The Shrew* has 2,394 lines (in the Arden 3 edition), whereas *Kunst* has 3,407.

dramatis personae and the plot of the German play correspond to and depart from Shakespeare's. The second explores in greater depth some of the specific ways in which *Kunst* adapts *The Shrew*'s plot, in particular the untangling and clarification of sequences which the adaptor may have considered potentially confusing. The third deals with a central feature of the adaptation, its addition to Shakespeare's play of many soliloquies and asides, and examines what effects this addition has. The fourth section takes a closer look at how the verbal, cultural and dramatic language of *Kunst* relates to that of Shakespeare's play.

Characters and plot: correspondences and differences

Kunst über alle Künste and *The Taming of the Shrew* have an intricate – and intricately related – plot, and *Kunst* renames almost all the characters. Only Katherina has a name that is recognizably the same: Catharina. Many characters in the German play have speaking names, and since their meaning is of some importance, we have usually translated them into English (see the List of Roles and notes). Table 1 provides a short guide to character correspondences between *Kunst* and *The Shrew*.

Apart from Sly and the other characters who appear in the Induction, all the significant characters in *The Shrew* have their equivalent in *Kunst*, with the exception of the Haberdasher, whose small part (in *TS*, 4.3) is conflated with that of the Tailor. *Kunst*, in turn, has two characters (apart from the Prologue) with no equivalent in *The Shrew*: Veit, Theobald's servant, appears in five scenes (1.1, 2.1, 3.1, 3.2 and 5.2) and is assigned thirty-one speeches, so his role is by no means small. Sybilla, Catharina's maid, enters the play quite late, in Act 3, Scene 3, and does not speak until her next appearance in Act 4, Scene 2, but she is an important character late in the play and has twenty-two speeches assigned to her (in 4.2, 4.4 and 5.2), including a soliloquy at the end of Act 4, Scene 4. While Veit is generally a

TABLE 1 Character correspondences between *Kunst über alle Künste* and *The Taming of the Shrew*

Kunst	*Shrew*
Patient Job / Prologue	
	Christopher Sly etc. / Induction
Catharina	Katherina
Sabina	Bianca
Theobald	Baptista
Alfons	Hortensio
Sebastian	Gremio
Hardman	Petruccio
Wormfire	Grumio
Hilarius	Lucentio
Felix	Tranio
Fabian	Biondello
Veit	
Sybilla	
Blasius	Merchant / Pedant
Adrian	Vincentio
Hardman's Servants	Petruccio's Servants
Matz	Curtis
Fritz the Tailor	Tailor
	Haberdasher
Widow Eulalia	Widow

commentator (many of his speeches are asides), Sybilla's relationship with Wormfire and consequent pregnancy make her an actress in a subplot in which Hardman and Catharina's servants mirror and contrast with their master and mistress.

Even though *Kunst*'s other characters have their correspondences in *The Shrew*, their degree of proximity to Shakespeare's parts varies considerably. Many of Alfons' speeches, for instance, are reasonably close to Hortensio's, and their total line number is not vastly different: eighty-four for Alfons and seventy for Hortensio. Structurally, the two characters correspond closely to one another, and each time Hortensio appears on stage in *The Shrew*, Alfons does so in *Kunst* in the parallel scene. At the other end of the spectrum, the part of Wormfire in *Kunst* vastly expands on that of Grumio in *The Shrew*. Apart from a single line in Act 3, Scene 2, Grumio's speaking part is confined to three scenes (1.2, 4.1 and 4.3). Wormfire, by contrast, has a significant presence in nine scenes (1.3, 2.1, 2.2, 3.2, 3.3, 3.4, 4.2, 4.4 and 5.2), including a scene, Act 2, Scene 2, that consists of a soliloquy from him, and several others in which he has many asides (see below, pp. 105, 110–13). Whereas Grumio has sixty-three speeches, the total for Wormfire is 166, more than any other character in the play except for Hardman. While *Kunst* thus adapts some parts rather lightly, it transforms others fundamentally.

Kunst's plot may be briefly summed up as follows: the opening scene skips the preliminaries of Lucentio's arrival in Padua and immediately dramatizes Catharina's confrontation with her father Theobald and Sabina's suitors, Alfons and Sebastian. This is followed by a brief exchange between Hilarius and his servants about the previously established disguise scheme, and the arrival of Hardman. The next act closely adheres to the structure of *The Shrew*. It introduces Felix, disguised as Hilarius, and Hardman as suitors of Sabina and Catharina, and it dramatizes the first meeting and the engagement of Hardman and Catharina. The play adds a soliloquy by Wormfire in which he mentions Sybilla, Catharina's maid, and his potential sexual partner. Act 3 includes Sabina's poetry and music lessons, as well as the mad wedding, together with the newly-weds' arrival at Hardman's home, where he puts his taming technique into action. Act 4 weaves together several plot strands. It shows Alfons' interruption of his suit to Sabina after seeing her flirt with Hilarius. It dramatizes the tailor's visit to Hardman's house and the couple's journey back to Theobald. The act also includes the disguise of Blasius as Hilarius' fake father, and his violent meeting with Hilarius' real father, Adrian, who swoons when it occurs to him that the schemers may have killed his son. The last act resolves all conflicts and disguises: Hilarius has married Sabina, and Alfons Eulalia; a mock-trial is set up for the offenders in the disguise scheme; and Wormfire is given permission to marry Sybilla (who is now pregnant). A wager on wifely obedience proves Catharina to be the most tamed of the three wives on stage. The play ends with the servants alone and an allusive song is sung by Fabian about sexual relationships and fidelity.

Anyone familiar with *The Shrew* will recognize in this summary many similarities with Shakespeare's play, while also noting plot elements that are absent. *Kunst*'s plot correspondences to Shakespeare's play are summed up in Table 2 (the symbol ~ indicates that the correspondence is relatively loose, whereas – means that there is no correspondence).

As the table shows, the scenic order of the two plays is largely the same. *The Shrew* has a total of twelve scenes, whereas *Kunst* has sixteen, but the difference is easily accounted for:[1] *Kunst* splits *The Shrew*'s Act 1, Scene 1 into two scenes, and Act 4,

---

[1] The scene division of both plays is editorial: the Folios and the 1631 quarto divide *The Shrew* into acts (except that the Act 2 break is missing) but not scenes, and so do the early editions of *Kunst*. The usual rationale for scene-breaks in the editorial tradition, which we have applied to *Kunst*, is that a new scene begins when the stage is cleared and the action is not continuous.

TABLE 2 Plot correspondences between *Kunst über alle Künste* and *The Taming of the Shrew*

Kunst	Content	*The Shrew*
Prologue	**Patient Job** laments conjugal life with a bad wife, and introduces the play as an example of how to tame a shrew.	~ Induction
1.1 1–35	**Theobald** rejects **Alfons'** and **Sebastian's** suit for **Sabina** until **Catharina** is married.	1.1.48–66
36–103	They promise to provide tutors for the daughters, and quarrel with **Catharina**.	~1.1.92–104
104–77	They secretly form a pact to find a suitor for **Catharina** in order to free **Sabina** for marriage.	1.1.112–44
1.2 1–49	Introduction of the disguise scheme involving **Hilarius** and **Felix**.	~1.1.185–235
50–67	After initial frustration for being left out, **Fabian** makes peace with **Felix**.	~1.1.236–42
1.3 1–61	**Hardman** arrives at **Alfons'** house, declaring his wish to marry a rich woman.	1.2.1–57
62–316	**Alfons** suggests **Catharina** and, together with **Sebastian**, promises **Hardman** financial reward for his suit. **Hilarius** is present, disguised as a poetry teacher.	~1.2.58–215
316–416	**Fabian** and **Felix** enter, and the latter joins in the quest for **Sabina**.	1.2.217–81
2.1 1–81	**Catharina** abuses **Sabina** and is stopped by her father.	2.1.1–38
82–259	The suitors and disguised tutors enter. **Hardman** introduces himself to **Theobald**. All are invited inside.	2.1.39–140
260–85	**Hardman** describes his taming technique in a soliloquy.	2.1.167–79

Kunst	Content	*The Shrew*
286–486	He and **Catharina** have an exchange of insults and fake praise.	2.1.180–282
487–574	**Catharina** rejects **Hardman**'s suit, but the latter pretends she has agreed.	2.1.283–328
575–670	**Felix** and **Sebastian** vie for **Sabina**'s hand, competing for age and wealth. **Theobald** favours **Felix** provided his father consents.	2.1.329–414
2.2	**Wormfire** talks about his flirting with **Sybilla**.	–
3.1 1–30	**Hilarius** and **Alfons**, disguised as tutors, quarrel, then give Sabina her lesson.	3.1.1–25
31–202	**Hilarius** teaches her dactylic composition, **Alfons** sings her a song on the metamorphoses of Jupiter.	~3.1.26–84
203–33	**Veit** and **Alfons** speculate about the relationship between **Sabina** and **Hilarius**.	~3.1.85–90
3.2 1–85	**Catharina** complains about the shame of being abandoned on her wedding day. Reports arrive of **Hardman**'s and **Wormfire**'s outrageous dress.	3.2.1–83
86–147	**Hardman** and **Wormfire** arrive, dressed in strange clothes.	3.2.84–126
148–76	**Felix**, **Hilarius** and **Fabian** reflect on **Hilarius**' disguise scheme.	–
176–232	**Sebastian** reports on the intimidating ceremony inside the house.	3.2.148–82
233–348	When **Catharina** refuses to leave with **Hardman**, he carries her out on his shoulders, leaving the perplexed guests behind.	3.2.183–253

Kunst	Content	*The Shrew*
349–98	**Hilarius** and **Sebastian** discuss the latter's love suit, followed by **Fabian** and **Veit** discussing their masters' illicit wooing.	–
3.3 1–95	**Wormfire** arrives at **Hardman**'s house and gives an account of the exhausting journey.	4.1.1–105
96–186	**Hardman** abuses the servants and refuses **Catharina** food and sleep.	4.1.106–67
3.4	The servants comment on Catharina's patient endurance.	4.1.168–76
3.5	In a soliloquy, **Hardman** explains his taming strategy as a random mixture of rage and affection.	4.1.177–200
4.1 1–20	**Sabina** expresses her longing for **Hilarius**.	–
21–85	**Hilarius** arrives, and they embrace and kiss. They are secretly watched by **Felix** and **Alfons** who abjures **Sabina**.	4.2.1–59
86–105	**Fabian** enters with the news that he has found someone to impersonate **Hilarius'** father.	4.2.60–72
4.2 1–72	**Wormfire** and **Sybilla** feast while **Catharina** enters starving.	~4.3.1–35
73–104	The women discuss their impressions of **Hardman** in private.	–
105–326	**Hardman** and **Alfons** arrive, again teasing **Catharina** with food. The tailor offers his wares, but **Hardman** rebukes him for bad work.	4.3.36–195
4.3	**Felix** and **Blasius** discuss how to perform the role of father convincingly.	~4.4

Kunst	Content	*The Shrew*
4.4 1–9	**Adrian** worries about his son.	–
10–30	Journeying to her father's house, **Hardman** tests **Catharina**'s obedience by insisting he decides what is the time of day.	4.5.1–26
30–98	They meet **Adrian**.	~4.5.27–77
99–150	**Adrian** meets **Fabian**, and **Blasius** and **Felix** in disguise. The impostors flee.	~5.1.15–101
150–75	**Adrian** swoons, thinking they have murdered his son. **Theobald**'s servants carry him inside.	–
176–95	**Hardman** and **Catharina** promise each other peace, and kiss in public.	5.1.132–41
196–205	**Sybilla** reflects upon **Catharina**'s improved future nights and her own impending wedding.	–
5.1 1–17	**Theobald** and **Adrian** grieve for the supposed death of the latter's son.	–
18–56	**Sabina** and **Hilarius** enter, married, and beg forgiveness from their fathers for deceiving them.	~5.1.102–31
57–70	**Catharina** and **Hardman** renew their mutual affection and respect.	–
5.2 1–71	**Felix**, **Fabian** and **Blasius** are punished for their disobedience in a mock trial.	–
72–193	**Wormfire** asks permission to marry **Sybilla**, who is pregnant.	–
194–216	**Catharina** and **Eulalia** have a disagreement.	~5.2.16–49

Kunst	Content	*The Shrew*
217–68	**Felix** sings an erotic hunting song about the love suits of his betters.	–
269–344	The men have a wager about whose wife is most obedient. **Hardman** wins, and **Catharina** provides a brief conclusion on marital love and respect.	~5.2.64–195
345–93	**Wormfire**, **Sybilla** and **Fabian** conclude the play; **Fabian** performs an explicitly sexual song.	–

Scene 1 into three. *Kunst*'s only scene that has no correspondence in *The Shrew* is Act 2, Scene 2, which consists of a soliloquy by Wormfire. What complicates matters slightly is that two act-breaks occur at different moments: *The Shrew* ends Act 3 after the 'mad wedding' scene, but *Kunst*'s third act continues until the end of *The Shrew*'s following scene. The two plays also differ in the final act-break: *The Shrew* ends Act 4 after Petruccio and Katherina, on their return to her father, have met Vincentio, Lucentio's father. *Kunst*'s act-break does not occur until later, after Adrian, Hilarius' father, has met his son's servants. Nonetheless, every scene in *The Shrew* has correspondences in *Kunst*, and the material *Kunst* adopts from *The Shrew* essentially occurs in the same order as in Shakespeare's play.

Adapting the plot of The Taming of the Shrew

While *Kunst* thus generally follows *The Shrew*, it restructures a number of passages and adds dramatic configurations that are absent from Shakespeare's play. In what follows, we wish to identify some of the key features of *Kunst*'s adaptation of *The Shrew*. An important effect of some of *Kunst*'s interventions is that it untangles *The Shrew*'s plot when it is potentially confusing, or difficult to stage. This applies in particular to the beginning of the play, when Hilarius falls in love and devises the disguise scheme; to the plot involving the fake father of Hilarius; and to the illicit wedding of Hilarius and Sabina. Other important adaptive interventions by *Kunst* are observable in the last act and, in particular, the final scene: the mock trial and the servants' coda are indicative of the adaptation's interest in issues of gender and class.

The Shrew begins with the Induction involving Sly the tinker; this presents the main action of the shrew taming as a play, a 'comonty' (*TS*, Induction 2.133), as Sly puts it – probably a malapropism for 'comedy'. *Kunst* preserves neither the Sly Induction nor its brief return at the end of the first scene (*TS*, 1.1.247–52), perhaps owing to a source that had already omitted them, although it is equally possible that *Kunst* deliberately cut the lengthy Induction as part of its adaptation. *Kunst* substitutes for the Induction an equally metatheatrical device, however, the Prologue of Patient Job, which frames the play as instruction for wife-taming. *The Shrew*'s Induction's concern with social rank, the porousness of social stratification but also its ultimate impenetrability are not, however, removed from *Kunst*, but receive sustained treatment, in particular through the servant figures (see below, pp. 103–4).

The main plot of *Kunst* starts by clarifying Lucentio's falling in love and the invention of the disguise scheme which frames the first appearance of Katherina and Bianca. Lucentio and his servant Tranio arrive in Padua from Verona in order to study (*TS*, 1.1.1–47). They '*stand by*' (*TS*, 1.1.47 SD) when a company of people enters and witness their conversation, in particular the complaint of Bianca's suitors, Gremio and Hortensio, about their situation (*TS*, 1.1.48–144). Lucentio also overhears Bianca's reference to her passion for learning which, together with her beauty, makes him fall in love with her. The audience only learns of Lucentio's falling in love when he and

Tranio, left alone on stage, speak about what they have just witnessed (*TS*, 1.1.145–219). Tranio gently mocks his master for the suddenness of his emotions and for his exaggerated praise of Bianca. As it becomes clear that Lucentio wants to marry her, he and Tranio invent the disguise scheme and exchange their clothes. When Biondello enters, he is shocked by the sartorial changes. Lucentio comes up with the explanation that he has killed a man in a quarrel and needs to remain incognito, but does not clarify why Tranio is to become a suitor to Bianca. Biondello briefly expresses discontent for missing out on Tranio's social promotion, but the two servants make up in Lucentio's presence (*TS*, 1.1.220–46).

Kunst omits the frame in *The Shrew*'s Act 1, Scene 1, in which Lucentio eavesdrops and falls in love. Instead, it presents consecutively the dialogue involving the suitors and the sisters on the one hand and the dialogue between servants and master on the other hand. Rather than staging Hilarius' arrival and falling in love in the main play's first scene, *Kunst* has Hilarius and Felix enter in the second, already in disguise (1.2.1–12). Hilarius reminds Felix of the reasons for the disguise, effectively dropping the audience into the middle of the subplot. Fabian appears and is amazed at the altered appearances, but rather than explaining the situation, Hilarius exits and lets Felix make sense of the situation to Fabian. Felix falsely suggests that Hilarius committed a crime and hence his consequent need for disguise, and the two servants discuss the unfairness of the change in Felix's station (1.2.15–67). *Kunst* thus creates a more linear dramatic sequence which eliminates some of *The Shrew*'s intricacies, notably the eavesdropping frame, the spontaneous invention of the disguise scheme by both Tranio and Lucentio, and Lucentio's bombastic use of love language which Tranio teases him about.

A result of the adapted beginning is that the initial character of Hilarius, unlike that of Lucentio, is not quite fleshed out, and the disguise scheme is introduced rather abruptly. In reorganizing the material, *Kunst* also, crucially, chooses to put

Catharina centre-stage. Whereas Bianca is central to Act 1 as the object of Gremio's and Hortensio's suit, and of Lucentio's love-struck gaze, her *Kunst* counterpart, the meek Sabina, is absent from the equivalent scene. *Kunst* delays Sabina's first appearance until Act 2, Scene 1, in which she is depicted in stark contrast to the domineering Catharina. The impression given of Sabina, then, is that she is a vaguely sketched obedient daughter, unlike Bianca who speaks up for herself in Act 1, Scene 1, however briefly (*TS*, 1.1.80–3). Sabina's development in the course of the play, then, is all the more remarkable: she evolves from a mere supporting role into a self-confident young woman with sexual desires and initiative, as shown most notably in Act 4, Scene 1. *Kunst*'s adaption of the beginning of the main play thus has a profound effect not only on dramatic arrangement but also on characterization; it is fundamentally different from its Shakespearean model.

Another of *The Shrew*'s plot lines which *Kunst* simplifies is that of the Merchant from Mantua who plays fake father to Lucentio. In Act 4, Scene 2 of *The Shrew*, Biondello enters to Lucentio, Bianca and Tranio and announces that he has spotted a man arriving in Padua who '[i]n gait and countenance' looks 'like a father' (4.2.66). Once Lucentio and Bianca have departed, the Merchant enters. Tranio then tricks him into dressing like Vincentio by convincing him that there is a ban on Mantuans arriving in Padua and that he needs to assume the identity of his master's father for his own safety (4.2.73–122). *Kunst*, on the other hand, omits the set-up of this third disguise plot. When Fabian enters to Hilarius and Felix towards the end of Act 4, Scene 1, Felix inquires whether he has 'found an honourable father' (4.1.87–8). Fabian reports that he has, that the 'grave gentleman . . . looks as honourable as Saint Valentine, is filled to the brim with imagined wisdom, and when it comes to natural philosophy, thinks he is the biggest pig in the sty' (4.1.91–4). Blasius, as Fabian adds, is 'willing to do anything for gain' (4.1.96–7) and so has agreed to the scheme. For the far-fetched idea of the ban on Mantuans, *Kunst* thus substitutes the simple idea of pecuniary profit.

The plot line of *The Shrew*'s Merchant is bound up with the secret wedding of Bianca and Lucentio. Shortly after being disguised as Lucentio's father, the Merchant meets Baptista, and the match between Bianca and the Merchant's supposed son is struck. Lucentio (as Cambio) is sent home to notify Bianca of her wedding which is to take place later in the day (4.4.19–71). Biondello then intercepts Lucentio and tells him that Tranio has prepared a secret wedding to take place between him and Bianca (72–106). The plot line of the secret wedding interacts with that of the fake father and his unmasking in Act 5, Scene 1, where the focus switches from one to the other with quick-changing entries and exits. While the confrontation between Vincentio and the Merchant rises in tension, brief sequences pertaining to the secret wedding (5.1.1–6, 36–9) punctuate the unmasking of the Merchant, each plot line increasing the other's pace and urgency until they both join when Lucentio and Bianca enter as a married couple (5.1.97 SD).

As part of the clarification and simplification of *The Shrew*'s complex dramatic structure, *Kunst* does away with the dramatization of the secret wedding. In Act 4, Scene 1, Sabina and Hilarius meet, kiss and promise each other their lasting love. Alfons, who has spied on them, gives up his wooing of Sabina and decides to 'reciprocate the friendliness and desire of a young rich widow' and to 'link [his] life to hers' (4.1.50–2). Sabina and Hilarius part with a kiss, and when we next meet them in Act 5, Scene 1, they enter '*well dressed*' (5.1.17 SD), presumably straight from their secret wedding, and apologize to their fathers for their transgressions. Between these two scenes, we see the fake-father scheme implode: in Act 4, Scene 3, Blasius reassures Felix that he 'will take care of everything and settle the business to my lord's [i.e. Theobald's] liking' (4.3.1–2). But in the following scene, Blasius, Fabian and Felix, in Hilarius' clothes, come face to face with Hilarius' real father, Adrian, who assumes they 'must have strangled [his] poor son' (4.4.150) and swoons, giving them the chance to escape. By the last scene, they have been arrested and are subjected to a mock trial. *Kunst* thus reduces the complications of *The Shrew*'s plot by focusing on the fake father scheme and eliminating the dramatization of Hilarius and Sabina's secret wedding.

The last scene of the German play weaves together the substantial, entirely original trial scene with a largely faithful adaptation of *The Shrew*'s wager sequence. It separates different sequences in *The Shrew* and skilfully blends them with original material. To appreciate the dramatic make-up of *Kunst*'s conclusion, one needs to see first how differently the two plays reach the final scene.

The Shrew's Act 5, Scene 1 brings together the several disguises: the fake father (the Merchant), the fake suitor (Tranio) and the fake tutor (Lucentio). Initially, the different storylines clash (5.1.15–99). The confrontation between the fake and the real father threatens to spiral out of control, and only abates upon the arrival of Lucentio and Bianca who are now married. Biondello, Tranio and the Merchant flee, realizing they are 'undone' (5.1.101). Vincentio's anger at being duped by his servant persists (5.1.110–11) as he ignores his son's explanations and requests for peace (5.1.114–20), and threatens violence: 'I'll slit the villain's [i.e. Tranio's] nose that would have sent me to the jail' (5.1.121–2). Baptista, too, is outraged at having his paternal authority thwarted by Bianca and Lucentio (5.1.123–4). With threats to 'be revenged' (5.1.126) on the servants and/or disobedient children, the scene uneasily concludes without any reconciliation. *The Shrew*'s last scene starts with a banquet presided over by Lucentio. Peace-making has thus occurred offstage and between scenes. Huge threats of revenge only a scene earlier have dissolved into 'kindness' (5.2.5) and tolerance towards the servants who are present, though without speaking roles.

Kunst's penultimate scene differs from that of *The Shrew* in that the fathers gladly accept their new children-in-law (5.1.25–

56) and pardon their offspring. Overall, the reactions to the fake father and the secret wedding are more benevolent and forgiving. Rather than showing aggression towards the fake father and Felix who has impersonated his son, Adrian is overcome by emotion and repeatedly swoons (4.4.144–70). When he revives, he and Theobald lament the loss of Hilarius both as son and as possible son-in-law (5.1.16–17). Once their children arrive alive and married, Theobald and Adrian forgive their breach of custom. Whereas *The Shrew* deals with the business of reconciliation behind the scenes, the audience of *Kunst* thus becomes its witness.

As for the transgressions by Felix, Fabian and Blasius, Hilarius, solicitous of their pardon, asks for forbearance, Hardman pleads for the preservation of harmony, and the fathers agree to mere mock-punishment:

> HILARIUS . . . I must now also beg forgiveness for all those who have acted in this, for my sake, as others than themselves.
>
> ADRIAN They should at least be frightened, especially that fool who wanted to make me mad.
>
> HARDMAN This day is a day of joy. We should mingle nothing upsetting or grievous with it.
>
> ADRIAN Then they should undergo an amusing kind of punishment, and all for their own good.
>
> THEOBALD I add my voice to this, because my house ought to be a place of pleasure and gladness. So bring them all in, please.
>
> (5.1.44–56)

While the breach of sumptuary law cannot go unprosecuted, nothing 'grievous' (5.1.51) is to interfere with the wedding celebrations. The punishment of the servants therefore takes the form of a communal ritual, so that those who attempted to rise unlawfully are restored to their proper place in society.

While *The Shrew* is keen to establish visual harmony through the banquet and Lucentio's pacifying words (5.2.1–11), *Kunst* performs the return to previous power structures through the trial (5.2.1–193), a long sequence that is wholly original to the German play. Sebastian first pronounces a harsh judgement: 'Master Blasius Nosewhite and Felix are condemned to sweat out the nobility they wrongfully assumed in a hot bath house for three days. Fabian will wait upon them and serve them food, but no drink' (5.2.23–6). When the offenders beg for mercy, Sebastian revisits the judgement and supposedly condemns them to assistance and participation in the wedding celebrations:

> Master Blasius shall join Ceres and Bacchus, and make friends with them for eight days and longer in Sir Theobald's lodgings in tolerable temperatures . . . Felix will hear an acceptably merciful judgment from his own master, and will behave like a modest guest. Fabian, on the other hand, will be handed over to Wormfire for his excesses, who will put him into the pillory, and run wine through him until he falls to the ground powerless, having done his duty to justice. When he has recovered his modest standing, he shall be made an inspector over the law of the jug. He shall diligently pour the cups overfull.
>
> (5.2.50–65)

The sentence takes the form of an inversion of the scapegoat ritual. Rather than creating social exclusion by assigning unmerited blame, there is social inclusion of the offenders in a prolonged post-wedding Bacchanalian feast.

Just as the trial seems to conclude, Wormfire, in characteristic mock-Latin, states that he 'must confer another more or less dirty thing to the *Sacro-Sanctae Justitiae*' (5.2.77–8), and so the trial scene transitions to its second part. As Sybilla is expecting a child, Wormfire asks for permission to marry her, his embarrassment masked by comically convoluted Latinate language (5.2.91–105). The attendants gently tease them, and Hilarius suggests that their punishment for pre-marital sex

100

should be a prohibition to be 'bedfellows' (5.2.115), but after some comical resistance from the couple, they are allowed to get married. They are to be 'handed over to the priest' (5.2.162–3) and to participate in the wedding celebrations, and, after the birth of their child, 'this whole company shall serve as godparents' (5.2.168–9). In both parts of the trial scene, the threat of punishment and mock humiliation are thus followed by forgiveness, benevolence and joyful social integration.

After this long and funny but linguistically complex additional material, *Kunst* returns to material dramatized in *The Shrew*'s final scene, in particular in the short altercation between Katherina and the Widow (5.2.16–38), and the wager sequence with the demonstration of Katherina's tameness (5.2.64–195). Interpolated within the passage based on *The Shrew* is the recitation by Felix of a poem – 'a little wedding wish' (5.2.218), as he puts it – that retells the story of the three suitors, Hilarius, Alfons and Sebastian, figured as huntsmen of Sabina, who is troped as a deer (5.2.224–55). Apart from adding to the comic conclusion through its recapitulatory effect, the poem also reminds us of Felix's predicament as a servant in his concluding plea to Hilarius for continued patronage and employment.

Kunst aligns itself closely with *The Shrew* for the men's wager on their wives' obedience (*The Shrew*, 5.2.64–195; *Kunst*, 5.2.267–344). It comes as a surprise to the modern reader, however, that, amid this faithful rendition of the English original, *Kunst* chooses to condense Katherina's famous speech on female obedience in marriage (*TS*, 5.2.142–85), the longest speech of the play (it has forty-four lines), into a two-line nugget of sober advice, borrowed from St Paul's Letter to the Ephesians: 'Let me put it briefly. You men, love your wives. And you women, obey your husbands' (5.2.340–1).[1] In *The Shrew*,

---

[1]   'Husbands, love your wives . . .' (5.25); 'Wives, submit yourselves unto your own husbands . . .' (Ephesians 5.22).

Katherina's long and rhetorically sophisticated speech, with its massive potential for different interpretations, is the moment towards which the play's conclusion moves. *Kunst*, by contrast, breaks the structure of the final scene into several smaller units: the mock trial of Felix, Fabian and Blasius; the mock trial of Wormfire and Sybilla; the performance of Felix's recapitulatory poem; and the men's wager on their wives' obedience.

One reason why the German play can afford to reduce Katherina's long and troubling speech to a succinct piece of advice is that it completes a reinterpretation of the relationship between Petruccio and Katherina which started some time earlier. Although Hardman makes Catharina undergo more or less the same treatment as Petruccio gives Katherina, *Kunst* stresses that the couple's relationship leads to mutual contentment and peace. In a significant departure from Shakespeare's play, Hardman, in his second soliloquy (corresponding to *The Shrew*, 4.1.177–200), says, 'I confess I love her dearly' (3.5.8). In keeping with this are the names Hardman uses for Catharina. Even though Shakespeare's female protagonist insists on her full name – 'They call me Katherine that do talk of me' (2.1.183) – Petruccio reduces her name to 'Kate', consistently during their first encounter and frequently after it too.[1] Hardman, however, uses the shortened 'Trina' during their first encounter but almost invariably calls her 'Catharina' elsewhere in the play, suggesting a more respectful attitude.[2] Catharina shows similar signs of benevolence towards Hardman in the course of the play. In her conversation with Sybilla, for instance, she says, 'I believe this man has bewitched me, because I have to be gentle to him almost against my will' (4.2.102–3). At the end of Act 5, Scene 1,

---

[1] After Act 2, Scene 1, Petruccio calls her 'Kate' thirty times and 'Katherine' only twice, in the last scene (*TS*, 5.2.127, 136).

[2] For the diminutive of the shortened form of Catharina's name which Hardman uses once in the penultimate scene, see 5.1.57 and note. See also 5.2.123, 206 and notes.

immediately after their kiss in public (cf. *TS*, 5.1.139–41), *Kunst* adds a short passage that sums up the stage that their relationship has reached:

> HARDMAN   Do you see now, my love, that this is
> much better than when we are at odds? So let us
> put away all tricks and stubbornness, and live in
> peace and pleasure after wearing down our horns.
> I will chase away the mad Hardman, and you must
> chase away the bad Catharina. Thus we shall be
> an honourable couple renowned in all the world.
> CATHARINA   I am content with you if you are content
> with me.
> HARDMAN   Amen.
>
> (4.4.186–95)

By the time we reach *The Shrew*'s last scene, then, the outcome of Petruccio's taming still hangs in the balance. In *Kunst*, by contrast, the last scene only confirms what the play has previously shown, which is that the couple have made peace.

An effect of *Kunst*'s reorganization of the final scene is the special prominence it gives to the servants. In keeping with this adaptive decision, *Kunst*, after the exit of the higher-ranking characters, adds a coda with the play's four chief servants, Felix, Fabian, Wormfire and Sybilla (5.2.345–93). For much of the final scene, then – the long mock trial, the performance of the poems and the coda – *Kunst* puts the servants centre-stage. While *The Shrew*'s festive conclusion is essentially about the newly-wedded couples – Petruccio and Katherina, Lucentio and Bianca and, to a lesser extent, Hortensio and the Widow – *Kunst*'s conclusion is socially more inclusive and gives considerable space to those servants (Felix and Fabian) who have helped bring about the marriages and to those (Wormfire and Sybilla) who serve as foils to the unions of their social superiors. Whereas *The Shrew* moves towards Katherina's parade of her new obedience as its defining moment, *Kunst* divides the scene into several smaller units where a significant exchange is limited to gentle mockery of the servants and their robust resistance to it. The weaving together of *The Shrew*'s last scene with *Kunst*'s substantial addition of the trial and the songs by and coda with the servants shows a sophisticated adaptor of Shakespeare's play who deftly interwove new material, while keeping the playful mood of the original.

Soliloquies and asides

To its often close adaptation of *The Shrew*'s text, structure and themes, *Kunst* adds many soliloquies and asides that offer subtle twists to the original in terms of meaning and theatrical pace. The soliloquies often precede or succeed versions of the Shakespearean material, adding anticipatory or retrospective perspectives on what we will soon see or have just witnessed. They elegantly create brief points of rest which allow for (re)consideration of action and motivation and result in dramatic progression at highly variable speeds.

One example of a soliloquy that slows down the progression of the plot is that of Fabian (3.2.164–76) when he compares his own lack of success with the rosy prospects enjoyed by Felix through the disguise scheme. Sandwiched between the passage where Hilarius and Felix discuss the fake father scheme and Sebastian's report of the mad wedding, *Kunst*'s soliloquy slightly halts the rapidly accumulating events of *The Shrew* where the entry of groom and servant, the discussion on the fake father, and Gremio's report of the ceremony follow each other thick and fast. The overhasty betrothal, wedding and impatient leave-taking of Petruccio overwhelm Katherina by presenting her with seemingly inevitable facts, tricking her into acceptance through the speed of theatrical sequencing. There is a logic to the overwhelming thrust of *The Shrew*'s forward-moving plot, and soliloquies would lessen its effect. *Kunst*, however, puts a premium on varied pace which permits the exploration of motivation and emotional state.

The Shrew's chief soliloquies give us access to Petruccio's reflections just before he meets Katherina (2.1.167–79), and after their shocking homecoming (4.1.177–200). Both instances concern his taming techniques of playing hot and cold with her, and of withdrawing even the most basic of physical comforts, food and sleep. Other than Petruccio, a few characters have short soliloquies at the end of scenes and, in one instance, at the beginning of a scene. Of these, *Kunst* provides versions of similar length by Felix (2.1.663–70; cf. *TS*, 2.1.407–14) and Wormfire (3.3.1–14; cf. *TS*, 4.1.1–10), and a considerably expanded version by Alfons (3.1.224–49; cf. *TS*, 3.1.85–90).[1] The two longest soliloquies in *The Shrew* are thus Petruccio's, which confers a special status on his 'taming of the shrew' and motivations.

Kunst includes largely faithful versions of Petruccio's soliloquies (2.1.225–46 and 3.5.1–30), but it also has six other characters give soliloquies with no equivalent in *The Shrew*, namely Wormfire (3.3.1–14), Catharina (3.2.1–12), Fabian (3.2.164–76), Sabina (4.1.9–18), Adrian (4.4.1–9) and Sybilla (4.4.196–205). These soliloquies have a considerable impact on pace, character and plot. The audience of *The Shrew*, for instance, first meets Vincentio as an unwitting actor in Petruccio's taming test concerning the sun and the moon (*TS*, 4.5.1–25). Hilarius' father Adrian, however, first enters the stage alone, worrying about his son's whereabouts (4.4.1–9). The first impression of him as loving father is confirmed throughout the last part of the play, setting up the mood for a conciliatory ending.

A similar change is discernible in *Kunst*'s addition of Catharina's reflection on her misery and her fear of the mockery

---

[1]   The short speeches by Lucentio and Hortensio when alone left on stage (*TS*, 4.4.103–6 and 4.5.78–80) have no equivalent in *Kunst*.

she will suffer if Hardman does not arrive at the wedding soon (3.2.1–12). Catharina blames her father for rashly giving her away, and confesses to herself that she has found her match in shrewishness. She admits that she would 'give [Hardman] the kindest words, and force [her]self to be friendly' if only he returned (3.2.9–10). This concession, lacking in *The Shrew*, anticipates future taming scenes, including the meeting with the tailor (4.2), where Catharina curbs her impulse in order to allow Hardman to end his raging. Through the soliloquy, *Kunst* thus strategically supports the plot and complicates Catharina's image, showing that she, who flouts traditional gender conventions, is no less bound by social expectations and reputation than those she scorns.

Kunst's soliloquies provide insights into the workings of the characters' minds, as well as their feelings. In its astonishing decision to add a soliloquy to Sabina's part in which she reveals her love for Hilarius, *Kunst* makes her character radically depart from its equivalent in *The Shrew*, showing her as being much more sexually forward. The German play preserves *The Shrew*'s configuration in which the servant disguised as his master hides with the suitor disguised as a tutor in order to witness the flirtatious lesson between a daughter and a poetry teacher (*The Shrew*, 4.2; *Kunst*, 4.1). Into the two sections of hiding and revelation from *The Shrew*, however, *Kunst* inserts a brief speech by Sabina who is waiting for Hilarius. Believing herself to be alone (although Felix and Alfons are in fact on stage), she expresses her love and physical desire:

Happy hour which will bring my soul to my body. O love, never tried by me before, how great is your sweetness! Everything else in the world is stale and miserable in comparison! True joy and pleasure lie in you alone, pervading all my senses, body and soul. Many things can be found to entertain the body, but the soul cannot find pleasure and contentment but through another soul, united in sweet love. But where is the comfort that I long for so much? Does his mind not feel the same yearning desire as mine?

(4.1.9–18)

Sabina remains teasingly vague about what it means to 'entertain the body' (4.1.14). The violence of her feelings and their expression, though, as well as her keenness to kiss and touch, even on her own initiative – '*She kisses him*' (4.1.84 SD) – point towards her awareness, if not necessarily knowledge, of sexual pleasure. Her remarkable frankness in word and deed differs significantly from the arch voice of Bianca. The equivalent scene of *The Shrew* has the latter exchange merely a handful of quick-witted lines with Lucentio before he, rather than she, confesses his love for her (*TS*, 4.2.10). And no stage direction in *The Shrew* alerts us to a kiss between the two.

The German adaptation's non-judgemental attitude and its greater interest in female desire and sexuality become evident not only in its depiction of higher-ranked characters like Sabina, but also in its remarkable addition of the female servant Sybilla, a character who seems to be an invention by the author of *Kunst*, although the idea of inserting a female servant into the play may have been prompted by Slobbetje in Abraham Sybant's Dutch adaptation of *The Shrew* of 1654, *De Dolle Bruyloft* (see below, pp. 125–7). As Catharina's maid, Sybilla provides a female equivalent to Wormfire, Hardman's servant, filling a comic vacuum in *The Shrew*. She is first mentioned by Wormfire, after Theobald has agreed to Catharina's marriage to Hardman. In his soliloquy, Wormfire muses on his flirting with Sybilla, and expresses confidence that she will eventually come around to having sex with him: 'I have set up my cause well. She is ready on certain conditions. If my lord says yes, and her lady yes, the whore will be mine. I thought my tool would have it my way, but not this time. Such an honourable tree will not fall with one stroke' (2.2.5–9). In her first speaking scene,

Act 4, Scene 2, in which she and Wormfire feast on leftover food at Hardman's house, it becomes clear that the couple has now had sex (she is pregnant) and are hoping to get married before the baby is born. They face the situation with jocular acceptance rather than anxiety, and are more interested in the food than in the precariousness of their circumstances (4.2.1–25). As she puts it, their extra-marital sex in fact 'conforms to *courtoisie*' (4.2.14) as practised by socially more distinguished people. This down-to-earth relationship between the two servants thus explores sexual mores, calling into question loftier but ultimately no less appetite-driven models of courtship. Her relationship with Wormfire is robust and frank but never condemned and, eventually, even blessed by marriage.

Later in Act 4, Scene 2, *Kunst* continues the theme of female sexual experience when Sybilla and Catharina discuss the wedding night (4.2.73–104). Sybilla frankly asks her mistress how the bedding was, and equally frankly receives a negative answer: 'He has left me all too pure so far' (4.2.86). The passage is not a soliloquy, but, like a soliloquy, it gives the spectators access to Catharina that is unrestricted by public norms of behaviour or expression, and so shares with them a private moment in which she is genuinely vulnerable. As there is no equivalent confidante in *The Shrew*, all we experience of Katherina is her starvation and lack of sleep; there is little emotional reflection. Catharina, by contrast, exposes her vulnerability and wonders about her changing relationship with and attitude towards Hardman who, she claims, 'has bewitched [her]' (4.2.103).

Sybilla returns to the theme of female sexual pleasure in her own soliloquy (4.4.196–205) which caps the busy final scene of Act 4. Having witnessed the public kiss between Hardman and Catharina, and their promise to be respectful towards one another, a breach of which would be followed by a ban from their shared bed (4.4.179–95), Sybilla humorously reflects on how their improved understanding must reflect a happier sexual life: 'Well, I take it she is content with him now. She has had better nights than the first' (4.4.196–7). Through the soliloquies, therefore, *Kunst* acknowledges female desire and sexuality with a degree of frankness that is absent from *The Shrew*. In sum, *Kunst* treats the female characters' desires and appetites with equanimity, allowing them to elaborate *for themselves* what they wish for, untrammelled by male observations *about* them.

Kunst's added soliloquies thus help to enhance characterization and function as a tool to control and vary the dramatic pace of the play, slowing it down in order to open up spaces in which characters articulate their emotional states, such as Fabian's social frustration, Catharina's fear of mockery, Wormfire's and Sabina's sexual desire and Vincentio's fatherly care. Whereas *The Shrew* employs soliloquizing chiefly to allow Petruccio to reflect on and rationalize his 'taming of the shrew', *Kunst* opens it up to many other characters, resulting in an introspective heteroglossia that is absent from Shakespeare's play.

The soliloquy as a dramatic device is closely related to the aside, in that both are only heard by (or even addressed to) the audience, and, indeed, *Kunst* adds not only many soliloquies to *The Shrew* but also many asides. The aside is a well-established convention on the early modern stage, although stage directions that render them explicit are rare in sixteenth- and seventeenth-century editions of Shakespeare's plays, and *The Shrew*'s early modern editions contain no instance of it.[1] The early editions of *Kunst*, however, mark twenty-four speeches as asides ('beyseits' in German),[2] almost all of them with material that has no

---

[1]   For the prominence of the aside on the early modern English stage, see Dessen and Thomson, 15–16. Note that many of *The Shrew*'s modern editors mark several speeches as asides, although Barbara Hodgdon, in the Arden 3 series, does so only once (5.1.37 SD), arguing that, on the whole, 'whether a line is or is not spoken "*aside*" is best left for performers to work out' (341).

[2]   This excludes the rare occasions where two characters speak aside to one another, unheard by others (so-called 'split asides').

equivalent in *The Shrew*. It is likely that asides are more pervasive still in the play but have been recorded unsystematically in the early editions. In Act 2, Scene 1, for instance, as Hardman and Sebastian speak to Theobald about their suit to his respective daughters (2.1.82–145), Wormfire makes ten interjectory comments during their conversation, none of which in any way registers with or is responded to by the other characters, and this despite the fact that many of the comments are so provocative that, if heard, they would elicit a rebuke or some other response. Yet the early duodecimos mark only four of Wormfire's ten speeches as asides. There is nothing about the nature of Wormfire's comments that would allow us to determine why those four should be spoken as asides and not the other six. Similar patterns can be observed elsewhere in the play (see, for instance, 1.1.17–32, 2.1.196-200). Given that these and similar comments – chiefly spoken by servants, as we shall see – play an important role in the play, we have usually marked them as asides (signalling the editorial intervention by square brackets), even though the early editions do not. It would be possible, of course, to perform many of these asides in such a way as to elicit a non-verbal response by other characters, but we nonetheless consider them to be asides insofar as they fail to register in the other characters' dialogue.[1]

Of the sixty-one (original or editorial) asides in the play, by far the greatest number, thirty-eight, are spoken by Wormfire, and of those that are not, the majority are assigned to two other servants: Veit and Fabian. Indeed, it is noticeable that *Kunst* frequently inserts asides by servants into faithfully translated passages from *The Shrew*, and it does so as part of a conscious strategy to make the servants reflect on the actions and motivations of the higher-ranked characters. For instance, in

---

[1] Our understanding of what is usefully considered an aside is here shaped by Morgan, *Turn-Taking*, 105–15.

the following passage, Sebastian tells Hilarius, disguised as Johannes, how to prepare for his teaching of Sabina:

> SEBASTIAN [*to Hilarius*]   The next thing I want is
> that you buy for her the best books about love that
> you can find. These have great power to enflame
> the fire of love in the hearts of maidens.
>
> WORMFIRE (*aside*)   But not for you.
>
> SEBASTIAN   And they should be bound in the
> daintiest and prettiest manner. The paper that you
> use must be well perfumed, for she whom my
> soul loves is worth more than all exquisite spices.
> And may I remind you, Johannes, to be as diligent
> in her service as you can. Your reward from me
> will exceed even Sir Theobald's generosity.
>
> WORMFIRE [*aside*]   He looks to me as if he would
> receive his salary from her without your
> knowledge or will.
>
> SEBASTIAN   But what matters will you treat with her?
>
> (1.3.158–72)

If we compare the passage to *The Shrew*, we notice that it corresponds to a single speech by Gremio, addressed to Lucentio disguised as Cambio, into which *Kunst* has inserted the two acerbic asides by Wormfire:

> GREMIO   O, very well; I have perused the note.[1]
> Hark you, sir, I'll have them very fairly bound
> (All books of love, see that at any hand)
> And see you read no other lectures to her:
> You understand me. Over and beside
> Signor Baptista's liberality,
> I'll mend it with a largess. Take your paper too,
> And let me have them very well perfumed,

---

[1]   Ard³ *TS* annotates, 'bill, account – presumably, for Lucentio's purchase of books'.

> For she is sweeter than perfume itself
> To whom they go to. What will you read to her?
>
> (*TS*, 1.2.142–51)

In *The Shrew*, the 'books of love' have already been purchased, whereas they have not yet in *Kunst*, but the German adaptation nonetheless preserves all the important elements of Gremio's speech: the plan to have the books bound and to use them in the teaching to further the wooing, the additional reward, the perfumed paper and the final question. The faithfulness in the adaptation of Gremio's speech contrasts with the innovation of Wormfire's comments. Clearly, they are both asides, although only the first is marked as such in the early editions: Wormfire's second comment anticipates Hilarius' wooing of Sabina for himself, which is precisely what remains hidden from Sebastian. *Kunst* thus adds a layer to the passage by having Wormfire comment on the ongoing action, increasing the complicity between the audience and the servant character (who understands Hilarius' plan), while exposing and undercutting the foolish project of Sebastian.

The same mechanism can be observed on a larger scale in the previously mentioned passage in Act 2, Scene 1, in which Hardman and Sebastian introduce themselves to Theobald as suitors to his respective daughters (2.1.84–143). The passage follows the equivalent dramatic sequence in *The Shrew* (2.1.39–86), and almost every speech by Petruccio, Gremio and Baptista has its corresponding speech in *Kunst*. What is radically different in the German adaptation, however, are the asides by Wormfire. In *The Shrew*, Grumio is simply absent from the scene; in *Kunst*, Wormfire provides a sarcastic running commentary, inserts daring jokes and exposes to the audience much of what the other characters try to keep hidden from one another, thereby deflating their motives and unmasking their ambitions.[1]

---

[1]   One could also point to other passages in which Wormfire (e.g. 1.3.235–7; 2.1.222–23; 3.2.117, 124–5; 4.4.59–60) or, less frequently, Veit (e.g. 2.1.569–70) or Fabian (e.g. 3.2.229) have asides that have been added by *Kunst* in passages that otherwise closely follow *The Shrew*.

The perspicacity and irreverence with which Wormfire frequently comments on and subverts the self-interested projects of the higher-ranked characters arguably make him the protagonist of the German play. This may seem surprising, given the Shakespearean source, but it is less so if we place *Kunst* in the context of the seventeenth-century theatre companies that travelled across Germany. In many of their plays, Pickelherring was typically the protagonist, and the actor playing him was often the company leader (see Katritzky, 'Pickelhering' and 'A plague'). Indeed, he was so prominent that his name became a generic word designating a fool.[1] Pickelherring, like Wormfire, is a servant figure who owes his importance to the place he occupies in the plays as witty, irreverent commentator and trenchant interrogator. Like Wormfire, the German stock character has a special relationship with the audience, often speaks aside and has a propensity for bawdy innuendos. Nor is *Kunst* the only early modern German Shakespeare play in which a version of the Pickelherring figure comes to occupy an important role. In *Romio und Julieta*, Pickelherring is a character himself, an amalgamation of the Nurse, Peter and another Capulet servant in Shakespeare's play (Erne and Seidler, 76–7). In *Der Bestrafte Brudermord*, he is called Phantasmo, a name that seems to be unique to this play but whose functions are clearly related to Pickelherring's (Erne and Seidler, 9–10). Wormfire, then, offers a late instance of a character whose adaptation to the German stage is shaped by the conventions of the Pickelherring figure. In *Kunst*, he complements several other servant figures, notably Felix, Fabian and Veit, and reinforces the play's more general interest in servants and their relationship to their social superiors.

[1]   For the clown figure in early German professional theatre more generally, see Asper, *Hanswurst*, 124–230.

Verbal, cultural and dramatic language

Apart from the addition of soliloquies and asides, another important feature of *Kunst*'s adaptation of *The Shrew* is its revision of the dramatic writing that makes up Shakespeare's play. Unlike *The Shrew*, which combines verse and prose, *Kunst* is written almost entirely in prose, although it contains two short verse passages during the poetry lesson in Act 3, Scene 1, a song that is performed during the music lesson in the same scene, and two poems that are recited in the last scene.[1] If we compare *Kunst* and *The Shrew* closely, we notice that the German adaptation sometimes follows Shakespeare's play speech by speech and almost word for word. The following excerpt, taken from the passage in which Hardman/Petruccio feigns dissatisfaction with the work of the tailor ('Fritz' in *Kunst*), serves to illustrate the occasional verbal proximity between the two plays. *The Shrew* reads as follows:

KATHERINA

    I never saw a better-fashioned gown,

    More quaint, more pleasing, nor more
       commendable.

    Belike you mean to make a puppet of me.

PETRUCCIO

    Why true, he means to make a puppet of thee.

TAILOR   She says your worship means to make a
    puppet of her.

PETRUCCIO

    O monstrous arrogance. Thou liest, thou thread,
      thou thimble,

    Thou yard, three quarters, half-yard, quarter, nail,

    Thou flea, thou nit, thou winter-cricket, thou!

    Braved in mine own house with a skein of thread?

---

[1] See 3.1.46–50, 3.1.67–70, 3.1.143–78, 5.2.224–60 and 5.2.352–79.

Away, thou rag, thou quantity, thou remnant,
Or I shall so bemete thee with thy yard
As thou shalt think on prating whilst thou liv'st.
I tell thee, I, that thou has marred her gown.

(*TS*, 4.3.103–16)

Here is the equivalent passage in *Kunst*:

CATHARINA   I say he has worked well. You want
to make a rogue of him, and a fool of me.

HARDMAN   You speak right. It's the rogue who wants
to make a fool of you.

FRITZ   She says, my lord, it is you who wants to
make a fool of her.

HARDMAN   O, great presumption by the shadow of a
man in my own house! You lie, you lie, you thread,
you Tom Thumb, you needle tip, you flaky-headed
clod of earth, you! I'll soon measure your mangy
back with your mete-yard and make you remember
it all your life. You've wasted everything that's
been given into your hands.

(4.2.202–14)

The four speeches occur in the same order, and each has its
easily recognizable equivalent. Catharina's speech condenses
and simplifies the first sentence in Katherina's, but the second
sentence remains close, except that it adds the idea that Hardman
mocks not only her but also the tailor. Hardman's first speech
closely follows Petruccio's and relies on the same feigned
misunderstanding. Fritz then, like the *Shrew*'s tailor, corrects
Hardman/Petruccio by explaining the misunderstanding.
Hardman's following outrage, or mock outrage, draws on many
of the same elements as Petruccio's. The initial exclamation is
followed by an accusation of lying, followed by a series of
apostrophes that belittle the tailor through references related to
his profession. The (feigned) resentment at being contradicted

in his own house also recurs, though in a slightly different position. *Kunst* omits Petruccio's order for the tailor to go away, but the two speeches conclude in the same way with the threat of beating the tailor with a yard rule and the charge that he has spoiled the work, although Petruccio's accusation that he has spoiled the 'gown' is more specific than Hardman's that he has 'wasted everything'. All in all, then, the relationship between the two passages in *Kunst* and *The Shrew* is close. To the extent that it is a translation, the translation is rather loose, but to the extent that it is an adaptation, the adaptation closely follows the original.

While occasional proximity is one feature of the relationship of *Kunst*'s language to *The Shrew*'s, the German play also contains distinct characteristics that depart from or go beyond Shakespeare's play. One such feature is its fondness for proverbs, some of which are inevitably lost in translation, although we use the commentary to draw the reader's attention to their presence in the original and to their literal meaning. In the opening scene, for instance, Catharina taunts Sebastian by telling him, 'Dann jhr ja nicht könnet einen Hund auß dem Ofen locken', of which a more-or-less literal translation might be that Sebastian 'could not tease a dog out from under the oven'. Given that Sebastian is unable even to make a dog move, he will be utterly unable, Catharina implies, to evoke desire in a young woman. Our translation, 'you couldn't tease a dog out from under the oven' (1.1.38–9), preserves the insult to Sebastian and the canine reference, but in the absence of a precise equivalent in English, it inevitably loses something of the colourfully proverbial original.

On other occasions, the German play uses expressions that have at least a proverbial appearance, although they cannot be found in the most comprehensive reference work of German proverbs, Karl Friedrich Wilhelm Wander's five-volume *Deutsches Sprichwörter-Lexicon* (1866–80), and may be idiosyncratic coinages by the German author. So in Act 1,

Scene 3, as the suitors are fighting over Sabina, Wormfire comments that 'where carrion is stinking, there the ravens will gather' (1.3.359–60), a characteristically irreverent comment that tropes Sabina as rotting flesh over which the suitor-ravens fight. The German text contains many such vivid expressions, often rooted in references to the animal world, in particular but by no means only spoken by Wormfire. In line with this feature of *Kunst*'s language is its proliferation and amplification of sexual allusions, often channelled through outspoken servants (notably Wormfire, Sybilla and Veit) but also through characters of higher rank, like Catharina. All these linguistic features contribute to making *Kunst* an earthier and more exuberant play than *The Shrew*.

While using many distinctly German expressions and proverbs, the author of *Kunst* also goes beyond this linguistic adaptation by fitting geographic and cultural references to the German context. For instance, Hardman is from Worms (1.3.249), not Verona, and he claims to be planning a trip to Frankfurt, not Venice, to purchase 'gorgeous robes and jewels' for the wedding (2.1.539–40). Wormfire affirms (perhaps fancifully) that he and Hardman served in the military at 'Bautzen' (1.3.310) in east Saxony, associated with various events during the Thirty Years' War, including a siege in 1620 and the town's destruction by fire during occupation by the Catholic imperial army in 1633. His interjection 'Leipzig surrenders' (2.1.128) likely alludes to another event in the Thirty Years' War, the Battle of Breitenfeld (1642), during which Leipzig surrendered to the Swedish forces. Elsewhere the same character refers to 'a market in Hanover' (2.1.112–13), in northern Germany, and to 'Bacherach wine' (3.2.250) from the wine-growing region of Bacherach in the Rhine-Palatinate. Geographic references thus range from west to east and from north to south, though what may well be the most regionally-specific reference, 'Bacherach', is compatible with the opinion of several German scholars that certain linguistic peculiarities point to western central Germany as the homeland of the play's anonymous author (see below, p. 143).

A specific instance of cultural translation may be observed in Act 3, Scene 1. In its endeavour to make the English play recognizable to German culture, the translator replaces the Ovidian Latin lesson with a tutorial on dactylic composition in German while keeping the romantically suggestive content and context of *The Shrew*. The line-by-line translation of Latin (to 'conster' is Bianca's word for it – *TS*, 3.1.30, 40) was a staple activity of humanist education and would have playfully activated school-time memories of many male readers or audience members (see Maurer). The Latin passage is from Ovid's *Heroides*, and the part on which Lucentio has Bianca focus is from Penelope's letter to Ulysses, recounting her difficult situation as wife left behind in their kingdom, beset with unwanted suitors. Shakespeare toys with the obvious inference that Bianca's suitors are just as unwelcome as Penelope's, and are, for the moment at least, rebutted by her translation. Elite references to classical literature are thus embedded in *The Shrew*'s scene in specific cultural practices that have implications for plot and characterization.

Kunst's adaptor realizes the particularity of the passage and adapts it to German literary culture of the seventeenth century in which use of the dactyl was rare.[1] The complex layers of intertextuality between Ovid and Shakespeare are sidestepped for a more straightforward situation-based adaptation that focuses on the flirtation between student and tutor. The German stresses the potentially sexual relationship between teacher and pupil by having Hilarius explain the dactyl in terms that suggest

---

[1] Martin Opitz (1597–1639), the leading theoretician of German literature of the seventeenth century, did not advocate use of the dactyl, but his contemporary and successor August Buchner (1591–1661) did. The author of *Kunst* may well have been aware of Buchner's posthumously published *Anleitung zur deutschen Poeterey*, sigs F10r–G6r ('Instructions for German Poetry', Wittenberg, 1665; VD17 39:121087A).

the male sexual organs (one long syllable and two short ones, for which the standard notation was —⌣⌣), and its composition in terms suggesting sexual intercourse: 'Although it may appear to you a little sour the first time, afterwards it will seem so sweet that your appetite will not be stilled' (3.1.49–51). The passage thus combines wit and daring at the same time as *Kunst* adapts it to its own cultural context.

Though *Kunst* thus eliminates *The Shrew*'s Latin lesson, it includes many Latin words and phrases elsewhere. It does so far more than Shakespeare's play, making the presence of Latin snippets another characteristic feature of *Kunst*'s language that distinguishes it from *The Shrew*'s.[1] This presence might be thought to pull the language of *Kunst* over towards sophistication and sober learning, but given the barely veiled mocking or suggestive undertone of many of the Latin words and phrases, it does not. Although its appreciation presupposes some learning, the Latin with which the play is peppered usually serves a comic or satiric purpose, such as the exposure of pretentiousness or the conveyance of mock formality. In Act 1, Scene 2, for instance, Fabian mocks Felix's newfound noble status through bragging in French and Latin: 'How now, my brand-new lord, *avec permission*, may I interrogate you and receive report through my *quaestiones*?' (1.2.40–2). In Act 2, Scene 1, as Hardman is getting ready to meet Catharina for the first time, he sends Wormfire away on the grounds that he 'need[s] to think', an idea his servant mocks by using Latin: 'I can well believe you: there will be brave *lectiones*, you will receive the *contra*' (2.1.248–51). Sebastian's pompous and self-righteous quotation from Ovid's *Fasti*, '*Magna fuit capitis quondam reverentia cani*' ('in the past there used to be great reverence for the white head'), is immediately countered by

---

[1]   For Latin in *The Shrew* outside the Latin lesson, see Grumio's '*Inprimis*' and '*Ergo*' (4.1.59, 4.3.129), the Tailor's '*Inprimis*' (4.3.133) and a phrase by Tranio (1.1.161) and by Biondello (4.4.91–2).

Veit's acerbic comment, 'Even if you gather all the maxims from Cicero and Seneca, you will not convince a pretty maid that you are more suitable for her than a fresh young gentleman' (2.1.613–17). In the tailor passage, Fritz reads out Wormfire's written instructions to defend himself against Hardman's accusations of professional incompetence (4.2.236–97), and the comedy of the passage partly relies on the note's combination of pompous diction, convoluted syntax and repeated use of Latin (and French). Latin is pervasive when, during the second part of the trial scene, Wormfire confesses that Sybilla is pregnant and requests permission to marry her (5.2.73–192). Struggling to come clean about Sybilla's pre-marital pregnancy, he hides his embarrassment in confusing syntax and Latin, with the result that his onstage (see 5.2.81) as well as his offstage audience find it hard to understand him.

In other passages, characters use Latin to give bawdy allusions a veneer of respectability, or mock respectability. Disappointed that his first close encounter with Sybilla has not led to full sexual intercourse, Wormfire rationalizes his disappointment by stating that 'one stays *in atrio* [i.e. in the entrance hall] the first time' and only later gets to 'drift into the Netherlands' (2.2.21–4). When Sybilla, in her soliloquy, concludes that Catharina, since her wedding, 'has had better nights than the first' (4.4.197), she attributes the change to the '*instrumentum pacis*', the instrument of peace, that is, the male member. In the music lesson, Alfons presents to Sabina his method of gamut teaching by using several Latin words that contain sexual innuendos: 'Here is the *scala* which I have devised in a perfect new manner. Women usually conceive better of *b flat major* than *b flat minor*, so I will first instruct you in the *ascendendo*, and then in the *descendendo* which teaches itself' (3.1.112–16). The German text reads 'dur' for '*flat major*', that is, Latin for 'hard', and '*scala*', '*ascendendo*' and '*descendendo*' allude to the erection and detumescence of the male sexual organ. Examples could be multiplied, but the point has been made: Latin, in *Kunst*, is not the language of learning but comedy. It serves to expose pretension, to deflate ambition or to give bawdy puns an air of (mock) respectability. It usually suggests pseudo-learning. That said, there is nothing pseudo-learned about the play's implied audience or readership which should be educated enough to appreciate the comic function of these Latin passages. *Kunst* might share this feature with a play like *Love's Labour's Lost*, but does not share it with *The Shrew*. The place of Latin in the play, in other words, is another feature through which the German play distinctly emancipates itself from the language of *The Shrew*.

In terms of stage action, by contrast, *Kunst* stays closer to *The Shrew* and usually follows the English play in the passages they share. For instance, both Katherina and Catharina, in Act 2, Scene 1, strike Bianca/Sabina (*TS*, 2.1.22 SD / 2.1.10 SD), and while Petruccio '*pulls [Grumio] back and forth by the ears*' (1.3.15 SD), Hardman similarly '*wrings [Wormfire] by the ears*' (*TS*, 1.2.17 SD). At other moments, however, the German play is more specific in what it records in stage directions. In particular, several characters who simply enter in *The Shrew* do so in *Kunst* in ways that are specified. So when Fabian enters and discovers that Hilarius and Felix have swapped clothes, he '*Looks at both in dismay*' (1.2.12 SD; cf. *TS*, 1.1.219 SD). Alfons, when Hardman and Wormfire have arrived at his house, enters '*hastily*' (1.3.22 SD; cf. *TS*, 1.2.19 SD). Felix, upon discovering his master's father, is '*all aghast*', and Adrian, seeing Felix in his son's clothes, looks '*shocked*' (4.4.143–4; cf. *TS*, 5.1.57–8). Such additional information can often be derived from the dialogue text, as when Hardman arrives before his wedding '*strangely dressed*' (3.2.85 SD; cf. *TS*, 3.2.83 SD) or when Sebastian, after the same wedding, enters '*laughing*' (3.2.176 SD; cf. *TS*, 3.2.147 SD), but these directions may well have been added for the benefit of readers who are thus allowed to apprehend the information at the same time as spectators would, rather than belatedly, through the dialogue.

Of particular interest are passages in which *Kunst* clarifies stage business that may – but does not have to – be implicit in *The Shrew*. During the forced engagement in Act 2, Scene 1, for instance, stage directions in *Kunst* clearly indicate that Hardman first '*extends his hand to* [*Catharina*]' and then '*takes her hand and presses it into his*' (2.1.543 SD, 546 SD). Petruccio encourages Katherina – 'Give me thy hand' (*TS*, 2.1.318) – but what stage action follows these words is not made clear. Something similar may be observed when the couple departs after their wedding in Act 3, Scene 2. In *The Shrew*, since Katherina is unwilling to leave, Petruccio claims to defend her against the dangerous advances of her friends and family: 'Grumio, / Draw forth thy weapon, we are beset with thieves; / Rescue they mistress, it thou be a man'; turning to Katherina, he pretends to reassure her: 'Fear not, sweet wench, they shall not touch thee, Kate; / I'll buckler thee against a million', at which point an unspecific '*Exeunt*' stage direction indicates that the couple leaves the stage (3.2.236–40), without clarifying how they do so. *Kunst*, by contrast, chooses to pinpoint the action: '*He carries her out in his arms*' (3.2.328 SD). A similar instance is the conflict between the two tutors at the beginning of Act 3. In *The Shrew*, Lucentio calls Hortensio a 'Preposterous ass' (3.1.9) and provokes him by belittling the importance of music. Hortensio threateningly responds that he 'will not bear these braves' at which point Bianca interrupts them: 'Why gentlemen, you do me double wrong / To strive for that which resteth in my choice' (*TS*, 3.1.15–17). Is Hortensio's threat followed by aggressive action, or does the conflict remain purely verbal? In *Kunst*, Hilarius responds to Alfons' threat and '*starts to beat him*', prompting Sabina's intervention: 'Hold, my lord. It's strange that you should quarrel about what lies in my choice alone' (3.1.19–20). In these cases, the German play spells out stage action that is left unclear in *The Shrew*, but is not incompatible with it.

In the passage dramatizing Hardman's arrival at his house, *Kunst*'s stage directions indicate a whole series of actions which *The Shrew* does not render explicit. In *The Shrew*, Petruccio objects to all his servants do and showers them with abuse, but the early editions add no stage directions concerning his physical treatment of them. As Barbara Hodgdon has pointed out, 'Most modern editions, following Rowe, introduce SDs at 134 ("*Strikes him*"), 141 ("*Strikes Servant*") and 154 ("*He throws the food and dishes at them*")', and 'performances often incorporate such stage business'. Yet, as she adds, 'the scene has also been played without some or all of the traditional physical action' (Ard³, 248); her edition therefore refrains from adding stage directions to this passage. The early editions of *Kunst*, unlike *The Shrew*'s, are perfectly explicit in directing Hardman's treatment of his servants. Shortly after their entrance, he first '*strikes them*' (3.3.104 SD), and a short time later, '*He strikes the [Second] Servant*' (3.3.127 SD) who tries to take off his boots. Another servant who has brought a bowl of water is beaten with the bowl itself (3.3.133 SD, 136 SD). Later in the scene, Hardman '*beats*' a servant whom he accuses of spilling the broth, and shortly before the end of the sequence he also '*strikes*' Wormfire (3.3.146 SD, 176 SD). Whereas the absence of stage directions in *The Shrew* leaves open the possibility that the abuse in the scene is purely verbal, *Kunst* has determined that it is also, and repeatedly, physical.

While the stage directions in *Kunst* are often similar to or at least compatible with *The Shrew*, there are passages where the German play adds stage business that has no equivalent in Shakespeare's play. In the scene just discussed, Petruccio, amidst the abuse he hurls at his servants, turns to Katherina and bids her 'welcome' (4.1.128) to his house. Hardman also does so – 'Be welcome, dearest darling' (3.3.119) – but follows up on his words with a kiss: '*He kisses her, while she stands still*' (3.3.119 SD). Similarly, after their wedding, and shortly before carrying her out in his arms, Hardman turns to Catharina and '*kisses her*' before telling her, 'You are my all, my nothing, my life and death depend on you' (3.2.315–16). No kiss accompanies Petruccio's equivalent words, and they are addressed, significantly, not to Katherina, but to the other men: 'She is my goods, my chattels . . . my anything' (*TS*, 3.2.231–3). Another case in point is the conflict between the two sisters in Act 2, Scene 1. In *Kunst*, Catharina not only beats Sabina once, as Katherina does Bianca, but Catharina then '*binds her hands*' (2.1.24 SD), after which she '*beats her*' (2.1.28 SD) again, suggesting a degree of (partly playful?) violence absent from the sisters' conflict in *The Shrew*. Beating and kissing are actions that are characteristic of comedy and, in particular, farce, and it seems significant that they figure prominently in *Kunst*. They contribute to stage action which the play scripts with greater frequency and precision than Shakespeare's play, a difference that can inform alternative and additional ways of understanding the dynamics among characters.

To conclude, the linguistic, dramatic and structural changes of *Kunst über alle Künste* reveal an incisive reconsideration of *The Taming of the Shrew*. At a time when we have become all too familiar with Shakespeare's play and the issues it raises, its seventeenth-century German adaptation offers untapped insights into the potential of the English comedy to signify anew when meeting a different cultural and yet still early modern context. *Kunst* allows us to witness complexities of intercultural exchange, in particular in its creative exploration of gender and social issues, adopting, adapting, omitting from, adding to and embracing the Shakespeare play it so aptly reconfigures.

THE TAMING OF THE SHREW IN GERMAN IN THE SEVENTEENTH CENTURY

The early history of *The Taming of the Shrew* is bound up with a similar play, *The Taming of a Shrew*, performed in *c*. 1592 and published in 1594 (Hodgdon, 12–14). Theories concerning the relationship between the two plays include: one, that *A Shrew* is an early draft by Shakespeare; two, that it is an anonymous source play that Shakespeare adopted and elaborated; three, that it is an adaptation of Shakespeare's play; and, four, that it is a memorial reconstruction that derives from and tries to record (a version of) Shakespeare's play (Hodgdon, 20).[1] Unlike *The Shrew*, *A Shrew* returns to Sly at the end of the play (as he awakens from his supposed dream) and thus treats as a frame what editions of *The Shrew* call an Induction. While *The Shrew*'s Katherina plot is close to *A Shrew* (in which the character is called 'Kate'), the Bianca plot is not. *Kunst über alle Künste* clearly follows *The Shrew*, and we have found no evidence to suggest that its author may have been aware of *A Shrew*.[2]

The Taming of the Shrew is assumed to have been written in or around 1591 (Taylor and Loughnane, 499–503). It first reached print in the First Folio of 1623, followed by a quarto reprint in 1631. It is unknown how the text found its way abroad. Its first appearance on the Continent is recorded in the Netherlands: a Dutch version of *The Shrew*, *De Dolle Bruyloft* ('The Mad Wedding'), was performed in 1654 at the Amsterdam Theatre and published the same year (Wiggins, 3.159; Hoenselaars and van Dijkhuizen, 55; Nassau-Sarolea, 44).[3] The translator-adaptor, Abraham Sybant (*c.* 1620–60), was associated with several Anglo-Dutch companies of itinerant

---

[1] For a close analysis of the relationship between *The Shrew* and *A Shrew*, see Miller, 12–31, 127–43.

[2] It has been argued that the Sly material in *The Shrew* and *A Shrew* received separate adaptations in two mid-seventeenth-century Dutch farces, the anonymous *Pots van Kees Krollen, hertogh van Pierlepom* ('Farce of Kees Krollen, Duke of Neverland', Leiden, 1649) and Melchior Fockens' *Klucht van dronkken Hansje* ('Farce of Hans the Drunkard', Amsterdam, 1657) (Helmers). See also Gstach, 428–30.

[3] The play received four performances in 1654 (9, 12, 16 and 19 November) and a total of three more in 1655 (4 February) and 1656 (24 February, 7 August) (Wiggins, 3.158).

players, which may have given him access to texts from England (Hoenselaars and van Dijkhuizen, 55). Neither *De Dolle Bruyloft* nor *Kunst* refer to Shakespeare or an English original, but, while the title page of *Kunst* mentions no author and the play's anonymous author acknowledges in a note the text's status as a translation-adaptation (see below, pp. 140–1), it is Sybant's name that is mentioned on the title-page of *De Dolle Bruyloft* and in three short celebratory verses preceding the play proper. The Dutch play is composed in rhyming hexameter couplets throughout. Unlike *Kunst*, Sybant generally retains the English names though he gives the servants Dutch names. Among these, he invents a female servant called Slobbetje for whom there is no precedent in the English. She has a brief speaking role at the beginning of Act 4, taking over a handful of lines from one of Petruccio's servants. The brevity of her role means that Slobbetje does not qualify as the source on which *Kunst*'s Sybilla is based, although it is possible that the presence of a named female servant in *De Dolle Bruyloft* gave the author of *Kunst* the idea for the character.[1]

Like *Kunst*, *De Dolle Bruyloft* slightly rearranges *The Shrew*'s act division and condenses parts of *The Shrew*'s first scene, notably Lucentio's falling in love with Bianca. Unlike *Kunst*, however, the Dutch play omits the Widow and the wager in the last scene, nor does it include the Induction, or any other prologue. This has been taken to suggest that the English copy Sybant was working from – perhaps a copy of the 1631 quarto – may have been damaged at its two extremities (Nassau-Sarolea, 55), as easily happened to unbound quarto playbooks. Ton Hoenselaars and Jan Frans van Dijkhuizen have argued,

---

[1]   Another possible hint of the acquaintance of *Kunst*'s author with *De Dolle Bruyloft* is the description in the List of Roles of Matz Trumper's function as 'well-established oven-raker and firekeeper'. Sybant amplifies Curtis' name to Curtus Stookebrant, literally 'the one that stokes the fire', a detail the author of *Kunst* may have remembered.

however, that the text of *De Dolle Bruyloft* suggests a conscious and deliberate reworking of the entirety of Shakespeare's play (56–7). What is clear, in any case, is that the author of *Kunst* did not work from *De Dolle Bruyloft* but from a text, no doubt a German text (see below, pp. 141–2), that was closer to Shakespeare's, although it is possible that he was familiar with the Dutch version or a German derivation from it.[1]

Although *Kunst* is the earliest text of a version of *The Shrew* in German, there are records of earlier performances that are likely to be related to Shakespeare's play. We owe the earliest such record to Johann Christoph Gottsched, the leading German literary scholar of the mid-eighteenth century. Gottsched compiled an overview of German drama from 1450 to his time, *Nöthiger Vorrath zur Geschichte der deutschen Dramatischen Dichtkunst* (Leipzig, 1757), in which he mentions four plays that were performed 'auf dem Zittauischen Schauplatze', that is, in the theatre in the Saxon town of Zittau, from 5 to 7 March 1658. The fourth play is 'Die wunderbare Heurath Petruvio, mit der bösen Catharine' – 'The Wonderful Wedding of Petruvio with the Bad Catharine' (210).[2] 'Petruvio' might be assumed to be the result of a simple copying error, but the name's reappearance in a later record (see below, p. 129) suggests that it is a conscious adaptation of the name in Shakespeare's play. Gottsched derives his information about the performances from

[1]   For *De Dolle Bruyloft*, see also Helmers, 125–8.
[2]   The titles Gottsched gives for the other three plays are 'Androfilo oder göttliche Wunderliebe', 'Sylvia, oder wunderthätige Liebe' and 'Der klägliche Bezwang'. The first two were written by Sigmund von Birken and jointly published in 1656, *Androfilo oder die Wunderliebe* and *Silvia oder die Wunderthätige Schönheit* (Lüneburg, 1656, VD17 23:284204W). The second is not known to survive, but it is likely to have been a translation of Lope de Vega's *La fuerza lastimosa* (Köhler, xii), produced by Georg Greflinger, who announces a forthcoming play of his called 'Der beklägliche Zwang' (sig. *2v) in a preface to his translation of Pierre Corneille's *Le Cid* (*Die Sinnreiche Tragi-Comoedia genannt Cid*, Hamburg, 1650, VD17 1:627142D). See also Gärtner, 135.

a now lost programme by Christian Keimann (1607–62), headmaster of the Zittau grammar school from 1638, suggesting that the performance was a school production (see Köhler, x).[1] Keimann is known to have produced plays from 1638, usually based on biblical material (Pescheck, 348). These included plays he translated and adapted, such as *Samuel* by Johann Förster (1646, originally published in Latin in 1604, VD17 39:139726E) and *Susanna* by Nicodemus Frischlin (1648, also originally published in Latin, VD17 7:710222Q) as well as plays he wrote himself, notably *Junger Tobias* (Freiberg, 1641, VD17 3:308439H) and *Der neugebohrne Jesus, den Hirten und Weisen offenbahret* (Görlitz, 1646, VD17 23:236006T).[2] Keimann was crowned poet laureate, 'Poeta Laureatus Caesareus', in 1651 (Flood, 973–8; see above, pp. 65–6). It is known that 'englische Komödien' had been publicly performed at the Zittau town hall by the 'kurfürstlich sächsische Comödianten' ('Elector of Saxony's Comedians') from 14 to 25 July 1650 (Pescheck, 348). Perhaps this offered an opportunity for Keimann to see plays of English origin or even to secure texts of some of them.[3]

Keimann's 1658 programme is lost, but a later programme made for a production in 1678 probably gives us information about the play that was performed under Keimann. The programme is for a school production in Görlitz, some twenty miles from Zittau, overseen by the headmaster Christian Funcke (1626–95).[4] Its title page mentions two plays that were to be performed 'auff offentlicher Schau-Bühne zu einer nützlichen und erbaulichen Schul-Ubung' ('on a public stage as a useful

---

[1] Gstach's mention of further Zittau performances of the play in 1661 (523) relies on a misunderstanding of a confusing footnote in Köhler (x–xi). See also Junkers, 249.

[2] The last of these plays has received a modern reprint (Markus).

[3] For Keimann, see also Kühlmann, 340–1.

[4] The programme is extant at the Oberlausitzische Bibliothek der Wissenschaften in Görlitz (call number Mil. II/131.60). It has been digitized and can be accessed at http://digital.slub-dresden.de/id1667619160.

and edifying school exercise'). The first is Christoph Kormart's *Polyeuctus*, a translation of Pierre Corneille's *Polyeucte*, published in Leipzig in 1669 (VD17 23:239720M). *Polyeuct* was to be performed, the programme continues, 'nebst der Wunderbahren Heyrath PETRUVIO mit der bösen KATHARINEN' ('alongside the Wonderful Wedding of Petruvio with the Bad Catharine') (sig. A1r). The fact that the title is the same as that of the Zittau production of 1658 and includes the surprising spelling 'Petruvio' offers strong evidence that the two plays were identical.

The 1678 programme contains no information about the contents of the plays, but, as well as giving the dates of the performances (20 and 21 October), it includes a list of roles with the names of the actors (sig. A2v).[1] The character names in the list suggest considerable proximity to Shakespeare's play: 'Baptista Minola', 'Catharina, Baptistae älteste Tochter' ('Catharina, Baptista's oldest daughter'), 'Bianka, Baptistae jüngste Tochter' ('Bianka, Baptista's youngest daughter'), 'Lucentio, ein junger Edelmann von Pisa' ('Lucentio, a young gentleman of Pisa'), 'Petruvio, Edelmann von Verona, der Catharinen Liebhaber' ('Petruvio, gentleman of Verona, suitor to Catharina'), 'Hortensio, ein Junger Edelmann in Padua' ('Hortensio, a young gentleman in Padua'), 'Vincentio, Lucentii Vater' ('Vincentio, Lucentio's father'), 'Vermummeter Vincentio' ('disguised Vincentio'), 'Grumio, alter Bürger zu Padua' ('Grumio, old citizen of Padua'), 'Die Wittib' ('the widow'), 'Curtas, Petruvii Diener' ('Curtas, Petruvio's servant'), 'Tranio, Lucentii Diener' ('Tranio, Lucentio's servant'), 'Bondello, Lucentii ander Diener' ('Bondello, Lucentio's other servant'), 'Grumio, Petruvii Diener' ('Grumio, Petruvio's servant'), 'Martinus, Baptistae Kammer-Diener'

---

[1] The address to the reader, which concludes the programme (sigs A3r–A4v), contains no information about the *Shrew* production. It is signed by 'Joh. He[i]nrich Oder, von Torau auß Nieder-Laußnitz' and dated 19 October 1678 (sig. A4v).

('Martinus, Baptista's valet'), and 'Der Schneider' ('the tailor').[1] We note the occasional departure in spelling, not only 'Petruvio' for 'Petruccio' (or 'Petruchio'), but also 'Grumio' for 'Gremio' (no doubt an error given the recurrence of 'Grumio' later in the list), 'Curtas' for 'Curtis' and 'Bondello' for 'Biondello'. On the whole, however, the names are close to Shakespeare's. The list excludes the smallest parts, such as attendants and some of the servants. It also excludes the haberdasher, as does *Kunst*, perhaps an unsurprising omission given that his role is easily omitted or conflated with the tailor's. On the other hand, it adds 'Martinus, Baptistae Kammer-Diener' ('Martinus, Baptista's valet'), probably the name given to Baptista's servant who, in Shakespeare's play, speaks three lines to Bianca to interrupt the music lesson (see below, p. 131). The list further shows that the Sly material was omitted and replaced by a 'Vorredner' ('Prologue'), again as in *Kunst*. Unlike *Kunst*, the play also had an epilogue, or even two, by a 'Schluss-Redner' ('Epilogue') and an 'Allgemeiner Schluss-Redner' ('General Epilogue').

The list of roles in the Grömitz programme of 1678 shows in fact a number of parallels to the list of roles (called 'Personaadjen', sig. A2v) in Sybant's *De Dolle Bruyloft*. The spelling of 'Catharina' and 'Bianka' is identical and slightly differs from the spelling in *The Shrew*. The descriptions in the programme of Lucentio as 'ein junger Edelmann von Pisa' ('a young gentleman of Pisa'), of Hortensio as 'ein junger Edelmann in Padua' ('a young gentleman in Padua'), of Petruvio as an 'Edelmann von Verona' ('a gentleman of Verona') and of Gremio as an 'alter Bürger zu Padua' ('old citizen of Padua') largely correspond to those of the same characters in Sybant, where Lucentio is an 'Edelman van Piza'

---

[1]   Nicholas Rowe's 1709 edition of Shakespeare's plays is the first English edition of *The Shrew* that contains a list of roles.

('gentleman of Pisa'), Hortensio an 'Edelman te Padua' ('gentleman in Padua'), Petrutio (note the spelling) an 'Edelman van Verona' ('a gentleman of Verona') and Gremio a 'Burger tot Padua' ('citizen of Padua'). Moreover, Lucentio's fake father is 'Vermummeter Vincentio' in the programme and 'gemomde Vincentio' in Sybant, both meaning 'disguised Vincentio'. Most compellingly, not only the programme but also Sybant give a name to Baptista's unnamed servant in Act 3, Scene 1 of *The Shrew*, which is virtually the same: 'Martinus, Baptistae Kammer-Diener' in the programme and 'Martijn, Dienaar van Babtista' in Sybant.[1] The evidence need not suggest that the play performed in Görlitz in 1678 (and, by extension, also the play performed in Zittau in 1658) are wholly derived from *De Dolle Bruyloft*. Indeed, the widow is absent from Sybant's play and list of roles, whereas she is mentioned in the 1678 programme, a clear indication that whoever produced the Zittau/Görlitz play knew *The Shrew* and not just *De Dolle Bruyloft*. Nor does the programme mention some of the other named characters in Sybant's play, notably 'Claas Slikom', 'Keen Partinentie', 'Pieter Zuykerzop' and 'Slobbetje' (Petrutio's servants). What can be said at the very least, though, is that some of the designations in the list of roles in the 1678 programme go back to the list of roles in Sybant's play. The

---

[1] Martijn is not named in Sybant's play beyond the list of roles. The characters appear in the list of roles in the order of their appearance, and the location in which 'Martijn' occurs in the list makes it clear that the name must designate Baptista's servant who, in Shakespeare, interrupts the music lesson to tell Bianca, 'Mistress, your father prays you leave your books / And help to dress your sister's chamber up; / You know tomorrow is the wedding day' (*TS*, 3.1.80–2). In Sybant, an unnamed 'Dienaar' appears at the same moment and speaks the equivalent of the first two of the three lines in *The Shrew* (*Dolle*, sig. B8v). The point is worth making since the existence of a named servant of Baptista's in Sybant and the 1678 programme might otherwise wrongly suggest that Theobald's servant Veit, one of *Kunst*'s fairly prominent additions to *The Shrew*, originated in Sybant's play or in the version performed in Zittau in 1658.

other conclusion that can be drawn is that, judging by the programme of 1678, the Zittau performance of 1658 was of a German version of *The Shrew* that stayed reasonably close to Shakespeare's play.[1] That *Kunst* derived from it, however, as Bolte ('Schulkomödie', 128) believed, is not made clear by the extant evidence.

On 3 March 1663, the Saxon court of Dresden saw the performance of a 'Komödie', called 'Amphitrione', and several 'Possenspiele' (farces), including 'die erste tolle Hochzeit, die andere tolle Hochzeit' ('the first mad wedding, the other mad wedding') (Fürstenau, 215–16). This raises several questions: is one farce here referred to or two? The title of Sybant's version of *The Shrew* is *De Dolle Bruyloft*, that is, 'The Mad Wedding', so was the Dresden performance (or were the Dresden performances) related to the Dutch play? What is implied by the generic designation 'Possenspiele' (as opposed to 'Komödie')? The difference may be partly one of length, a 'Komödie' being the main performance at an entertainment, with a 'Possenspiel' serving as an afterpiece, as was sometimes the case. If so, is it possible that *De Dolle Bruyloft* was adapted to serve as two 'Possenspiele' (perhaps for performance on subsequent days), the first leading up to Petruccio and Katharina's wedding, the second focusing on Lucentio and Bianca's? The evidence is too inconclusive to allow for clear-cut answers.

What increases the likelihood that the 1663 record is of a two-part play is a performance of 'der erste und zweite Theil "von der bösen Katharina"' ('the first and second parts of "Bad Katharine"') (Fürstenau, 251–2) among several other comedies at the Saxon court of Dresden in May 1678. Another play

---

[1] Bolte ('Schulkomödie', 125–8) did not notice the connections between Sybant's play and the 1678 programme and therefore argued that the Zittau 'Wonderful Wedding' of 1658 and *De Dolle Bruyloft* derived from Shakespeare's play independently.

performed in early 1678 was 'die Komödie "von Amphitryone"' (Fürstenau, 251), which may suggest that this and the two-part play may have belonged to the same repertory both in 1663 and in 1678. The later performances were by a company led by Johannes Velten, and, indeed, a repertory list of Velten's company of 1679 includes 'Die böse Catharina' ('Wicked Catharina'), although the list makes no mention of its being a two-part play (Gstach, 651).

Other records that can confidently be associated with a German version of Shakespeare's *Shrew* date from 1667. A company led by Johann Ernst Hoffmann and Peter Schwartz, the 'Churpfälzische Compagnie Comoedianten' ('Elector Palatine Company of Comedians'), performed at the court of Charles Louis, Elector Palatine (1617–80), in the spring of that year. A list of their repertory has survived, listing fifteen plays, including 'Die tolle Hochzeit von der böß Katharina' ('The Mad Wedding of Wicked Katharina') (Gstach, 646). They were back at the Mannheim court in December of the same year, when they are known to have performed several plays from their repertory, including 'Die tolle Hochzeit von der böß Katharina' on 20 December (Gstach, 647).[1] It is notable that the title of the play performed in 1667 by the Elector Palatine's Company of Comedians includes an element of the title of the 1663 'Possenspiele', namely 'tolle Hochzeit', but also anticipates the title of the play in the 1679 list of Velten's company, 'Die böse Catharina'. Another record of a performance prior to the publication of *Kunst* in 1672 dates from 6 July 1668, when the prolific German poet Sigmund von Birken, who lived in Nuremberg, noted in his diary that he had seen a performance of the 'Comoedie von der bösen aber frommgemachten Br[aut]' ('Comedy of the Bad Bride who was Made Pious'), quite possibly another reference to a German

---

[1]   For Hoffmann and Schwartz's company connections, see Rudin, '"Zwei Mal"'.

version of Shakespeare's play (Kröll, 1.381; Gstach, 523). The performance record is patchy and the relationship of the different titles ultimately inconclusive, but what seems clear is that in the years prior to the writing of *Kunst*, a German version of *The Shrew* could be witnessed in various theatres.

Kunst über alle Künste appeared in 1672, probably in Frankfurt (see below, pp. 147–9). Whether it was ever performed and if so, where, is not known. It would have required at least fifteen actors, a reasonably large cast (see the Appendix). Little can be inferred from the stage directions about any implied performance space, as most characters are simply said to enter and exit. When Hilarius' real father, Adrian, meets the fake father, Blasius, the latter appears at a '*window*' (4.4.101 SD), like the Merchant in *The Shrew* (5.1.14 SD), but Blasius later simply runs out, not down, to the main stage (see 4.4.132 SD and note), which may imply that no second level 'above' is involved. There is one stage direction, however, that might suggest that *Kunst*'s author imagined performance in a fairly specific theatrical space. Early in Act 4, Scene 1, Sabina enters and '*sits down at a table on the inner stage*' (4.1.8 SD, '*setzet sich bey einen Tisch in der inneren Scene*'). At the equivalent moment in *The Shrew* (4.2.5 SD), Bianca simply enters, and no inner stage is mentioned or implied. Inner stages are referred to in a number of contemporary German plays (see the note to 4.1.8 SD), and it has been suggested that their usage may 'derive from the practice of English companies touring in Germany' (Brandt and Hogendoorn, 34). *Kunst*'s anonymous author relates in an address to the reader that he had seen the play from which he adapted his *Kunst* (see below, p. 141) in the theatre, so it is possible that Sabina's appearance on the inner stage corresponds to what he had seen performed.

The documentary record of the seventeenth-century German reception of *The Taming of the Shrew* starts in the town of Zittau, and ends there, too, with Christian Weise's play *Die böse Catharina* ('Bad Catharina'). Weise (1642–1708) was headmaster of the Zittau grammar school from 1678 to 1708, as Keimann had been from 1638 to 1662. Formerly a pupil of Keimann's in this same school, Weise had probably witnessed and may even have acted in the 1658 'wunderbare Heurath', and so may have returned to the material later in his life. Weise's output was vast: apart from poetry and satirical novels, he wrote some sixty plays for performance by his pupils of which about two-thirds have come down to us (Watanabe-O'Kelly, 'Early Modern', 136–8). *Die böse Catharina* was not printed but survived thanks to two manuscripts which are now at the Christian-Weise-Library in Zittau (call numbers 4° Mscr. 47 (B) (1) and 4° Mscr. 50a (B); see Keller et al., 648–50). The play is dated between 1689 and 1702 by Ludwig Fulda (lxxiv), its first modern editor (Fulda, 103–272).[1] Fulda (lxxii) speculates that the unnamed comedy performed in Zittau on 28 October 1693 in honour of the Elector of Saxony, John George IV, may have been Weise's *Böse Catharina*, but there is no evidence to confirm this. The play follows the basic outline of Shakespeare's play but significantly departs from it by adding subsidiary plot strands and characters. It has none of the dramatic intensity and verbal wit of *Kunst*. Weise replaced most of Shakespeare's names with German equivalents, except for Baptista, Bianca and Catharina. It is noteworthy that the Petruccio character is called Harmen, which closely resembles *Kunst*'s Hardman, suggesting that Weise was familiar with *Kunst über alle Künste*.

The first faithful translation of Shakespeare's *Taming of the Shrew*, by Johann Joachim Eschenburg, appeared in 1775, and its title testifies to *Kunst*'s legacy more than a century after its publication. *Die Kunst eine Widerbellerin zu zähmen* ('The Art of Taming a Back-Barking Woman') adopts the first key word of the title of the seventeenth-century adaptation by

---

[1] For a more recent but unannotated reprint, see Roloff and Kura. As Fulda shows (lxxi), Köhler's suggested date, 1705 (xiii), relies on a misunderstanding.

conceptualizing the taming as an *art* (Eschenburg, 147).[1] The Schlegel-Eschenburg translation (1810–12, 18 vols) essentially reprinted Eschenburg's text but changed the title to *Zähmung eines bösen Weibes* (1811, vol. 14, p. 1). While the new title eliminated the word 'Kunst', it introduced part of the subtitle of the seventeenth-century adaptation: *ein bös Weib gut zu machen* ('to Make a Bad Wife Good'). The title in the famous Schlegel-Tieck translation (vol. 6, 1831), *Der Widerspenstigen Zähmung*, still current today, finally eliminated any echo of the title of *Kunst* and no doubt accelerated the play's descent into the oblivion from which the present edition aims to raise it up.[2]

TEXTUAL INTRODUCTION

The early editions and their contexts: publication, paratext and authorship

Kunst über alle Künste was published in duodecimo format in 1672. The title page of the first edition (see p. 150) reads:

> Kunst über alle / Künste / Ein bös Weib gut zu machen. / Vormahls / Von einem Jtaliänischen / *Cavalier practici*ret: / Jetzo aber / Von einem Teutschen Edel- / man glücklich nachgeahnet / und / Jn einem sehr lustigen Possen- / vollem Freuden-Spiele / fürgestellet. / Samt / Angehencktem singenden / Possen-Spiele / Worinn / Die unnötige Eyfersucht ei- / nes Mannes artig betro- / gen wird. / Rapperschweyl / Bey Henning Lieblern 1672.

---

[1] Eschenburg mentions *Kunst* in the appendix to his translation and quotes from it extensively (397–409).

[2] For a list of translations of *The Shrew*, see Blinn and Schmidt, 219–22.

The English translation reads:

> An Art beyond All Arts, to Make a Bad Wife Good,
> formerly composed by an Italian knight, but now
> happily imitated by a German gentleman and presented
> in a very amusing comedy full of merriment. With an
> appended singing-jig, in which the unnecessary
> jealousy of a husband is prettily deceived.
> Rapperschweyl, at Henning Liebler's, 1672.[1]

The printed title page, with which some extant copies start,
appears in fact on sig. A2r, and it was originally preceded by an
engraved title page, which was pasted onto the otherwise
blank sig. A1r, of which some copies are extant (see below,
pp. 156–7). At the top of the copper engraving, the following
title appears: *'Kunst über alle Kunst, Ein bosweib* [sic] / *guth
Zu machen'*. Below it, the background shows a house on a cliff
and windy clouds. In the foreground there is a woman to the left
with snake hair and bare breasts, who is being tickled in the
mouth with a fox tail by a man who stands to the right with his
back to the viewer. He has thrown the noose in his left hand
around her neck, and holds a club in his right hand. With his left
foot, the man stands in a circle on a checkerboard floor made of
a Latin inscription in capital letters: 'In verbis et herbis et
lapidibus magna consistit virtus' – 'there is great power in
words, herbs and stones'.

The engraving shown in Fig. 6 depicts a scene of the taming
of a fury-like female by a well-dressed male; its relationship to
the play is clear. The relevance of the Latin inscription, however,
is not immediately obvious. It derives – as does the second half
of the play's title, *'ein bös Weib gut zu machen'* ('to Make a Bad
Wife Good') – from a Shrovetide play by Hans Sachs, printed

---

[1]   The final 'n' in 'Lieblern' is a dative flexion.

6 Copper engraving, *Kunst über alle Künste* ('Rapperschweyl', 1672, 2nd edn), sig. A1r (Austrian National Library, shelfmark: 23387-A).

in the third volume of his works, *Das dritte Buch. Sehr Herrliche Schöne Tragedi, Comedi vnd schimpff-Spil, Geistlich vnd Weltlich* (Nuremberg, 1588, VD16 S 151; 'The Third Book: Very Delightful, Beautiful Tragedies, Comedies and Farces, Religious and Secular'): *Das bös Weib mit den Worten, Würtzen, vnd Stein gut zu machen* (sigs ³H6r–I2v; 'To Make a Bad Wife Good with Words, Herbs and Stones'). In Sachs's play, a man complains to his neighbour about his bad wife, who remembers the advice King Solomon gave to someone who had the same complaint, namely to use the wholesome effect of words, herbs and precious stones to cure her. The man tries all three, to no effect, before throwing stones at her until she drops to her knees and swears to improve.

At the end of the duodecimo volume appears a twelve-line poem called 'Erklärung dess Kupffer-Tittels' (sig. K12r), 'Explanation of the Copper-Title'.

> To rule a woman you must use your *status ratio*
> Act like a man who plays a flute and let the notes
> you blow
> Be sometimes harsh and rough and coarse, then soft
> and sweet-refined,
> You must see everything, and yet with open eyes be
> blind.
> Your ears too must be firmly closed and yet hear
> every sound.
> Then, *hocus pocus*, change your tactics when the
> time comes round.
> Mix bad words with the good ones if you want your
> bride to dance;
> With Hercules' Club and Reynard's tail you'll stand
> a better chance.
> Outside you'd take me for a fool, within I'm shrewd
> and smart;
> My noose is ready; club and tail are poised to play
> their part

> In catching this bad cat at last. You bet they'll serve
>   my turn;
> If you seek wit and daring, this is the place to learn.[1]

The German poem is in octameters, whereas the English translation, produced for us by Anthony Mortimer, is in fourteeners. The translation is not literal, but it conveys the sense and manner of the original. It provides a kind of Epilogue to the play from the position of the male tamer figure and, like the Prologue, comments on its ability to teach readers the ability to apply its insights.

The play's anonymous author ('a German gentleman' according to the title page) seems to have assumed that the play was of Italian origins ('by an Italian knight'), probably for the simple reason that the setting and the names in Shakespeare's play are Italian.[2] This is suggested by an address to the reader, printed after the end of the play, in which the anonymous author's voice is clearly audible:

> Favourable reader, I can say of this comedy that it is someone else's, but also my own. It is someone else's, not only because it was often performed in the theatre by comedians, but also because it is an invention whose

---

[1]   The original reads:

> Jst auch wohl in einem ding *Status ratio* von nöthen
> So ist es im Weiber-Zwang: Man muß wunderlich die Flöthen
> anzusetzen und zu blasen wissen, bald starck, bald gelind,
> grob und rein: bald muß man sehen, bald mit ofnen Augen blind
> Gleichsam seyn: Das Ohr muß nicht hören, und doch alles hören:
> Man muß, *hocus pocus* gleich, alles nach der Zeit umkehren
> Gute Wort mit bösen mischen, Herkuls Keul' und Reinckens Sch[w]antz,
> so man gantz *polit* gebrauchet, führen offt die Braut zum Tanz.
> Aussen Narr, von innen klug, steh' ich jetzt im Zirck umkreiset
> Meine Schlinck' ist zugericht, Keul' und Schwäntzchen sich auch weiset,
> meine böse Katz zu fangen. Was gilts, es gelinget mir,
> Wer Witz und auch Kühnheit heget, folge nach und lerne hier.

[2]   Given the reference to a 'gentleman', we assume that *Kunst* was written by a man, but the author's anonymity means that it is impossible to be certain.

old names and ways of speaking indicate to those who have already seen and heard it that it is of Italian origin. I can call it mine because, in view of its pleasant manner, I have recomposed it, altering and writing what I liked, with quick inventions that easily came to me. The jig is known to anyone who knows actors, and is attached as a coda, according to current fashion. Enjoy yourself with it, as I enjoyed myself in watching it, and fare well until things get better.[1]

(For the appended jig, see below, p. 144.) This address answers some questions, but raises others. The play which formed the basis of the anonymous author's adaptation had been frequently performed, in German, and had been witnessed in performance by the author. But where the play was performed and by whom remain obscure. The process of adaptation seems to have involved both copying and original composition, but the details of this process are not clarified. It may well be that the version the author witnessed in performance was essentially a German translation of Shakespeare's *Taming of the Shrew*, but just how close the translation was to the original and how often the author

---

[1]   The original reads:

Gunstgeneigter Leser.

Von diesem Freudenspiele kan ich sagen, daß es eines andern, und doch auch mein seye. Eines andern ist es, weil es nicht allein schon offt von *Comoedianten* auff dem Schauplatz fürgestellet worden, sondern auch die Erfindung, alte Nahmen, und Redens-Arten, deme, so es zuvor angesehen und gehöret, zeigen, daß es von Jtaliänischem Ursprunge: Mein kan ich es nennen, dieweil ich solchs, wegen seiner artigen Manier, gefasset, und auß meinem Kopffe, wie es mir gefallen, geändert, und hingeschrieben, nach dem es die geschwinden Einfälle, ohne Kopff brechen gegeben. Das Possen-Spiel kennet ein jeder, so *Comoedianten* kennet. Und ist an statt des Schwantzes, nach jetziger Manier, angehencket. Belustige dich hiermit, wie ich in derer anschauen gethan, und lebe wohl, biß es besser wird.

(sigs I12v–K1r)

The word 'Schauplatz' could refer to any theatre. There is no reason to believe, pace Gstach (522), that there is any reference to the theatre in Zittau.

of *Kunst* simply followed it are unclear. Nor do we know anything about the process of textual transmission: did the author of *Kunst* have access to a manuscript, perhaps thanks to the actors who performed the play, as has been assumed by Ellinger (267)? Or did the author work from a (now lost) printed text, as conjectured by Bolte ('Schulkomödie', 124–7)? Or might another form of transmission, such as shorthand, have been involved?

Little is known about the anonymous author, but we do know that he can be credited with two other playbooks. One of them contains another address to the reader which also comments on *Kunst*:

> To this and the preceding jig, esteemed reader, the same applies as to *Kunst über alle Künste, ein bös Weib gut zu machen*: I saw them performed by actors in the theatre, preserved them because of their pleasantness, and have written them down for your useful amusement, as they please me according to my judgement. I see no point in racking my brain over new inventions, and thereby losing time that is better spent on something else, and so here only *inventis addo* [add inventions]. Whoever else has seen or heard them will notice the difference between the old and the new, and will profitably recognize that, with such grotesquery, I show the world and its vanity (whose change and improvement I, and all of us, heartily desire).[1]

---

[1] 'Mit diesem und vorigen Possenspiele, Geehrter Leser, gehet es, wie mit der Kunst über alle Künste, ein bös Weib gut zu machen: Ich habe sie von *Comoedianten*, auf dem Schauplatz fürgestellet, gesehen, wegen ihrer Artigkeit behalten, und schreibe sie, zu deiner nützlichen Belustigung, hin, wie sie mir, nach Gutküncken beyfallen. Ich mag meinen Kopff hierin nicht wegen neuer Erfindungen zerbrechen, und hierüber Zeit verlieren, welche ich besser in andern anwenden, und hier nur *inventis addo*: Wer diese sonst gesehen, oder gehöret, wird den Unterscheid, unter dem alten und neuen, finden, und dass ich in solchen Fratzen auch die Welt und ihre Eitelkeit zeige (welcher Ender- und Besserung ich, mit unser aller, hertzlich wünsche) erspriesslich erkennen' (*Alamodisch*, sigs 2B8v–2B9r).

The anonymous author thus on at least two occasions adapted dramatic texts of plays or jigs he had seen in the theatre, but the precise nature of the adaptive process remains obscure. A lot depends on what the author means when writing that he 'preserved' (in German, 'behalten') the playtexts. It may imply that he got his hands on manuscripts which provided the texts he adapted, but in the absence of further evidence, it is impossible to be certain.

The author of *Kunst* addresses his readers in each of his playbooks, but he consistently refrains from revealing his identity. In one of them, he makes a point of commenting on his deliberate anonymity: 'The reader has no need to know my name, for it does not matter whether a kitten be called Mignon, Weinzchen, Heinz, Murner, Novazemblisch or Australisch, provided it catches mice.'[1] While his name thus remains unknown, it can be gathered from linguistic features in his plays that he was probably from Hesse or an adjacent part of Germany (see Köhler, xxv–xxvi; Bolte, 'Görlitzer Schulkomödie', 128; Ellinger, 267). His writings also reveal considerable learning, and show that he was steeped in German literature of the sixteenth and seventeenth century (Ellinger, 267; Scheitler, 1056–7).

In keeping with the author's deliberate anonymity is the fake imprint at the bottom of the title page: 'Rapperschweyl, at Henning Liebler's, 1672'. No information about a printer or bookseller called Henning Liebler has come down to us, and no printing press is known to have existed in the Swiss town of Rapperswil (to which 'Rapperschweyl' seems to refer), nor is there a plausible connection to the Alsacian town Rappoltsweiler. As we shall see below, the place of publication was probably Frankfurt.

---

[1] 'Meinen Namen hat der Leser nicht nöthig zu wissen: dann ein Kätzchen Mignon, Weinzchen, Heinz, Murner, Novazemblisch oder Australisch mag genennet werden: wann es nur wol mauset' (afterword to *Irrthum*, sig. L9r).

A version of the same fake imprint was used for the anonymous author's other dramatic publications. In the year after *Kunst, Der Pedantische Irrthum des überwitzigen doch sehr betrogenen Schulfuchses* (*The Pedantic Error of the would-be clever but much deceived Schoolfox*) was published in duodecimo: a satirical play in three acts about bad, pedantic schoolmasters (see Ellinger, 268–74). The imprint reads, 'Rappersweil, Bey Henning Lieblern, Im Jahr 1673' (VD17 23:252481T). This was followed two years later by *Alamodisch Technologisches Interim* (*Fashionable Technological Interim*), also in duodecimo, a satirical three-act play about clerical abuse and hypocrisy (see Ellinger, 274–8), with an analogous imprint: 'Rappersweil, Bey Henning Lieblern. Im Jahr 1675' (VD17 23:235914D). Many of the characters in *Irrthum* reappear in *Alamodisch*, and a minor character in *Alamodisch* is 'Blasius Nasenweis . . . *Rector paganus*' (sig. A4r), who also appears in *Kunst* as the character who corresponds to the Merchant, that is, Lucentio's fake father, in *The Taming of the Shrew*. Stylistically, the three plays are closely related, characterized by the same rough, often bawdy and typically proverbial or proverbial-sounding language, although the plots of *Irrthum* and *Alamodisch*, unlike that of *Kunst*, recede for much of the time behind dialogues whose relevance to the plot is tangential.

Each of the three plays is followed by a jig, reflecting the performance practice of (or in the tradition of) the itinerant English players (Ellinger, 278). The play appended to *Kunst* (sigs K1r–11r) is called *Singendes Possenspiel Die doppelt betrogene Eyfersucht vorstellend* (*Singing Jig Presenting Doubly Deceived Jealousy*). Fearing to be made a cuckold, Pickelherring, before leaving on a journey, tells his wife to say 'no' to all wooers. She turns away the first two accordingly, but the third, the 'Kavalier', cleverly asks her whether she would turn down his presents, to which she responds 'no' and gives herself up to him. Different printed versions of this jig survive in German, Dutch and Swedish (Wiggins, '*Jig of a Miller*', vol. 4, pp. 6–7). The jig appended to *Irrthum* (sigs L11r–N11r) is *Die seltzame Metamorphosis der Sutorischen in eine Magistrale Person* (*The Strange Metamorphosis of a Shoemaker into a Teacher*). Its central character is good-for-nothing Jan Pint who escapes from his shoemaker's apprenticeship, marries a prostitute and, despite his ineptness, is offered a position as a teacher by a headmaster who is interested in seducing his wife (in which he succeeds). The jig appended to *Alamodisch* (sigs 2B7r–2E4v), finally, is *Der viesierliche Exorcist* (*The Peculiar Exorcist*). It deals with an adulterous relationship that is witnessed by a friar who, upon the cuckolded husband's return, pretends the lover is a devil using a would-be exorcism to allow him to escape. Versions of this material are well known (Ellinger, 284–6), including one from the fifteenth-century comic poem *The Friars of Berwick*.[1]

Apart from the three closely-related playbooks of 1672, 1673 and 1675, only one other publication is known to have a similar imprint, and it contains what we believe is a false lead concerning the author's identity. *Donum nundinale oder Meß-Gaabe; allerhand merkwürdige Lähren, Fragen u. scharfsinnige Beantwortungen* (*Donum Nundiale, or Fair Stuff: All Kinds of Strange Instructions, Questions and Shrewd Replies*) appeared in 1673, also in duodecimo, and was, according to the imprint, 'Gedruckt zu', that is, printed at, 'Rapperschweyl, bey Henning Lieblem [sic]' (VD17 1:642505G). 'Lieblem' is clearly a misprint for 'Lieblern', and 'Rapperschweyl' is identical in spelling with the place name in the imprint of *Kunst*. *Donum nundinale* is not a play but a collection of anecdotes about ancient and more recent historical figures in which Socrates and Xanthippe – who feature prominently in the Prologue to *Kunst* – make several appearances (e.g., sigs A10r–v, B9r). The straightforward prose of *Donum nundinale* differs stylistically

---

[1]   For the three jigs, see Bolte, *Singspiele*, 110–37.

from the rougher style of the plays, but we do not think that the differences are such that they preclude common authorship. Also, linguistic features and geographical references in *Donum nundinale* point to the author's origins in or near Hesse, as is the case with *Kunst* and the other two anonymous plays (Bolte, 'Schulkomödie', 129). This along with the fake imprint suggest that the author of *Donum nundinale* may well be the author of *Kunst*.

Unlike the three plays, *Donum nundinale* contains a pseudonymous authorship attribution on the title page – 'Von dem Freygebigen' – followed by the Greek letters mu, beta and chi.[1] It is unclear what the Greek letters designate. 'Von dem Freygebigen', which might be translated as 'by the generous one' or 'by the munificent one', has been interpreted as a reference to the Count Ulrich von Kinsky, a member of the Fruchtbringende Gesellschaft (the Fruitbearing Society; Latin, *societas fructifera*), a German literary society, founded in Weimar in 1617, whose chief purpose it was to promote German as a literary and scholarly language (see Ball). Members adopted pseudonyms, among them Ulrich von Kinsky, who went under the name 'der Freigebige'. He had joined the Society in 1658 and died in 1687, so he was alive and active in the first half of the 1670s when *Kunst* and the other 'Rapperschweyl' publications appeared. Based on the coincidence of the title-page reference to the 'Freygebigen' and von Kinsky's pseudonym, VD 17, the standard short-title catalogue of seventeenth-century printed titles published in Germany, attributes *Donum nundinale* to von Kinsky. Yet there are good reasons to be sceptical about the attribution. Von Kinsky belonged to a distinguished Bohemian family that had been elevated to the rank of nobility in the early seventeenth

---

[1]   Bolte ('Schulkomödie', 129) reads the small initials on the duodecimo title page as 'M. B. K.', but after analysis with a magnifying glass, we think they are more likely to be the Greek letters mu, beta and chi.

century. He occupied important positions in the Electorate of Saxony, and is known to have been the commander of the Königsstein Fortress near Dresden (*Akademie*). He was a member of the Saxony-Weimar branch of the Fruchtbringende Gesellschaft.[1] Nothing connects him to Hesse or other western parts of Germany, and what is known about the dialectal features of the works with the fake 'Rapperschweyl' imprints is difficult to reconcile with the assumption that he wrote them. The ascription to the 'Freigebige' on the title page of *Donum nundinale* is thus probably a false lead put in place by someone who was determined to preserve his anonymity.[2] The author of *Donum nundinale* may well have written *Kunst* and the other anonymous plays, but it seems unlikely that the author is Ulrich von Kinsky. In the absence of further discoveries, it thus remains impossible to identify the author of the German adaptation of Shakespeare's *Taming of the Shrew*.[3]

The place of publication of *Kunst* has repeatedly been assumed to be Hamburg (Weller, 22–3; Hayn, 134, 138), and VD17 conjecturally agrees with this assumption (VD17 32:677848D). Thanks to a bibliographic accident, however, it can be shown that the place of publication was probably Frankfurt. Three copies (of which one is now lost; see below, pp. 157–8) of the second edition of *Kunst* feature a copper engraving which has no relationship to the play. It contains a

[1] The Weimar archives of the Fruchtbringende Gesellschaft, extant in three volumes at the Thüringische Hauptstaatsarchiv Weimar (Kunst und Wissenschaft: Hofwesen 11817.1 and 2, and 11818), contains no document by or addressed to von Kinsky. We are grateful to Andreas Herz for this information.

[2] There is one other German society of the seventeenth century whose members took on similar pseudonyms, the Deutschgesinnte Genossenschaft. The member directory published in volume 12 of the works of Philipp von Zesen suggests that this society had no member who used the pseudonym 'der Freigebige' (van Ingen).

[3] It should be noted that none of the playbooks with the 'Rappersweil' imprint is listed in any of the Frankfurt or Leipzig book fair catalogues; *Donum nundinale*, however, is mentioned in the Leipzig book fair catalogue of autumn 1672, as published by 'Henning Lieblem' (sig. B4v).

view across a gate onto an alley of poplars with a coach drawn by horses. Above the gate are a naked woman and a skeleton holding a wreath that surrounds the following text: 'Die wieder kommende ANGELICA' ('the returning Angelica'; see Bolte, '*Kunst*', 446). This is the title of a short anonymous novel, conjecturally dated *c*. 1680 on VD17 (23:665989F) but in fact mentioned in the Leipzig book fair catalogues in 1671 (*Catalogus* Spring 1671, sig. C3v; *Catalogus* Autumn 1671, sig. B3v). Two copies of *Die wieder kommende Angelica*, a slight duodecimo, are known to survive, and both contain the copper engraving.[1] As has been pointed out, 'The simple and probable explanation is that the *Angelica* novel and the *Kunst über alle Künste* were printed about the same time at the same print shop . . . Some careless workman confused the two copper plates' (Jantz). The catalogues contain the following information about the publication of *Die wieder kommende Angelica*: 'Frankf[urt] bey Joh. Hoffmann' (*Catalogus* Spring 1671, sig. C3v) and 'Franckfurt bey Jac. Gottfr. Seylern' (*Catalogus* Autumn 1671, sig. B3v). Based on the evidence in the Leipzig book fair catalogues, it thus seems likely that *Kunst* (and thus probably also the other 'Rapperschweyl' publications) appeared in Frankfurt. This place of publication squares well with dialectal features in the anonymous publications (see above, p. 143). It may be added that Frankfurt is one of the rare place names mentioned in *Kunst*: in Act 2, Scene 1, Hardman intends to 'travel to Frankfurt now, and buy the most gorgeous robes and jewels' (1.2.469–70) for Catharina. All things considered, then, Frankfurt is a plausible place of publication for *Kunst über alle Künste*.

What complicates matters is that of the two publishers mentioned in the Leipzig book fair catalogues, only one, Jakob

---

[1] Herzog August Bibliothek Wolfenbüttel, call number QuN 943 (2), and Hamburg, Staats- und Universitätsbibliothek, call number Scrin A/1613, the third item in a Sammelband.

Gottfried Seyler, can be associated with Frankfurt. Johann Hoffmann, a known publisher whose activities have been thoroughly researched and documented (see Deneke; and Benzing, 1173), was in fact based in Nuremberg. In the *Catalogus* of spring 1671, three lines below Hoffmann's mention as the publisher of *Angelica*, appears a title that is correctly said to have been published in 'Nürnb[erg] bey Johann. Hoffmann' (sig. C3v). What is likely to have happened, then, is that the information regarding Hoffmann's publication of *Angelica* is erroneous and resulted from eye-skip. The manuscript from which the spring book fair catalogue was printed probably mentioned Seyler as *Angelica*'s publisher, as the autumn catalogue did, but the compositor's eye accidentally turned to Hoffmann's name slightly further down in the list when setting the type.

Independently of what happened in the printing of the spring 1671 Leipzig book fair catalogue, there is no reason to doubt the information in the autumn catalogue according to which Jakob Gottfried Seyler was the publisher of *Angelica*. By extension, given the *Angelica* engraving, he is also likely to have been involved in the publication of *Kunst*. Seyler was active in Frankfurt as a publisher from 1667 until 1683 and is known to have published at least 129 titles there during that period (Benzing, 1268). Although he seems to have moved some of his business to Kassel in the course of the 1670s, he kept a bookshop in Frankfurt at least until 1678 (Paisey, 172). In the absence of information about the play's author, he is the one and only person we can associate with some confidence with the origins of *Kunst*.

The order of publication of the two editions of 1672

There are two early duodecimo editions of *Kunst*, both dated '1672'. The title pages of the two editions are identical in text and font, and the layout is very similar. The easiest way of telling the title page of the first (see Fig. 7) from that of the

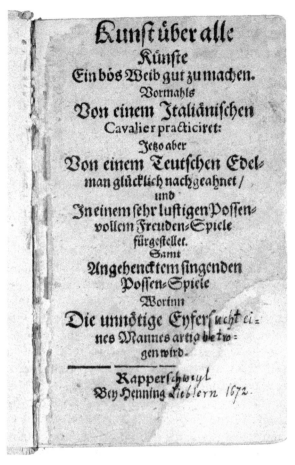

7 Title page of *Kunst über alle Künste* ('Rapperschweyl', 1672, 1st edn), sig. A2r (Herzogin Anna Amalia Bibliothek, Weimar, shelfmark: O 9: 246).

second (see Fig. 8) edition is that at the end of line nine, the slash ('/') that follows the word 'nachgeahnet' is followed by a blank space in the first edition, whereas it is not in the second where the bottom of the slash almost touches the lower part of the final 't'. Both editions have some misnumbered pages,

8 Title page of *Kunst über alle Künste* ('Rapperschweyl', 1672, 2nd edn),
sig. A2r (Austrian National Library, shelf mark: 23387-A).

especially towards the end, and the last page number in what
we will show below is the first edition ('D1' short for the first
duodecimo edition; VD17 32:677848D) is '138' (instead of
'238'), whereas the last page number in the second edition
('D2'; VD17 23:236440V and VD17 23:252479X) is '337'
(instead of '237').

It is unclear from the title pages which is the earlier of the two editions, so bibliographic analysis is needed to establish the order. Typographic arrangement turns out to be an important source of information, since it points to one edition trying to replicate as far as possible the line breaks and page breaks of the other. On sig. A4r, for instance, the compositor of D2 falls slightly behind in line 3 (D1 ends with 'An-', for which D2 lacks space). In the next few lines, we see the compositor of D2 trying to catch up, or at least not fall behind further. In line 4, the last word is printed as a two-letter word (the second letter seems illegible), although the equivalent word in D1 is 'daß'. There are various contractions in D2 (and none in D1), 'eyterbissigē' (line 6), 'dē' (line 9) and 'gestochē' (line 10). When it becomes apparent to D2's compositor that his line breaks will be before D1's despite the contractions, he seems to have stopped using contractions and resigned himself to using an extra line of type at the end of the page (D1 has twenty lines of text, not counting the catchword and the signature, whereas D2 has twenty-one). As he is approaching the end of the page, D2's compositor has actually not fallen behind quite enough (i.e., not quite a whole line), which means he decides to waste space, as shown by the large spaces before and after 'Hosen' in the penultimate line. At the end of the last line, D2 has 'an Beseeli-'. D1, however, only has 'an', with 'Beseeli-' following on the next line as the catchword. D2 fails to have a catchword on a separate line and, even more surprisingly, also omits the signature present in D1, 'A jv'. The following page then starts identically, 'Beseelingungsstatt', D2 thus repeating not the catchword but the last word on the last line of text on the preceding page. All these oddities in D2 are clearly attempts to keep the printing process as simple as possible by making it a line-by-line or, when that fails, at least a page-by-page reprint of D1.

Something similar may be observed on sig. A4v. From the first line, we see D2's compositor use a contraction, 'vō', to have the same line break as D1. The same happens in the next line, with D2's 'welchē'. D2's compositor nonetheless falls behind in line 6, which ends with 'lassen/' in D1, but with 'las-' in D2. But the difference remains small for much of the page, and a series of contractions close to the bottom of the page ('vō', 'Jungē', 'uň' (for 'und') and 'Dāck') allows D2's compositor to catch up with D1's line breaks. D1, by contrast, uses no contractions, nor any extra-large spacing, suggesting that its compositor, unlike that of D2, is not trying to work to line and page breaks imposed by an earlier edition.

Similar evidence could be adduced from later in the book, but the important point has been made: recurrent space-wasting and space-saving devices in D2 and the absence of such devices in D1 show that D2 was set up from D1. D1 is thus the first of the two editions dated 1672; D2 the second.

D1 collates A-K12. Leaf A1 is blank, with the engraving pasted onto sig. A1r. The title page is on sig. A2r. After a blank verso follows the List of Roles ('Personen dieses Freuden-Spiels', sigs A3r–v) (see Fig. 9). The text of *Kunst* (sigs A4r–I12v; for a sample page, see Fig. 10) is directly followed by the address to the reader ('Gunstgeneigter Leser', sigs I12v–K1r) which is in turn directly followed by the jig, whose title appears at the bottom of sig. K1r, followed by a List of Roles ('Personen dieses Possen-Spiels') and a short argument in verse ('Einhalt'), both on sig. K1v. The text of the jig (sigs K2r–K11v) is followed by the 'Erklärung des Kupfer-Tittels' (sig. K12r). The last page is blank (sig. K12v). Several pages are mis-signed: sigs B7r 'Bvj', H5r 'Hiij', K2r 'Kiij', K3r 'Kij' and K4r 'Kv'. Sig. H4r is unsigned. Page numbers start on sig. A3r ('5'), and, with the exception of '218' lacking on sig. K1v, follow consecutively until '230' (sig. K7v). The page number then jumps to '331' (sig. K8r), then follows consecutively until '337' (sig. K11r) and ends with '138' (sig. K11v). There are no page numbers on leaf K12.

The make-up of D2 corresponds to that of D1, with a few exceptions. The text of the jig is made to fit on sigs K2r to K11r, with the 'Erklärung des Kupfer-Tittels' printed on sig. K12r.

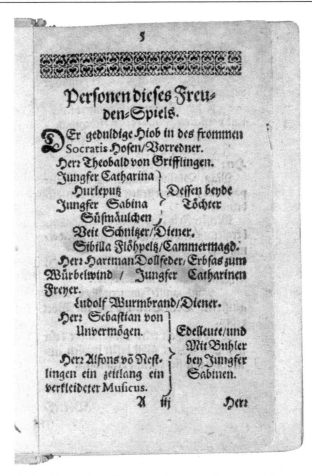

9 List of roles, *Kunst über alle Künste* ('Rapperschweyl', 1672, 1st edn), sig. A3r (Herzogin Anna Amalia Bibliothek, Weimar, shelfmark: O 9: 246).

Sig. B7r is mis-signed 'Bvj' and sig. H5r 'Hiij'. Sigs A4r, E4r and H4r are unsigned, and, after K1r, the last sheet is entirely unsigned. Page numbers are at first identical with those in D1, except that 164 is misnumbered '184'. As in D1, '218' is lacking on sig. K1v, and the numbering jumps from '331'

127

Hartman. Ich sehe wohl wir seynd hier mit Schelmen und Dieben besetzt/die wollen uns den Paß sperren. Hilff deine Frau retten/ mein treuer Diener/ wofern du Hertz im Leibe hast.

Wurmbrand. Das ist leider sehr wenig.

Hartman. Fürchte dich nicht mein liebstes Kind/ es soll dir keine Seele schaden thun/ du bist in meinem Schutz sicher (Er trägt sie im Arm hinaus.)

Wurmbrand. Der Teuffel dancke meinem Herren daß er so eine truckene Hochzeit hält. Der Galge möchte jhn beherbergen/ hinterliesse er mich nur zum Pfande hier.(Gehet ab.)

Sabina Das ist mir ein tolles Völckchen/ es stehet aber über auß übel/ daß wir zum wenigsten die Braut nicht sollen auff der Hochzeit haben. Es wäre doch gut wann man sie noch auffhielt.

Felix.Dieses halte ich nicht für gut/zu dem würde sich auch sein eigensinniger Kopff hieher nicht bändigen lassen.

Theobald. Wir müssen sie mit einander

F iv

10 Sample page of *Kunst über alle Künste* ('Rapperschweyl', 1672, 1st edn), sig. F4r (Herzogin Anna Amalia Bibliothek, Weimar, shelfmark: O 9: 246).

(sig. K8r) to '337' (sig. K11r). Since the text of the jig ends on sig. K11r, not on sig. K11v as in D1, the final page number is '337'. The page with the 'Erklärung des Kupfer-Tittels' has no page number, as in D1.

Extant copies of the early editions

There are five extant copies each of the two 1672 duodecimo editions of *Kunst über alle Künste*:

First edition (D1):

- Herzogin Anna Amalia Bibliothek Weimar (call number O 9: 246). Lacks the copper engraving. The bottom-right corner of the title page is missing, with some loss of text.[1]

- Austrian National Library, Vienna (call number 4679-A ALT MAG). Lacks the copper engraving. Bound up with another play, Laurentius Postel, *Traur-Freudenspiel von Almadero und Liarta* (Hamburg, 1652), which precedes it. Postel's play does not appear in VD 17.

- Russian State Library, Moscow (call number MK IV-нем. 8°). This copy was previously in the Saxon State Library in Dresden (call number Lit. Angl.A.661), from which it disappeared after the Second World War.

- Staatsbibliothek Bamberg (call number: 14 N 2#2). With the copper engraving.

- Beinecke Rare Book & Manuscript Library, Yale University (call number Zg17 G88 672r). Lacks the copper engraving. The second of three titles in a

---

[1]   It is from this copy that our German text (see above, p. xvii) has been prepared.

Sammelband, preceded by anon., *Malus Mulier, Das ist Neue Böser Weiber Legenden* (n. pl., 1671, VD17 1:668937W) and followed by Hans Jakob Christoffel von Grimmelshausen, *Rathstübel Plutonis oder Kunst Reich zu werden* (Samarien: 1672, VD17 12:653071C).[1]

Second edition (D2):

- Herzog August Bibliothek, Wolfenbüttel (call number QuN 847 (1)). With the copper engraving. Bound up with *Der Pedantische Irrthum* (1673; see above, p. 144) and *Der seltzame Springinsfeld* by Hans Jakob Christoph von Grimmelshausen (1670, VD17 23:233338F).

- Herzog August Bibliothek, Wolfenbüttel (call number Lo 4098.1). With the *Angelica* engraving (see pp. 147–8) in initial position, and the *Kunst* engraving inserted between sigs I12v and K1r. An early ownership note reads, 'F[erdinand] A[lbrecht] H[erzog] z[u] B[raunschweig] u[nd] L[üneburg] . . . 1682'.

- Privately owned. Previously on loan at the Universitäts- und Landesbibliothek Sachsen-Anhalt, Halle (call number AB 40 19/h, 19) but returned to its owner in 2010.

- Austrian National Library, Vienna (call number 23387– A). With the copper engraving and, before it, the *Angelica* engraving (see pp. 147–8).

- Landesbibliothek Coburg (call number Rara / Cas A 2532). With the copper engraving.[2]

---

[1] We are grateful to Sara Powell from the Beinecke Rare Book & Manuscript Library, Dr Stefan Knoch from the Staatsbibliothek Bamberg and Kerstin Schellbach from the Saxon State and University Library in Dresden for information about these copies.

[2] We are grateful to Gerd Schramm from the Landesbibliothek Coburg and Bettina Lampel from the Universitäts- und Landesbibliothek Sachsen-Anhalt, Halle, for information about these copies.

A copy of the second edition previously known to exist at the Landesbibliothek Kassel (call number Fab. Roman. Duodez 114) almost certainly burnt in a fire in 1941.[1] It included both the *Angelica* and the *Kunst* engraving (Bolte, 'Schulkomödie', 129).

Editorial history

The modern editorial history of *Kunst* is very brief and confined to the edition published by Reinhold Köhler in 1864. Köhler's text is mostly a faithful reprint, although spelling and punctuation are somewhat modernized. Köhler followed the original division into acts and added no scene division, or any stage directions. The major exception to his otherwise conservative editorial policy is that he omitted from his text what he considered a few 'particularly dirty passages' ('besonders schmutzige Stellen', xxxviii). The first is from Wormfire's soliloquy at the end of Act 2 ('One ... better', 2.2.19–23), and the other three are from the final scene (5.2.110–40, 146–54, 345–93). Köhler also bowdlerizes a couple of other passages (see 2.2.7–8, 17–18 and notes) by changing 'die Hure' ('the whore') to 'sie' ('she'). He prints some of the corresponding Shakespeare passages at the bottom of the page and provides a scholarly introduction (v–xliii) and commentary (213–60). Cohn did not include an edition of *Kunst* in *Shakespeare in Germany*, but he devoted a number of pages to it in the introduction (cxxiv–cxxx) and printed three short passages, with English translation (cxxvii–cxxix). Prior to the present publication, no translation of the play had been undertaken.

---

[1]   We are grateful to Heike Homeyer from the Universitätsbibliothek Kassel-Landesbibliothek und Murhardsche Bibliothek der Stadt Kassel for this information. Attention was drawn to the Kassel copy by Bolte, '*Kunst*', 446.

A NOTE ON THE
TRANSLATIONS

The translations in this volume have been undertaken by the three editors, with extensive help from Anthony Mortimer, whose vast experience in translating from various languages into English (including Petrarch and Michelangelo from Italian, Villon from French, and Silesius from German) has been invaluable. The translation of the verse passages in *Kunst über alle Künste* (see below) is essentially Mortimer's, and he also much improved the prose text.

Like any translation, ours needs to steer a course between a literal, word-for-word version, which would come at the cost of readability, and a more free approach which would not preserve enough of the linguistic and semantic make-up of the original. Our edition is particularly concerned with the relationship between the German adaptations and the Shakespearean originals, and this can only be revealed by a reasonably close translation. On the other hand, we have tried to arrive at a text that feels natural and is easily readable in English, and that occasionally entails a departure from what the German text literally says. When such departures are significant, we draw attention to our translation choices in the commentary.

Of the two previous translations of *Tito Andronico*, one (see below) adopts now archaic second-person familiar pronouns (thou, thee, etc.) and corresponding verb forms. There may be good reasons for this: the English playtext of which *Tito* is a translation and adaptation included those linguistic features, and so a retranslation that reproduces them may reflect a significant aspect of the relation between German adaptation and English original. Yet any attempt to translate a text into early modern English or an approximation thereof also comes with a series of problems. Early modern English is a language no one now speaks, and its supposed recreation runs the danger of coming across as pastiche. Many early modern terms would need notes since they are not familiar to all readers, and it seems more sensible to translate into a language that does not sound alien to modern readers. Other words have changed their meaning since the early modern period, and a translation into pseudo-early-modern English would raise the question of which meaning is intended and create the need for more notes. The decision to translate a text into the English language of another period would also raise the question of which period to choose: the late sixteenth century, when *Titus Andronicus* and *The Taming of the Shrew* came into being; the early seventeenth century when *Tito* was printed; or the later seventeenth century, when *Kunst* came into being? Any one of these options would be hard to justify and even harder to maintain in any consistent and coherent fashion.

We have therefore decided to translate the texts into modern (British) English. Yet while we have tried to steer clear of the awkwardly archaic, we have also favoured options that do not feel aggressively modern. Given the origins of the texts we have translated, we think there is a limit to how modern the translations should sound. We also make an exception in our avoidance of early modernisms by using 'exit' and 'exeunt' in stage directions, in keeping with Arden Shakespeare practice. Apart from this exception, we have striven for diction that is neither recognizably archaic nor specifically of the twentieth and twenty-first century.

We use contracted verb forms (don't, isn't, he'll, etc.) when there seems to be a good reason to do so. For instance, short forms may indicate a more relaxed mood, a class difference or a certain absence of emphasis, and of course they impact the overall rhythm of a sentence. The German text of *Kunst* has a fairly colloquial feeling throughout, and contracted forms thus often seem appropriate. In *Tito* the short form is reserved for Morian (it suits his sardonic nature) and the midwife (as a matter of class difference). We similarly used short forms for Pickelherring in the translation of *Romio und Julieta*.

The translation of *Kunst* comes with challenges over and above those of the other seventeenth-century German Shakespeare adaptations. The language is often idiosyncratic, with passages that are hard to make sense of, and many phrases sound proverbial but are not recorded and explained in any of the standard reference works (see pp. 116–17). Even the play's only previous editor, Reinhold Köhler, a well-known German scholar in his time, who was the head librarian of the Duchess Anna Amalia Library in Weimar, was repeatedly left nonplussed by the text (e.g. pp. 215, 220, 224, etc.), though, in the 1860s, he was still considerably closer in time to the German of *Kunst* than we are today. Translating *Kunst* thus occasionally involves conjectures, as acknowledged in the commentary.

Tito is exclusively in prose, but *Kunst* contains several passages in verse (3.1.46–50, 3.1.67–70, 3.1.143–78, 5.2.224–60, 5.2.352–59), which we have translated as verse. The first two passages, dactylic compositions by Felix and Sabina during the poetry lesson, have been translated so as to preserve the dactylic metre. In the third, Alfons' song performed for Sabina during the music lesson, the translation preserves the original's iambic trimeter couplets. The fourth, Felix's hunting poem, has rather rough iambic octameter couplets in the original, which our translation renders as fourteeners to convey the impression of a fairly rudimentary verse technique. In the last verse passage, a poem by Fabian, our translation preserves the original's (rather awkward) iambic trimeter couplets. We have rhymes where the German does, although we make occasional use of half rhyme where the German has full rhyme (e.g., 3.1.143–6).

Kunst has not been previously translated, but there are two earlier translations of *Tito* into English. We have benefited from them but have also tried to improve on them. Moritz Lippner's translation in Cohn's *Shakespeare in Germany* (1865) is generally reliable, although its English is partly archaic, not least in its adoption of second-person familiar pronouns (thou, thee, etc.) and corresponding verb forms. The translation by Ernst Brennecke in *Shakespeare in Germany 1590–1700* (1964) is considerably less formal than Lippner's and sometimes rather loose. We have tried to avoid the former's archaisms and the latter's looseness, striving for a text that combines readability with conservative modern English.

A NOTE ON THE
COMMENTARY AND
COLLATION

The commentary and collation located below the text of the two plays in this volume have several purposes. An important aim of the commentary is to shed light on the relationship between the German adaptations and the texts of *Titus Andronicus* and *The Taming of the Shrew*. The commentary on each scene begins with a short note that synthetizes correspondences to and differences from Shakespeare's play. Other notes comment on local similarities and dissimilarities between *Tito Andronico* and *Titus Andronicus* or *Kunst über alle Künste* and *The Taming of the Shrew*. In instances that seem significant, we also annotate *Tito*'s relationship to other early (English and Continental) Titus texts, in particular the English ballad, the English chapbook and Jan Vos's Dutch play *Aran en Titus*.

While an important part of the commentary relates the German adaptations to Shakespeare's plays, another part situates them within their cultural, theatrical, literary and linguistic contexts in the German-speaking territories of the seventeenth century. Although our texts are English translations of the German *Tito Andronico* and *Kunst über alle Künste*, we sometimes find it necessary to comment on features of the German text. In notes where the German word or phrase is important, we insert it between parentheses after the English headword. To explain early modern German, we often draw on the *Deutsches Wörterbuch* initiated by Jakob and Wilhelm Grimm (hereafter, 'Grimm'), the most comprehensive dictionary of the German language. Its examples from primary sources reach back to the fifteenth century, making it the closest equivalent to what the *OED* is for the English language.

The language of *Kunst über alle Künste* is sometimes idiosyncratic: there are many proverbs and idioms, or passages that at least sound proverbial or idiomatic, even though the most comprehensive reference work of proverbs in the German language, Karl Friedrich Wilhelm Wander's *Deutsches Sprichwörter-Lexicon* (hereafter, 'Wander'), does not always contain them, or records the passage in *Kunst* as the only known occurrence. The approximate meaning of the passages in question can often be inferred from the context, but our translation usually makes no attempt to render them literally. Instead, we often try to explain in the commentary how the passage works in German by providing its literal meaning, thereby striving for readability in the translation while conveying a sense of the characteristically proverbial-sounding German via the commentary.

The chief purpose of the collation is to provide our sources in instances where our text does not simply translate but departs from the first edition of *Tito Andronico* (1620) and *Kunst über alle Künste* (1672). At the end of Act 2, Scene 1 of *Tito Andronico*, for instance, the 1620 edition provides no exit stage direction for Morian, Helicates and Saphonus. Brennecke is the first editor to change this, so our collation note reads: '108 SD 1 *Exeunt*] *Brennecke; not in 1620*'. (We have made no attempt to record in the collation readings in later editions of *Tito Andronico* that have not been adopted in the present edition.) Similarly, at 3.3.79 of *Tito Andronico*, we add the following stage direction to clarify whom Aetiopissa addresses in the last part of her speech: '[*to Saphonus*]'. This stage direction is not in the text of 1620, nor in any of the later editions and translations of the play. Accordingly, we have a collation note that reads: '79 SD] *this edn; not in 1620*'. In the case of *Kunst über alle Künste*, we slightly depart from this policy, for the following reason: the play has not been translated before and has been edited only once, by Reinhold Köhler (1864). Köhler often modernizes spelling and punctuation but otherwise adheres closely to the original text. What this means is that almost all editorially added stage directions (there are well over a hundred) and parts of stage directions (there are over thirty) as well as all explanatory additions to the 'List of Roles', marked by brackets, have been added by us. We have also divided the play into scenes (the early editions are divided into acts but not scenes) on the understanding that a new scene begins when the stage is cleared and the action is not continuous. On all these occasions, we have considered it unnecessary to mention in the collation that the editorially added text or scene division, in brackets, originates with us. In other words, when a change to the original text is marked by brackets and there is no collation note accounting for its origins, the material in brackets has been added by us. When, on the other hand, a stage direction or speech heading in brackets substitutes for material in the early editions or when a stage direction or emendation originates with Köhler, then that change is recorded in the collation.

We standardize names in stage directions and speech prefixes, and our collation does not record the many instances where this standardization takes place. The standardized name appears in small caps in speech prefixes and entrance directions, in keeping with Arden 3 policy, and it does so even when the name does not appear in the equivalent speech prefix or stage direction in the original German text. So, for instance, the name 'TITO' is editorially supplied in cases where the 1620 text only has 'Andronicus', as is sometimes the case. In *Kunst über alle Künste*, to give another example, Alfons is referred to as 'Musicus' (i.e., Musician) in stage directions and speech headings when in disguise. In stage directions, we clarify the character's identity by adding his name in brackets: '[ALFONS *as*] *Musician*' (4.1.0 SD). In the speech prefixes, we systematically opt for 'ALFONS'. Significant variations in speech headings are discussed in the notes accompanying the 'List of Roles'.

TITO ANDRONICO IN ENGLISH TRANSLATION

A VERY LAMENTABLE TRAGEDY
OF TITO ANDRONICO AND
THE HAUGHTY EMPRESS

VESPASIANUS	*[son of Tito Andronico]*	
Roman EMPEROR		
TITO ANDRONICO		
ANDRONICA	*[daughter of Tito Andronico]*	
AETIOPISSA	*Queen of Ethiopia, [later Roman]*	5
	Empress	
MORIAN	*[servant and secret lover of Aetiopissa]*	
HELICATES	*elder son of Queen of Ethiopia*	
SAPHONUS	*other son of Queen of Ethiopia*	
Andronica's HUSBAND		10
VICTORIADES	*[brother of Tito Andronico]*	
[Two] MESSENGERS		
MIDWIFE		
[SOLDIER]		
[ROMANS]		15
[Attendant, Servants, Soldiers]		

LIST OF ROLES In *1620*, headed 'Personae', and in the identical order to that reproduced here. The order of the main characters is close to the order of appearance but does not quite correspond to the order of their first mention in SDs (Tito is named before the Emperor, and Andronica after Aetiopissa, Morian, Helicates and Saphonus), nor to the order in which they first speak (Andronica does so after Aetiopissa, Morian, Helicates and Saphonus). The material in brackets has been added in the present edition. The first edition of *TA* with a list of 'The Persons' Names' was Ravenscroft's (1687). For characters who appear only in *TA*, see Introduction, p. 2.

VESPASIANUS Lucius in *TA*. Lippner and Brennecke have 'Vespasian', but this edition follows the original spelling.

Roman EMPEROR Saturninus (sometimes 'Saturnine') in *TA*. Tito does not give this character a proper name. Although the opening SD has '*the* EMPEROR *also enters, but at this time he is not yet the Roman Emperor*' (1.1.0.3–4), the first speech delivered by this character nevertheless has the SP 'Emperor' (1.1.14).

TITO ANDRONICO Titus Andronicus in *TA*. In *1620* the SPs vary between 'Titus', 'Titus Andron.' and 'Titus Andronicus'. This edition follows the form of the name used in the title of the German play.

ANDRONICA Lavinia in *TA*.

AETIOPISSA ... **Empress** The 'Personae' list indicates both of her titles: Queen of Ethiopia and Empress ('Königin auß Mohrenlandt. Käyserin'). Grimm defines 'Mohrenland' as the land where the Moors live, namely Mauritania and Ethiopia, which is supported by Aetiopissa's name in this instance. However, some seventeenth-century German texts use 'Mohrenland' to refer to the Northern African coast (see Schuster, sig. A1r). Her SP is 'Ætiopis.' (for 'Aetiopissa') before she is crowned, and usually 'Keyserin' or 'Käyserin' ('Empress') thereafter, although on two occasions (3.3.51 and 3.3.63), when she addresses her sons, her SP is 'Mutter', i.e. mother; we regularize to 'AETIOPISSA'. The name is linked to Ethiopia, whereas Tamora's name does not mark her out as a Goth. Despite being Ethiopian, Aetiopissa is described as '*lovely and white*' ('schön und weiß') in the opening SD (1.1.0.5), suggesting that, unlike Morian, her part is not to be performed in blackface. See Introduction, pp. 20–3. In Thomasius' 1661 German adaptation of Vos' *Aran en Titus*, Thamera becomes 'Tomyris', in reference to the Scythian queen.

MORIAN Unlike 'Aaron' in *TA*, Morian's name (from the German 'Mohr, Moriane, Morianer' for 'Moor') marks him out as a black African. This is supported by the opening SD, which identifies him as black ('schwartz'). While Aaron is not located in a specific African country, Morian reveals that he was hailed as the 'Thunder and Lightning' of Ethiopia on account of his martial prowess (1.1.111–12). In the chapbook and the ballad, the equivalent character is referred to simply as 'Moor'.

HELICATES Demetrius in *TA*. 'Helicates' has classical Greek connotations and suggests 'follower' or 'agent of' the sun (from 'helios' for 'sun' and the -της suffix, which is used to form agent nouns). Aetiopissa's sons are presumably white, like their mother, although there are no explicit comments on their whiteness as in *TA* (e.g. 4.2.99–100, 118–20, 156).

SAPHONUS Chiron in *TA*.

Andronica's HUSBAND (Andronicæ Gemahl) This character differs considerably from Lavina's husband Bassianus in *TA*; he has no proper name (which is also the case in the chapbook and the ballad), and there is no evidence that he is the brother of the Emperor. After the Emperor rejects Andronica in favour of Aetiopissa in 2.1 there is no mention of her subsequent marriage, yet she appears with her husband in 3.3 (see Introduction, p. 10). In the chapbook (39) and the ballad, Titus' daughter is betrothed to the son of the Emperor, which is also the case in Thomasius' adaptation *Titus und Tomyris* (1661).

VICTORIADES The 'Personae' list has 'Victeriados', but the spelling in the dialogue and the SPs is 'Victoriades'. Corresponds to 'Marcus' in *TA*.

169

MESSENGERS In *Tito*, 5.1 and 5.2, one of the messengers performs largely the same function as the Clown in *TA*, 4.3 and 4.4, who delivers Titus' insulting letter to Saturninus. In both cases the bearer of the message is punished by death. The other messenger in *Tito* (8.1) has no equivalent in *TA*. The 'Personae' list in *1620* mentions a single 'Bote', i.e. messenger.

MIDWIFE The 'Personae' list in *1620* and *1624* have 'Weise Wächter', which Lippner mistakenly translates as 'White Guards', while Brennecke corrects to 'Midwife'. 'Weise' is best translated as 'wise', not 'white' (German: 'weiß'). 'Wächter' means 'guard' or 'guardian' but is used here to refer to a guardian or carer in a broader sense. The SP in 6.1 is 'Weise Mutter' (literally, wise mother), a designation occasionally used for a midwife (see Grimm, 'Hebamme'). The SD introducing this character calls her 'weise Muhme' ('Muhme' usually referring to a female relative; Grimm). This character corresponds to *TA*'s 'Nurse'. 'Cornelia the midwife' (4.2.143) is mentioned in *TA* but does not appear onstage.

SOLDIER Not mentioned in the 'Personae' list in *1620* or *1624*. In 7.1, he delivers Morian and his child to Vespasianus as his prisoners.

ROMANS An unspecified number of 'Romans' are addressed in the opening scene by Vespasianus (1.1.1), the Emperor (1.1.16–17) and Tito (1.1.20), and they 'ALL' (1.1.34) acclaim the Emperor when he is crowned. Not in the *1620* 'Personae' list.

Attendant This non-speaking part is required in 5.2. Not in the *1620* or *1624* 'Personae' list.

Servants An unspecified number of non-speaking servants who prepare the banquet at the beginning of 8.2. Not in the *1620* 'Personae' list.

Soldiers The play requires two non-speaking soldiers in 7.3. Not in the *1620* 'Personae' list.

LIST OF ROLES 1 *son . . . Andronico*] Brennecke (son of Titus Andronicus); *not in 1620*

4 *daughter . . . Andronico*] Brennecke (daughter of Titus Andronicus); *not in 1620*

5 *later Roman*] *this edn*; *not in 1620*

6 *servant . . . Aetiopissa*] Brennecke (an Ethiopian, secret lover of Aetiopissa); *not in 1620*

11 VICTORIADES] *Cohn*; Victeriados *1620*; Victoriados *1624*

11 *brother ... Andronico*] Brennecke (brother of Titus Andronicus); *not in 1620*

12 Two MESSENGERS] *this edn*; Messenger (Bote) *1620*

13 MIDWIFE] *Brennecke*; White Guards *Cohn*; Weise Wächter *1620*

14 SOLDIER] *this edn*; *not in 1620*

15 ROMANS] *this edn*; *not in 1620*

16 Attendant, Servants, Soldiers] *this edn*; *not in 1620*

TITO ANDRONICO

1.[1]   VESPASIANUS *enters, the Roman crown in his hand. Enter* TITO ANDRONICO *wearing a laurel wreath, the* EMPEROR *also enters, but at this time he is not yet the Roman Emperor. Also enter* AETIOPISSA, *the Queen of Ethiopia, who is lovely and white, with her two sons* HELICATES *and* SAPHONUS, *and* MORIAN, *who is black and has a humble cloak pulled over his magnificent clothes, being a servant to the Queen and her secret consort. The last four to enter are the prisoners of Tito Andronico. Also enter* ANDRONICA [*and* ROMANS].

VESPASIANUS   Noble Romans, you are aware that our imperial throne is now empty and unfilled, and so to

---

1.1 generally corresponds to *TA* 1.1 (with some parallels to Aaron's speech about his villainies in 4.3), although it is much shorter, and several of the more elaborate details of *TA* are omitted. Whereas *Tito* has all the principal characters except for Victoriades enter onstage at once, *TA* staggers the action, presenting the initial dispute between Saturninus and Bassianus, followed by Titus' entry, the execution of Alarbus and the burial of the fallen Andronici sons in the family tomb. *Tito* has no equivalent to the dispute between Saturninus and Bassianus, which makes the transition of the crown from Tito to the Emperor simpler than that from Titus to Saturninus. Likewise, the absence of the rival brother figure makes the betrothal of Andronica to the Emperor more straightforward than the equivalent action in *TA*. Whereas in *TA*, Saturninus has cause to reject Lavinia in favour of

Tamora later in the same scene (because the Andronici sons and Marcus choose to support Bassianus' abduction of her), in *Tito* the Emperor has no cause to reject Andronica, whom he leads away at the end of the scene without challenge. Aetiopissa has only two sons, who are never threatened with death, unlike Tamora's three sons, one of whom is killed (which gives her a motive to be revenged on Titus and the Andronici). In *Tito* there is no explicit or sustained ill will between the principal characters, unlike in *TA*, where a significant portion of the lengthy opening scene is devoted to peace-keeping between various factions.

0.1–2 VESPASIANUS ... *hand* In *TA*, Marcus, not Lucius, holds the crown, '*aloft*' (1.1.18 SD). Victoriades is absent from the first scene, perhaps because of casting exigencies (see Appendix). The opening is proleptic in that the play will end when

---

1.1] *this edn*; Actus Primus *1620*   0   SD11 *and* ROMANS] *this edn*; *not in 1620*

avoid great discord and strife among the people, we
must soon elect another Emperor. Because I know of
no other man to whom this honour is more due than   5
Tito Andronico, who is now the most distinguished
and most eligible candidate, and since no-one in this
city of Rome has achieved more than him in bloody
and perilous combat, and also as everyone proclaims
that the crown of Rome is his by right, so let us all   10
wish him good fortune, place the Roman crown upon
his head, and for all time hold and honour him as our
most gracious Emperor.

EMPEROR   What? Shall Tito Andronico wear the crown
upon his head, and not I? No, that must never be! I am   15

Vespasianus agrees to 'receive the crown
in the presence of all' (8.2.75–6). For the
importance   of   Vespasianus,   see
Introduction, pp. 14–15, 39–40.

0.2 **laurel ... wreath** In *TA*, in his first
speech, Titus mentions that he is returning
to Rome 'bound with laurel boughs'
(1.1.77). Laurel is the foliage of the bay-
tree, used as an emblem of martial victory
in Rome.

0.3–4 **at ... Emperor** For the narrative and
descriptive nature of some of the SD in
Tito and elsewhere in the Leipzig volume,
see Introduction, pp. 69–70.

0.5 **white** ('weiß') Lippner and Brennecke
translate this as 'fair complexion', but
'white' seems significant in the context of
the play's treatment of race (see
Introduction, pp. 19–28).

0.9 **secret consort** Nothing in the subsequent
dialogue allows an audience to identify
Morian as Aetiopissa's secret lover until he
reveals it at 1.1.89–90. In *TA*, the relationship between Aaron and Tamora is also
revealed late in the first scene (1.1.512).

1–13 **Noble ... Emperor** It is unclear how
Vespasianus' position puts him in charge
of the election of the new Emperor.

Braekman suggests that the speech is
'wrongly ascribed' to Vespasianus and
that Victoriades 'is meant' (9.48), but
there is no evidence for this, and the character of Vespasianus is also foregrounded
elsewhere (see Introduction, pp. 14–15).
In *TA*, Saturninus speaks first and Marcus,
brother of Titus and Tribune of the
people, holds the crown (1.1.18.1). Like
Marcus in *TA*, Vespasianus attempts to
influence the process by advocating the
election of his kinsman.

2   **imperial   throne**   ('Keyserthumb')
Lippner has 'Empire', but we follow
Brennecke, which is supported by
Bassianus' reference to the 'imperial seat'
(1.1.14) and Tamora's comment on
Saturninus being 'but newly planted in
your throne' (1.1.449). The chapbook
also makes mention of Rome's 'imperial
Throne' (35).

2   **empty and unfilled** The first of many
hendiadyses in the play, the second following later in the sentence: 'discord and
strife'.

4   **elect** As in *TA*, Rome is an elective monarchy, although the exact modalities of
the succession are not spelled out.

next in line and the crown is rightfully mine. So, Romans, consider well and wisely what you do, so that no rebellion break out among us to trouble and endanger this noble city of Rome.

TITO   Romans, you must know that this imperial throne   20
is of no interest to me. I am now an old man and have spent all my life in constant and most perilous wars. Even if all the votes are cast for me, and everyone confers on me the imperial throne, you shall see that for the sake of peace I will give it to another, for it is   25
through *concordiam* and unity between the Emperor and the council, and also the common people, that Rome has become the head of the entire world. If dissension and strife now arose within its walls, the city would perish. Therefore, I shall cast aside my   30
pride and turn instead to humility. So come together

---

16 **next ... line** ('der neheste') literally, the next one. It is unclear if he, like *TA*'s Saturninus (1.1.5–8), is insisting upon his right of primogeniture.

17–18 **Romans ... us** The veiled warning about armed intervention is weaker than Saturninus' explicit invitations to cause civil unrest: 'Defend the justice of my cause with arms' (1.1.2) and 'Romans, do me right. / Patricians, draw your swords and sheathe them not / Till Saturninus be Rome's emperor' (1.1.207–9).

20–1 **this ... man** In *TA* Titus similarly states that 'A better head her [i.e., Rome's] glorious body fits / Than his that shakes for age and feebleness' (1.1.190–1). As in *TA*, 'old' is a recurrent epithet for the protagonist, used both by himself and others.

22 **all my life** ('die Zeit meines Lebens') literally, the time of my life. Compare Titus, who indicates a specific duration: 'Rome, I have been thy soldier forty years' (1.1.196). The duration of Tito's Ethiopian campaign is not specified, whereas

Marcus points out in *TA* that 'Ten years are spent since first he [i.e., Titus] undertook / This cause of Rome' (1.1.31–2).

23–31 **Even ... humility** Tito foregrounds the avoidance of civil unrest and the common good in his decision to renounce the crown. Titus, by contrast, insists on his age when explaining his decision (1.1.192–5).

26 *concordiam* Latin: harmony, concord, union.

27 **council** ('Rathe') Lippner and Brennecke translate this as 'Senate'. Whereas *TA* mentions the 'senate' (1.1.27, 44), '*the Senate House*' (1.1.66 SD1) and the 'Capitol' (1.1.44), which was often assumed to be the site of the Senate House, *Tito* has the vague 'council' ('Rathe') and mentions neither Capitol nor Senate House. Nor does *Tito* mention '*Tribunes ... and Senators*', whereas *TA* does (1.1.0.1–2). *Tito*'s dramatization of Rome's political institutions remains very vague.

29 **dissension** ('*despennation*') a Latinism.

173

now and let us crown the Emperor, loudly wishing
him good fortune and well-being.

> *Tito Andronico places the crown upon*
> *the Emperor's head.*

ALL *(cry)*   We wish long life, good fortune, and well-
being to the invincible and all-powerful Roman   35
Emperor.

EMPEROR   Well, my dear followers, since you elect and
uphold me as your Emperor, I in turn commit myself
to favour you with special liberties, to venture life and
blood with you for our fatherland, and always to act   40
in good faith. – As for you, Tito Andronico, who have
gladly and willingly conferred this imperial throne on
me for the common good and peace, I bear you great
love and loyalty. Therefore, I desire your lovely
daughter, Andronica, as my Empress, and today she   45
shall be crowned as Empress and married to me, if it
pleases you.

TITO   Most mighty and invincible Emperor, it gives me
special pleasure that you desire my dearest daughter,
Andronica, as Empress, which will establish yet more   50
peace and friendship between us. I hereby give you

---

33 SD In *TA* it is Marcus rather than Titus
who crowns Saturninus, presumably
during or after his speech at 1.1.234–7
(see Ard³ 1.1.237 SD note).

34 ALL *(cry)* *1620* typographically incorporates this passage into the SD that precedes
the cry. We derive the SP and the SD '*cry*'
from 'vnd sagen alle mit lauter Stimme'
(literally, and all say with a loud voice).

41–7 As ... you Like Saturninus (1.1.238–
47), the Emperor moves directly from his
expression of gratitude ('I give thee

thanks', 1.1.240) to his desire to marry
the daughter of his benefactor ('Lavinia
will I make my empress', 1.1.244). In
both speeches the Emperor ends by
asking for Tito's/Titus' agreement ('doth
this motion please thee?', 1.1.247). The
Emperor's desire to marry and crown his
Empress 'today' is only in *Tito*.

48–51 Most ... us Titus says that he is
'highly honoured' (1.1.249) by the match,
but only Tito insists (again) on peace (see
23–30).

my daughter and wish you both a peaceful, long, and
happy life.

Presents his daughter to him. The Emperor takes
her by the hand.

EMPEROR   I shall hold her in great respect and honour.
But tell me, please, who are these that stand behind   55
you?
TITO   Most mighty Emperor, this woman is the Queen of
Ethiopia, these two are her sons, and the Moor is her
servant, all of whom I have brought as prisoners from
Ethiopia.   60
EMPEROR   They please me greatly, especially the female
creature, and I could wish that they were mine.
TITO   Most mighty Emperor, since they please your
Majesty, I willingly give them to you.

He takes Aetiopissa and leads her to the Emperor.

Queen of Ethiopia, I hereby pronounce you free and   65
unyoked from me, and present you to my gracious
Lord Emperor.
AETIOPISSA   Great and mighty Emperor of Rome, I, my
sons, and my servant have now been handed over

52–3 **my ... life** The equivalent moment in
TA has Titus give away not only Lavinia
but also a number of other entitlements:
'My sword, my chariot, and my prisoners, / Presents well worthy Rome's
imperious lord: / Receive them then, the
tribute that I owe, / Mine honour's
ensigns humbled at thy feet' (1.1.253–6).

58 **the Moor** ('der Schwartz'; literally, the
black one). The distinction between 'her
sons, and the Moor' implies that the skin
colour of Helicates and Saphonus, like
their mother's, is considerably lighter
than Morian's.

61–2 **They ... mine** In *TA*, Saturninus
focuses more explicitly on Tamora, 'A
goodly lady, trust me, of the hue / That I
would choose were I to choose anew'
(1.1.265–6). This comment is made *after*
Titus bestows the prisoners upon him,
whereas in *Tito* the loosely corresponding
comment leads Tito to present his prisoners as a gift to the Emperor.

64 SD The early editions of *TA* have no
equivalent SD, but Ravenscroft inserted
'*Presents his Captives to the Emperor*'.

68–72 Tamora does not address Saturninus at
the equivalent moment.

175

as your Majesty's captives, and we offer ourselves to   70
your Majesty as your humble servants. Do with us
as you please.

EMPEROR   Lovely Queen of Ethiopia, I am well disposed
towards you and yours. So do not be melancholy and
distressed but of good cheer for I shall raise you to   75
great things, and you shall be maintained according to
your former status as a high-born queen.

AETIOPISSA   All-gracious and most mighty Emperor, I
humbly thank your Majesty for this great favour.

EMPEROR   Well, time flies, so let us all now go inside.   80

Exeunt. Morian remains.

MORIAN   Let me throw off these old rags now, for I see
that my secret mistress holds favour and grace with
the Emperor.

He pulls off the old cloak.

I hope she will attain even greater grace and *gratia*
with him, and that she will win his love with her   85

75–7 **I ... queen** Titus similarly assures
Tamora, 'for your honour and your state /
[Saturninus] will use you nobly and your
followers' (1.1.263–4).

81–130 The equivalent speech in *TA* is part of
the opening scene in Q1, but F introduces
an act division before it, which many subsequent editions followed, although Ard[3]
includes it in 1.1. Whereas Aaron's equivalent speech outlines his ambitions for personal advancement at the Roman court via
Tamora, Morian's concerns focus on adultery (his former involvement with
Aetiopissa), and on his former military
career and the Roman invasion of Ethiopia.

83 SD With this action, Morian reveals the
'magnificent clothes' mentioned in the
opening SD, which have so far been
hidden under his cloak. There is no equivalent SD in *TA*, although note Aaron's

'Away with slavish weeds and servile
thoughts! / I will be bright, and shine in
pearl and gold' (1.1.517–18). Morian thus
enacts (a version of) what Aaron says.
Tito's presentation of Morian in sartorial
finery can be read in the wider context of
Continental visual representations of black
Africans (see Introduction, pp. 25–6). For
the racial coding of Ethiopian dress mentioned elsewhere in the Leipzig volume,
see Introduction, p. 26 n. 2.

84 *gratia* Latin: grace, mercy.

85–7 **and that ... Rome** Aaron's 'Now
climbeth Tamora Olympus' top' (1.1.500)
follows after Saturninus has taken
Tamora as his consort. In *Tito*, the
Emperor has only told Aetiopissa that he
is 'well disposed towards' (73–4) her, and
Morian expresses no more than specula-
tive hopes at this point.

flattery and caresses and become the Empress of
Rome. If that happens, I shall truly cuckold the
Emperor and have far more pleasure and joy with her
than he will. Everyone thought I was merely the
Queen's servant – but no, I was her secret lover and   90
slept more often with her than the King of Ethiopia,
her husband, so that at last he noticed the mischief
between me and the Queen, and had me closely
watched so that I could not go near her. The Queen
became very impatient with her husband, for I could   95
not come near her for fourteen days, being guarded so
closely, and the King could not pluck her strings half
as vigorously as I. Therefore, she took poison and
gave it to the King in a goblet of wine so that again I
had free access to her. Yes, many who looked with   100

87–9 **I . . . will** more detailed and cruder than
Aaron's plans 'to wanton with this queen'
(1.1.520).

89–90 **merely . . . lover** Morian's designation
of himself as a mere 'servant' need not be
contradicted by his later account of his
fame as a soldier. He is insisting that he
was not just Aetiopissa's servant (as soldier and perhaps otherwise) but her lover.

90 **secret lover** Aaron speaks more specifically of Tamora's amorous enslavement
to him, describing her as a 'prisoner held,
fettered in amorous chains / And faster
bound to Aaron's charming eyes / Than
is Prometheus tied to Caucasus'
(1.1.514–16).

91 **King of Ethiopia** No equivalent Goth
king is mentioned in *TA*. In the chapbook
the Goth King is called Tottilius.

91 **King** The German text has 'Keyser'
('Emperor'), but Morian otherwise refers
to Aetiopissa's former husband as 'König'
('King'), so 'Keyser' seems erroneous
here, perhaps a confusion with the Roman
Emperor referred to earlier in Morian's

speech as 'Keyser'. It is possible that the
word was abbreviated ('K') in the MS
from which *1620* was set up, which
would explain the confusion.

97 **pluck . . . strings** ('die Lauten schlagen')
literally, beat (i.e. play) the lute. Creizenach
notes that this expression was used in an
obscene sense by the English comedians,
and points to an eighteenth-century dictionary that supports this usage (21, n. 36).
The sexualized 'Lauten schlagen' is mentioned again by Morian later in the play
(6.1.66). The phrase appears a third time
when it is used literally by Tito in lament
of Andronica's inability to play the lute
following her mutilation: 'But how will
you pluck the lute now' (5.1.10, 'Aber
wormit wiltu nun die Lauten schlagen').

98 **poison** The German text has '*veniam*',
flawed Latin derived from 'venenum'
('poison'; see Fredén, 149). No mention
is made of Tamora's husband in *TA*. In
Aran en Titus, Thamera simply mentions
that she killed her husband at Aran's
behest (Buitendijk, ll. 535–6).

displeasure on me and my paramour I have secretly
killed in their bedchambers by night. I have committed
thousands and thousands of villainies and robberies,
and yet it seems to me that I have not done enough
mischief yet. Yes, everyone, even the King himself,   105
was very afraid of me because of my great, valorous
deeds and military might. In battles and perilous wars
I fought like a formidable lion – not like a man but
like a very devil. Thus, eventually, I became known
throughout the whole world for my great, superhuman,   110
manly exploits and was given the title of 'Thunder
and Lightning of Ethiopia'. My fame finally reached
the Romans, who armed themselves mightily and
came for us in Ethiopia, devastating and destroying
the land with unheard-of cruelty. I went out against   115
them with my army and thought they would cause me
little trouble and be driven back so that none would
return to Rome alive. But when the fight began, I saw
how dreadfully old Tito Andronico hit back; he
surpassed me and was ten times more fierce. In all my   120
life I had not seen an army more warlike and battle-
hardened than these Romans. This frightened me, and

102–5 **committed ... yet** Compare 'Tut, I
have done a thousand dreadful things / As
willingly as one would kill a fly, / And
nothing grieves me heartily indeed / But
that I cannot do ten thousand more'
(5.1.141–4). Unlike Aaron, Morian does
not elaborate on these villainous acts
beyond the account of his involvement in
the murders at the Ethiopian court.

105–12 **Yes ... Ethiopia** This passage, in
which Morian portrays himself as a
former military champion of his country,
has no equivalent in *TA*, where Aaron's
account of his past life is a catalogue of
crimes and not rooted in a geographical
location (5.1.125–44).

111–12 **Thunder ... Lightning** Compare
Aaron's comment that Tamora is 'Secure
of thunder's crack or lightning flash'
(1.1.502). In *Aran en Titus*, Aran declares
that he 'did terrorize the Roman
army with the thunderings of my voice,
with the lightnings of mine eyes'
(Buitendijk, ll. 176–9; trans. quoted from
Fuller, 25).

116 **my army** That Morian, like Tito, was a
military leader establishes a parallel
between the two antagonists that *TA*
lacks.

119–20 **he ... me** This may provide a motive
for Morian to be revenged upon Tito,
which is not in *TA*.

I saw my ranks dissolve, beaten like dogs. Before
long, old Tito rushed at me and – something that no
man had ever done before – struck me off my horse   125
with his lance so fiercely that I didn't know whether
I were dead or alive. They cut everyone down, so
that no-one escaped. They took many spoils, among
them me, the Queen, and her sons, and brought us to
Rome. But now I shall go and see what comes about.   130
                                                                        Exit.

[2.1]   *Enter the* EMPEROR, AETIOPISSA *with her two
                    sons* HELICATES *and* SAPHONUS, *and* MORIAN.

EMPEROR   Lovely Queen, my desire and lust for you is
ten times greater than for Tito Andronico's daughter.

---

125 **struck ... horse** Black Africans were
associated with expertise in horsemanship in early modern European culture
(see Introduction, p. 25). This detail parallels the chapbook history, where
Tottilius, the Goth King, 'desperately
charged by Andronicus', is 'thrown from
his Horse and much wounded' (36).

127–8 **They ... escaped** This account of
cruelty in warfare anticipates the ferocity
with which Vespasianus' forces attack
Rome (see 7.1.1–15 and 7.2.1–19).

128 **many spoils** In the chapbook the Goth
King 'caused the Retreat to be sounded'
and 'left the rich Spoils of his Camp, the
Wealth of many plunder'd Nations' to
Andronicus and his soldiers (36).

2.1 The beginning of this scene corresponds to
the second half of the opening scene in *TA*
(1.1.304–635), or the end of 1.1 and 2.1 in
editions that follow F's act divisions. In *TA*,
Saturninus has cause to fall into a dispute
with the Andronici because Marcus and his
nephews support Bassianus' claim to
Lavinia (1.1.280), but in *Tito*, given the
absence of the brothers' rivalry, the
Emperor's decision to abandon his promise
to marry Andronica (3–4) is more unexpected and seems based on his sexual
attraction to Aetiopissa. The dispute
between Helicates and Saphonus that follows (18–95) generally corresponds to that
of Demetrius and Chiron in *TA*, although
Morian's motivation in appeasing the
brothers is different from Aaron's. Whereas
Aaron rebukes Chiron and Demetrius for
the danger they run in publicly fighting
over the wife of Bassianus, the Emperor's
brother (1.1.545–69), Morian expresses his
irritation over their physical violence
towards one another and threatens to
punish them if they do not desist (96–8).
Aaron devises a detailed plan for the
brothers (1.1.612–31), but the scene in *Tito*
ends without a plan though Morian gives a
general promise to assist the brothers.

2.1] *this edn; not in 1620*; Act II *Cohn*   108 SD1 *Exeunt] Brennecke; not in 1620*

179

I have sent her back and informed him that she does
not please me and will not be the Empress of Rome.
From now on you shall no longer be called the captive   5
queen but the Empress of Rome. So now I place the
crown upon your head, and you shall be my faithful
consort, for the goddess Venus has wounded me so
much in your favour that I shall have no peace until I
have possessed your proud body.   10

Places the crown upon her head.

AETIOPISSA   Most mighty Emperor, I am unworthy of
the great honour and dignity your Majesty confers
upon me. Although the goddess Venus has likewise
roused in me an ardent passion for your Majesty,
modesty did not allow me to reveal it.   15

1–10 This speech seems to follow directly
from the opening scene (especially
1.1.73–87), yet the fact that Andronica
now has a husband (see 2.1.36–7 and
note) suggests that considerable time has
elapsed. This inconsistency may be the
result of imperfect revision or some form
of textual corruption. Compare *TA*, where
Lavinia asserts that Tamora's 'slips have
made him [i.e. Saturninus] noted [i.e.
branded with disgrace] long' (2.2.86),
although Tamora and Saturninus have
only been married for one day; this suggests a similar 'double time scheme',
'slip', or 'corruption' (Ard³, 214).

3–4 I ... Rome When Saturninus rejects
Lavinia, he does so in response to the per-
ceived dishonour he received when
Bassianus, Marcus and Titus' sons
removed Lavinia: 'No, Titus, no, the
emperor needs her not, / Nor her, nor
thee, nor any of thy stock. / I'll trust by
leisure him that mocks me once, / Thee
never, nor thy traitorous haughty sons, /

Confederates all thus to dishonour me'
(1.1.304–8). By contrast, in *Tito*, the only
reason the Emperor gives for rejecting
Andronica is that 'she does not please
me'.

5–6 From ... Rome The Emperor's proposal is more assertive than that of
Saturninus in the equivalent passage,
which is phrased conditionally and leads
to a question, 'If thou be pleased with this
my sudden choice, / Behold, I choose
thee, Tamora, for my bride, / And will
create thee empress of Rome. / Speak,
queen of Goths, dost thou applaud my
choice?' (1.1.323–6).

8, 13 Venus the classical goddess associated
with sexual desire. See also 3.3.125, 128.

12 dignity (*'digniteten'*) a Latinism.

13–15 Although ... it Tamora makes no
mention of any attraction to Saturninus
when she accepts his offer of marriage,
stating only that she 'will a handmaid be
to his desires, / A loving nurse, a mother
to his youth' (1.1.336–7).

EMPEROR   So let us now go in, my lovely Empress, and
while away our time in delights.

> *He takes her by the hand and they go within.*
> *Morian follows.*
> *The two sons Helicates and Saphonus remain.*

HELICATES   Dearest brother, let us now live in joy and
bliss, for this prison of ours holds neither harm
nor disadvantage for us, but instead brings us great   20
honour. I ask you, dearest brother, where could
our mother have come to greater and higher honours
than here, where she has become the Empress of
Rome?

SAPHONUS   Yes, dearest brother, I cannot rejoice enough   25
at the great cheer in my heart, for in Ethiopia we
would never have been as highly exalted as here –
thanks to our mother – among these noble Romans
who are renowned throughout the world. So I would
like to rejoice with you, but one thing torments and   30
sorely pains my heart.

HELICATES   Dearest brother, I would like to know the
sorrow in your heart.

SAPHONUS   O dearest brother, then know that I am so
greatly overcome with fiery lust for lovely Andronica   35

---

17 **while . . . delights** In the equivalent passage in *TA*, sexual activity is referred to when Saturninus invites Tamora to ascend the Pantheon (a temple in Rome dedicated to all the gods) in order to 'consummate [their] spousal rites' (1.1.342).

17.3 **remain** In *TA*, Aaron remains onstage after his soliloquy, and the quarrelling brothers enter to him; in *Tito*, Morian exits at the end of Act 1, and the brothers quarrel alone at the beginning of Act 2, until Morian enters to them (66.2–3). Chiron and Demetrius enter '*braving*' (1.1.524.1) and their argument over who has the better claim to Lavinia is already underway. In *Tito*, by contrast, their relationship is at first harmonious but then gradually deteriorates.

25 **rejoice** ('*jubiliren*') a Latinism.

that I do not know what to do. What grieves me most
is that she is already married to another.

HELICATES   Dear brother, I am very sick for the same
reason. I will not believe that your love for her is as
fierce as mine. Therefore, give up such thoughts; I am   40
the eldest and will possess her body. I must consult
with our mother's servant to think up a secret way of
taking her husband's life.

SAPHONUS   How, brother! Though you are older than I,
you shall not thwart me. I hope I have as much of   45
what becomes a man as you, and if we should make a
wager over who would best acquit himself in the
tournament of Venus, truly, I know I would defeat
you. Therefore, dear brother, leave this to me and find
yourself another, for I will not give her up and no-one   50
shall have her but I.

HELICATES   O you poor fool, could you ever satisfy a
woman? Indeed not, you are incapable of it! Leave
off, brother, leave off. She must be mine and you are
much too weak to make me yield. Or shall we fight for   55
her in such a way that dogs may lick up our blood?

36–7 **What ... another** It is unclear how
much time has passed since 1.1, when
Andronica would have been free to marry
the Emperor. Either Andronica's marital
status is dramatized inconsistently or her
marriage must have taken place since Act
1. There is no indication that she was previously betrothed to a man other than the
Emperor, as is the case with Lavinia and
Bassianus (1.1.280–90). See 2.1.1–10
and note.

41 **eldest** Demetrius, as the elder brother,
similarly draws attention to his superi-
ority by belittling and insulting Chiron:
'thy years want wit, thy wits want edge /
And manners to intrude where I am
graced' (1.1.525–6). In *TA*, Demetrius'
argument for the elder brother's superi-
ority mirrors Saturninus' (1.1.5–8), a

parallel not operative in *Tito* where
the Emperor is not known to have a
brother.

41–2 **consult ... servant** (*'consuliren'*) a
Latinism. In *TA* the brothers have no
intention to approach Aaron for help with
their undertaking.

44–5 **Though ... me** This parallels Chiron's
assertion that ''Tis not the difference of a
year or two / Makes me less gracious, or
thee more fortunate' (1.1.530–1). As elsewhere, *TA* indicates a temporal duration,
'a year or two', where *Tito* does not (see
1.1.22 and note).

55 **too weak** Helicates' condescension
towards his younger brother mirrors
Demetrius' in *TA*, where Chiron is called
'boy' (1.1.537, 544) and 'Youngling'
(1.1.572).

SAPHONUS   Brother, I say there's no bigger fool in the
world than you! That I would give her up and let you
have her? That must never be. But it is true that she
can have only one of us, therefore draw and let us   60
fight valiantly for her, since I would rather give my
life than yield her to another.

HELICATES   Yes, brother, with pleasure, since one of us
must be swept away. And I say likewise that I would
rather give my life than let you have her. So let us   65
fight and not hold back. Lay on!

They strike at one another.
In the midst of the scuffle enter MORIAN,
who runs between them.

MORIAN   No, no, my lords! By a thousand devils, what
are you doing? Are you brothers so incensed that
you seek each other's lives? That simply must not
be while I am here. Be content, or else I'll beat   70
you both so soundly that you'll think the elements
wage war upon you! Once I begin, I'm worse than
the devil himself. But tell me, what's the reason for
your quarrel?

HELICATES   My dear Morian, you must know that I am   75
fiercely in love with Andronica; my brother says that

60 **draw** ('ziehe vom Leder') literally, draw
from the leather, an expression designating the removal of a sword or other
large blade from a scabbard, which was
often covered in leather.

66 SD1 *They strike* In *TA*, '*They draw*'
(1.1.544 SD). Since Saphonus has just
invited his brother to 'draw' (60), it may
be assumed that the fight in *Tito* involves
a bladed weapon. In *TA*, Demetrius identifies his weapon as a 'rapier' (1.1.553).
In *Tito* 3.3, both brothers have a sword.

66 SD2 *enter* MORIAN Unlike Morian, Aaron
does not leave the stage and witnesses the
quarrel between the brothers.

70–2 **I'll ... you!** Aaron does not threaten the
brothers with violence but draws their
attention to the likely consequences of
openly quarrelling over the wife of
Bassianus, 'a prince's right' (1.1.563), in
the vicinity of the Emperor's palace: 'I tell
you, lords, you do but plot your deaths /
By this device' (1.1.577–8). The identity
of Andronica's husband is not known,
which means that there is no occasion in
Tito for Aaron's concern over Demetrius
and Chiron's desire for someone as
distinguished as the Emperor's brother's
wife.

he also is greatly in love with her, and that's why we
quarrelled. I want to have her, as does he; so he offered
to fight me, since she can only be had by one of us.

MORIAN   I can only laugh at the two of you fighting over   80
a young lady who already has a husband! But listen
to me, Saphonus, I think it would be best if your
brother, who is the elder, takes Andronica and you
find yourself another – there are Roman women far
lovelier than Andronica!   85

SAPHONUS   No, my dear Morian, that's impossible, for
I am far too much in love with Andronica and shall
never give her up. So let's fight.

> *Saphonus starts attacking his brother again;*
> *Morian intervenes.*

MORIAN   No, not so! Listen further. What do you think,
Helicates, of giving up Andronica and finding yourself   90
another – the best in all of Rome? I'll help to get her
for you.

HELICATES   No, I cannot give her up – I am too much in
love with her. So let's fight and not relent till one of us
is killed.   95

> *They attack one another. Morian separates*
> *them forcibly.*

MORIAN   What the devil! Are you so determined to fight?
Once more I advise you to be content or, indeed, I'll
beat you both until you howl. Now, listen again to
what I have to say, and if you remain unsatisfied, then

---

83 **elder** Morian echoes Helicates' earlier
claim as the elder brother (40–1). Aaron
does not favour one brother's claim over
the other's.

84 **find ... another** This corresponds to
Demetrius' suggestion to Chiron, 'learn thou
to make some meaner choice' (1.1.572).
However, where Demetrius instructs his

brother to find a *less* attractive woman,
Morian goes on to suggest that there are, in
fact, *more* attractive women in Rome.

88 SD–95 SD In *TA* there is nothing to suggest that the brothers attempt to fight one
another physically again. The second
scuffle in *Tito* may be for the benefit of
spectacle.

I don't know what else I can do. If neither of you 100
wants to give her up, don't lose your lives over it. I'll
help you take her husband's life, and then both of you
may have her and satisfy yourselves.

HELICATES   My dear Morian, this pleases me; assist us in
this purpose.   105

SAPHONUS   I am also content with this.

MORIAN   Then follow me, my lords, and let's consider
how to go about the matter.   [*Exeunt.*]

3.[1]   *Enter* EMPEROR *and* AETIOPISSA,
also TITO ANDRONICO.

TITO   Great and mighty Emperor, I have arranged a fine
stag-hunt for tomorrow in honour of your Majesty
and your beloved Empress, and I humbly ask your

104–5 **My ... purpose** This respectful form
of address is markedly different from
Chiron's response to Aaron: 'Thy counsel,
lad, smells of no cowardice' (1.1.632).

107 **let's consider** In *TA*, Aaron makes his plan
known before the stage is cleared: the
brothers are to 'strike [Lavinia] home by
force' (1.1.618) during the hunt the next day.
In *Tito* their eventual attack on Andronica is
instigated by their mother, following their
chance encounter with her in the forest on
the day of the hunt (3.3). Much later in the
play, we find out about Morian, Helicates
and Saphonus' unsuccessful plot against
Andronica and her Husband (7.1.55–60).

3.1 This very brief scene parallels *TA*,
1.1.496–9 and looks ahead to *TA*, 2.1.14–
15. In *TA* the hunt takes place on the day
after the opening scene (cf. 1.1.496). In
Tito, we later find out that, following 2.1,
Morian, Helicates and Saphonus plotted
together that Morian was to kill
Andronica's Husband, but that he 'never

had the opportunity to do so' (7.1.59–60),
which suggests that some time elapses
between Acts 2 and 3.

1–6 **Great ... pleasure** In *TA* the invitation is
offered to Saturninus before the arrange-
ments for the hunt are made: 'Tomorrow,
and it please your majesty / To hunt the
panther and the hart with me, / With horn
and hound we'll give your grace *bonjour*'
(1.1.496–8). The point in the scene at
which the offer is made in *TA* fits in with
the conciliatory tone that follows the violence and quarrels earlier in the same
scene. It is less clear why Tito should
arrange a hunt after the Emperor's flippant
rejection of Andronica. He explains later
in the play that he was hoping to 'increase
[his] favour with the Emperor' (5.1.35).

2   **stag-hunt** *Tito* does not have *TA*'s exotic
panthers (1.1.497), which were of course
not hunted in the Roman woods (although
they may have been imported for the
circus; see Barton, 57).

3.1]   *this edn*; Actus Tertius *1620*

Majesty and the lovely Empress to arrive at the
hunt in the early hours and spend the day in joy and   5
pleasure.

EMPEROR   Dear Tito Andronico, I shall set out at an
early hour with my beautiful Empress and be present
at the hunt. But tell me, will many Romans ride
with us?   10

TITO   Yes, most mighty Emperor, there will be a
considerable number, including my brother, Victoriades
Brutus, and the husband of my daughter, Andronica.

EMPEROR   Very well then, my dear Tito Andronico. We
shall prepare ourselves for the occasion.   *Exeunt.*   15

[3.2]   *Morning dawns. The hunting horns and*
                  trumpets are sounded.

Enter TITO ANDRONICO.

TITO   How sweetly and pleasantly the birds sing in the
air, each seeking his sustenance; the hunt has begun

---

5   **early hours** parallels Titus' remark on the
earliness of the hour: 'The hunt is up, the
morn is bright and grey' (2.1.1).

9–10 **will ... us?** Saturninus does not enquire
about the size of the retinue in *TA*, but in
Tito the 'considerable number' (12) emphasizes the stateliness of the occasion and provides a context for the insults about large
numbers of followers later (see 3.3.8–18).

13 **Brutus** ('Brutinen') the only instance in
which this Latin cognomen appears in
connection to Victoriades.

13 **husband ... Andronica** the first mention
of this character, who greatly differs from
TA's Bassianus (see above, p. 169). *Tito*
has 'Androva' instead of Andronica here,
probably a printer's error.

3.2 The speech that makes up this scene corresponds to *TA* 2.1.1–10.

0.1 ***Morning dawns*** It is unclear whether
this SD would have been realized
onstage and if so, how it could have
been. It parallels the opening line of
the equivalent scene in *TA*, Titus' 'The
hunt is up, the morn is bright and grey'
(2.2.1).

0.1–2 ***The ... sounded*** The first of four
occasions when offstage music or sound
effects are called for (see the opening SDs
of 3.3, 7.1 and 8.2).

0.3 ***Enter*** TITO ANDRONICO Tito immediately
re-enters. For the only other occasion when
characters do so, see 5.1.0 SD and note.

1–3 **How sweetly ... splendour** This passage recalls the protagonist's speech in
TA: 'The hunt is up, the morn is bright
and grey, / The fields are fragrant and the
woods are green' (2.1.1–2). The singing

3.2] *this edn; not in 1620*

in delight and splendour. Yet my heart is troubled and
heavy, for last night I had a most frightening dream
and do not know what it may portend. Now I must   5
ride to the Emperor, who attends the hunt.   *Exit.*

[3.3] *Enter* ANDRONICA, *hand in hand with her* HUSBAND.
Also enter AETIOPISSA, *walking towards them.*
The hunters sound their horns.

ANDRONICA   Dearest husband, in all my days, I have
never seen a finer and merrier hunt.

HUSBAND   I too, my lovely wife, can say in truth that
I have been at many hunts but never a merrier or
more joyful one. But what extraordinary thing do I   5
behold! The Empress walks alone and comes quickly
towards us.

of the birds is commented on by Tamora
when she is alone in the woods with
Aaron: 'The birds chant melody on every
bush' (2.2.12); she also refers to 'sweet
melodious birds' (2.2.27).

3–5 **Yet ... portend** Cf. Titus: 'I have been
troubled in my sleep this night' (*TA*, 2.1.9).
Tito comments later in the play: 'the
frightful dream I had the night before the
hunt foretold this misfortune' (5.1.37–8).

6   SD The German text adds 'etc.' after
'Gehet weg' (i.e., exit). The meaning of
'etc.' here is unclear. See 4.1.23–4 and
5.2.65–6 and notes.

3.3 largely corresponds to *TA* 2.2, although
there is no equivalent to Aaron's scheme to
blame the murder of Bassianus on Quintus
and Martius. Whereas the encounter of
Morian and Aetiopissa is placed at the end

of the scene, that of Aaron and Tamora
occurs early on (2.2.10–50). In *TA*,
Bassianus first addresses Tamora (2.2.55–
9), whereas the Husband remains silent in
Tito after Aetiopissa has entered, and only
Andronica speaks with her. The conversa-
tion is quite different in the two plays: in
TA, Tamora's indiscretion with Aaron is
brought to light (2.2.67–83), whereas
Andronica expresses no awareness of the
secret relationship between Aetiopissa and
Morian.

0.1 **hand in hand** The equivalent SD in *TA*
does not provide this detail, although
physical intimacy between Lavinia and
her husband is suggested in the allusion
to the consummation of the newlyweds'
marriage (2.1.14–17).

0.3 **The ... horns** See 3.2.0.1–2 and note.

3.3] *this edn; not in 1620*

Aetiopissa approaches them.

AETIOPISSA   I am amazed, Andronica, to see you walking
alone with your husband like this. Have you not a
thousand knights and footmen that follow and serve   10
you?

ANDRONICA   Fair Empress, I ask you the same: why
do you walk alone and have no crowd of servants
waiting upon you? But I take your mockery to be
nothing but a trifle, and, as it comes from you, I put up   15
with it easily. I trust that if it were necessary I could
summon a thousand knights and foot-soldiers as
readily as you.

AETIOPISSA   Andronica, since you ask so impudently
and craftily why I am walking alone thus, let me tell   20
you that it is because I want to do so. But a question
for you: how is it that you answer me with such
insolence and defiance? Am I not your Empress and
do you not know how much you ought to honour me?
Do not think that I shall let this rest!   25

ANDRONICA   Indeed, Empress, if one shouts into the
woods then one will hear an echo, and as you

8–40 In *Tito*, Andronica and her husband say
nothing of the Empress' adultery (unlike
Lavinia and Bassianus in *TA*, 2.2.51–88).
The present quarrel is, then, necessary to
explain Aetiopissa's later cruelty to
Andronica. Fredén (368) argues that in
Tito, unlike in *TA*, the quarrel is poorly
motivated, but Aetiopissa's haughtiness
along with her discomfort at being surprised alone in the forest may provide some
basis for it.

8–11 I . . . you? The speech recalls Bassianus'
feigned surprise at finding Tamora alone in
the forest, having just witnessed Aaron's
departure from the scene (2.2.55–9). In *Tito*,
however, the Husband's surprise at finding

Aetiopissa alone seems genuine. Late in the
play, Morian explains to Vespasianus why
Aetiopissa was alone in the forest: 'your
father, Tito Andronico, held a great stag-
hunt ... the Empress walked alone in
search of me to satisfy her lust' (7.1.61–5).

15–16 **nothing . . . easily** In *TA* it is Tamora
who tells Lavinia, 'Why, I have patience
to endure all this' (2.2.88).

23–5 **Am . . . rest** Like Aetiopissa, Tamora
asserts her rank, calling Bassianus 'Saucy
[i.e. 'insolent towards a superior', Ard³]
controller of my private steps' (2.2.60).

26–7 **if . . . echo** ('wie man ins Holz ruffet,
also krieget man ein Wiederschall') proverbial (Wander, 'Holz').

questioned me with a haughty spirit, I will answer
you in a similar manner. Although you are indeed the
Empress, I shall not grovel at your feet. Remember   30
that you were first my father's prisoner, and now that
you have become an empress you do not know how to
control your pride. So continue in your pride, and let
me remain as I am. I wonder, what good has this city
of Rome received from you and yours? And what   35
benefits from my father and mine? Indeed, had he not
fought with his valorous hands as he did, the imperial
throne and all of Rome would long ago have been
razed. Yet hurt me as much as you like if you can't
help it.   40

AETIOPISSA   O, my heart will burst within me! Get out of
my sight, you damned creature! If I am unable to
punish your arrogance, I shall kill myself! I swear by
all the gods that I shall neither eat nor drink nor lay

28 **haughty** ('hoffertigen') echoing the
play's full title, *Eine sehr klägliche
Tragœdia von Tito Andronico vnd der
hoffertigen Käyserin* (*A Very Lamentable
Tragedy of Tito Andronico and the
Haughty Empress*). The same epithet is
used for Aetiopissa by Tito (4.3.10, 19,
79; 8.2.47), Vespasianus (7.1.13, 96) and
even Morian (7.1.49). In the chapbook,
Attava, the Goth Queen, is called 'an
imperious Woman, and of a haughty
Spirit' (38). The adjective 'haughty' is not
applied to Tamora.

30–1 **Remember ... prisoner** Lavinia
reminds Tamora of her former captivity

later in the scene, when threatened with
rape, begging her to have pity 'for my
father's sake, / That gave thee life when
well he might have slain thee' (2.2.158–9).

41 **heart ... burst** a recurrent conceit, used
elsewhere by Tito (4.3.61, 5.1.1–2 and
8.2.40) and Vespasianus (8.2.63).

41–6 In *TA*, Tamora's last speech before her
sons enter (or possibly prompted by their
entrance) is simply, 'Why, I have patience
to endure all this' (2.2.88). Aetiopissa is
unaware of her sons' plan to rape
Andronica, whereas Tamora has been
apprised of it earlier in the scene, so her
smug response makes sense.

my head to rest until I have taken my fill of vengeance   45
and triumphed joyfully over you.

She steps away.

Enter her two sons HELICATES *and* SAPHONUS, *who*
come to her. Andronica speaks aside with her Husband.

HELICATES   Gracious mother, we are amazed that you
are all alone and wandering away from the others. But
we are even more surprised to find you so troubled
and melancholy.   50

AETIOPISSA   O my dear sons, open your ears, listen to
my words, and know that I was walking not far from
here, where Andronica was with her husband; she
assailed me with scornful and jeering words, enough
to drive me frantic and insane. Therefore, come and   55
take revenge on her; be ruthless with her, and, if you
love me, kill her husband by her side. If you fail to do

---

46 SD1 *She . . . away* The German SD reads
'Gehet ein Schritt sex fort' (in *1620* and
1624). 'Sex' was an accepted spelling for
'sechs', that is, six, so translated literally,
the sentence means 'Walks a step six
away', perhaps meaning *walks about six*
steps away (Kaulfuss-Diesch, 65, 73).
Brennecke translates '*She walks six paces*
away', which makes sense of 'sex' but
seems an awkwardly precise direction.
Lippner translated, '*She walks a little fur-*
ther'.

46 SD2–64 Two conversations take place
during this episode on two sides of the
stage, one heard by the audience, the
other not. Andronica and her Husband,
'*aside*' (46.3), are clearly unaware of
what Aetiopissa and her sons are saying,
and the two brothers do not even know
where Andronica and her Husband are
(see 61–2). In *TA* the brothers simply
enter to the other characters (2.2.88 SD).

48–50 **But . . . melancholy** Demetrius' first

speech after his entrance ends with a
similar expression of surprise: 'Why doth
your highness look so pale and wan?'
(2.2.90).

51 **listen** ('*observiret*') a Latinism.

51–5 **O . . . insane** Whereas Aetiopissa gives
her sons a biased account of what really
happened, Tamora concocts a fictitious
story of how she was lured to a dismal pit in
the forest and threatened by Bassianus and
Lavinia (2.2.91–115). See note at 4.1.5–8.

55–9 **Therefore . . . sons** Tamora's equivalent speech ends similarly: 'Revenge it as
you love your mother's life, / Or be ye not
henceforth called my children' (2.2.114–
15).

57 **kill . . . husband** There is no explicit
command to slay Bassianus in *TA*. Since
the Husband in *Tito* remains silent during
Andronica's dialogue with Aetiopissa yet
still needs to be disposed of for the sake
of the plot, the instruction is necessary to
clarify the action.

so, I will curse you and never more take you to be my
sons.

HELICATES *and* SAPHONUS   Gracious mother, we are   60
willing to obey you. Only come and show us where
they are, so that I can take his life immediately.

AETIOPISSA   Well then, follow me, and have no mercy on
them.

> *They go to Andronica and her Husband. Helicates*
> *draws his sword.*

HELICATES   Here we find you both. You have lived far   65
too long.

> *Stabs him.*

[HUSBAND]   O, murder, murder!

> [*Dies.*]

ANDRONICA   Alas! Alas! Will no-one cry out and denounce
this murderous deed?

> *She goes to sit on the ground with the corpse.*

AETIOPISSA   Look, you haughty woman! How do you   70
like this? What do you think, have I not kept the oath

---

60 SP *1620* reads 'Söhne' ('Sons') and so
does not clarify how the characters share
the speech.

61–2 **Only . . . are** See note above, 46 SD2–
64.

66 SD The elder brother commits the
murder, whereas in *TA* both sons stab
Bassianus in turn (2.2.116–17).

67 SP The SP is missing in *1620* and *1624*;
we follow Lippner in assigning the speech
to Andronica's Husband, although it is
possible that Andronica is the speaker.

67 **murder, murder** ('*mordio, mordio*') A
call, derived from 'Mord' ('murder'), that
proclaims murder and charges a pursuit of
the perpetrator (Grimm). It is unclear
what is done with the corpse, since *Tito*
lacks the pit device. In *Aran en Titus*,
Bassianus' body is hung on a shrub; the
German adaptations of Vos from 1656
and 1661 have him hung from a tree, and
the 1699 programme has him bound to a
tree.

69 SD a vivid SD with no equivalent in *TA*.

67 SP] *Cohn; not in 1620*   67 SD] *this edn; not in 1620*

I swore? Indeed, this is but a trifle! I will tame you so
that you will lie at my feet, and I will tread on your
corpse. I will murder your entire kin, including your
parents and brothers, and shall prevail upon my   75
gracious Lord Emperor with cunning and guile to let
them all die a miserable death. I am your mortal
enemy, haughty woman, and it is impossible for me to
see you live any longer. [*to Saphonus*] Therefore, my
dear son, give me your sword so that I myself may   80
take away her life.

She attempts to take his sword.

SAPHONUS   Dearest mother, I can perform this act, so
think about it first.

ANDRONICA   O, you most merciless woman! Is there
no spark of pity in you? Should my father learn of   85
this, his vengeance would be grim beyond your
reckoning; he would leave no stone upon another
but tear down the very earth on which you stand.
Alas, you haughty Empress, have pity on me and take

74–5 **murder ... brothers** corresponds to
Tamora: 'Ne'er let my heart know merry
cheer indeed / Till all the Andronici be
made away' (2.2.188–9).

75 **parents** ('Väteren') may stand for 'kin'
more generally, since Andronica's mother
is not mentioned or alluded to elsewhere
in the play.

77–8 **mortal enemy** ('spinne feindt') literally,
spider enemy, an expression derived
from the action of large spiders who
devour smaller ones (see Grimm,
'spinnefeind').

79–81 **Therefore ... life** recalls Tamora:
'Give me the poniard. You shall know,
my boys, / Your mother's hand shall right
your mother's wrong' (2.2.120–1).

82–3 At the equivalent point in *TA*, Demetrius
and Chiron suggest raping Lavinia before
murdering her (2.2.122–30); in *Tito*, rape
is suggested by Aetiopissa later in the
scene (101–5).

84 **you** Here Andronica switches from using
the formal form of address ('sie') to the
informal ('du'). Her use of 'sie' before
this point contrasts with Aetiopissa's
insistence on 'du' when addressing
Andronica throughout the scene.

89–90 **have ... now** This plea comes before
any threat of rape is verbalized in *Tito*
(although Aetiopissa's later reference to her
sons' 'great urge for lustful pleasure and ...
libidinous sap' (102–3) may suggest that
unscripted stage action is making their

79 SD] *this edn; not in 1620*

my life now, for I cannot live on; it brings me infernal   90
anguish.

AETIOPISSA   Indeed, I believe it is so. Your father and
brothers do not fight in the manner of men but more
furiously than devils, and if they knew of this, they
would tear down to the ground the whole of Rome,   95
with its imperial palace, and rage like fierce lions. But
I must prevent this from happening, and consider
how to keep them from finding out. Since I now hear
that to live any longer is infernal anguish for you,
and that you cannot think of anything more terrible,   100
I shall let you live on for a while. And you, my dear
sons, I know you have a great urge for lustful pleasure
and are full of libidinous sap. So I give her to you;
go with her to the most frightful place in these woods
and take your fill of pleasure with her and use her   105
so harshly that she no longer resembles a human
being. But if you have mercy on her, remember that
my anger will be unleashed on you and promise little
good.

[HELICATES *and* SAPHONUS]   Gracious mother, we shall   110
obey your command.

> *They go to Andronica, attempting to lift her*
> *up and take her away.*

ANDRONICA   O, is there no help? O, is there no pity? I
beg you, leave me, and take my life!

---

intention known). Lavinia begs for death
after the threat is made: ''Tis present death
I beg' (2.2.173).
96   **rage** ('*rumoren*') a Latinism.
102–3 **I ... sap** Tamora similarly refers to
her 'spleenful sons' (2.2.191), the spleen
being considered 'the seat of strong

passions' (Ard³).
112–13 Andronica's final speech calls to
mind the beginnings of Lavinia's last two
speeches: 'No grace? No womanhood?'
(2.2.182); ''Tis present death I beg'
(2.2.173).

110 SH] Cohn; Söhne *1620*

AETIOPISSA   No, I shall certainly have no pity on you.
Now, sons, take her out of my sight.   115

They take her away and go into the forest with her.

Enter MORIAN.

MORIAN   I see a wonder of all wonders! What the devil
does this mean, Empress, that you walk alone in
the forest? The Emperor has ordered me to search
for you.
AETIOPISSA   My faithful paramour, do not be amazed 120
and angry because I had a desire to walk alone; I shall
return with you to the Emperor presently. But, my
dearest paramour, we are now quite alone in this fine
and delightful forest, and I have a great appetite for
the sport of Venus. So let me sport with you and make 125
merry.
MORIAN   No, lovely Empress, even though the goddess
Venus is tempting you to her games, I am ruled and
mastered by the god Mars. Therefore, this cannot be,
and you may not have my body at this time. So let us 130
now go to the Emperor, who has been waiting for you
for a long time.   *Exeunt.*

116–32 *TA*, which places the encounter of Tamora and Aaron early in the scene (10–50), ends it with Aaron's plot against Quintus and Martius (2.2.192–306).

117–18 **alone ... forest** Morian is the third character to remark on the impropriety of Aetiopissa being unaccompanied, after Andronica (12–13) and Helicates (47–8).

118–19 **ordered ... you** Not in *TA*, where Tamora comes to meet Aaron in the forest.

123–4 **fine ... forest** In *TA*, Tamora delivers a lengthy description of the forest as an idyllic space for amorous encounters (2.2.10–29).

124–5 **I ... Venus** In *TA* it is Aaron who tells Tamora, 'though Venus govern your desires . . .' (2.2.30).

129 **Mars** Roman god of war. In *TA*, Aaron says he is ruled by 'Saturn' (2.2.31), 'saturnine' meaning gloomy, melancholy. *Tito*'s decision to invoke Mars here may be an allusion to Morian's first speech, in which he recounts his military exploits (1.1.107–18).

4.[1]   *Enter* TITO ANDRONICO, VESPASIANUS *and*
VICTORIADES. *They stand, dejected.*

TITO   O, dearest ones, it troubles my heart that the
Emperor has put my sons in prison. I have no idea
what the cause may be. I have written to the Emperor,
asking him the reason for my sons' sudden
imprisonment; he has answered that my sons are   5
prisoners of the Empress, that they have grossly
offended her, insulted her with mockery and libels,
and therefore must die a swift death. It would cause
me great pain and anguish to see my own flesh and
blood executed. But whom do I see coming towards   10
me? The Empress' Morian!

Enter MORIAN *to Tito Andronico.*

MORIAN   God speed you, old Tito Andronico! Have hope
and be of good cheer; I bring you good news.

4.1 The opening speech has no correspondence in *TA*, where Titus' sons Quintus and
Martius are imprisoned because of their
alleged murder of Bassianus, not for allegedly insulting Tamora. The rest of the
scene is similar to *TA*, 3.1.151–206, but
Aaron conveys to Titus the Emperor's
request for a severed hand *after* the mutilated Lavinia has been discovered, whereas
in *Tito* Morian arrives with his message
before Andronica is found. *Tito* does not
dramatize the procession with Titus' bound
sons to the place of execution, nor the pleas
of the distraught protagonist to the tribunes
and senators (*TA*, 3.1.1–58).

5–8 he ... death The fact that the brothers are
imprisoned and sentenced to death due to
Aetiopissa's (presumably untrue) report of
their insults contributes to the play's depiction of her as the principal antagonist. Note

that her allegations against Tito's sons
mirror those against Andronica at 3.3.53–5,
where Aetiopissa goes on to announce that
she will eliminate Andronica's 'entire kin,
including your parents and brothers'
(3.3.74–5). In *Aran en Titus*, Thamera
falsely claims that two of Titus' sons
abused her in the forest, where they pulled
her hair and called her a whore (Buitendijk,
ll. 761–72). The 1656 programme notes
that Aran and the Empress concoct a story
about the latter being antagonized by two
disguised persons in the forest, whom Aran
pursues and recognizes as Titus' sons (2.7).
For the 1699 programme, see Cohn,
'Breslau', 280.

12–13 Aaron is more direct in delivering the
message: 'Titus Andronicus, my lord the
emperor / Sends thee this word' (*TA*,
3.1.151–2).

4.1] *this edn*; Actus Quartus *1620*

TITO   You have my thanks, Morian. Say, what news do
    you bring?   15
MORIAN   The Empress has sent me to tell you that if
    you love your sons and want to save them from death,
    you should cut off your right hand and send it to
    her by me. Then they shall be sent back to you
    immediately.   20
TITO   O my dear Morian, what good news you bring me!
    No, if the Empress desired both my hands I would
    gladly cut them off. I shall cut off my hand and give it
    to you.
VICTORIADES   Dearest brother, I beg you, let me cut off   25
    my hand, for it would be a great shame for you to cut
    off your noble hand!

16 **Empress** Aaron claims he is sent by the
Emperor (*TA*, 3.1.151), although his comments later in the play suggest otherwise
(5.1.111–20). In *Tito* the command
clearly does come from Aetiopissa (see
5.2.4–10). In the chapbook, Attava is said
to have 'sent the Moor in the Emperor's
Name' (41).

16–18 **if you ... hand** The instruction in *TA* is
less specific: 'Let Marcus, Lucius, or thy-
self, old Titus, / Or any one of you, chop
off your hand' (3.1.153–4). There is an
unresolved   contradiction   between
Morian's request for *Tito's* hand, and the
subsequent argument between Tito,
Vespasianus and Victoriades about who is
to cut off his hand (in keeping with *TA*,
3.1.163–86). If *Tito* and *TA* both derive
from an earlier Titus play (see Introduction,
pp. 36–40), then it seems likely that the
reason for the argument (i.e. that the protagonist, his son and his brother are left to
choose whose hand should be cut off) was
in that earlier play but was accidentally
removed in the process of adaptation that
led to *Tito*. See also Fredén, 369–70.

21–4 Titus is equally enthusiastic about the
proposal: 'With all my heart I'll send the
emperor my hand' (*TA*, 3.1.161). Unlike
Tito, *TA* may have prepared the audience
for the protagonist's response through his
earlier affirmation, upon seeing his mutilated daughter, that he is willing to 'chop
off [his] hands too' (3.1.73).

23–4 **give ... you.** The German text adds
'etc.' at the end of the speech. The
meaning of the expression is unclear
here. See 3.2.6 and 5.2.65–6 and notes.

25–7 **Dearest ... hand!** In *TA* it is Lucius
who initially offers to sacrifice his hand in
place of his father, to which Marcus
responds 'Which of your hands hath not
defended Rome /. . . / O, none of both but
are of high desert. / My hand hath been
but idle: let it serve' (3.1.168–72). This
distinction is important because Marcus
is a tribune, and there is no evidence to
suggest that he has ever engaged in military combat like Titus and his warlike
sons. In *Tito* it is unclear whether
Victoriades holds a civic or military rank,
and he does not refer to his 'idle' hand.

VESPASIANUS   O, dearest father, I implore you, let me
 chop off my hand, for they are my dearest brothers!

TITO   No, my dearest brother, and my dear son, neither   30
 of you shall give up your hand; that is for me
 to do.

They fall on their knees before him.

VICTORIADES   Dearest brother, we kneel before you and
 implore you to leave your hand unhurt, and to let me
 cut off my hand.   35

TITO   Rise and do not kneel before me. As you plead
 so earnestly, I must yield against my will. Decide
 amongst yourselves who shall lose his hand.

VICTORIADES   Yes, dearest brother, let us draw lots for it.
 Let us go within and fetch an axe. He who gets the lot   40
 shall cut off his hand immediately for the sake of us all.
 Exeunt Victoriades and Vespasianus.

TITO   No, now I'll outwit you both, for whilst you draw
 lots and fetch an axe, I'll cut off my hand.   *Exit.*

25–41 The passage is quite close to *TA*, although it is notable that Lucius and Marcus there have four pairs of successive speeches (3.1.163–86), whereas in *Tito* Victoriades has three speeches and there is only one by Vespasianus.

28–9 Lucius similarly appeals to brotherhood when asking his father, 'Let me redeem my brothers both from death' (*TA*, 3.1.181). On the other hand, Vespasianus does not, like Lucius, comment on the advantage of being younger: 'My youth can better spare my blood than you, / And therefore mine shall save my brothers' lives' (3.1.166–7).

32 SD not in *TA*. The act of kneeling in *Tito* is an effective way of condensing and intensifying the pleas.

39 **let ... it** This detail is not in *TA*, where Lucius and Marcus exit the stage without deciding whose hand shall be sacrificed or how the decision will be made.

43 **I'll ... hand** In *TA*, Titus asks Aaron to help him cut off his hand: 'Lend me thy hand and I will give thee mine' (3.1.188). It may be fitting that Aaron severs the hand, given that he is the play's principal villain, unlike Morian (see Introduction, p. 12).

43 SD Tito cuts off his hand offstage, perhaps because it would have been difficult to stage. In *TA*, the corresponding SD has Aaron cut off Titus' hand (3.1.192 SD1), but in *Aran en Titus* Titus also cuts off his own hand (Buitendijk, ll. 1256–84).

MORIAN   Now, if that's called deceit, this is how the
devil deceives his dam. Yet even though I have a   45
pitiless heart, I pity you, old Tito Andronico, for the
Empress tricks you out of your hand so that you'll be
unable to overthrow Rome. When you think you'll
receive your sons, you'll only get their heads.

Enter TITO *with his hand cut off. Also enter*
VICTORIADES *and* VESPASIANUS.

VESPASIANUS   Gracious father, I've won, so now I may   50
– Alas! Alas, why have you cut off your hand? This is
indeed a piteous sight, dearest father!
TITO   Please say no more, for it is done. – Look here,
Morian, take this hand of mine to the Empress and
bring my dear sons back to me immediately.   55
MORIAN   Well, adieu. [*aside*] I shall indeed bring back
something of them.   *Exeunt.*

44–5 **this ... devil** 'so pfleget der Teufel
seine Muttel aexieren', corrected to
'Mutter zu vexiren' in *1624*. Literally,
'this is how the devil is wont to deceive
his mother', which here refers to Tito's
deception of his son and his brother. In
TA, Aaron later refers to Tamora as 'the
devil's dam' (4.2.67). The devil and his
mother (dam) is proverbial in German
(Grimm, 'Teufel', *m*. II 3) as well as in
English (Dent, D225).
45–8 **Yet ... Rome** Morian's pity sharply
contrasts with Aaron's admission that
'this villainy / Doth fat [i.e., delight] me
with the very thoughts of it' (3.1.203–4).
48 **you** ('du') When he is alone onstage
Morian uses the informal form of address.

When he addresses Tito directly he uses
the formal 'sie'.
48–9 **When ... heads** The equivalent of
Morian's soliloquy is dramatized in *TA* as
a speech by Aaron addressed to Titus, followed by an aside: 'Look by and by to
have thy sons with thee. / [*aside*] Their
heads I mean' (3.1.202–3).
50–2 In *TA*, Lucius and Marcus do not ver-
balize their reaction to Titus' severed
hand.
54 **take ... Empress** Titus asks Aaron to
'give his majesty my hand' (*TA*, 3.1.194).
56–7 **I ... them** This is a veiled reference to
his earlier mention of the heads (49). In
TA, Aaron makes one such reference, also
in an aside (3.1.203).

56 SD] *this edn; not in 1620*

[4.2]   *Enter* HELICATES *and* SAPHONUS, *with* ANDRONICA
between them, coming from the forest. Having
satisfied their lust upon her and horribly mutilated
her, they have cut off both her hands and torn
out her tongue.

HELICATES   This is what a man must do when he has had
sex with a beautiful woman to stop her revealing it.
He must cut off her tongue so that she can say nothing,
and cut off both her hands so that she can write
nothing, as we have done with this one. But what   5
shall we do with her now? We must leave her in this
wild forest to be torn in pieces by savage beasts.

4.2 parallels *TA* 2.3. The initial sequence with
Chiron and Demetrius (2.3.1–10) has its
equivalent in a single speech by Helicates
(1–9), while Marcus' long speech
(2.3.11–57) has its equivalent in the much
shorter speech by Victoriades (10–16).
Tito differs from *TA* by its lack of reference to classical mythology; it does not
invoke Ovid's tale of Philomel and has
none of the poetic language that charac-
terizes Marcus' description of his niece.

0.1–2 **with ... them** In the German text, the
SD ends by mentioning that the brothers
'haben sie zwischen sich' (i.e., have her
between them); we transfer this indication
to the beginning of the SD to clarify the
staging. Lippner and Brennecke mistakenly believed that 'sie' is not the third-
person singular feminine pronoun (i.e. *her*)
but the third-person plural pronoun (i.e.
them), and that it refers not to Andronica
but to her severed hands and tongue.

Lippner: '*Having also barbarously mutilated her, cut off both her hands, and torn
out her tongue, they now bring them with
them*'; Brennecke: '*They have cut off both
her hands and torn out her tongue, which
they carry with them*'. However, the next
SD (9 SD2) clarifies that when the brothers
exit, '*Andronica   bleibet   alleine*'
('*Andronica remains alone*'), which
implies that they earlier entered with her,
not just with her severed body parts.

0.4–5 **torn out** Andronica's tongue has been
'torn out' according to this SD but 'cut
off' according to Helicates (2). Morian
later says that the brothers 'tore out'
(7.1.81) the tongue.

6–7 **We ... beasts** In *TA* there is no plan to
dispose of Lavinia in this way. After
Chiron mockingly tells her to go home
and wash her hands (2.3.6), Demetrius
adds, 'And so let's leave her to her silent
walks (2.3.8).

4.2] *this edn; not in 1620*

Come, dear brother, let us go. – Now farewell,
Andronica, farewell.

Exeunt Helicates and Saphonus.

*Andronica remains alone, sighing and looking
wretchedly up to heaven.*

Presently enter her uncle VICTORIADES, *who sees
her; but when she sees him, she flees into the forest.*

VICTORIADES   Alas, alas! What great affliction do I find   10
here! Andronica, but no longer resembling a human
being. O, do not hide from me.

He runs within and brings her back.

O, you poor creature, who has abused you with such
malice and barbarity? Alas, your tongue is torn out;
both your hands are cut off. O, alas, this would rouse   15
a stone to pity! O, come with me, do not remain here.
Exeunt.

9   SD2 ***Andronica ... heaven*** This is
     another SD with no equivalent in *TA*. See
     Introduction, p. 6.

9   SD3 ***uncle*** 'Vater' (father) in *1620* and
     1624 must be a misprint for 'Vetter',
     which today means 'cousin' but in early
     modern German could mean 'uncle'
     (Grimm, 'Vetter', 1).

9   SD3 ***when ... forest*** In *TA*, Lavinia simi-
     larly attempts to flee from her uncle who
     says, 'Who is this – my niece that flies
     away so fast?' (2.3.11).

12   SD Modern editors of *TA* have suggested
     that Lavinia '*turns*' to Marcus (Ard³) or
     that 'either he blocks her escape or she is
     too weak and disoriented to get away'
     (*NOS*). But in *Tito*, Andronica does get
     away; she is pursued by her uncle who
     '*brings her back*'.

15–16 **this ... pity** The reference to a
     stone may anticipate the next scene,
     where Tito laments to the stone (4.3.63–
     5). In *TA*, Marcus makes no mention of
     a stone.

[4.3]   *Enter* TITO ANDRONICO *and* VESPASIANUS.
                Also enter MORIAN, *who brings the heads*
                of both sons and Tito's hand.

MORIAN   Behold, old Tito, I pity you, for you have been
tricked out of your noble and valiant hand. The
Empress sends it back to you. And here are the heads
of your sons.

> *Lays them down before him. Tito and Vespasianus*
> *are struck dumb with horror and stand as*
> *though lifeless.*

Now I shall go. If you let this rest, the Empress will   5
destroy you and your kin with affliction and treachery,
and thus put you out of the way.   *Exit.*

4.3 Apart from Tito's long speech, the first part of this scene (1–54) remains close to *TA*, 3.1.235–301, except that Morian, not a messenger, brings the severed heads. The second part of the scene (55–86), where Andronica is brought in by Victoriades, corresponds to an earlier passage in *TA* (3.1.59–150). *Tito*'s order of these episodes is identical with that in the chapbook, which places the mutilation of Titus before Lavinia's rape and discovery by her uncle.

1–4 In *TA*, a Messenger delivers the message along with the severed heads, not Aaron. Whereas the Messenger tells Titus, 'ill art thou repaid' (3.1.235), without specifying by whom, Morian affirms Aetiopissa's responsibility for the devious plot, which she later confirms (see 5.2.7–12). In *Titus und Tomyris*, Aran also delivers the hand, whilst in Vos' *Aran en Titus* (and the 1656 programme), it is Aran's page, Quintus (a Moor), who does so.

5 **If ... rest** ('wirstu aber dieses also darbey bleiben lassen') Morian's affirmation that the Empress will punish Tito if he lets things rest may seem surprising. Lippner inserts a tentative emendation: 'if you rest (not?) satisfied with this the Empress will exterminate you and your stock'. Brennecke emends more confidently: 'if you will not be content with this ...'. Our translation follows the German text because its reading is defensible. Morian, who was earlier moved to pity by Tito, may be giving sincere advice by warning Tito against inaction. Alternatively, Morian may be provoking Tito to retaliate in the hope of precipitating his downfall. What is at stake in this crux is the conception of Morian's character, on which there are differing views.

4.3] *this edn; not in 1620*

TITO   O, O, O, let there be an outcry for you, bloodthirsty
        and treacherous woman! Was there ever a more
        perfidious, haughty, and bloodthirsty woman than this   10
        detestable Empress? O, I could spit at myself because
        I let her live and did not cut her throat when she was
        my prisoner. – O, you most ruthless and ungrateful
        woman, how is it that the stars in heaven are not your
        enemies? Even brute beasts will wail and lament with   15
        me. – O you heavenly gods, you cannot suffer such
        iniquity. Ah, grant me the wit and cunning to consider
        shrewdly how to take a double vengeance on the
        haughty Empress. – O you damnable creature, how
        maliciously you have robbed me of my hand.   20

        Takes the hand up from the ground.

        Yes, you valiant hand, how have you been repaid for
        your faithful service? – O ungrateful Rome, this hand
        often saved you from cruel enemies. Yes, had it not
        done so, you would have been razed long ago, and no
        Roman would still be spoken of. O noble hand, how   25
        often did you have to fight against a thousand hands;

---

8 **let ... outcry** ('zeter vnd mordio') The
German expression is a cry for help
(Grimm, 'Zeter', m. 1), similar to the now
archaic English expression 'hue and cry'.

8–20 This passage is important for presenting Aetiopissa as Tito's nemesis (see
Introduction, p. 12).

8–35 Tito's long speech, in which he succes-
sively apostrophizes Aetiopissa, the gods,
his hand, Rome and his sons' heads, has
no equivalent in *TA*, where the protagonist responds with a rhetorical question –
'When will this fearful slumber have an
end?' (3.1.253) – and laughter: 'Ha, ha,
ha!' (3.1.265).

12 **cut her throat** proleptically announces
his killing of Aetiopissa's sons in 7.3.

16–19 **O ... Empress** Tito does not drama-

tize the protagonist's shooting of arrows
with messages to the gods, but the present
appeal to the gods resembles the following passage in that scene: 'We will
solicit heaven and move the gods / To
send down Justice for to wreak our
wrongs' (*TA*, 4.3.51–2).

21 **how ... repaid** *TA*'s Messenger who
brings Titus his hand expresses a similar
sentiment: 'ill art thou repaid' (3.1.235).

22 **ungrateful Rome** Titus uses the same
phrase in the arrow-shooting scene (*TA*,
4.3.17). See the note at 16–19 above.

26 **a ... hands** Hand synecdoches are frequent in *TA* but much rarer in *Tito*, so the
present instance, with no equivalent in
TA, is exceptional.

you were victorious in the most perilous, bloody wars.
– Ah, my dear sons, what anguish and pain it gives
me to see your heads lying in front of me like this. O,
never shall you be laid to rest until I behold my   30
enemies' heads in front of me in the same way. Alas,
alas, you fought valiantly and manfully for Rome, and
inherited a brave heart from me. – But you, ungrateful
Rome, how have you repaid them? O ungrateful
Rome, how swiftly you hasten to your doom.   35

VESPASIANUS   O dearest father, such tyranny and devilish
ingratitude have not been heard of since the world
began. I would not be worthy to tread upon the earth
if I did not avenge it; and I can no longer hold back.
Please, let me put on my armour and weapons, and   40
give me a long, warlike sword for each hand, so that I
may go to the palace and cut down all that comes in
front of me. I shall fight not like a man but like a
raging devil. No iron door will be impregnable, for
I'll assail and shatter it, and when I have slain the   45
Emperor and the Empress, I'll cut down the ungrateful
Romans as long as I have strength and will, until I am
struck down myself, as I no longer value my life.

29–31 **O . . . me** Compare the protagonist's
words in *TA*: 'For these two heads do
seem to speak to me / And threat me I
shall never come to bliss / Till all these
mischiefs be returned again / Even in
their throats that hath committed them'
(3.1.272–5). Tito speaks to the heads,
whereas the heads 'seem to speak' to
Titus. In *Aran en Titus* the heads may
have spoken onstage (see Fuller, 31;
Baldwin, 437; Braekman, 10.46).

36–48 Vespasianus' fantasy of almost limit-

less power in solo revenge, which comes
before he discovers his raped sister, is followed in the next scene by his pledge 'by
the god Mars' (5.1.69) to gain revenge
after raising an army. In *TA*, Lucius promises revenge in a soliloquy at the end of
3.1.

38–9 **I . . . back** In *TA*, Lucius articulates his
desire for revenge in a similar conditional
sentence: 'If Lucius live, he will requite
your wrongs / . . . / To be revenged on
Rome and Saturnine' (3.1.297–301).

TITO   No, dearest son, it is impossible, you would not get
        into the palace alive. You are now my only dearest   50
        son. We must consider wisely how to avenge
        ourselves. Although I have only one hand, I shall do
        plenty of harm and damage with it. But you, dearest
        son, you must do your best.

            Enter VICTORIADES, *leading* ANDRONICA.

VICTORIADES   O dearest brother, look at this, the most   55
        dreadful spectacle that you ever saw. Here is your
        daughter Andronica, whom I found in the forest, her
        tongue torn out and both her hands cut off.

            Tito is struck with horror; he shudders and
            trembles, overcome with distress.

VESPASIANUS   Alas, alas!

            He falls to the ground in a swoon. Victoriades
            approaches the heads and weeps bitterly.
            Tito falls to his knees.

49 **No ... impossible** In *TA*, Young Lucius
    (who has no equivalent in *Tito*) imagines
    immediate revenge 'with my dagger in
    their bosoms' (4.1.118), and Titus' tem-
    pering response is not unlike Tito's present
    answer to Vespasianus: 'No boy, not so;
    I'll teach thee another course' (4.1.119).

50–1 **my ... son** In *TA*, Lucius is likewise
    Titus' only remaining son, although Titus
    does not point this out in the equivalent
    scene. In the absence of a character
    equivalent to Young Lucius, Vespasianus
    is the character on whom all hope for the
    future hangs, as these words stress. See
    also Tito's words to his son at 5.1.80–1:
    'In you I place all my hope'.

52–3 **Although ... it** Titus does not refer to
    his remaining hand until later, when he is
    about to kill Chiron and Demetrius: 'This
    one hand yet is left to cut your throats'
    (*TA*, 5.2.181).

56–8 **Here ... off** Victoriades narrates and
    describes the spectacle, which contrasts
    with Marcus' powerfully simple 'This
    was thy daughter' (3.1.63).

58 SD Tito's shuddering and trembling has
    no equivalent in *TA*, where Titus instead
    calls Lucius a 'faint-hearted boy' (3.1.66)
    because of his strong reaction.

59 SD *He ... swoon* Lucius' response to the
    sight of his sister is 'Ay me, this object
    kills me', and in the subsequent line Titus
    asks him to 'arise and look upon her' (*TA*,
    3.1.65–6). According to an added SD in
    Ard³, Lucius '*fall[s] to his knees*' (3.1.65
    SD), whereas *NOS* comments that
    'Lucius must have sat, fallen, or knelt, or
    perhaps fainted at the sign of Lavinia's
    injuries'. *Tito* supports the last possibility
    (see Introduction, p. 7).

59 SD *Victoriades ... bitterly* Marcus is
    onstage when the messenger delivers the

TITO   O! O great misfortune, how quickly you overtake   60
my chest. O, murder! O, murder! These barbarous
misdeeds! – Alas, alas, I lament to you, O stone, and
although you cannot help me, at least you do not
chide me and remain silent. I will lie here and will not   65
cease my bitter laments until a great tide of tears
pours from me. In winter I will melt the snow and
frost with my tears. Alas, alas, these grim and
overwhelming thoughts are too dismal!

Rises and goes to Andronica.

O you, my dearest daughter, who has torn out your   70
tongue? I may well guess that you have been robbed
of your chastity and had your tongue torn out so that
you cannot denounce the villain, and your snow-
white hands cut off so that you cannot reveal it in
writing. Is it not so, dearest daughter? Alas, alas, you   75
can say nothing.

She sighs and nods her head.

Perhaps you can tell me with signs that this is so.

---

heads of his nephews (*TA*, 3.1.235–41), but Victoriades is not and only discovers them at this point. The SD has no equivalent in *TA*.

61   **heart . . . burst** See note at 3.3.41.

62   **murder . . . murder** See 3.3.67 and note.

63–5   **I . . . silent** In *TA*, Titus tells his 'sorrows to the stones' (3.1.37) earlier in the play, when Quintus and Martius have been sentenced to death. Titus develops the conceit over a passage of some length (3.1.37–47).

65   **I . . . lie** In *TA*, Titus prostrates himself as he pleads with the Judges and Senators for his sons' lives (3.1.11 SD).

71–2   **I . . . chastity** An implied SD, indicating that visual signs suggest Andronica's loss of chastity.

70–6   **O . . . nothing** Tito is more active than Titus in attempting to ascertain the identity of the attacker(s). In *TA*, Lucius is the one who asks his sister, 'who hath martyred thee?' (3.1.82).

75   SD–77 SD These SDs are not in *TA*, where Lavinia has no scripted reaction to the questions by her father (3.1.67–8) and her brother (3.1.82, 88).

77   **tell . . . signs** corresponds to Titus' observation that he understands her signs (3.1.144), although it is unclear whether the signs in *TA* are wholly imagined by Titus, or whether Lavinia makes some physical gesture or facial expression.

She nods her head once more.

But look, dearest daughter, here are the heads of your
two brothers, which the haughty Empress caused to
be cut off.   80

*She stands appalled, moans and looks up to heaven,
then goes to the heads and kisses them.*

VICTORIADES   O, this great unhappiness could move
stones to pity. But what good does it do to stand here
and weep? Let us all go in and consider how we can
find out who has abused her thus.

TITO   Yes, dearest brother, that is the best advice. Let us   85
go in and have no rest until we have found them out.

Exeunt.

5.[1]   *Enter* TITO ANDRONICO, ANDRONICA
                   and VICTORIADES.

TITO   Alas, alas, dearest daughter, my old heart is ready
to burst in my breast as I see you so wretched before

80 SD No equivalent SD appears in the early
editions of *TA*. Shortly after the messenger has set down the heads and Titus'
hand (3.1.241 SD), Marcus says, 'Alas,
poor heart, that kiss is comfortless'
(3.1.251). Editors have interpreted the
line by inserting various SDs, suggesting,
for instance, that Lavinia kisses Lucius,
or Titus (Ard³, 47), or that Lucius kisses a
head (Ravenscroft). Bate suggests that
Tito is an important witness to the likely
performance of this moment in *TA* (see
Ard³, 47–8) and inserts a SD that is based
on it: '*Lavinia kisses the heads*' (3.1.250
SD). Note that Capell also had Lavinia
kissing the heads, although he does not
seem to have been aware of *Tito*.

83 **weep** an implied SD, though who weeps is

not clarified. Titus weeps at the equivalent
moment, and Lucius asks him to stop, where-
upon Marcus offers him a handkerchief:
'good Titus, dry thine eyes' (*TA*, 3.1.139).

5.1 continues the action of the previous scene
(see 0 SD n.): 4.3 ends as Andronica's
relatives wonder how to find out who
mutilated her, and 5.1 dramatizes the solu-
tion. The scene largely corresponds to
parts of *TA*, 4.1 (in which Lavinia reveals
the identity of her rapists) and 4.3 (where
the Clown is sent by Titus to the Emperor).

0 SD Three of the four characters who exited
at the end of 4.3 re-enter (for the only other
immediate re-entry, see 3.2.0.3 and note).
Tito is an eight-act play, and there may
have been a break between Acts 4 and 5.

1–2 **heart ... burst** See note at 3.3.41.

5.1] *this edn*; Actus Quintus *1620*

me. I have had such love and esteem for you all my
life, I have reared you with such trouble and care!
Yes, when I returned to Rome in triumph, my body   5
greatly wounded by the enemy and suffering terrible
pain, I would see you run cheerfully towards me with
your lute to welcome me, and you would drive out
painful sorrow and refresh my old heart with your
sweet voice. But how will you pluck the lute now   10
with which you rejoiced me? And how will you
speak? You are robbed of all this. O, O, a terrible deed
has been done upon you! O, alas, if only I knew who
committed it and abused you so barbarously, I would
have some peace. But it is impossible for you to   15
reveal it. Look, here comes your brother. – Tell me,
what do you bring?

Enter VESPASIANUS *with a basket of sand and a stick.*

VESPASIANUS   Dearest father, I have some sand here, to
enable my dearest sister Andronica to write with this
stick and reveal who has maimed her so shamefully.   20
TITO   O, dearest son, if she could bring it to light in this
way then I would find a little peace for my sick old
heart. Now pour the sand on the ground, and give her
the stick.

*He pours the sand on the ground. Tito Andronico
puts the staff between his daughter's stumps.*

7–8   **see … welcome me** This reminiscence
of familial tenderness is not in *TA*.
Marcus mentions Lavinia's skilful lute
playing when he finds her earlier in the
play (2.3.45).

17   SD In *TA* no basket of sand or stick are
brought in. Marcus finds a suitable part of
the ground on which to write – 'This sandy
plot is plain' (4.1.69) – a task he carries out
with '*his staff*' (4.1.68.1). Lucius, being

banished, is absent from the scene.

18–20   Vespasianus initiates the revelation
of Andronica's rapists, whereas in *TA*
Lavinia initiates the process by using one
of Young Lucius' books to alert her
family to the similarities between her and
Ovid's Philomel (4.1.30–58).

24   SD In *TA*, Marcus offers Lavinia the staff
(4.1.73–6), and Titus has no active part in
the action.

Look here, dearest daughter, and write with it in the   25
sand the names of those who robbed you of your
tongue and hands.

She takes the stick and writes with it.

O, dearest daughter, this is enough for me. There is
'Helicates' and also 'hunt'. O, dearest daughter, did
Helicates and Saphonus maim you at the recent hunt?   30

Andronica inclines her head.

Show me also, dearest daughter, is the Empress
likewise to blame?

Andronica nods her head.

O, cursed be this hunt and the day on which it was
held! I thought it would be a joyful occasion and that
it would increase my favour with the Emperor, but   35
now I see it has caused my greatest misfortune. O,
the frightful dream I had the night before the hunt
foretold this misfortune. Come now, if we must
perish then hear me, dearest brother and dearest

---

26 **names of those** Earlier references to
Andronica's attacker were in the singular
(which corresponds to *TA*, 2.3.26–50,
3.1.67, 69, 92 and 4.1.36). The present
plural has its equivalent in *TA*, where
Lavinia has gestured with her arms to
indicate that 'there were more than one'
attacker (4.1.38). In *Tito* the reason for
the shift to the plural is unclear, as she
only writes one name. Braekman commented on the passage that 'the text is
very corrupt' (9.88).

29 **'Helicates' ... 'hunt'** corresponds to
Lavinia's writing of '*Stuprum – Chiron –
Demetrius*' (*TA*, 4.1.78).

29–30 **did ... hunt?** corresponds to Marcus'
speech after both names have been

written and read out: 'What, what? The
lustful sons of Tamora / Performers of this
heinous bloody deed?' (4.1.79–80). In
Tito, however, only Helicates' name has
been written, and it is unclear why Tito
assumes that Saphonus was also involved.

31–2 **Show ... blame?** Titus does not ask
about Tamora's involvement, but he does
demonstrate an awareness that taking
revenge on Chiron and Demetrius will
incur their mother's wrath and invite
retaliation (*TA*, 4.1.96–100).

38–54 **Come ... grasp** Tito pronounces a
call to arms, which is approved by his
brother, whereas in *TA* Marcus calls for
revenge and Titus warns him that they
must proceed with care (4.1.83–100).

son, and listen closely to my words. We must prepare 40
for perilous, bloody war and raise many soldiers to
overthrow Rome and cause such ravage and ruin
for them as was never heard before. Not one stone
shall be left upon another. So let us all unite here
and swear to our gods not to cease bloody, perilous 45
warfare until Rome is overthrown and we have in our
grasp the Emperor and the murderous Empress with
her two damnable sons. Likewise, let us conclude
no peace with them nor have pity on them, but treat
them in the most cruel and dreadful way that can be 50
imagined.

VICTORIADES   Dearest brother, I swear by all the gods in
heaven not to cease my vengeance until we have the
Empress and her sons in our grasp. I shall sell all my
possessions and levy warlike men. 55

TITO   O, my dearest and faithful brother, how it makes
me glad that you promise such great and powerful
assistance. I will now swear never to cease my
vengeance for as long as I live. First, I will swear by
the warlike hand that once was mine, then by the 60
heads of my sons, and then by my daughter.

52–5 **Dearest . . . men** While Marcus swears
revenge along with Titus and Lucius (*TA*,
3.1.279 SD), he does not mention a prag-
matic means of achieving it.

58–61 SD **I . . . rise** Whereas Tito swears by
the various severed body parts and by
Andronica, Titus invites his family to
form a circle to swear to right their
wrongs (*TA*, 3.1.276–9).

61 SD No equivalent SD appears in the early
editions of *TA*. Bate argues that *Tito* may
offer an insight into how the oath in *TA*

would have been performed (see
Introduction, p. 4, and Ard[3], 46).

61.1 **dirge** ('Klagelied') a song of lament.
While some of the entertainments in the
Leipzig volume contain musical notation,
there is none for *Tito*.

61.2 **the . . . heads** This suggests that the
characters do not form a circle around
Tito, as is the case in *TA* (3.1.277).

61.6–8 **approaches . . . others** that is, aligns the
severed body parts with Andronica from
whom body parts have also been severed.

209

*Tito Andronico kneels and begins to sing a dirge;
the others sit down by the heads. He takes up his hand,
raises it, and looks to heaven, sighs, utters an oath,
strikes his breast, and puts down the hand after
having sworn. He then takes up the heads and swears
by each of them in turn. Finally, he approaches
Andronica and swears by her as before with the
others. This done, they all rise.*

Now that I have taken this oath and sworn, I shall
sell all my property and goods so that my son
may raise the bravest and most valiant men. Listen,
dearest son, take all the vast store of my treasury; set   65
out with it directly and enlist as many men as you
can get.

VESPASIANUS   Dearest father, I am eager for it, and so
I swear by the god Mars that I shall not cease my
rage and fury until pale Death has triumphed over   70
my heart. Now, farewell, beloved father, I go from
here to raise brave men. Before long, you will hear
the blast of trumpets and in this way know that
I bring ruthless men who shall pillage, burn, and
kill, like the god Mars himself. And so, farewell,   75
farewell.   *Exit.*

TITO   Dearest son, may the gods favour you. Although I
have lost my hand, I hope that my dearest son will
fight the better, for in the recent battle with the Moors

62–5 **I shall ... treasury** In *TA* there is no
indication of how Lucius is to finance the
raising of an army (3.1.286), nor of Titus'
wealth. Tito's plan to sell his property
corresponds to the chapbook, where Titus
'got together Friends, and sold whatever
he had of value to hire Soldiers' (36). See
Introduction, p. 43.

68–76 Lucius' final speech before he departs
from Rome is a soliloquy that concludes
the scene (3.1.289–301).

69, 75 **god Mars** the Roman god of war, previously mentioned by Morian (3.3.129).

70 **pale Death** a rare personification. The
triumph of death was a popular medieval
and early modern conceit.

73 **blast of trumpets** Compare the '*flourish
of trumpets*' (7.1.0.1) as Vespasianus
enters on his approach to Rome.

74–5 **ruthless ... kill** reminiscent of
Morian's account of the Roman invasion
of Ethiopia (1.1.112–15, 120–2).

I saw him fight like a fierce tiger. In you I place all my   80
hope, and if I must end my old life here, I know that
you will take vengeance on our enemies. But now I
shall send the Emperor word of eternal enmity. –
Holla, messenger! Come here.

Enter MESSENGER.

MESSENGER   I am here, my lord. Have you any orders   85
for me?

TITO   Listen, and mark the words I speak to you. Go to
the Emperor and deliver to him this sword with these
words: that I am, and ever will be, his eternal enemy,
that I will loose my military forces upon him, and not   90
cease until I have him in my grasp, together with the
Empress and her two sons. Go now, and deliver this
clearly.

MESSENGER   Gracious lord, it will be done accordingly.

He takes the sword.

TITO   But listen further; when you have spoken this, give   95
him this letter together with its contents.

---

80 **fierce tiger** There are several references
to tigers in *TA*, always in relation to the
enemies of the Andronici, notably Tamora
(2.2.142, 5.3.194), Aaron (5.3.5) and
Rome (3.1.54–5).

80–1 **In . . . hope** See Tito's earlier comment
at 4.3.50–1 and note.

84 **Holla . . . here** No messenger is sum-
moned in *TA*; instead, Titus mistakenly
chooses a Clown as the messenger to
whom he entrusts a message for
Saturninus (4.3.77–119).

88 **deliver . . . sword** cf. the swords that
Young Lucius delivers to the court (*TA*,
4.2.1–17).

88–9 **with . . . words** Tito sends his message
orally, whereas Titus writes it down on
paper (*TA*, 4.3.105).

95–6 **when . . . contents** The letter may seem
redundant, since Tito has conveyed his
missive orally to the Messenger, but it is
necessary because the 'contents' alludes
to the naked blade within it. Titus writes
the letter onstage and asks for a knife to
fold into it (*TA*, 4.3.114–15), whereas the
letter seems to have been prepared earlier
in *Tito*, which means that the blade sealed
in the letter may not be visible to the
audience.

Messenger takes the letter.

Address him roughly, as suits a messenger of the
enemy.

MESSENGER   Very well, gracious lord, I shall deliver
everything to him.   *Exeunt.*   100

[5.2]   *Enter* EMPEROR *and* AETIOPISSA.

EMPEROR   Lovely Empress, I admire the cunning with
which you had the heads of Tito Andronico's sons
struck off, who so grossly sinned against you, as you
say. And in order that we may not be harmed by him,
you cheated him out of that right hand with which he   5
caused terrible bloodshed all his life.

AETIOPISSA   Yes, gracious lord and Emperor, this is how
we must prevent misfortune. I know well that if I had
not taken his hand, he would have razed the imperial
palace to the ground. But now we may scorn his might   10
and resist it, though he will probably not rest, but
wage war upon us.

EMPEROR   Indeed, lovely Empress, Tito shall never more

97–8 **Address … enemy** Titus, by contrast,
gives instructions to the Clown to make
his delivery as polite as possible (*TA*,
4.3.109–12).

5.2 corresponds to *TA*, 4.4. *Tito* conflates
the two separate messages brought to
Saturninus by the Clown (4.4.39–48) and
Emillius (4.4.60–106).

0.1 In *TA*, Chiron, Demetrius and attendants
are also onstage.

5.2] *this edn; not in 1620*

1–8 **Lovely … misfortune** confirms
Aetiopissa's responsibility for the earlier
plot against Tito and his sons, as affirmed
by Morian at 4.3.1–4. The passage also
provides a rationale for her earlier
actions. In *TA*, Saturninus enters with the
arrows that were fired by Titus in the previous scene, and Tamora reassures him
(4.4.1–38).

perform great deeds. Yet I fear his son, Vespasianus,
who is said to be his father's equal in battle.   15

AETIOPISSA   Yes, gracious lord and Emperor, it is true
that in Ethiopia, where his father made me his captive,
it was said that he fought with a ferocity equal to his
father's. But, gracious lord and Emperor, do not fear
him, for I shall contrive a means how to put him out   20
of the way. But what news does this man bring who
makes such haste towards us?

[*Enter* MESSENGER, *with an attendant.*]

MESSENGER   Almighty Emperor of Rome, I am a
messenger from Tito Andronico, who sends a sword
to signify eternal war between you and him. He will   25
forever seek revenge and be your extreme enemy, and
will never rest until he has you, the Empress, and her
two sons in his grasp and in his power.

EMPEROR   Well now, messenger, you deliver your
message defiantly enough. I would never have thought   30

14–15 **Yet ... battle** Whereas the Emperor
fears Vespasianus' military prowess,
Saturninus is concerned about Lucius'
popularity with the populace: 'Ay, now
begins our sorrows to approach. / 'Tis he
the common people love so much; /
Myself hath often heard them say, / When
I have walked like a private man, / That
Lucius' banishment was wrongfully' (*TA*,
4.4.71–5).

19–21 **gracious ... way** Aetiopissa does not
elaborate on how she plans to eliminate
Tito. In *TA*, after news of the Goth forces
is brought by Emillius, Tamora notes that
Titus is the key to stopping Lucius: 'know
thou, emperor, / I will enchant the old
Andronicus / With words more sweet and
yet more dangerous / Than baits to fish'
(4.4.87–90). At the end of the scene she

makes explicit the need to work upon
Titus in order to prevent Lucius from
causing them harm: 'Now will I to that
old Andronicus, / And temper him with
all the art I have / To pluck proud Lucius
from the warlike Goths' (4.4.107–9).

22 SD ***attendant*** The Emperor later asks an
attendant to deliver the Messenger to the
hangman (see 56–66), and it seems likely
that he enters with the Messenger.

23–8 In keeping with Tito's instructions, the
Messenger addresses the Emperor
'roughly' (5.1.97), which is also reflected
in his use of the German familiar second-
person singular pronouns ('du' and 'dir').
In *TA*, the Clown simply presents the
letter, which Saturninus reads before
ordering that the Clown be taken away
immediately and hanged.

22 SD] *this edn; not in 1620*

213

that Tito Andronico could wage a bloody war against
me. Give me the sword.

Takes it.

And tell him roundly, that since strife is what he
wants, I shall be enemy enough, and that I shall now
resist his insufficient might with ease and shall not   35
honour it.

MESSENGER   O almighty Emperor, a great misfortune is
in store for you and yours, and although he no longer
has his hand, his warlike son even now travels through
many kingdoms and raises great, powerful, warlike,   40
and choice men, in order to rage and better assault
you. I know for certain that he will soon attack the
palace with a powerful force and lay siege to it; he
will not stop until he has overthrown it and has you
and yours in his grasp. I have a letter here which you   45
must read.

The Emperor takes the letter.

EMPEROR   You insolent messenger, how dare you address
me in so bold and brazen a manner. I swear by all the
gods that on account of your brazen words you will
never leave this place and I shall give you fitting   50
punishment.

33–6 Whereas Saturninus orders the hanging
of the Clown straight after reading the
letter (*TA*, 4.4.43–4), Tito's Emperor
does so only after seeing the naked blade
(52–3).

37–46 corresponds to the speech of Emillius
(*TA*, 4.4.61–7), who brings news about
Lucius and the Goths. While the
Messenger's earlier speech (23–8) reflects
the message Tito asked to be delivered
(5.1.87–93), the present one does not.

39–41 **travels ... men** The chapbook mentions that the Roman Emperor 'raised a
mighty Army in Greece, Italy, France,
Spain, Germany, and England' (35). See
Introduction, p. 45.

Opens the letter.

What do I find here in this letter but a naked
blade! May the gods never help me again if I do not
avenge this great outrage and maliciousness. You,
messenger, shall be sent away immediately to be   55
hanged on the gallows – Attendant, take him away
and deliver him to the hangman, so that he may hang
this very minute.

MESSENGER   Gracious lord Emperor, I hope I shall not
have violence done to me and shall not be entrusted to   60
the hangman, for it would be contrary to the customs
of war. I have done nothing but deliver my lord's
message as he asked me to do.

EMPEROR   This will not help you, your life is lost. – Do
you not hear me, attendant? Get him out of my sight   65
at once.   [*Exeunt.*]

52–3 **What ... blade!** In *TA*, Saturninus
does not remark on the knife inside the
letter, but Bate suggests that his strong
reaction after opening the letter is 'pro-
voked by the knife' (Ard³, 280).

54–8 **You ... minute** This parallels *TA*,
where Saturninus, upon reading the letter,
immediately bids an attendant to 'Go,
take him away and hang him presently'
(4.4.44).

59–63 **Gracious ... do** Whereas the
Messenger draws attention to the
Emperor's lack of regard for the customs
of war, the Clown in *TA* makes a punning

response to the announcement that he
must be hanged: 'Hanged, by'Lady?
Then I have brought up a neck to a fair
end' (4.4.47–8). See also 7.1.114–15 and
note.

61–2 **customs of war** 'By the seventeenth
century, England had a full system of
Articles of War', and 'Similar codes
existed . . . in Germany' (Green, 23).

65–6 **Get ... once.** The German text
adds 'etc.' at the end of the speech.
The meaning of the expression is
unclear here. See 3.2.6 and 4.1.23–4 and
notes.

66 SD] *this edn; not in 1620*

6.[1]   *Enter* MIDWIFE *cradling a black child which has*
             been fathered by Morian on the Empress.

MIDWIFE   I search everywhere for Morian, to whom I
     must present this child, so that he may secretly put it
     out of the way. This night it was born by the Empress
     into this world. It was fathered by Morian, her secret
     paramour. Alas, I cannot find him anywhere and I   5
     don't know where to go with the child.

             [*Enter* HELICATES *and* SAPHONUS.]

     But here come the Empress' sons, who mustn't know
     of this. Alas, I don't know what to do!
HELICATES   Let me see, midwife, what you have there.
     – Dearest brother, come and see this great prodigy: 10
     here is a young black devil!
SAPHONUS   I am amazed at it. But listen, midwife, tell us
     the truth if you want to leave from here with your life.

6.1 largely corresponds to 4.2.52–182. In *TA*,
Tamora's sons and Aaron are already
onstage when the Nurse arrives, and they
remain onstage until after the Nurse's
murder. In *Tito*, the Midwife enters alone,
is joined by the two brothers and eventually Morian, who argues with Saphonus
and Helicates and then orders them to
leave before murdering the Midwife.
The brothers leave, unlike Chiron and
Demetrius, who agree to cooperate with
him in his efforts to save his child and
keep the scandal from becoming public.
Unlike Aaron (4.2.100–5 and 118–20),
Morian does not deliver a diatribe against
whiteness, and less is made of the child's
blackness.

3–4 it was . . . Morian The birth of the mis-
cegenated child is also in the chapbook. It
is absent from Vos' *Aran en Titus* (and
its subsequent German adaptations),
although in Vos' play Aran has a young
Moor named Quintus, who serves as his
page.

5 cannot . . . anywhere In *TA*, Aaron is
onstage when the Nurse enters, but she
does not immediately recognize him,
asking instead, 'O tell me, did you see
Aaron the Moor?' (4.2.53).

7–8 who . . . this There is no indication in *TA*
that Tamora wishes to keep the birth
secret from her sons.

11 here . . . devil anticipates Morian's later
remark about the likely response that the
infant's appearance will prompt: 'men
will say "There sits a devil"' (6.1.112–
13). In *TA* the Nurse similarly describes
the infant as a 'devil' (4.2.66).

6.1] *this edn*; Actus Sextus *1620*   6 SD] *this edn; not in 1620*

Who is this child's mother? I see that he is the father,
so with whom has our Morian slept?   15

MIDWIFE   Gracious lord, I shall readily reveal it to you if
you can keep it secret, for no-one knows of it but I. If
she should learn that this came from me, I would die
a miserable death.

SAPHONUS   No, midwife, it shall never be made known   20
by us, we shall keep it secret. Confess and tell us the
truth, but should you tell us anything other than the
truth, expect nothing but a cruel death.

MIDWIFE   No, I'll tell you the truth. Black Morian, your
mother's secret paramour, fathered this child, and   25
when she saw that the child was black she was very
frightened, and asked me go in secret to Morian and
take the child to him, so that he can have it brought up
in secret to make sure that no-one knows about it; but
I cannot find him anywhere.   30

They stand, amazed at her words.

SAPHONUS   Alas, what great shame! A curse on the
treacherous villain Morian, who has brought our

---

14 **Who ... mother?** In *TA*, Demetrius and
Chiron know that Tamora is the new-
born's mother. Demetrius remarks upon
Tamora's labour pains; the trumpets then
sound, which Chiron interprets as a sign
that Tamora has given birth to a son,
following which the child is brought
onstage (4.2.46–51).

14 **I ... father** The infant's black skin
makes him easily recognizable as
Morian's offspring, which corresponds
loosely to the Nurse's identification of
Aaron's child as 'thy stamp, thy seal'
(4.2.71).

25 **this child** This neutral reference to the
infant is very different from the Nurse's
description in *TA*: 'A joyless, dismal,

black and sorrowful issue. / Here is the
babe, as loathsome as a toad' (4.2.68–9).

28–9 **that he ... it** This clarifies the
Midwife's earlier comment in lines 2–3
about putting the baby out of the way.
Aetiopissa's desire to preserve her baby's
life is not to be found in *TA*, where
Tamora wishes to have the baby killed
(see 84–8 and note).

32–46 **brought ... us** Unlike Tamora's sons
in *TA*, Saphonus and Helicates are worried about how the discovery of the infant
will impact on their own reputations and
bring 'dishonour' and 'shame' upon them.
TA's Nurse exclaims 'we are all undone'
and considers the wider implications of
'stately Rome's disgrace' (4.2.56, 61).

217

mother to shame, for which we must suffer mockery
and scorn. Dearest brother, let us no longer suffer the
detestable rogue, but instead kill him miserably as   35
soon as we lay eyes upon him.

HELICATES   O, dearest brother, my heart is troubled. I
do not know what to do about the murderous and
treacherous rogue, who has brought us such great
dishonour. He deserves to be boiled in hot oil. But   40
what are we to do with the damnable villain? For if
we strike against him, we shall not escape from his
hands alive.

SAPHONUS   Indeed, I do not know what can be done. If
the child remains alive, all will be known and bring   45
shame upon us. Therefore, give me the child, so that I
may kill it at once.

*He takes the child from the midwife, draws his
sword and is about to kill the child.*

Enter MORIAN, *who, seeing that Saphonus is about to
kill the child, rushes at him and snatches the child
out of his hands.*

35   **kill him** In *TA*, Demetrius and Chiron do
not consider murdering Aaron.
40   **boiled ... oil** Since the Middle Ages,
boiling in oil had been used as a form of
capital punishment in parts of Europe,
usually for the crime of coin counter-
feiting (Miethe and Lu, 42). Helicates
may be implying that Morian has coun-
terfeited a child, and therefore deserves to
be punished in this manner.
46–7 **give ... once** In *TA*, Chiron states that
the child cannot be allowed to live, and,
after responses from Aaron and the
Nurse, Demetrius offers to murder the

infant (4.2.82–8). Since Morian is not
present in this scene, the action is condensed.
47   SD1 There is no indication in *TA* that
Demetrius manages to seize the infant
when he demands 'Nurse, give it me'
(4.2.88). Ravenscroft inserted a SD,
'Aron *takes the child from the Woman*',
and Hughes comments that 'Aaron probably takes the child from the Nurse'
(126). The stage action in *Tito* is different
and arguably more dramatic, Saphonus
taking the child from the Midwife before
having it snatched from him by Morian.

MORIAN   No, no, stop, for I see that it is my child; don't
kill it or I'll give you such a box on the ears that you
will not escape alive.   50

SAPHONUS   O you treacherous villain! What shame have
you brought upon us and our mother! How could you
be so bold as to take your pleasure with our mother?
Did you not know that you would pay for it with your
life?   55

MORIAN   Why, my lords, there is no need to be half so
angry with me; it is uncalled-for. But if you insist on
satisfying your wrath, you should know that you are
bringing an angry devil onto your backs, and that you
will thank the gods if you have my friendship once   60
again. I made love to your mother and she bore this
son to me. I ask, was I not above all her servant and
bound to obey dutifully whatever she commanded?
Let me tell you that she urged and compelled me to
make love to her because neither your father nor this   65
present Emperor could pluck her strings as vigorously
as I. Therefore, make peace, you lords, and be content
with me, for I have become your stepfather and this,
my son, is your stepbrother. How can you be angry
with your father and your brother?   70

48 **for ... child** At the equivalent moment in
TA, Aaron appeals to a different kindred relationship: 'will you kill your brother?'
(4.2.90). It is not until later in the scene that
Morian reminds Helicates and Saphonus that
'this, my son, is your stepbrother' (68–9).

51–2 **What ... mother!** Demetrius similarly
exclaims that 'By this our mother is for
ever shamed' (*TA*, 4.2.114). For the sons'
concern for their own reputations, see
32–46 and note.

54–5 **Did ... life?** Saphonus' sword may still
be drawn (cf. 47 SD1) and his words thus

accompanied by an appropriately men-
acing gesture. In *TA*, no equivalent punishment is considered for Aaron.

61–5 **I ... her** Morian's feigned innocence
has no equivalent in *TA*, where Aaron is
defiant and unapologetic.

66 **pluck ... strings** ('die Lauten ...
schlagen') See 1.1.97 and note.

68–70 **stepfather ... brother?** Aaron
repeatedly reminds Demetrius and Chiron
that the newborn is their 'brother' (*TA*,
4.2.90, 124, 128), but he does not refer to
himself as their (step)father.

SAPHONUS   O treacherous villain! You are the devil's
father and not ours. I advise you to stop your insolent
words, or else you shall come to harm. It is enough
that you have brought such insult and disgrace
upon us.   75

MORIAN   What, you lords, are you getting more and more
angry? I swear by all the gods that if you don't get out
of my sight I shall beat you both so soundly that
someone will have to come and gather up the pieces.

Morian begins to speak to the midwife.
Helicates and Saphonus shake their heads in
anger and exeunt.

But listen, midwife. How is it with the Empress? Was   80
she happy to become a mother, and where are you
taking the child?

MIDWIFE   Yes, gracious lord, she is well and content, and
a happy mother. But she told me to search for you,
deliver the child, and instruct you to take it in secret   85
to Mount Thaurin, where your father lives, so that he

71–5 **O ... us** Saphonus' outrage contrasts with
the reaction of Demetrius, who peacefully
goes along with Aaron's plan: 'Advise thee,
Aaron, what is to be done / And we will all
subscribe to thy advice' (*TA*, 4.2.131–2).

77–9 **if ... pieces** At the equivalent point in
TA, Aaron similarly threatens the two
brothers in a conditional clause: 'if you
brave the Moor, / The chafed boar, the
mountain lioness, / The ocean, swells not
so as Aaron storms' (4.2.139–41).

80–1 **How ... mother** Aaron also talks to
the Nurse (*TA*, 4.2.142–5) but does not
enquire about Tamora's well-being and
post-natal condition.

84–8 **But ... Empress** Tamora has different
plans for the infant: 'The empress sends it
thee, thy stamp, thy seal, / And bids thee
christen it with thy dagger's point'

(4.2.71–2). Aaron's father is not mentioned in *TA*.

86 **Mount Thaurin** ('Berg Thaurin') Morian
is later caught on Mount Thaurin (7.1.16–
18) by Vespasianus, who is levying men
(see 5.1.71–2). Marti suggests the location refers to Monte Taurino or Pizzo S.
Michele, which is part of the Picentini
mountain range in the Campanian
Apennines, south-east of Naples (384, n.
19). Fredén (377) argues that the implied
location is the 'Taurisani montes', a designation that goes back to the 'Taurini',
an ancient Celtic people in what is now
northern Italy. Alfred Noe proposes that
'Thaurin' designates Turin (Brauneck and
Noe, 6.40), but apart from the difference
in spelling, it is not clear what 'Mount'
would refer to.

can raise it; no-one must know that it was born of the
Empress.

MORIAN   Very well, I shall do so. But hear me further
and tell me, does any other creature know that this   90
child belongs to the Empress? Tell me also, who was
in attendance when the child was born?

MIDWIFE   Gracious lord, there is not a creature alive that
knows the child belongs to the Empress except myself
and the Empress' sons, who met me when I was   95
searching for you, made enquiries and then threatened
to kill me if I did not confess the truth. But let me tell
you that when the child was delivered, I was alone
with the mistress.

MORIAN   It pleases me ten times over that none but you   100
were there, but you must lose your life for it.

Draws his sword and stabs her.

MIDWIFE   Alas, alas!

Falls dead to the ground.

MORIAN   So, lie there. I know that you will reveal
nothing; your death is my guarantee. Had there been
more who knew of it, they should also have died by   105

90–2 **does ... born?** In *TA*, Demetrius
enquires about the number of women
who saw the child (4.2.137), and Aaron
repeats the question (4.2.142).

93–4 **not ... Empress** *TA*'s Nurse admits
that Cornelia the midwife also knows
about the child (4.2.143). In *TA* there are
two women who aid Thamora's delivery:
the Nurse and Cornelia the Midwife, who
does not appear onstage.

100–1 **you ... it** There is no equivalent in *Tito*
to Aaron's farcical jesting at the dying
Nurse: '"Wheak, wheak!" – so cries a pig
prepared to the spit' (*TA*, 4.2.148).

103 **So ... there** Morian makes no plans to
dispose of the body, unlike Aaron: 'Hark
ye, lords, you see I have given her physic,
/ And you must needs bestow her funeral;
/ The fields are near and you are gallant
grooms' (4.2.164–6). See 3.3.67 and
note.

103–4 **I ... guarantee** a pithier statement
than Aaron's ''tis a deed of policy: / Shall
she live to betray this guilt of ours? / A
long-tongued, babbling gossip? No, lords,
no' (4.2.150–2).

my hand. None but the Empress' sons know of it, and
I hope they will keep quiet and not reveal their
mother's shame, but instead help to cloak it.

He pauses and looks at his infant son
sleeping in his arms.

But you, my dearest newborn son, did your brothers
wish to kill you? No, they must not do it or they will   110
die. You have a shape like my own, except for a sharp
nose and chin like your mother's, but men will say
'There sits a devil'. You are indeed flesh of my flesh
and bone of my bone. I must now consider how to
rear you so that you may one day emulate your father.   115
Dog milk and whey will be your food till you can

109–11 **But ... die** Morian's intimate
address to the infant calls to mind Aaron's
'Sweet blowze, you are a beauteous
blossom, sure' (*TA*, 4.2.74), which occurs
earlier in the corresponding scene.

111–12 **a sharp ... mother's** Aaron does not
comment on his son's facial features, but
he does state earlier in the scene that he is
'myself, / The vigour and the picture of
my youth' (*TA*, 4.2.109–10).

112–13 **men ... devil** This echoes Saphonus'
words in lines 9–10: 'here is a young
black devil!

113–14 **flesh ... bone** This inverts the structure of Adam's comment about Eve after
her creation from one of Adam's ribs:
'This is now bone of my bones and flesh
of my flesh' (Gen. 2.23).

116 **Dog ... whey** The German text reads,
'Hundemilch Käse vnd Wasser'. The reference to dog milk may allude to the story of
Romulus and Remus, the mythical founders
of Rome, who were succoured by a wolf in
a cave. The absence of a comma between
'Hundemilch' (dog milk) and 'Käse'
(cheese) raises the question of whether the
words form a compound (cheese of dog's

milk) or not (dog milk and cheese). Fredén
(378) convincingly argues for a third possibility, namely that 'Käse vnd Wasser' is a
mistake for 'Käsewasser' (i.e. whey; see
Grimm), with the implication that the word
'vnd' (and) was misplaced in the sentence:
'Hundemilch Käse vnd Wasser' instead of
'Hundemilch vnd Käsewasser'. If so, the
implied meaning is neither 'dog milk,
cheese and water' nor 'cheese of dog's milk
and water' but 'dog milk and whey', which
partly corresponds to the 'curds and whey'
(*TA*, 4.2.180) Aaron intends to make his son
consume. Marti (385, n. 20) uses the *OED*
to argue that 'Hundemilch' is a literal translation of 'whey' and that *TA*'s 'curds and
whey' correspond to 'Hundemilch' and
'Käse' (cheese). In the process of making
cheese curd, the milk separates into the
solid curd and watery whey, which, as the
OED suggests, was historically fed to dogs
('whey', *n.* 1a, 1600), probably because of
its low lactose content. However, we have
found no evidence in Grimm or elsewhere
to suggest that 'Hundemilch' was used as a
synonym for 'whey' (Molke) in early
modern German.

walk. I will teach you all kinds of exercises so that
you learn how to put up with hardship, how to fight
and battle bravely, and tear a suit of armour apart with
your hands, as I can. I will tutor you in all villainies 120
and bloody business so that you will fear no devil,
and, like myself, obtain much grace and favour from
high-born ladies, so that in the end they will revere
you. – Now, I shall go away from here, and take the
child to my father, who is a black devil like myself 125
and lives on Mount Thaurin, to let him raise it and say
it is his own, so that nobody will know to whom it
belongs. The Empress can now think about another
one for next year. *[Exeunt.]*

116–17 **Dog ... walk** Aaron envisages a
slightly more varied diet: 'I'll make you
feed on berries and on roots, / And fat on
curds and whey, and suck the goat' (*TA*,
4.2.179–80).

117–18 **all ... hardship** a loose parallel to
Aaron's desire to have the infant 'cabin in
a cave' (4.2.181), which implies harsh
conditions.

118–19 **fight ... bravely** corresponds to
Aaron's intention to 'bring [his son] up /
To be a warrior and command a camp'
(4.2.181–2).

119–24 **tear ... you** After a sequence (see
116–19 and notes) with obvious resem-
blances to Aaron's soliloquy at the end of
4.2, the present passage (which adds to
Morian's vision of what it means for him

to rear his child successfully) has no correspondence in *TA*.

119–20 **tear ... can** perhaps an example of
the 'great, superhuman, manly exploits'
('grosse, vnmenschliche Mannliche
Thaten') that Morian mentions at
1.1.110–11.

120–1 **I will ... devil** Morian's intended
tutoring may be modelled on his own villainous deeds as described at 1.1.102–5.

124–8 **Now ... belongs** not in *TA*, where
Aaron outlines a plan secretly to exchange
his son for a white infant born to his
countryman (4.2.154–63). However, the
proximity of Morian's father's home
loosely parallels Aaron's assertion that
'Not far one Muly lives, my countryman'
(4.2.154).

129 *Exeunt] Brennecke (Exit); not in 1620*

7.[1] *Beating of drums and flourish of trumpets. Enter*
VESPASIANUS *advancing on Rome with his
army, which has raged cruelly and devastated
all the cities of the Romans.*

VESPASIANUS   I march against Rome with a great and
valiant army of choice and seasoned troops. I have
sixty thousand horsemen in full armour, and a hundred
thousand men on foot, with whom I have marched
across the whole of Italy and razed all the cities we   5
came upon, with the result that no stone was left on
another. We have unnerved all Italy so that the people
run about to no avail, like fugitives. We have already
slaughtered a horrendous and vast number, so now
they cry 'oh, no!' wherever we come. But this is   10
nothing yet, for we shall attack them with ten times
greater cruelty. Once more, I swear by all the gods
never to withdraw my army until the haughty Empress

7.1 corresponds to *TA* 5.1, although the last
part of the scene in *TA*, with Emillius, the
messenger from Rome, has no equivalent
in *Tito*. Morian does not share Aaron's
glee at being a villain (5.1.124–44), and
Vespasianus, unlike Lucius, promises to
spare Morian's life only to subsequently
break his promise. Whereas Morian is
presumably executed immediately after
this scene and makes no further appearance in the play, Aaron's execution is
postponed and he is brought onstage
again at the end of *TA* (5.3.175–89).

0.1 *Beating ... trumpets* See 3.2.0.1–2 and
note.

0.3 *army* In *TA*, Lucius enters 'with an army
of Goths' (5.1.0.1). The loyalty of
Vespasianus' soldiers has presumably
been secured with the store of wealth
from Tito's treasury (see 5.1.64–7),

whereas Lucius' Goths in *TA* are motivated by their personal grievances against
Rome (cf. 5.1.7–8).

1–15 **I ... now?** parallels Lucius' conversation with the Goth soldiers (5.1.1–19).

3–4 **sixty ... foot** In *TA*, Lucius does not
specify the type or number of soldiers at his
disposal. The chapbook recounts that the
Emperor levied men from different countries when trying to fight off the invading
Goths but notes that he lost 'threescore
thousand of his Men' in the fight (35).

7–10 **We ... come** Vespasianus' indiscrimi-
nate slaughter of innocent people contrasts with Lucius' mission to aid Rome in
ousting an unpopular emperor: 'I have
received letters from great Rome / Which
signifies what hate they bear their
emperor, / And how desirous of our sight
they are' (*TA*, 5.1.2–4).

7.1] *this edn*; Actus Septimus *1620*

and her two sons are in my power. But what wondrous
sight greets me now?   15

Enter SOLDIER, *with* MORIAN *and his son as prisoners.*

SOLDIER   Gracious prince and lord, I humbly deliver up
to your highness this Moor, whom I made prisoner on
Mount Thaurin.

VESPASIANUS   My dear and trusty soldier, I rejoice at this
prisoner, for he is one of our greatest enemies; he is   20
the Empress' attendant, I know him well. – Listen,
black devil, you are a welcome guest to me. But tell
me, what were you doing on Mount Thaurin? And
what kind of a black devil is that in your arms?

MORIAN   Never in my life has a lone fellow so shamefully   25
taken me prisoner as this man. I must say that you and
your followers are like devils in battle and combat.
I am so madly enraged that I don't know what to do. I
could curse myself for the fact that I am now your
prisoner. If you spare my life and show me mercy,   30
I shall fill your ears with wonder and amazement at
what the Empress and her two sons have done to your

16–18 **Gracious . . . Thaurin** The equivalent
account of Aaron's arrest by the second
Goth is considerably more detailed
(5.1.20–39).

18 **Mount Thaurin** See note at 6.1.86. This
is the geographical location of the
'ruinous monastery' (5.1.21) where
Aaron is captured is not specified.

20 **greatest enemies** Unlike Lucius, who
knows that Aaron 'robbed Andronicus of
his good hand' (*TA*, 5.1.41), Vespasianus
only knows at this point that Morian was
the bearer of the severed hand and heads
at the beginning of 4.3.

22 **black devil** Lucius also calls Aaron 'devil'
(*TA*, 5.1.40, 145) though not 'black devil'.
Morian uses the word for himself (and his

father) in the preceding scene (6.1.125).

24 **black devil** echoes the type of response
imagined by Morian in 6.1.112–13.

25–37 Morian's verbosity contrasts with
Aaron, who refuses to speak until Lucius
threatens to kill his son (5.1.46–8).

30 **If ... mercy** Morian's desire for self-
preservation has no equivalent in *TA*; the
only life Aaron wants to preserve is his
son's.

31–4 **I ... lives** Aaron makes a similar
promise ('I'll show thee wondrous
things', 5.1.55), but gives a non-specific
list of things he will divulge: 'murders,
rapes and massacres, / Acts of black
night, abominable deeds, / Complots of
mischief, treasons, villainies' (5.1.63–5).

sister, Andronica, and how your brothers lost their
lives. I will also serve you faithfully and help you
fight the Emperor; but if you show me no mercy, I   35
shall reveal nothing, for here I am. Having surrendered
myself, I can now meet my death.

VESPASIANUS   Although a prisoner, you do not lack
defiance. But tell me everything and speak the truth:
say who, in which place, at what time, and for what   40
reason, robbed my sister Andronica of her hands and
tongue. Likewise, say how my brothers were taken
prisoner and for what reason they were condemned to
death. When I have heard all this, then you shall keep
your life.   45

MORIAN   Then open your ears, and listen to me carefully.
Know that I have always been the Empress' secret
lover, when she was the Queen of Ethiopia as well as
here. And because she always had a haughty and
highly arrogant disposition, she could not suffer a   50
rival, and when she saw that you and yours stood in
such great and high renown, and were as mighty and
rich as the Emperor, she could not suffer it in her
proud spirit, but persecuted you to the utmost at every
turn. But the Empress' sons were overcome with love   55

34–5 **I ... Emperor** Morian's offer to cooperate contrasts with Aaron's defiance
throughout 5.1.

38–45 **Although ... life** Since Morian does
not refuse to speak, there is no need for
Vespasianus to threaten the child's life
and to utter the oaths that Aaron makes
Lucius swear (5.1.51–86).

40 **who** Vespasianus already knows who
mutilated Andronica and when (see
5.1.24–7.1), and Morian has just stated
(32–4) that Aetiopissa and her sons are
responsible for the attack.

46–91 Morian's account corresponds to

Aaron's in *TA* (5.1.87–120). The chief
villain in Morian's account is Aetiopissa,
whereas in Aaron's account it is Aaron
himself.

47–9 **Know ... here** Lucius is aware of the
affair (5.1.42–43), but there is no reason
to suppose that Vespasianus suspects
Morian of being Aetiopissa's lover.

49–55 **because ... turn** The sacrifice of
Alarbus (*TA*, 1.1.99–150) provides a motive
for Tamora's revenge for which there is no
equivalent in *Tito*. The present passage provides the clearest motive for Aetiopissa's
villainous actions against the Andronici.

for your sister Andronica, and instructed me to keep
watch on her husband and kill him, so that they could
satisfy their lust on her. I waited with all diligence on
him so that I could murder him, but never had the
opportunity to do so, and could not kill him. Now   60
your father, Tito Andronico, held a great stag-hunt,
attended by the Emperor and Empress, her two sons,
and also your sister, Andronica, and her husband. And
at that time the Empress walked alone in search of me
to satisfy her lust. She could not find me but came   65
across Andronica and her husband, who were alone.
She addressed them with arrogant words to which
Andronica did not submit and answered defiantly. So
the Empress left discontentedly, swearing a high oath
that she would neither eat nor drink until she had   70
satisfied her rage on Andronica. Her sons happened to
meet her, and she commanded them to take vengeance
on Andronica, and to stab her husband at her side,
or she would not consider them her sons any more.
They willingly went with her to the place where   75
Andronica was, and there stabbed her husband to
death at her side. Then she commanded them to
take Andronica and spend their lust on her, and
afterwards to maim her so that she would no longer
look like a human being. So they took her away, and   80
afterwards they cut off her hands and tore out her
tongue. The Empress then resolved to annihilate your
kin, and so had me take your brothers prisoner on

58–60 **I ... him** The audience has no previous knowledge of Morian's unsuccessful plot against Andronica's husband.

60–80 **Now ... away** is a condensed version of 3.3.8–109 (but see 64–5 and note).

64–5 **the ... lust** Aetiopissa does not spell out in 3.3 that she has gone to the forest in search of Morian, although when he finds her, she does attempt to engage him in an amorous encounter (3.3.120–6).

81 **tore out** See 4.2.0.3–5 and note.

trivial grounds and beheaded them. To secure herself
against future harm from your father, she sent him 85
word that his sons had insulted her roughly and would
consequently have to die for it, but if he loved them,
he should give up his hand for them, and then they
would be returned to him alive. Thus she cheated him
out of his warlike hand and sent it back to him with 90
the heads. So now you have heard the entire business
from me. You must also know finally that I fathered
the Empress' child, which I was going to take to
Mount Thaurin.

VESPASIANUS Your words have filled my ears with 95
wonder upon wonder. – Alas, haughty Empress, may
you and your sons never be well; I rejoice because
I now know how everything came about and how
I may act accordingly, for you shall suffer the same in
everything, and ten times worse. [*to Morian*] I have 100
no need to keep the promise I made you, since the
damnable Empress robbed my aged father of his
warlike hand, and promised him the lives of his sons
but did not keep her word. So, Morian, you must die
without any grace or mercy. – Attendant, take him 105
away from here. Deliver him to the hangman, so that
he may hang him and his child immediately.

84–91 **To … heads** Whereas Aetiopissa is
responsible for devising the scheme in
Tito, it is Aaron's idea in *TA* (5.1.111–20).

92–3 **know … child** Aaron begins his narrative with the equivalent information:
'First know thou I begot him on the
empress' (*TA*, 5.1.87).

96–100 **Alas … worse** There is no equivalent apostrophe to Tamora in *TA*. It reinforces Aetiopissa's status as the principal

enemy of the Andronici (see Introduction,
p. 12).

97 **sons** The singular 'son' ('Sohne') in the
German text must be an accidental error,
perhaps a confusion with Morian's one son.

105–6 **Attendant … here** ('Diener nimb jhn
von hinnen') is presented typographically
as a SD in the German text. The use of the
imperative suggests that the sentence is
part of Vespasianus' speech.

100 SD] *this edn; not in 1620*

MORIAN   What now, though the devil sends me to hang,
I don't think it would become me! Is there no mercy?
I beg you, spare my life.   110

VESPASIANUS   No, I shall not spare your life nor have the
least mercy. – Therefore, take him away so that he
may hang, and his child with him.

MORIAN   Well now, wait a little. If I am to eat hanging
pears, there is time enough for that. If there is nothing   115
else but death in store for me, I shall be willing, for I
have long deserved it. But I beg you, pity my child
and do not let it die with me, for it has done no evil
yet. Just let him be brought up as a soldier and I am
certain he will be a brave and valiant hero.   120

VESPASIANUS   I will pity this child and have it brought
up to fight and battle; but you, get you away from
here.   *Exit.*

108–10 **What ... life** Cf. Aaron: 'If there be devils, would I were a devil, / To live and burn in everlasting fire, / So I might have your company in hell / But to torment you with my bitter tongue' (*TA*, 5.1.147–50). Whereas Aaron remains defiant, Morian pleads for mercy.

112–13 **take ... him** is the first time that a threat is posed to the infant. Cf. Lucius: 'A halter, soldiers! Hang him on this tree, / And by his side his fruit of bastardy' (*TA*, 5.1.47–8).

114–15 **If ... pears** ('sol ich Hangelbeeren fressen') Creizenach (46) suggests that 'Hangelbeeren' refers to a type of pear with a long stem (see Grimm, hängelbirne) and that the expression is synonymous with hanging from the gallows (see also Marti, 389, and Fredén, 146). Lippner's translation makes the pun on 'henge' (i.e. hang) explicit: 'if I must eat gallows pears'; Brennecke spells out the meaning: 'If I'm to swing by the neck on the gallows'. Fredén (391–2) argues that Morian's comic

reaction as he finds out that he will be hanged corresponds to the Clown's similarly comic response to Tamora's announcement that he 'must be hanged': 'Then I have brought up a neck to a fair end' (*TA*, 4.4.46–8). See also 5.2.56–63 and note.

117–18 **I ... me** Morian's show of concern for his son comes late in the scene compared to that of Aaron who repeatedly pleads for his son's life and makes Lucius swear that the boy will live (*TA*, 5.1.49, 53–4, 67–8, 70, 78–85).

118–19 **has ... yet** Rather than emphasizing the child's innocence, Aaron insists on his royalty: 'Touch not the boy, he is of royal blood' (*TA*, 5.1.49).

119–20 **let ... hero** Aaron asks Lucius 'To save my boy, to nurse and bring him up' (*TA*, 5.1.84). Morian's desire for the child to have a military upbringing is in keeping with his earlier hopes for his son (6.1.103, 106–8).

121–2 **I ... battle** Lucius similarly promises that the boy shall live (*TA*, 5.1.60, 69, 86).

MORIAN   In all my days I never thought I would be
hanged in the end. Now, let us go, and hang me   125
quickly before I have time to think more about it.

Exeunt.

[7.2]   *Enter* EMPEROR.

EMPEROR   Such great bloodshed and so dangerous a war
have never been heard of. Rome has never stood in
such fear and peril before. Vespasianus has devastated
the city so violently and ravaged the surrounding
lands so cruelly that it moves one to pity. We have   5
fought four battles with him, but he has won them all
and slaughtered a great host of people. He fights so
fiercely that no-one comes near him in battle, all flee
before him. Yesterday, he took the whole imperial
palace in defiance of me. Yes, all my troops have   10
become so fearful that they refuse to go out against
him, saying they witness daily that all who venture

124–6 **In ... it** has no equivalent in *TA*.
Since Aaron is gagged following 5.1.151,
he is unable to speak at the end of the
scene.

7.2 is not in *TA*, where the action moves from
Lucius and Aaron straight to Tamora's
visit to Titus with her sons (5.2). This
brief scene confirms that Vespasianus is
ravaging the empire (see 7.1.1–9) and sets
up the next scene by mentioning the disguises worn by Aetiopissa and her sons.

5–7 **We ... people** In *TA*, Lucius does not
attack Rome before he is invited for a
parley (5.1.156–9).

9–10 **he ... me** ('Mein Keyserlichen Pallast
hat er gestriges Tages mir zu trotze voller
Flenten geschlossen') The German passage is probably corrupt. Fredén (370–1)
and Marti (389) conjecture that 'Flenten'

refers to the arrows of *TA*, 4.3, and propose
that 'geschlossen' is a printer's error for
'geschossen' (i.e., shot). Yet 'Flinte'
('shotgun') was not in use before the
second half of the seventeenth century
(Grimm), and 'Flenten' has no separate
entry in Grimm. Brauneck and Noe conjecture that it means 'Klagen' (lament, complaint). The Emperor's report of the attack
fulfils Vespasianus' earlier promise in
4.3.41–5. It is not clear where the present
scene takes place, since the Emperor may
have been forced to flee the palace either
before or during the attack.

10–12 **all ... him** implies that the troops are
otherwise loyal, which is significantly
different from Saturninus' fears that 'the
citizens favour Lucius / And will revolt
from me to succour him' (*TA*, 4.4.78–9).

7.2] *this edn; not in 1620*

out against the enemy never return. My heart is so
alarmed that I do not know what to do, for my power
diminishes day by day, and the enemy grows stronger.   15
So we shall no longer be able to resist his forces
unless we weaken him with cunning and treachery,
and unless he is deceived by my Empress, who,
together with her sons, is disguising herself. Even
now they are gone; may the gods favour them and   20
give them grace! I shall leave and eagerly wait to hear
what they accomplish and bring about.

Exit.

[7.3]   *Enter* AETIOPISSA, *with her two sons,* SAPHONUS
and HELICATES, *in disguise.*

AETIOPISSA   Dearest sons, now no-one will know us, for
we are well disguised. But hear me, and note what
you are to do with Tito Andronico. Lend careful
attention to the cunning stratagems he will use in

17–19 **weaken . . . sons** In *TA*, Tamora states,
'Now will I to that old Andronicus, / And
temper him with all the art I have, / To
pluck proud Lucius from the warlike
Goths. / And now, sweet emperor, be
blithe again / And bury all thy fear in my
devices' (4.4.107–11). The wording in *Tito*
leaves the exact nature of the plan unclear.
7.3 corresponds largely to 5.2 in *TA*, but the
scene is condensed and no information is
provided about the types of disguise worn
by Aetiopissa and her sons. Tito readily
welcomes Aetiopissa's sons (21–3),
without the extended dialogue between
Titus and Tamora in *TA* (5.2.9–69).
Andronica is not present when Tito kills
her attackers, unlike Lavinia, who is
onstage during Titus' long speech to the
brothers (5.2.166–205), and collects their

blood in a receptacle. In *Titus und Tomyris*,
Titus' daughter is similarly uninvolved in
the slaughter of her attackers, whereas in
Aran en Titus, Titus orders her to bite out
Quiro's heart (Buitendijk, ll. 1896–906).
2–3 **we . . . Andronico** Cf. Tamora: 'Thus, in
this strange and sad habiliment, / I will
encounter with Andronicus, / And say I
am Revenge, sent from below / To join
with him and right his heinous wrongs'
(*TA*, 5.2.1–4). There is no explicit indication in *Tito* that Aetiopissa disguises herself as Revenge.
3–6 **Lend . . . guard** Whereas Aetiopissa
plans to have her sons gather intelligence
about the Andronici's military strategies,
Tamora intends to busy Titus and Lucius
so that their Goth army may be disbanded
in the meantime (*TA*, 5.2.75–9).

7.3] *this edn; not in 1620*

battle to overthrow the Emperor, so that we can   5
recognise them at once, and be on our guard. So if you
see that he continues to rage and ravage, and that this
cruel bloodshed against us does not stop, contrive to
murder secretly Tito and his valiant son, Vespasianus,
so that this perilous war can end in victory. Follow me   10
now, we will go to his palace at once.

They go to the palace. Aetiopissa calls to old Tito.

Holla! Holla, good friend Tito Andronico, come down
to me.

[*Enter* TITO *above.*] *He looks down.*

TITO   Who are you that call on me like this?
AETIOPISSA   Old Tito Andronico, we are your good   15
friends, and the gods have sent me to you with these

8–10 **contrive . . . victory** This suggestion is
not made in *TA*. Marti (390) argues that
this is the only point where the German
play dramatizes motivation with greater
clarity than the English version.

11 **his palace** In *TA*, Tamora and her sons
visit Titus 'at his study' (5.2.5).

11 SD In *TA*, Tamora and her sons '*knock,
and* TITUS . . . *opens his study door*' (5.2.8
SD). Editors since Capell (1767–8) usually indicate that Titus appears 'above', as
implied in Tamora's later request for Titus
to come down (5.2.33, 43).

13 SD The use of a space '*above*' is rare in
the German plays of the English comedians. Of those in the 1620 *Engelische
Comedien vnd Tragedien, Fortunato* and
A King's Son of England perhaps make
use of it, but only *Tito* clearly does,
whereas the other plays do not (Kaulfuss-
Diesch, 66–7, 69, 74, 76).

15–20 Since Aetiopissa's plan is to deliver her
sons to Titus, it is fitting that she includes
them in the introduction, unlike Tamora,

who introduces herself as someone who
would like to speak with Titus (5.2.16), then
presents herself as Revenge (5.2.30–40),
and only introduces her sons as Rape and
Murder when prompted by Titus (5.2.45–
64). Aetiopissa identifies her children as
Tito's 'good friends' but does not comment
on their disguise. Marti (390) notes that
'good friends' may refer to the Eumenides
in Greek mythology, whose name literally
(and ironically) meant 'the kindly ones'. In
Aran en Titus, Thamera introduces herself
as Vengeance ('Wraakzucht'; l. 1781);
the 1656 programme simply states that
Thamera and her sons disguise themselves
(4.3 and 4.4); in *Titus und Tomyris*, the
Empress disguises herself as Justice,
accompanied by Revenge and Mercy (sig.
L1v); and the 1699 programme notes that
Thamera and her sons disguise themselves
as ghosts (Cohn, 'Breslau', 281).

16 **gods . . . me** is not in *TA*. In her disguise as
Revenge, Tamora claims that she has been
'sent from th'infernal kingdom' (5.2.30).

13 SD *Enter . . . above*] *this edn*; Titus siehet von oben hinunter *1620*

fellows so that I may deliver them to you, for they
were ordained by the gods to help you with good
counsel in these wars, to ensure that the enemy may
be speedily overthrown.   20

TITO   O, they shall be most welcome, and be held in
great honour. I shall come down to you now to receive
them with pleasure.

                              He goes down, [exit].

AETIOPISSA   Now, my hearts, I have presented you to
him, farewell. I shall go now.   *Exit.*   25

               Enter TITO ANDRONICO, *below.*

TITO   Tell me, where is the third?
HELICATES   She left after presenting us to you.
TITO   Yes, indeed, you shall be the most welcome guests
I ever had. – Holla, soldiers, come here, quick!

               Enter two soldiers.

Come here and lay hold on them both, steady and   30
fast. – Now, you cursed and murderous villains, do
you think I have lost my senses and cannot recognize
you?

---

17   **deliver them** Tamora does not intend to
leave her sons with Titus: 'Now will I
hence about my business, / And take my
ministers along with me' (*TA*, 5.2.132–3);
she only lets them stay after Titus
demands it (*TA*, 5.2.134).

21   **they ... welcome** Titus is less welcoming
to his visitors (*TA*, 5.2.17–19) and first
refuses to go down to Tamora: 'Do me
some service ere I come to thee' (*TA*,
5.2.44).

22–3   **I ... pleasure** corresponds to Titus' 'O
sweet Revenge, now do I come to thee'

(*TA*, 5.2.67) and 'Welcome, dread Fury,
to my woeful house; / Rapine and Murder,
you are welcome too' (*TA*, 5.2.82–3).

24–5   **Now ... now** In *TA*, Tamora remains
onstage for some time after Titus has come
down and confers with her sons before
bidding Titus farewell (5.2.137–47).

29   **Holla, soldiers** Titus calls Publius, Caius
and Valentine, kinsmen of the Andronici
(*TA*, 5.2.151).

33   SD There is no equivalent SD in *TA*, and
it is not clear whether masks are worn by
the brothers.

23   SD *exit*] *this edn; not in 1620*

He takes the masks from their faces.

Are you not the Empress' sons? And do you not seek
to take my life with treachery? Yet now I have means   35
to take my revenge. – One of you, bring me a sharp
knife and a butcher's apron at once.

                   [Exit first soldier.]
Yes, now I have thought up a secret stratagem
whereby I shall ensnare all my enemies and satisfy
my rage on you.   40

*Enter [first soldier], bringing a sharp knife and a
butcher's apron. Tito puts on the apron,
as if he would slaughter them.*

Go and get a vessel, too.

                   [Exit first soldier.]
[to second soldier] And you, come here with that
murderer and hold his throat here, so that I may cut it.

      [Enter first soldier,] bringing a vessel.

– And you, come here with your bowl, hold it under
his throat and catch all the blood in it.   45

36–7 **bring ... apron** In *TA*, Titus fetches the knife himself and does not call for an apron. He may wear an apron only in the final scene, when he enters '*like a cook*' (5.3.25.2).

41 **Go ... vessel** In *TA*, Lavinia enters 'with a basin' (5.2.165.2).

43 **hold ... here** Titus asks the bound brothers to 'prepare your throats' (*TA*, 5.2.196).

44–5 **come ... in it** Titus has Lavinia hold the basin (*TA*, 5.2.182–3, 196–7), which establishes a link between the blood lost by the ravished and mutilated Lavinia

earlier in the play and the blood that she collects from her attackers, a link that is missing from *Tito*.

45 SD–46 SD These SDs are considerably more detailed than in *TA*: '*He cuts their throats*' (5.2.203 SD).

45 SD *He ... stopped* Whereas in *Tito*, the brothers' mouths are stopped as a reaction to their attempts to speak shortly before they are killed, in *TA*, once the brothers have been gagged, Titus makes them listen to a lengthy speech about their crimes (5.2.167–205).

37 SD] *this edn; not in 1620*   40 SD1 *first soldier*] Brennecke (a soldier); einer *1620*   41 SD *Brennecke* (The soldier goes); *not in 1620*   42 SD] *this edn; not in 1620*   43 SD *Enter first soldier*] *this edn*; Bringt Gefäß *1620*

Helicates is first held down. He tries to speak, but his
mouth is stopped. Tito cuts his throat. The blood
runs into the bowl. Once the blood has drained,
they lay him on the floor, dead.

– Now, the next fellow, bring him too.

Holds his throat in the same way. Saphonus violently
attempts to resist death and tries to speak, but they
stop his mouth. Tito cuts his throat, and the blood is
collected; then they lay him on the floor, dead.

Now I have cut their throats. What I have slaughtered
I shall cook myself. I shall mince these heads and
bake them into pies, and then invite their mother and
the Emperor. A messenger of peace shall be sent to   50
the Emperor at once. – But you, make haste and
bring the bodies to me in the kitchen.

                             Exeunt with the dead bodies.

8.[1]   *Enter* EMPEROR *and* AETIOPISSA.

EMPEROR   Lovely Empress, pray tell me, was Tito
   Andronico pleased with your sons when you presented
   them as being sent to him by the gods?
AETIOPISSA   Gracious lord and Emperor, old Tito was
   delighted; he came down to them immediately.   5

47–50 **What ... Emperor** is a condensed
version of *TA*, 5.2.186–205. Unlike Tito,
Titus shares his plan with his captives
before he kills them.

48–9 **mince ... pies** Titus describes this
process twice in *TA*, at 5.2.186–9 and
5.2.197–200.

49–50 **invite ... Emperor** In *TA*, the disguised Tamora proposes earlier in the
scene that Titus invite Lucius to a banquet
while she, as Revenge, will bring all of

Titus' enemies so that revenge may be
taken (5.2.111–19).

8.1 This scene, which follows directly from
7.3, has no equivalent in *TA*: Tamora
plans the banquet even before Titus kills
Chiron and Demetrius (4.4.99–102;
5.1.156–61), so it is not necessary for
Titus to send an invitation. The scene
dramatizes the Emperor and Aetiopissa's
misplaced joy about the apparent success
of the disguise scheme.

8.1] Actus Octavus *1620*

Meanwhile I departed, trusting that my sons would be held in great honour by him, and that he would follow all their advice. But here comes a messenger; what good news does he bring us?

Enter MESSENGER, *to the Emperor.*

MESSENGER   Fortune, health, and all prosperity to your   10
imperial majesty, almighty and invincible Emperor of
Rome. I am a messenger sent from my gracious lord,
Tito Andronico, to your imperial majesty to proclaim
peace and amity. He will never take arms against your
majesty again, but wishes to make a peaceful alliance   15
with your majesty. Likewise, he requests your majesty
and your fair Empress to come to a banquet, so that
peace and unity may be established all the better.

EMPEROR   The message you deliver brings me great
pleasure, and it cheers my heart that old Tito   20
Andronico desires to make peace with me. Tell him
this from me: I am very pleased and shall immediately
come in person with my Empress.

MESSENGER   Almighty Emperor, I shall deliver this
message faithfully.   *Exit.*   25

AETIOPISSA   It is quite certain, gracious lord and
Emperor, that my two sons have advised this peace
and old Tito has followed their suggestions.

6–7 **trusting ... honour** echoes the sons' reflection upon their newfound position at the Roman court in 2.1.18–29.

10–18 **Fortune ... better** Tito's proclamation of peace and his invitation of the Emperor and Aetiopissa to the banquet mean that he has complete control over the circumstances of his revenge. This is unlike *TA*, where Tamora first has Saturninus invite Lucius to a parley at his father's house (4.4.99–102) and then, in disguise, effectively invites herself to the banquet (5.2.111–19). Tito seems to offer unconditional peace; the message sent to Lucius does not (5.1.159–61).

19–23 **The ... Empress** While their belief in Titus' 'lunacy' (*TA*, 5.2.70) explains why Saturninus and Tamora go to Titus' banquet, the Emperor's acceptance of the invitation seems comparatively simplistic and naive.

EMPEROR   If they have arranged this for me, I promise
to advance them to the highest honours. But, lovely   30
Empress, let us no longer delay but go to Tito
Andronico at once.   [*Exeunt.*]

[8.2]   *Music. Enter servants who dress a table and
bring out the pies. Not long thereafter, enter*
TITO ANDRONICO *wearing the blood-stained
apron, with a knife in his hand. After him, enter*
EMPEROR *and* AETIOPISSA, *followed by*
ANDRONICA, VESPASIANUS *and* VICTORIADES.

TITO   Almighty Emperor and fair Empress, my greatest
thanks for accepting my invitation. Please, your

8.2 chiefly corresponds to *TA* 5.3.26–65.
Vespasianus has presumably been in
Rome for some time, and peace has
already been established through Tito's
message in the previous scene, so there is
no need for an equivalent of the opening
part of the scene in *TA* (5.3.1–25). *Tito*
dramatizes the banquet as a private,
domestic event and swiftly concludes
after the killings, unlike *TA*, where Lucius
and Marcus, after Saturninus has been
killed (5.3.65 SD), withdraw to a space
above, protected by the Goths, from
where they justify their deeds to the
Romans, who then proclaim Lucius
emperor (5.3.66–147). Nor does *Tito*
have an equivalent of the Andronici's
mourning of dead Titus (*TA*, 5.3.148–74),
or of Aaron's return onstage '*under
guard*' (*TA*, 5.3.174.1–89).

0.1 ***Music*** The play's other SDs that call for
offstage music or sound effects designate
specific instruments, horns, trumpets and
drums (see 3.2.0.1–2 and note). At the
equivalent moment in *TA*, there are
'*Trumpets sounding*' (5.3.25.1).

0.1–4 ***Enter ... hand*** *TA* has Titus set the

dishes on the table himself (5.3.25.2).

0.3–4 ***wearing ... hand*** Tito put on the apron
at 7.3.40.2, before murdering Saphonus
and Helicates. In *TA*, Titus enters '*like a
cook*' (5.3.25.2–3). The '*knife*' may be the
same as the '*sharp knife*' (7.3.40.1) with
which Tito cut the throats of Saphonus
and Helicates. No knife is mentioned in
the equivalent SD in *TA* (5.3.25).

0.6 **ANDRONICA** In *TA*, Lavinia wears '*a veil
over her face*' (5.3.25.3), which Titus presumably removes at 5.3.44–5. There is no
evidence in *Tito*'s SDs to suggest that
Andronica is also veiled.

1–23 The issue of sitting down occupies
much of the beginning of the scene. Like
the opening of the Banquet Scene in *Mac*
(3.4), it follows a hierarchical order, first
the Emperor and Aetiopissa (2–4), then
Victoriades (8 SD) and Vespasianus (18
SD), the last of these only after his father
asks him to do so. Tito is asked to sit
down (by the Emperor) or to let his
daughter sit down (by Aetiopissa) but
refuses. *TA* does not foreground the
action of sitting down, and Ard³ simply
has an added SD: '*They sit*' (5.3.25.1).

32 SD] *this edn; not in 1620*   8.2] *this edn; not in 1620*

majesty, sit with the Empress, and help yourselves to
my offerings.

EMPEROR   My good friend, Tito Andronico, I am delighted   5
that this bloody, perilous war has come to an end and
that we have arrived at peace and harmony.

He goes to sit at the head of the table; Aetiopissa sits
next to him.

But tell me, why do you wear this apron?

Victoriades sits down.

TITO   Almighty Emperor, I myself have been the cook
and have made these pies for your majesty.   10

EMPEROR   Now, this is very good. I say, Tito, come with
your son and sit beside us.

TITO   No, almighty Emperor, I will not sit down now, but
rather wait upon your majesty. – But you, dearest
son Vespasianus, go and sit, and keep the Emperor   15
company.

VESPASIANUS   Yes, dearest father, I am always willing to
obey your command.

He sits.

AETIOPISSA   Dear Tito Andronico, please, let your
daughter Andronica also sit.   20

5–7 **I ... harmony** is not in *TA*, where
Lucius and Saturninus have a hostile
exchange and Marcus encourages them to
make peace at the banquet (5.3.17–24).

8   Saturninus similarly asks, 'Why art thou
thus attired . . .?' (*TA*, 5.3.30).

9–10 **I . . . majesty** In *TA*, Titus does not state
that he has baked the pies himself.

19–22 **let ... you** Aetiopissa is aware of

Andronica's presence, and it is unclear
whether the Empress pretends not to
know about her mutilation, or whether its
fact is known but Aetiopissa assumes that
its perpetrators have remained unidentified. In *TA*, Tamora is presumably unaware of Lavinia's presence until Titus
unveils her immediately before killing
her (5.3.44–6).

TITO No, fair Empress, I cannot do that; she must stand
and wait upon you. I beg your majesty, eat and be
merry.

> *He goes to the pies, cuts portions for the*
> *Emperor and Aetiopissa, but Vespasianus eats*
> *nothing. Old Tito walks sorrowfully*
> *about the table.*

AETIOPISSA Truly, in all my life I have never eaten better
pies than these. I cannot imagine how they have been   25
prepared or what is baked inside them.
TITO O lovely Empress, please eat more of them if they
are to your liking. [*aside*] I'll tell the Empress later
what they are made of.

> *He cuts another piece and places it*
> *before Aetiopissa.*

AETIOPISSA But please tell me, my dear Tito Andronico,   30
why are you so melancholy and do not eat?

23 SD *He ... Aetiopissa* In *TA*, Titus
'*plac[es] the dishes*' (5.3.25.2) as soon as
he has entered, and the business of cutting
the pie is not mentioned in *TA*'s SDs.
23 SD–29 SD In keeping with its emphasis
on physical action and spectacle, *Tito*
emphasizes the point at which Tito's
Thyestean revenge succeeds. In *TA*,
Tamora does not comment upon the pie,
and it is only after killing his daughter
that Titus mentions that Tamora 'daintily
hath fed' on the pie (5.3.60).
28–29 **I'll ... of** ('worvon er aber gemachet,
wil ich der Keyserinnen darnach

28 SD] *this edn; not in 1620*

erzehlen') Brennecke alters 'Empress' to
'you', but the sentence is probably an
aside.
30–8 **But ... afflicted** In *TA* the dialogue
leading up to Titus' killing of his daughter
is between Titus and Saturninus. It is initiated by Titus and is about the legendary
slaying of Virginia by her father (5.3.35–
42), whereas in *Tito*, it is between Tito
and Aetiopissa, is initiated by Aetiopissa
and deals with the reason for Tito's grief.
As with Ovid's tale of Philomel, the reference to classical literature is thus absent
from *Tito*.

TITO   O lovely Empress, eat your fill. But I am too full of
        grief for it. Yes, the most distressed in all the world! I
        do not know what I may do in my anguish.

AETIOPISSA   I ask you, tell me, why are you so sad, what   35
        has driven you to such grief?

Tito goes to Andronica.

TITO   Empress, it is for this wretched creature, for my
        dearest daughter, that I am so sorely afflicted. [*to
        Andronica*] But now it is impossible for me to see you
        so wretched before me; my heart wants to burst within   40
        me! Take this.

*Thrusts his knife into her heart. She falls to
the ground, dead.*

EMPEROR   Alas, alas, Tito Andronico, have you lost your
        wits? Why do you murder your own flesh and blood?
        Alas, this pitiful creature.

TITO   Yes, Emperor, I suffered the greatest pain and   45
        infernal anguish because of her. But hear what I say,
        your cursed and haughty Empress is the sole cause,
        for she made her sons hew off the hands and cut out

32 **eat ... fill** In *TA*, it is not until after Titus'
    killing of Lavinia that Titus asks
    Saturninus, 'Will't please you eat? Will't
    please your highness feed?' (5.3.53).

39–41 **it ... me!** In *TA* there is a similar
    emphasis on the tremendous pain that
    Lavinia's condition causes Titus, but he
    identifies shame as the principal motive
    for her murder: 'Die, die, Lavinia, and thy
    shame with thee, / And with thy shame
    thy father's sorrow die' (5.3.45–6).

40 **heart ... burst** See note at 3.3.41.

43 **Why ... blood?** At the equivalent
    moment in *TA* this question is posed

twice, first by Saturninus ('What hast thou
done, unnatural and unkind?', 5.3.47) and
then by Tamora ('Why hast thou slain
thine only daughter thus?', 5.3.54).

45–61 The order of actions and speeches cor-
    responds to that in *TA*, with the exception
    of Aetiopissa's exclamation at l. 54,
    which has no equivalent in *TA*.

47–9 **your ... daughter** In *TA*, Titus holds
    the Empress' sons responsible: ''twas
    Chiron and Demetrius: / They ravished
    her and cut away her tongue, / And they,
    'twas they, that did her all this wrong'
    (5.3.55–7).

38–9 SD] *this edn; not in 1620*

the tongue of my unfortunate daughter. – But know,
cursed Empress, even now you have feasted on your   50
sons' heads, which I baked in the pies.

Aetiopissa shakes and trembles violently in fright.

Now you shall never again afflict any other man as
you have afflicted me. Take this for it!

> *He attacks her with his knife and stabs her at*
> *the table beside the Emperor.*

[AETIOPISSA]   O, murder, alas!

> *Falls to the ground, dead.*

EMPEROR   Alas, shall I suffer such a murder? Impossible!   55

> *Draws his sword, stabs Tito Andronico, who falls*
> *dead to the ground in front of the table. Vespasianus*
> *leaps over the table at the Emperor.*

VESPASIANUS   Emperor, now you must die, even if you
had a thousand lives.

> *He stabs the Emperor, who falls to the ground dead.*

50–1 **you . . . heads** Titus tells Tamora that
her sons have been 'both baked in this
pie' (*TA*, 5.3.59) but only Tito singles out
the 'sons' heads'.

51 SD There is no equivalent SD in *TA* (see
Introduction, p. 5).

52–3 **Now . . . me** In *TA*, Titus makes no
equivalent comment to Tamora before
stabbing her (5.3.62).

53 SD *TA*'s SD is less detailed: '*He stabs the
Empress*' (5.3.62 SD). Tito's knife ties
together the key actions in this scene:
after entering with it '*in his hand*' (0.4),
he '*cuts*' the pie with it (23.1, 29.1),
'*Thrusts*' it into his daughter's '*heart*'

(41.1) and here '*stabs*' Aetiopissa with it.

54 SP The SP is missing in *1620* and *1624*;
we follow Lippner in assigning the speech
to Aetiopissa. See 3.3.67 SP and note.

54 **murder** ('mordio') See 3.3.67 and note.

55 SD Ravenscroft ('*Emp. stabs* Titus') and
Rowe ('*He stabs* Titus') are the first ones
to add a SD at the equivalent point in *TA*,
but neither is as detailed as *Tito*'s.

56–7 Saturninus likewise points out that his
killing is retaliatory: 'Die, frantic wretch,
for this accursed deed' (*TA*, 5.3.63).

57 SD There is no equivalent SD in the early
quarto and Folio texts of *TA*; Ravenscroft
added 'Lucius *stabs the* Emperour'.

54 SP] *Cohn* (EMPRESS); *not in 1620*

VICTORIADES   Alas, alas, this wretched and despicable
creature. Alas, I will never find peace. – Now,
Vespasianus, the empire belongs to you. Set the crown   60
on your head, and rule in peace.

VESPASIANUS   O gracious lord uncle, how can I rule the
empire? My heart is ready to burst at this tragedy, the
most pitiful that has ever been heard of. I do not know
what to do in my wretchedness, so bear the imperial   65
crown upon your head, for your claim to it is the
strongest.

VICTORIADES   O, no. I have no wish to wear it. You are
the rightful heir to it, and your brave deeds have won
you much renown throughout the world; you have no   70
equal. And you know that the empire faces many
troubles and enemies, and lacks a strong ruler. So do
not refuse, accept the imperial seat, make a universal
peace, and rule in harmony and joy.

VESPASIANUS   Then let us go in, so that I may receive the   75
crown in the presence of all, though I shall never be
happy again.   [*Exeunt.*]

58–9 **this ... creature** It is unclear whether
Victoriades is referring to the Emperor or
to Aetiopissa.

59–77 **Now ... again** The ending in *Tito* is
very brief by comparison with the pro-
tracted ending of *TA* (5.3.66–199). See
Introduction, pp. 17–18. *Tito*'s final
moments are reminiscent of the conclusion
of *Lear* (5.3.318–25): the imperial crown
is offered to two characters; the older one
declines and the younger accepts.

68 **I ... it** In his unwillingness to accept the
crown, Victoriades resembles his brother,
Tito, in the play's opening scene.

69 **rightful heir** In Act 1, Rome is an elec-

tive monarchy, whereas only Vespasianus
and Victoriades are involved in choosing
the new emperor at the play's close. In
TA, the election of Lucius is legitimized
by the 'common voice' (5.3.139), and
'ALL ROMANS' (5.3.145) acclaim him as
their new emperor.

71–4 **And ... joy** Similar ideas are expressed
by Marcus, 'O let me teach you how to
knit again / This scattered corn into one
mutual sheaf, / These broken limbs again
into one body' (*TA*, 5.3.69–71), and
Lucius, 'May I govern so / To heal
Rome's harms and wipe away her woe'
(*TA*, 5.3.146–7).

77 SD] *not in 1620*

KUNST ÜBER ALLE KÜNSTE, EIN BÖS WEIB GUT ZU MACHEN

IN ENGLISH TRANSLATION

AN ART BEYOND ALL ARTS,
TO MAKE A BAD WIFE GOOD

LIST OF ROLES

PATIENT JOB	*in the trousers of pious Socrates. Speaks the prologue.*
THEOBALD	*of Grifflingen, gentleman*
CATHARINA	*Hurlyburly, [his older daughter]*
SABINA	*Sweetmouth, [his younger daughter]* 5
VEIT	*Carver, [Theobald's] servant*
SYBILLA	*Fleafur, maid [to Catharina]*
HARDMAN	*Madfeather, gentleman, heir and owner of Whirlwind Heights, Catharina's suitor*
Ludolf WORMFIRE	*[his] servant* 10
SEBASTIAN	*of Inability, gentleman, [suitor to Sabina]*
ALFONS	*of Nistlingen, gentleman, disguised as musician, [suitor to Sabina]*
ADRIAN	*of Liebenthal, the elder, gentleman*
HILARIUS	*of Liebenthal, the younger, gentleman,* 15 *suitor to Sabina, disguised as Mr Johannes*
FELIX	*Muchwind, [Hilarius'] servant, acting as [Hilarius of] Liebenthal, the younger*
FABIAN	*Apetail, [Hilarius'] servant* 20
Mrs EULALIA	*of Hohunk Wittib, Mr Alfons' confidante*
Magister BLASIUS	*Noseyparker, Rector paganus, acting as [Adrian of] Liebenthal, the elder*
Master FRITZ	*Thimble of Scratch-Hill, artful tailor*
MATZ	*Trumper, well-established oven-raker and* 25 *firekeeper*
Three SERVANTS	*who only speak one word [called] Lazypaunch, Alwayswet, and Noosehalter*

LIST OF ROLES Headed 'Personen dieses Freuden-Spiels' ('The Persons of this Comedy') in D1 and D2, and reproduced here in identical order. In keeping with the play's relocation, *KK*'s names are Germanized where *TS* offers Italianate names. *KK* thus does not preserve *TS*'s names with the exception of Catharina, a German name that closely resembles Katherine/Katherina (both names are used of her in *TS*). Telling names (e.g., 'Hartman', 'Wurmbrand') have been translated (e.g., 'Hardman', 'Wormfire').

PATIENT JOB Character added by *KK*, perhaps as a replacement for *TS*'s Induction. Job is the protagonist of the eponymous book in the Old Testament, and is often referred to as an archetype of patience in the face of undeserved adversity. The German describes him as appearing 'in the trousers of pious Socrates' ('in des frommen Socratis Hosen'). Socrates, the ancient Greek philosopher, was famous for having a shrewish wife, Xanthippe; see Prologue, 12–13n.

THEOBALD of Grifflingen 'Baptista' in *TS*. The name may be derived from 'Grüfflingen' (a village at the Belgian–German border) or 'finger, pen' (Grimm, 'Griffling').

CATHARINA Hurlyburly 'Katherine'/ 'Katherina' in *TS*. The diminutive 'Trina' ('Trine') is used by Hardman during their first encounter in 2.1 as a means of belittling her. 'Trine' was a generic name for a woman of low rank, represented as common and stupid (see Grimm). The English equivalent scene (2.1) plays on 'Kate' and 'cates' (food, dainties, *OED* 1, 2). Catharina's epithet 'Hurlyburly' ('Hurleputz') only occurs in the List of Roles. 'Hurliburli' is a person who hurries around headlessly (Grimm). It may be derived from 'to roll' ('hurlen'). The second part of 'Hurleputz' may come from 'to tumble' ('purzeln') (Grimm). Similarly spelt words exist in French ('hurluberlu', a scatterbrained person) and English ('hurlyburly', commotion, *OED* 1.a). Their connection is unclear (see *OED*, etymology of 'hurlyburly').

SABINA Sweetmouth 'Bianca' in *TS*. An allusion to the classical myth of the rape of the Sabines may be implied. After declining to marry their daughters into the burgeoning Roman city, the Romans invite the Sabines to a supposedly peaceful festivity. They rob the unarmed Sabines of their unmarried women, a moment often represented in sculpture and painting. The women largely integrate into their new families, and make peace between their husbands and fathers after subsequent battles. The name here is presumably ironic, implying that she will be an obedient wife, while also gesturing towards the surreptitious marriage scheme in which she actually engages with Hilarius. For the classical myth, see Livy's *Ab urbe condita libri* 1,9–13. 'Sweetmouth' (in German the diminutive 'Süsmäulchen') only occurs in the List of Roles. The name has an ambiguous ring, referring both to a pet name like 'darling' and to a flatterer, who makes things sweet by talking (Grimm, 'süßmaul', 1).

VEIT Carver Servant to Theobald, a character with no direct equivalent in *TS*. 'Carver' translates the German 'Schnitzer'.

SYBILLA Fleafur Maid to Catharina, and lover and wife of Wormfire; there is no equivalent in *TS*. 'Old Sibylle' was a condescending expression for a woman (Grimm, 'Sibylle'). The name may contain an ironic allusion to the classical Sybils, female oracles in ancient Greece. There are several spelling variations of Sybilla's name in D1 and D2, including 'Sibilla' and 'Sibylla'. 'Fleafur', which translates the German 'Flöhpeltz', only appears in the List of Roles and may mockingly refer to a lack of cleanliness (Grimm, 'Pelz', 3, for human skin).

HARDMAN ... Heights 'Petruccio' in *TS*. 'Hardman' translates 'Hartman', while 'Madfeather' is a translation for 'Dollfeder', and 'of Whirlwind Heights' of 'Zum Würbelwind'. The only other two mentions of 'whirlwind' in the play in connection to Hardman are when Wormfire brags about his master's ability to tame Catharina at 1.3.124, and when Hardman introduces himself as 'Hardman Madfeather ... heir of Whirlwind Heights' (2.1.118–20).

Ludolf WORMFIRE 'Grumio' in *TS*. 'Wormfire' (in the German text 'Wurmbrand') is a general insult, perhaps alluding to an illness such as a rash (see Grimm, 'Wurmbrand'). It could also refer to one who will burn in hell, or indeed to the devil himself (Grimm, 'Höllenbrand'). The name 'Ludolf' only appears in the List of Roles.

SEBASTIAN of Inability 'Gremio' in *TS*. 'Inability' translates the German 'Unvermögen'. The character is reminiscent of the Pantaloon, a stock figure of the Italian *commedia dell'arte*, often a miserly old man who intends to marry a young woman.

ALFONS of Nistlingen 'Hortensio' in *TS*. 'Nistling' is a bird of prey caught in a nest, a young and inexperienced person (Grimm). As in 'Grifflingen', the suffix may indicate a place name. In 3.1, when Alfons is disguised as a musician, his SPs in D1 and D2 are 'Musicus' throughout, which contributes to the play's interest in being and seeming. Our edition standardizes the SPs.

ADRIAN of Liebenthal 'Vincentio' in *TS*. The last name could be roughly translated as 'love dale'.

HILARIUS of Liebenthal 'Lucentio' in *TS*. As a poetry tutor, Hilarius takes on the name of Johannes. D1 and D2 consistently call the disguised Hilarius Johannes in SDs and SPs, switching to Hilarius once he reassumes his real identity, thereby perpetuating the play's interest in being and seeming. Our edition standardizes the SPs.

FELIX Muchwind 'Tranio' in *TS*. 'Muchwind' is a translation of 'Vielwind', referring to a braggart (Grimm).

FABIAN Apetail 'Biondello' in *TS*. 'Apetail' is a translation of the German 'Affenschwantz'.

The word may contain a sexual allusion to an ape's penis or refer to the proverb 'to lead one on an ape's tail', i.e., to mock someone (Wander, 'Affenschwanz', 2).

EULALIA ... Wittib 'Widow' in *TS*. 'Eulalia' comes from the Greek and means 'the one that speaks well', a rare first name. 'Wittib' means 'widow', whereas the meaning or origin of 'Hohunk' is unclear. The List of Roles calls her Alfons' 'confidante' ('Vertraute'), though by 5.2, the only scene in which she appears, she is his wife.

BLASIUS Noseyparker a 'Merchant' in *TS*. The German second name reads 'Nasenweis', literally 'nose-wise', a conceited meddlesome person that seeks to put their nose into everything, here translated as 'Noseyparker' (Grimm, 'nasenweis'). The designation '*Rector paganus*', i.e. 'rustic rector', is not fully clarified by the play.

FRITZ ... Scratch-Hill The tailor in *KK* is a conflation of the 'Haberdasher' and the 'Tailor' in *TS*. The name is a translation of the German ('Fingerhut vom Kratzenberg'). Calling the tailor 'Thimble' makes fun of his profession and connotes something small enough in quantity to be placed in a thimble (Grimm, 'Fingerhut', 2).

MATZ Trumper 'Curtis' in *TS*. The meaning of 'Trumper' is unclear. Perhaps it refers to a 'drummer' or a 'trumpet player' (Grimm), or originates in 'to stomp' (Grimm, 'trumpeln'). The word 'oven-raker' is a literal translation of 'Ofenschürer' (not recorded in Grimm).

Three ... Noosehalter. 'Petruccio's Servants' in *TS*. In both plays, the servants are named, though not consistently either in the *dramatis personae* or in the play itself. The edition translates the German literally, including 'Faulwamst' ('Lazypaunch'), 'Immernaß' ('Alwayswet') and 'Schlingenstrick' ('Noosehalter').

AN ART BEYOND
ALL ARTS,
TO MAKE A BAD
WIFE GOOD

[Prologue]

[*Enter* PATIENT JOB.]

[PATIENT JOB]   *Multa tulit fecit que sudavit et alsit*, most
honoured audience, *multa tulit*, I say it again, the man
who has been oppressed by an evil, shrewish wife,
and who has been her poor patient martyr all day,
stung by her biting tongue, plagued by her murderous   5
mood, and often tortured by her untameable hands; at
night, when the cards lie still after many quarrels by
day, has this reward – that when the *vires corporis* has
been given to someone else – patience puts horns on
his head. Unfortunately, I have experienced a lot of   10
this, and more than a lot, I, patient Job who have

Prologue *KK* does not translate *TS*'s
induction, but has a similarly metatheatrical prologue, setting the play
within a context of patient men and
shrewish wives.

1   *Multa ... alsit* Latin, 'He has suffered
and achieved much, he has sweated and
frozen' (from Horace's *Ars Poetica*, l.
413). For Latin in *KK*, see Introduction,
pp. 119–21.

3   **shrewish** ('eyterbissigen', literally 'pus-
biting'). See 2.1.403–4 and note.

7–8 **when ... day** Proverbial. When a couple
quarrels during the day, they will reconcile at night, and lie quietly in bed, much
like playing cards that have been mixed
and distributed in a game, and afterwards
lie calmly next to each other in their box
(see Köhler, 214).

8   *vires corporis* Latin, bodily strength; presumably an allusion to sexual intercourse.

9–10 **horns ... head** horns are the proverbial attribute of the cuckold (see Grimm,
'Horn', 58).

Prologue 0 SD] *this edn*; Vorredner *D1, D2, Köhler*

247

always worn the trousers of pious Socrates. Rather
than being blessed, I have been tortured by a wife
who must have been made from a rib without the
addition of one ounce of flesh. Her stubborn, sullen   15
behaviour and her deliberate neglect bear ample
witness to the fact that she is one of the evil seven.
Whether the other six are still alive I do not know.
Would to God that in my time there had lived the
teacher of morals who will now appear; I would have   20
wanted to go to his school in order to learn how to
chase out madness from the obstinate brain of an evil
wife, or how to exorcize the devil's head which she
has put on, as she herself admits. You find yourselves
in happier times; you can learn from him, because he   25
will show you the best way to go about it. This is
especially useful for you young people who have
someone young to handle and shape, and are not
trying to tame some evil old dog. Understand that art
well, and thank me for the good advice and for   30
reminding you of it. But if there is anyone who cannot
conceive of such an art or cannot apply it, let him
come, and be instructed in patience by me, who have
as my symbol *perfer perpatienda.*

12–13 **Socrates ... wife** Xanthippe, the wife
of the ancient Greek philosopher
Socrates, was believed to have been
shrewish and cantankerous, giving rise
to the stereotype of the recalcitrant wife.
Petruccio uses Xanthippe for comparison with Katherina (*TS*, 1.2.70) in a passage which *KK* omits.

14 **made ... rib** According to Genesis 2.22,
Eve was created from Adam's rib.

17 **evil seven** Perhaps a reference to a satiric
poem about seven evil female characters by
Joachim Rachel, 'Das Poetische Frauen-
Zimmer oder Böse Sieben' (1664; 'The
Poetic Woman, or the Evil Seven'), published
in Rachel's *Teutsche Satyrische Gedichte*
(Frankfurt, 1664; VD17 23:244496T).

29 **art** the art of wife-taming.

34 ***perfer perpatienda*** Latin, you shall
suffer what is to be suffered.

1.[1]   *Enter* THEOBALD, CATHARINA, SEBASTIAN,
                     ALFONS *and* VEIT.

THEOBALD   To speak frankly with you, my lord, it is to
no avail that you continue to make your suit to me. I
am determined not to make my younger daughter's
dowry known before the elder is married. Should any
of you be interested in the latter, she shall not be   5
denied you, for I know of your good name as well as
of your honourable character and wealth.

SEBASTIAN   My good Sir Theobald, may I give you great
thanks for such an offer. You know well, however,
that my waning forces would be a little too weak to   10
endure her untamed nature. Sir Alfons is younger and
stronger, she will not be unsuitable for him.

1.1 is presumably set in front of Theobald's
house, although no location is specified.
The scene is divided into four parts, a
long one followed by three shorter: 1–76
(to Theobald's exit), 77–103 (to
Catharina's exit), 104–40 (to Veit's exit)
and 141–77 (Sebastian and Alfons
alone). The first part starts by following
TS quite closely (1–35; *TS* 1.1.48–66) but
then diverges. The second part is largely
independent of *TS*: in Shakespeare,
Katherina exits right after Baptista does
(1.1.101–4), whereas Catharina remains
onstage longer, engaging in an aggressive
verbal give and take with Sebastian and
Alfons. The third part, in which Sebastian
and Alfons discuss with Veit Catharina's
shrewishness and Sabina's desirability,
has no equivalent in *TS*. The fourth part,
except for the first speech, again follows
TS quite closely (153–77; *TS* 1.1.112–
44). *TS*'s opening scene is framed by two
passages with Lucentio and Tranio
(1.1.1–47, 145–246, joined by Biondelio

from 1.1.220), who remain onstage,
unnoticed by the other characters for the
rest of the scene. These two passages
have no equivalent in *KK*.

0   SD *TS*'s Bianca also enters at this point,
whereas *KK*'s Sabina does not appear
until 2.1. In *TS*, Lucentio and Tranio
remain onstage; they '*stand by*' (1.1.47.3).

1   **you, my lord** It is unclear to which of the
two suitors Theobald's first sentence is
addressed; Baptista speaks to both
'Gentlemen' (*TS*, 1.1.48).

5–6 **she ... you** In *TS*, Baptista encourages
the two suitors to 'court' (1.1.54)
Katherina, but only Theobald promises
that his daughter shall not be denied
them.

8–11 **My ... nature.** The politeness and
indirection of Sebastian's response to
Theobald's offer contrasts with the harsh
directness of Gremio's 'To cart her
rather. She's too rough for me' (*TS*,
1.1.55) in response to Baptista's invitation to court Katherina.

1.[1]] *this edn*; Erste Handlung. *D1, D2, Köhler*

ALFONS   Please, sir, mind your own business. I am not
your ward, and I am no longer a minor.

CATHARINA   Father, I am amazed at your gross negligence,   15
that you will offer me to these fools with such disdain.

VEIT *(aside)*   What the merchant can't sell needs a
bargain like this.

ALFONS   As for us, the maid is mistaken: we are not such
fools as to take pains over her, and, indeed, I would   20
think twice before buying such stuff as a wife. Though
the colour may be good, the worth is small.

CATHARINA   My high-ranked lord has no reason to run
away from someone who is not in the least eager to
follow him. Indeed, I have no intention to be bound   25
with you. But if I were, my greatest care would be to
comb your bristles with a three-legged stool, to ruffle
your rabbit-beard with the fire tongs, to die your face
scarlet with a pan, and to show you around to everyone
as the fool you are.   30

VEIT *[aside]*   Now she's armed, now blows will rain
down! Strike him, strike him!

15–16 *TS*'s question, 'sir, is it your will / To
make a stale of me amongst these mates?'
(1.1.57–8), becomes an accusatory statement in *KK*. Katharina's 'sir' (1.1.57) suggests a politely distant relationship to
Baptista, whereas Catharina's 'Father'
renders her accusation all the more striking.

19–22 **we ... small**. The beginning of the
speech corresponds to Hortensio's (*TS*,
1.1.59–60), but *KK* adds Alfons' description of Catharina as goods on the marriage market.

21–2 **Though ... small**. Alfons presumably
means that although Catharina has
beauty (the 'colour'), her behaviour
reduces her worth.

23–5 **My ... him**. *KK* adapts *TS* ('I'faith, sir,
you shall never need to fear', 1.1.61) but
adds an imaginative insult, 'Mein hoch-

geöhrter Herr' ('My high-ranked lord'),
which puns on 'highly honoured' ('hoch
geehrt') and 'having big ears' ('hoch
geöhrt'), like a donkey (see Grimm,
'geöhrt').

25–30 **Indeed ... are.** *KK* is close to *TS*
(1.1.62–5) but adds to the triplet of insults
a fourth, threatening to 'ruffle [Alfons']
rabbit-beard with the fire tongs' (27–8).
For another 'rabbit' insult, see 1.3.182.

31–2 Added by *KK*. Veit relishes the
increasing tension, characterizing
Catharina as being, literally, 'in the
armour' ('im Harnisch') like a soldier.
He expects yet more volleys of insults
from her, which follow promptly. For our
editorial decision to consider this and
other speeches of his as asides, see
Introduction, p. 110.

ALFONS   Her maidenly modesty will be above such
trouble. I will always include her in the litany. May
the good Lord protect us from such evil.   35

SEBASTIAN   Amen.

CATHARINA   You grey-bearded ass, you'd better stay at
home with your poor servants; you couldn't tease
a dog out from under the oven. You're a lame old
horse, you can do nothing but neigh. A fine Sir   40
Sebastian, indeed! Touching her with his little stick.
Why, you may believe the girls gaze greedily at
you, but you will have to run after them. My sister
will certainly leave 'it' open for you, you know
where.   45

SEBASTIAN   Your sister has better virtues making her
lovelier than you. Sir Theobald would be wise to
bring her out sooner, since he is acquiring a bad name
because of your lack of virtue.

CATHARINA   Your wisdom sits nowhere except in your   50
ass-grey hair. You have not yet been made judge
between me and my sister, that silly child. Even if she

---

34 **I . . . litany.** ('Dann ich sie stets mit in
die Litaney setze') *TS*'s Hortensio quotes
from the Litany in *The Book of Common
Prayer* (1559), 'From all such devils,
good Lord deliver us!' (1.1.66). Alfons
presumably means he will pray for protection against Catharina's assaults.

37–57 A passage with no equivalent in *TS*,
offering more space for Catharina's eloquent insults, but also reflecting on expected
behaviour in young, unmarried women.

37   **grey-bearded ass** ('ein graubartiger
gEsel') With its unusual captialization of
the second letter, D1 puns on 'fellow'
('Gesell') and 'ass' (Grimm, 'Esel',
15e). D2 reads 'Esel'.

38–9 **you . . . oven** ('Dann jhr ja nicht könnet
einen Hund auß dem Ofen locken'), a

proverb   (Wander,   'Hund',   1399)
implying that if Sebastian cannot even
make a dog move, he will not be able to
evoke desire in a young woman.

40–1 **A . . . stick.** ('ein feiner Herr Sebastian,
grif jhr mit den Spänchen dran') The
German's rhyming couplet enhances
Catharina's mockery of the old suitor's
lack of virility.

43–5 **My . . . where.** It is not clear what
Catharina (sarcastically?) claims Sabina
will leave open for Sebastian. She may
mean a window to her chamber or perhaps this is a more directly sexual metaphor. There is no equivalent statement in
TS.

52   **silly child** Katherina mocks Bianca as a
'pretty peat' (*TS*, 1.1.78), a spoilt child.

were not brought out into the open for your pleasure,
I would still wish her burnt by the sun, ruffled by the
wind or stung by a fly when she's exposed under   55
the open sky. My father knows better how to watch
over her.

THEOBALD   Unnatural child, would to God you had a
single vein in you like hers. She does not run around
the streets like you, but practises all womanly virtues.   60

CATHARINA *(aside)*   That lazy girl will pay for such
hatred towards me when I find her alone.

THEOBALD *[to Alfons and Sebastian]*   I intend to offer
her some delight and have her instructed in poetry
and music.   65

CATHARINA   This is needed above everything, so that she
can please men, for she lacks certain courtly qualities.

ALFONS   I would gladly be of use for such instruction.

THEOBALD   I fear the gentleman would ask too much for
his wages.   70

SEBASTIAN   And I would say no to it.

CATHARINA   O, how the fools quarrel about what isn't
theirs, and above all not even worth the trouble.

THEOBALD   Gentlemen, make peace. In the meantime,
I shall excuse myself. I remain at your service,   75
gentlemen.   *Exit.*

52–6 **Even . . . sky.** Young women of rank kept
to the house in order to safeguard both
their chastity and the whiteness of skin,
considered a sign of beauty. Catharina taps
into these cultural norms while mocking
them as producing someone weak and
spoilt. Catharina's concern with the proper
spaces for young women may originate in
Baptista's order that Bianca return to the
house, followed by her obedient consent,
which evokes Lucentio's inflamed aside,
praising her wisdom (*TS*, 1.1.75–84). This
sequence is missing in *KK*, which chooses
to introduce both the lover and the younger

sister in subsequent scenes.

61 **lazy girl** ('Schleppsack', literally 'a bag
to drag around') a lazy, untidy woman
(Grimm, 2.b), or a kept mistress
(Wander). There is no indication of a
threat in *TS* at this point, but the elder hits
the younger sister in 2.1 of both plays.

63–5 It is Theobald who seeks instruction for his
younger daughter, while *TS* clarifies that it is
Bianca who takes 'delight / In music, instruments and poetry' (1.1.92–3). Unlike in *KK*,
Baptista tells the men of his request for
schoolmasters, encouraging the two suitors
to send him possible candidates (1.1.95–7).

SEBASTIAN   We remain ever obedient to your lordship.

VEIT [*aside*]   I'll listen a little longer, she's got more in
her yet!

SEBASTIAN   Will you not follow your father?   80

CATHARINA   This old ape-face is surely called to be the
tutor. [*to Sebastian*] You're very concerned about
what's not your business; go about your own, if you
like, you old vagabond, and let me go about mine.
Unless you want to have a good mouthful of what   85
comes from my behind. Pull in your snout, mouse-
beard, or else it is going to rain muck, I warn you.

SEBASTIAN   I had rather deal with evil spirits than with
such a one.

CATHARINA   If I were a spirit, I'd torment you.   90

ALFONS   The holy cross is good for protection from that,
and he who gets her will have no need to make it
himself. She'll bring it to him soon enough.

CATHARINA   You're much too dishonourable an ass to bear
such a cross, and may the devil protect you from it.   95

---

76   SD In *TS*, Baptista leaves the stage at
1.1.101, shortly afterwards followed by
Katherina (1.1.104 SD). *KK*'s Catharina
stays for another twenty-seven lines and
exchanges abuse with Sebastian and
Alfons (77–103). Baptista explicitly
allows his daughter to remain onstage,
which she understands as an attempt to
control her movements (*TS*, 1.1.102–4),
while Theobald simply exits.

77–152   Before reverting to a closer rendition
of the original (153–77), *KK* considerably
enlarges the insults between Catharina
and the suitors, and the conversation
between Sebastian and Alfons in which
they seek to use Theobald's servant Veit
as a means to enter the household.

82–3   **You're ... business** Catharina uses an
evocative proverb, literally saying 'you
are much occupied with unhatched eggs'
('Ihr bekümmert euch sehr um ungelegte
Eyer'; Wander, 'Ei', 124).

84   **old vagabond** ('Staudenhecht') high-
wayman (literally 'shrub pike', a long
thin fish) ambushing travellers on roads.
In Germany, as in other European countries, travellers were criminalized as rob-
bers owing to their nomadic lifestyle.

86–7   **mouse-beard** For another insult
mocking beard size, see note at 25–30.

90   **you** ('dich') Catharina's use of the
second-person singular pronoun adds to
the impoliteness of her remark, given
that Sebastien is her senior in age though
probably not in rank.

91–3   Alfons first suggests that a holy cross
protects against evil spirits such as
Catharina, before alluding to the expression 'to bear one's cross', i.e. accepting
the trials of life.

ALFONS   I'd rather call upon God.

CATHARINA   I'll waste no more time with this fantastico.

SEBASTIAN   And we won't force you to stay with us.

CATHARINA   Hold your tongue, old man, or I'll pluck off
your beard.   100

ALFONS   Be not swayed by anger, maid.

CATHARINA   You rude milksop, pull in your pipe, or I'll
give you some food for your snout.   *Exit.*

VEIT [*aside*]   I bet the gentlemen have enough for the
time being. That will keep them busy.   105

ALFONS   Let us part now. Sir Sebastian, should you
be interested, I will let you have my part of the
proceedings, for I know that you are a lover of all that
concerns the ladies.

SEBASTIAN   Keep what you have, sir, and have my part   110
for free.

ALFONS   Thanks, sir. I know well that you are sometimes
a little short-winded. Therefore make yourself a
poultice for the chest from these spices. – But, Veit,
what do you think about the civility of your maid?   115

VEIT   She speaks in a certain manner that I don't
understand, and which is perhaps only familiar to

---

97 **fantastico** ('Fantasten') raver, fool
(Grimm). See also 2.1.434, 496, 5.2.150,
154.

102 **milksop** Catharina makes fun of Alfons'
youth by calling him a 'Milchmaul', literally 'a milk maw', which could refer to
someone with downy beard hair
appearing at puberty (Grimm). For beard
jokes, see notes at 25–30 and 86–7.

102 **pull ... pipe** ('ziehe nur die Pfeiffe ein')
keep quiet (see Grimm, 'Pfeife', 1.c, in
reference to bagpipes)

103 **food ... snout** literally, 'nose food'

('Nasenfutter'). Grimm records no relevant meaning for the German word, but
it seems clear that Catharina threatens
Alfons with violence.

108 **proceedings** ('Traictements') Alfons
may offer to keep Sebastian informed of
how he fares in his courtship of Sabina.

113–14 **Therefore ... spices.** Alfons may
hand Sebastian spices, or pretend to do
so in order to provoke him.

114 **poultice** ('Umschlag') A medicinal sub-
stance put on the skin and held in place
with a bandage.

gentlemen. I am at your service if you seek to insinuate
yourself into her company, or to leave something with
her. I am more than willing if it is lawful.   120

SEBASTIAN   My goodness, that lady can go to the gallows
and the hangman can insinuate himself into her
company.

ALFONS   I ask you nothing except to write my name in
the book of exemptions. But if you truly wish to do   125
something, appeal to her mild-mannered sister. Your
reward will be good.

VEIT   Ha ha! There's a cat in the nest! Will she be easier
to deal with? I'd rather lodge by her than with the
dean, no matter how holy he may be.   130

SEBASTIAN   Ho, that morsel would be a little too good
for you.

VEIT   However delicious it may be, neither you nor I will
be allowed to have a little nibble. But I shall be off
now. Adieu, gentlemen.   135

ALFONS   Commend me to my lady.

SEBASTIAN   Commend me first, I am next in line.

---

118 **insinuate** ('*insinuiren*') Veit mockingly
uses the Latinate word in the sense of
wheedling himself into Catharina's trust,
probably with a sexual connotation,
especially in the context of his following
words, 'to leave something with her'.

125 **book of exemptions** ('Buch der
Verschonung') Meaning unclear. Grimm
('Verschonung') paraphrases the expression as 'if one wants to have nothing more
to do with someone' ('wenn man mit
jemand nichts mehr zu thun haben will').

128 **There's . . . nest!** ('saß da die Katze im
Nest', literally 'is that where the cat sat
in the nest') Veit mocks the suitors' sly-
ness. For the proverb, see Wander,

'Katze', 988: 'Da sass die Katze im
Nest', meaning 'das war der Grund'
('that was the reason').

129–30 **I'd . . . be.** Meaning unclear.
Presumably, Veit would rather commit
the sin of fornication with Sabina than
receive a blessing from the dean (in
German, 'Superintendent'), an overseer
of any larger ecclesiastical unit (Grimm).
The term refers to Protestant Church
structures.

131 **morsel** Sebastian warns Veit against his
interest in Sabina while equating her
with a tasty bit of food ('Bischen', literally 'a little bite') or a small person
('Bischen', literally 'a little one').

VEIT   That shall be my work. I will remember one thing,
         and forget the other. I'll seek money for my pains.
         Nothing is free.   *[Exit.]*   140

SEBASTIAN   I am glad at heart that the monster's gone. I
         wonder greatly that such a fine house has such an
         evil owner, but more about the difference between
         the sisters, for their characters are so opposite. What
         one possesses in virtue, the other lacks, and what one   145
         lacks in vice, the other possesses. And the more one
         makes herself loathed through her disobedience, the
         more the other makes herself beloved through her fair
         and commendable behaviour. I am angry that we must
         forget about modest Sabina because of this savage   150
         animal, this raging Catharina. I wish she were out of
         my sight altogether.

ALFONS   Not so fast, I have good advice on how to open
         the way to our lady: we need to find a man for the
         elder sister.   155

SEBASTIAN   A man? A devil!

ALFONS   I say a man.

---

139 **I'll . . . pains.** ('Den Danckhabt bring ich
nun ein Trinckgelt', literally 'I'm carrying a tip to the thanks') Veit seems to
suggest that he may obey the suitors if he
is paid for it. One or both of them may
hand him money.

141 **I . . . gone.** After *KK*'s interpolated flyting
between the suitors and Catharina, and the
dialogue with Veit, *KK* reverts to *TS* at the
moment Katherina has left the stage
(1.1.105). Owing to this textual patchwork,
Sebastian's 'monster', adapting 'the devil's dam' (*TS*, 1.1.105), refers to Catharina
rather than to Veit who has just exited.

150–1 **because . . . Catharina** Sebastian
portrays Catharina as a wild animal
('unbändiges tier', literally 'untameable
animal') and introduces her epithet
'raging' ('rasend'), which substitutes for

the English 'curst' (see *KK* 1.3.134–5;
TS 1.2.127).

151–2 **I . . . altogether.** The German uses an
evocative proverb, 'Ich wolte daß sie
wäre, wo der Pfeffer wächset', literally 'I
wished she was where the pepper grows',
meaning in foreign countries, as far
away as possible (Wander, 'Pfeffer', 37).

153–4 **Not ... lady** Alfons condenses
Hortensio's speech (*TS*, 1.1.112–17),
offering Sebastian a pact in order to
enable the wooing of Sabina. Both *KK*
and *TS* use the first-person plural pronoun, 'our lady' (1.1.154) and 'our fair
mistress' (*TS*, 1.1.115).

154–7 **we ... man.** Closely adapted from *TS*
(1.1.119–24). *KK*'s 'Mann' exploits the
fact that the German word can mean both
'husband' and 'man'.

SEBASTIAN   And I say a devil. What man would throw
himself into hell in good faith, and all for the sake of
riches?   160

ALFONS   It seems to me, Sir Sebastian, you still don't
know that nowadays *ratio status* governs marriage as
it does every other thing that follows people's fancy.
Whereas you and I don't care about the money when
someone is peevish and unworthy, there are some   165
who put their need for gold before the bride. Well,
God willing, may this succeed.

SEBASTIAN   I don't object to anyone taking her as long
as he's not one of my friends. I'd marry her for her
money as readily as I'd stand on the pillory every   170
morning, whipped bloody with rods. And while I
don't usually waste money, I would be generous with
any man who agrees to be joined with her in order to
release the younger.

158–60 adapts Gremio's speech in *TS*
(1.1.122–4), which equates Katherina
with 'hell' itself.

161–7 Alfons' speech adapts Hortensio's
(*TS*, 1.1.125–9), but adds reflections on
economic motivations for marriage.

162 *ratio status* Latin, 'reason of state', 'a
purely political ground of action on the part
of a ruler or government, esp. as involving
expediency or some departure from strict
justice, honesty, or open dealing' (*OED*,
reason, P1 b.). '*Status ratio*' appears in the
poem explaining the copper engraving on
the title page (see Introduction, pp. 139–
40). *Simplicianischer Zweyköpffiger Ratio
Status*, a tract in the 'mirror for magistrates'
tradition by the German author Hans Jakob
Christoffel von Grimmelshausen (best
known for his picaresque novel *Simplicius
Simplicissimus*), was published in 1670
(VD17 23:233095F).

165–6 **there ... bride** ('so ist doch man-
chem der sein bedarff, welcher dieses
Samen Metall für, und die Braut nach-
setzet'). The German literally says 'there
are some who put their need for this seed
of metal before the bride'. The expression 'the seed of metal' for 'gold' originates in the proverbial concept of God
planting metal seeds in mountains for
mining (Grimm, 'Same', 4.a).

171–4 **And ... younger.** The passage contains the gist of lines spoken by
Hortensio (*TS*, 1.1.133–40), but cancels
TS's reiterated affirmations of a tempo-
rary support between the two suitors
(1.1.134–5), which is in line with
Sebastian's distrust of Alfons elsewhere
(see 1.3.190–216 and note).

ALFONS   Time will tell. I know that some hungry fellow   175
          will come who'll do the work for us, so let him come,
          we'll have liberal hands.

                                                    [*Exeunt.*]

[1.2]   *Enter* FELIX *disguised [as Hilarius] and*
                   [HILARIUS] *disguised as Johannes.*

FELIX   My lord, the more I think about your behaviour,
          the less I understand it. O, strange effects of love that
          can change minds in one short moment!
HILARIUS Remember now, you are none other than
          myself, and bear yourself as I told you. Your good   5

175–7 In *TS*, Gremio speaks the equivalent lines (1.1.141–4), including the proverbial triplet 'woo her, wed her, and bed her' (1.1.143).

175 **Time ... tell.** *KK* employs the common proverb 'kommt zeit kommt rat', literally 'when time comes, advice comes' (Grimm, 'Zeit', 3a, and Wander, 'Zeit', 374). The end of the scene prepares for Hardman's arrival in 1.3.

1.2 In *TS*, 1.1 consists of three scenic movements: one, Lucentio and Tranio are newly arrived in Padua (1–47); two, they remain onstage, unnoticed by Baptista and the other characters, while Lucentio falls in love with Bianca (48–144); three, their dialogue resumes when the other characters have left, and they are joined by Biondello (145–246). This scene corresponds to the third part of *TS*'s 1.1, but unlike in the Shakespeare play, the characters appear onstage for the first time. Hilarius' explanation for his disguise is significantly shorter than Lucentio's (4–12; *TS*, 1.1.185–219). Hilarius has already fallen in love with Sabina, and he and Felix have already exchanged clothes so that Hilarius can woo her. *KK* adds dialogue between the two servants (Felix and Fabian, corresponding to Tranio and Biondello in *TS*) on the (in)ability of clothes to turn a servant into a master (15–31; 60–67). The

scene in *TS* ends on a brief dialogue between Sly and two servants (1.1.247–52) which has no equivalent in *KK*.

0   SD Lucentio and Tranio exchange clothes onstage (*TS*, 1.1.205–6), whereas Felix and Hilarius enter already in disguise. For Hilarius' name in SDs and SPs, see the List of Roles.

1–3 In *TS*, the audience witnesses Lucentio fall in love with Bianca while she is onstage, and he verbalizes this process when he and Tranio are alone (1.1.147–55), using lavish rhetoric and Petrarchan clichés. In *KK*, Hilarius enters already in love, and Felix's mystified response to his master's strange behaviour with which the scene begins mirrors the audience's initial loss of its bearings.

4–12 Hilarius recaps his plans to Felix, collapsing the invention of the disguise scheme by Lucentio and Tranio (*TS*, 1.1.184–206) into a summary of the planned proceedings. In *KK* the respective roles are more clearly demarcated than in *TS*: Felix is to 'do what [he] can' (10) with the father, and 'leave wooing' (12) the daughter to Hilarius. The threat posed by the other suitors is conveyed through the proverbial-sounding 'Chase away the wasps that swarm around the honey' (10–11), a passage with no equivalent in *TS*.

nature shall not fail you. I will and must aim straight
and hit the target. I know no other means than this. I
will play my part to my lady in this lowly disguise as
best I can. You, meanwhile, present a sumptuous show,
and do what you can for me with her father. Chase   10
away the wasps that swarm around the honey. Drive
off my fellow suitors, and leave wooing her to me.

Enter FABIAN. *Looks at both in dismay.*

But here he is, the dull rogue. Where have you been
so long?

FABIAN   Where have I been? My lord, first tell me where   15
you are? Or where my companion here is going? Circe
has effected a wondrous transformation! One who was
almost my equal not long ago has become a lord, or
rather an ape in disguise, and a noble lord a miserable
tutor. It's a mad world! O, it is my misfortune that I   20
have erred and travelled so long. Had I arrived in time,
I might have bettered myself as well.

FELIX   That could easily have happened, that a jester
becomes a fool.

FABIAN   *Horres morres* it is with you. I see nothing to   25
make me lift my hat but my lord's garments. A thief

---

8   **my lady** Sabina's name is not mentioned
in this scene, and Hilarius is not explicitly identified as a suitor of Sabina until
the subsequent scene.

12   SD ***dismay*** The surprise Biondello
expresses in *TS* (1.1.221–3) is conveyed
by *KK* in a SD.

15–31 In *TS*, Biondello addresses his master
with a series of brief questions about what
has happened (1.1.221–3). *KK* amplifies
the passage by having the servants talk to
each other, elaborating the seemingly
magical power of clothes to make the man.
There is a hint of aggression between the
servants (26–31) that is absent from *TS*.

16   **Circe** Fabian alludes to the mythological
enchantress in Homer's *Odyssey*, Book X.

20   **tutor** ('Pedant') Like the English word
'pedant', the German term designated a
teacher or tutor in the early modern period.

21   **erred ... long** perhaps an allusion to
Odysseus given the preceding reference
to Circe

25   ***Horres morres*** Probably a corruption of
the proverbial 'honores mutant mores'
('honours change customs'; see Köhler,
218). Fabian accuses Felix of behaving
proudly towards his former equal after
rising socially, if only by way of disguise.

might steal and wear these. I could pretend to be a
prince in such a worthy fashion, and I wouldn't need
to borrow your hare's head for that.

FELIX   Ho, not so fast. Remember who I have become,   30
and what you are.

HILARIUS   There's no time for such foolery now. Fabian,
I order you to obey your formerly equal fellow servant
who replaces me as your master. Obey him, and hold
your tongue. The reason why we proceed like this is   35
important, as you will learn from him. [*to Fabian and
Felix*] For the sake of your real master, behave
yourselves well. You will not lack reward.   *Exit.*

FABIAN   Now I am the fool of a fool! Fortune will smile
on me from now on. How now, my brand-new lord,   40
avec permission, may I interrogate you and receive
report through my *quaestiones*? What does this
Shrovetide mummery mean?

FELIX   A misfortune has happened to your lord: on his
arrival, he quarrelled with a noble gentleman and   45
gave him a deadly wound. That is why he disguises
himself to avoid danger. He has given me his best
clothes so that I, who am a stranger in this place, may
plead his cause.

---

26 **lift my hat** a sign of respect
29 **hare's head** ('Hasenkopf') an insult (see
2.1.288n)
32–8 Hilarius' speech follows Lucentio's (*TS*,
1.1.224–33), particularly the admonition
to the servants to behave according to
plan. Hilarius delays the revelation of the
'reason why we proceed like this' (35),
however, and leaves it to Felix to give
Fabian an invented explanation. This adds
to the swiftness of Hilarius' exit, conveying a sense of urgency to his scheme.
KK thus condenses Lucentio's falling in
love and invention of the wooing scheme,
but amplifies the servants' dialogue.

41–2 *avec ... quaestiones* Fabian mocks
Felix's newfound noble status through
bragging French ('*avec permission*',
'with permission') and Latin (e.g.
'*quaestiones*', 'questions').
43 **Shrovetide mummery** ('Fastnachts
Mummeren') Shrove-tide, the three days
before Ash Wednesday, designates the carnival season of merriment, which includes
dressing up in costumes ('Mummeren')
and inverting the social order.
44–9 Felix explains to Fabian the supposed
reasons for the identity swap. The speech
is closely modelled on *TS* where, however,
it is spoken by Lucentio (1.1.226–30).

FABIAN   If I had been with him, I might well have become   50
a lord.

FELIX   I would willingly let you have that mock power
if I were permitted to act as he does with the dear
angel. [*aside*] But hands off the vat while the grapes
are inside.   55

FABIAN   What are you murmuring to yourself?

FELIX   I must remind you to obey your lord's orders
when we are in company. When we're alone, we'll
make merry as before.

FABIAN   And so shall it be, says the fool. Well, I can   60
endure your lordship that way. Should you become
too great, it would be over, and we'd fall out of
friendship. But you shall let me enjoy your under- or
quasi-lordship without harm to your greater prosperity
and that of our master.   65

FELIX   I understand you, too, will enjoy the master's
prosperity. All shall be well.   *Exeunt.*

50–9 The dialogue between the servants runs
roughly parallel to *TS* (1.1.236–42) but
adds proverbial diction characteristic of
KK (see Introduction, pp. 116–17).

52 **mock power** The German 'Spiel-
Herrschaft' (literally, 'play rule') draws
attention to the play's concern with how
clothes produce social rank.

54–5 **hands ... inside** ('die Hand von der
Bütte, es seynd Weinbeer darinnen')
Having imagined wooing Sabina in the
person of his master, Felix chastises himself by saying, literally, that he must
'take his hands off the wine tub, there are
grapes inside', a proverbial expression,
meaning to desist from something
(Grimm, 'Butte', 1).

58–9 **we'll ... before** ('so geht es auff den
alten Kayser in gutem Vertrauen los')
Felix promises Fabian to behave like the
servant he is and drink with him when
they are alone, literally living 'in trust of

the old Emperor'. This proverbial
expression constitutes an excuse for irre-
sponsible behaviour on the grounds that
it occurred during the reign of the former
emperor and was therefore expunged
with the accession of the new (see
Köhler, 219–20).

60–7 has no equivalent in *TS*.

60 **And ... fool.** ('Es bleib darbey sagt
Spalter-Hans.') literally 'it remains thus,
says Cleaver-John', an obscure proverbial expression that refers to a rude and
loutish person (Grimm, 'Spalterhans').

62 **it ... over** ('würde der Hund auff dem A.
reiten') Proverbial (Köhler, 220). The
German literally means 'the dog would
ride on the a.', i.e. 'arse', when he is too
tired to hunt any longer.

64 **your ... prosperity** Felix exploits the
ambiguity created by the disguise since
'master' can refer both to himself and to
their actual master, Hilarius.

[1.3]   *Enter* HARDMAN *and* WORMFIRE.

HARDMAN   If I'm not mistaken, this is Master Alfons'
house. Ho, you, go knock.
WORMFIRE   Knock what? When, what shall I knock? I see
no one. Nobody has hurt you whom I should knock.
HARDMAN   Villain, knock, I say, and knock soundly.   5
WORMFIRE   This is another cause *pro more* of Jauer, to
burden my back with knocking. Shall I knock you?
St Nicholas forbid!
HARDMAN   Fool, I tell you, knock there for me, and do it
soundly, or I'll knock off your villainous head.   10

1.3 This scene closely corresponds to *TS*,
1.2. It has four main movements: the first
shows Hardman and Wormfire's arrival
at Alfons' house (1–22; cf. *TS*, 1.2.1–19);
in the second, Alfons joins them and
recaps the wooing situation, proposing to
Hardman the scheme to marry Catharina
in order to free up Sabina for the suitors
(23–153; cf. *TS*, 1.2.20–135); in the
third, Sebastian and the disguised
Hilarius arrive, and Sebastian commits
to the scheme (154–316; cf. *TS*, 1.2.136–
216); and the fourth brings onstage
Fabian and the disguised Felix, who is
accepted as third suitor by Sebastian and
Alfons (316–416; cf. *TS*, 1.2.217–81).
KK adds a brief dialogue between
Sebastian and Wormfire on the latter's
origins (299–316), and ends on a short
exchange of fellowship between
Wormfire and Fabian (417–28).

0   SD As in 1.1, *KK* omits Petruccio's indication of place (he has arrived at Padua
from Verona, *TS*, 1.2.1–2).

1–22 This farcical passage closely corresponds to *TS* (1.2.4–19). The humour
depends on the now archaic dative in
'knock me here' (*TS*, 1.2.8), meaning
'knock for me', which Grumio chooses

to understand as 'hit me here'. The dative
is also possible in German grammar, so
KK replicates the joke: 'knock there for
me' (line 9; 'da schlag mir an').

6   *pro ... Jauer* ('*pro more*, vom Jauer')
Meaning unclear, as acknowledged by
Köhler (220). Cohn translates 'according
to the custom of Jauer' (cxxviii) but provides no explanation. 'Jauer' might refer
to the town of Jauer in Silesia (today
Jawor, Poland), to a person (perhaps
Nikolas Magni of Jauer, a fifteenth-century Silesian theologian who wrote about
superstitious practices and the reform of
the Church), or to a Romansh dialect in
Switzerland. We have found no evidence
to support any of these hypotheses.

8   **St Nicholas** A fourth-century bishop of
Myra in Turkey, St Nicholas was a popular saint in the Middle Ages and the
early modern period, and a patron of
diverse groups of people. The reference
here is probably a general invocation for
protection.

9   **there** *KK* substitutes a deictic adverb for
TS's 'at this gate' (1.2.11). Both versions
play with the possibility of referring to
the knocking about of Hardman and
Petruccio, rather than the door.

WORMFIRE   I knew the song would end on such a note. My master must have noise in his head, hornets must have ravaged his brain. Me knock him? May the devil knock him! Yes, so he may, as long as I am spared.   15

HARDMAN   I see that the bell will not ring, so I shall pull the handle. I'll pull your ears and see if you can sing *fa, sol, la.*

He pulls him back and forth by the ears.

WORMFIRE   Murder, murder! Alarm in all the streets! Help, ho, help! My master has parted with his wits,   20 and wants to lodge with me!

HARDMAN   You reckless bird, will you sing now?

Enter ALFONS, *hastily.*

ALFONS   What does this mean? Do my eyes deceive me? Is it my lord, my brother? What does this brawl mean?   25

---

11   **I ... note.** *KK* adds Wormfire's musical metaphor which anticipates Hardman's subsequent speech.

12–13   **My ... brain.** *KK* turns Grumio's 'My master is grown quarrelsome' (*TS*, 1.2.13) into two related metaphors for madness, anticipating Grumio's 'My master is mad' (1.2.18) slightly later in the scene.

18   *fa, sol, la* 'sol-fa' in *TS* (1.2.17). Syllables in the solmization system in which each syllable indicates a note in the scale.

18   SD The corresponding SD in *TS* plays with the preceding musical conceit: '*He wrings* [spelt '*rings*' in F] *him by the ears*' (1.2.17 SD). *KK* adds the vivid detail of Hardman who '*pulls*' Wormfire '*back and forth*' like the handle of a bell.

19   **Murder, murder** ('Mordio, Mordio') derived from 'Mord' ('murder'). A call that proclaims murder and encourages pursuit of the perpetrator (Grimm).

22   SD Hortensio simply '*Enter*[s]' (*TS*, 1.2.19.1), whereas Alfons does so hastily ('Springet heraus', literally 'jumps out').

23–4   **Do ... me?** *KK* amplifies Alfons' surprise by adding this question (cf. *TS*, 1.2.20–2).

24   **Is ... brother?** *KK* omits *TS*'s greeting of Grumio (1.2.20–1). Whereas Hortensio and Petruccio address each other by their first name, Alfons and Hardman repeatedly call each other 'brother' (cf. 29, 52, 68, etc.), here a term of address rather than an indication of consanguinity.

HARDMAN [*to Wormfire*]   I'll spare you the reckoning
until later, you rogue.

WORMFIRE   May that time never come.

HARDMAN [*to Alfons*]   I beg your pardon, brother, I am
sorry that you find me in such labour.   30

WORMFIRE [*aside*]   May the hangman pay you for it.

HARDMAN [*to Alfons*]   How do you like this life?

WORMFIRE   I am weary of such a life. May the devil take
the master or the servant.

HARDMAN   I still hear you, you marmot.   35

ALFONS   Hush, Wormfire. I will help to settle this quarrel.

WORMFIRE   Then you should have come before I received
the blows. The hangman thanks the arbitrator after
the broil. If I had knocked my mad master soundly,
perhaps I would not have been knocked at all.   40

HARDMAN   You brainless villain! I said you should knock
on the door, but I could not get this service from you,
you deaf thick-skinned ass.

WORMFIRE   Knock on the door, *o mon dieu*! Knock here,
knock there, knock soundly. Is this what knock on the   45

26–7 Hardman delays his punishment of
Wormfire with a proverbial saying ('Ich
will dir Schelmen bis zu ander zeit die
Zeche borgen', literally 'I will lend you,
knave, the tap until some other time', i.e.,
I will let it pass (Wander, 'Zeche', 5)).
Wormfire develops Hardman's conceit,
wishing to postpone the punishment indef-
initely ('Der Teuffel hole solchen Wirth',
literally 'May the devil fetch such a host').

31 Proverbial (Wander, 'Henker', 30). The
first of Wormfire's many asides in the
play, with no equivalent in *TS*, demon-
strating *KK*'s interest in how the servants
reflect on the play's themes (see
Introduction, pp. 103–4, 107–8, 110–13).

35 Hardman likens Wormfire's interruptions to the murmuring sounds made by a
marmot (a large ground squirrel), which
may have given rise to its German name

(Grimm, 'Murmeltier', literally 'murmuring animal').

37–9 **Then ... broil.** *KK* substitutes this passage for several lines from a speech by
Grumio on the legitimacy of leaving
service due to bad treatment by the
master (*TS*, 1.2.28–33).

38–9 **The ... broil.** Proverbial (Wander,
'Henker', 54). Wormfire alludes to his
earlier proverb (31), suggesting he (the
hangman) would only thank Alfons (the
arbitrator) if he had done his duty of
judging. The meaning is opaque:
Wormfire may intimate that a quarrel and
a death sentence would be good business
for a hangman, but since Alfons has
arrived too late to prevent him from getting hit, he will not thank him.

44 *o mon dieu* French, 'oh my God'. *TS* has
'O heavens' (1.2.39).

door means? My master's wits run away from him,
and he means to find them by knocking me, but he'll
sooner chase away my own wits too.

HARDMAN   Do I hear you still? I shall have to go back to
where I left off.   50

WORMFIRE   No need, my lord, you may save the labour.

ALFONS *[to Hardman]*   Brother, accept my plea for your
entertaining servant. Release him from blows, and
instead tell me what good wind brings you here.

WORMFIRE *(aside)*   A stormy, whizzing wind.   55

HARDMAN   The same wind that spurs so many young
people around the world. My father is dead, and I am
heir to all his estate. I lack nothing except a fitting
wife. Until I get one, I have put a hundred ducats in
my purse to go out into the world and see what is   60
lacking in my fatherland.

ALFONS   I would be happy to help my brother to a wife
who is young and rich enough, but –

HARDMAN   Give me your hand on these words. An
honest man keeps his word.   65

46–8 **My ... too.** Wormfire develops his
earlier conceit at lines 19–21. Neither
passage has an equivalent in *TS*.

50 **left off** Our translation relies on Köhler's
emendation of 'gewendet' (i.e. turned) in
D1 and D2 to 'geendet' (i.e. ended, left off).

54 **here** *TS* provides geographical locations
at this point ('to Padua ... from old
Verona', 1.2.48) and elsewhere (e.g.,
1.1.2 and 1.2.2), while *KK* is careful to
omit them.

55 **whizzing wind** ('Sausewind') perhaps
an allusion to Hardman's title, 'heir and
owner of Whirlwind Heights' ('Erbsas
zum Würbelwind'); see List of Roles.

'Sausewind' could designate a skittish
person (Grimm).

56–61 The speech follows Petruccio's (*TS*,
1.2.49–57) but adds Hardman's insistence on his status as lord over his lands.
KK does not mention the father's name
('Antonio', *TS*, 1.2.53), which is in
keeping with its omission of names elsewhere (see 2.1.104–5 and note).

59 **hundred ducats** Cf. 'Crowns in my
purse I have' (*TS*, 1.2.56). The ducat was
the main trade coin in early modern
Germany. In the wager passage,
Hardman raises the stakes from twenty
to a hundred ducats (5.2.272–5).

1.3.50 left off] *Köhler* (geendet); *D1, D2* gewendet

265

WORMFIRE [*aside*]   She'll be good enough if she's rich
enough. Money, money.

ALFONS   Brother, don't be overhasty in this bargain. You
should have let me finish speaking. She is extremely
evil.   70

WORMFIRE [*aside*]   Then she's right for him. They're
birds of the same feather.

HARDMAN   Evil is the least impediment, my lord. If she
were as evil and grim as a lion, as roaring and sullen
as a bear, as unfriendly as a marmot, as prone to bite   75
and scratch as a dog or a cat, it would be a small
impediment; indeed, it is no blemish at all if there is
money enough.

ALFONS   I don't know if you are joking or not.

WORMFIRE   No, my lord, by our old maidservant's   80
undershirt, he's absolutely serious. He's telling you
his true heart. Just marry him with the money, and

71–2 **They're ... feather.** The German uses
an evocative, presumably proverbial
expression (see Köhler, 220): 'Gleich
und gleich, sagt der Teuffel zum Köhler'
(literally, 'like to like, says the devil to
the charcoal-burner'). The devil and the
charcoal-burner are imagined as black
(and sinister) in the same way as
Catharina and Hardman are both rough
and evil, according to Wormfire.

73–8 Hardman's speech is modelled on
Petruccio's (*TS*, 1.2.64–75). It preserves
the general emphasis on money as the
main reason for marrying the shrew but
omits Petruccio's insistence on Padua
(1.2.74–5). Like Petruccio, Hardman
chooses four elements for hypothetical
comparison to Catharina, but *KK* replaces
TS's literary allusions to undesirable
women ('Florentius' love ... Sibyl ...
Socrates' Xanthippe', 1.2.68–70) with
undesirable animals. For Socrates and
Xanthippe in *KK*, see the Prologue.

75 **unfriendly ... marmot** Wander records
an expression, 'Es ist ein altes
Murmelthier' (i.e., 'she is an old
marmot'), that suggests that marmots
were associated with unfriendly women.

80–91 Wormfire's speech is modelled on
Grumio's (*TS*, 1.2.76–81), but expands
on the original with colourful elabora-
tions on the undesirability of Hardman's
imagined wife.

80–1 **by ... undershirt** Wormfire's mock
oath makes fun of Hardman's previous
grandiloquence, bathetically swearing
by the least expensive or elegant bit of
clothing women would wear. Wander
cites *KK* as unique witness to this expression ('Magd', 84). There is a similar
mock oath in the same author's *Der
Pedanthische Irrthum* ('Ich schwüre bei
unser Magd Mäusefallen', literally 'I
swear by our maid's mousetrap', p. 273).
See Introduction, p. 144.

you can give him either a silly puppet or an old
withered hag without a tooth left in her chops, and no
hair on her skull, making the shameful head shiver,   85
and the ugly legs shake. If she were fouler than the
devil's dam, and had more diseases than fifty-two old
rotten nags, it's no impediment as long as there's
money, and money enough. Money passes through
the world, rules the world, seduces the world, and my   90
lord is a child of the world.

ALFONS   What I started as a joke I will end seriously if
you are serious, although I do not wish a friend like
you anything but what I wish for myself, namely only
good. She is young enough, has beauty enough,   95
money enough. The only blemish, and that is blemish
enough, is that she is so very shrewish and brawling,
which is why I would not have her for all the wealth
in the world.

83 **silly   puppet** ('eine   läppische
Kinderpuppe', literally a slight children's doll). *KK* condenses two elements
in *TS*, 'a puppet or an aglet-baby'
(1.2.78) is unclear; perhaps it designates a decorated tag (Ard³, 180). The translator may
not have known the word but understood
that it functions as a contemptuous term.

84–6 **and ... shake** This addition to *TS*
shows the adaptor expanding on the
effect of ugliness. Inspired by 'ne'er a
tooth in her head' (*TS*, 1.2.78–9), he
moves from 'no hair' and 'shameful
head' to ugly 'legs' in a kind of anti-
blazon (see Hillman and Mazzio, 3–22).

87 **devil's dam** Hardman also hypotheti-
cally compares Catharina to the devil's
mother at 2.1.266.

87–8 **and ... nags** *KK* surpasses its original
by turning 'as many diseases as' (*TS*,

1.2.79) into 'more diseases than', and
'two and fifty horses' (*TS*, 1.2.80) into
'fifty-two old rotten nags' ('alte verdorbene Schindmehren').

89–91 **Money ... world.** In *TS*, Grumio caps
his flamboyant speech with a memorable
parallel construction on money's power
to persuade: 'nothing comes amiss – so
money comes withal' (1.2.80–1). *KK*
surpasses the original in rhetorical
amplification by paraphrasing it with
four sayings on the theme.

92–9 Alfons' speech follows Hortenio's (*TS*,
1.2.82–91) while also integrating the end
of Hortensio's previous speech: 'But
thou'rt too much my friend, / And I'll not
wish thee to her' (1.2.62–3). The only
element *KK* omits is Hortensio's assurance of Katherina's social acceptability
since she has been '[b]rought up as best
becomes a gentlewoman' (1.2.86).

HARDMAN   O, my good brother, you don't know the   100
efffects of money. Just tell me who she is, and
it's enough. I will marry her, even if she has the
biting tongue of a dog, yes, even if her shrewish
voice rattles more than thunder rolling through high
mountains.   105

ALFONS   Her father is Sir Theobald, a noble and affable
gentleman. Her name is Catharina.

WORMFIRE   It would be a good sign if she were called
Margaret.

HARDMAN   I know this gentleman well. I have heard   110
enough and shall not rest until I have finished this
affair. I take my leave, unless my brother chooses to
accompany me.

ALFONS   Do not start this business too hastily.

WORMFIRE   My lord, for your life's sake, don't fight this   115
storm but let him be, since he is stung by these wasps.
His mind is set now. He will go about the thing
properly. If she knew him as well as I do, she would

100–5 A close adaptation of Petruccio's
speech (*TS*, 1.2.92–5), except that
Petruccio asks for 'her father's name'
(1.2.93), not 'who she is' (101).

106–7 *KK* omits the surname ('Minola', *TS*,
1.2.96, 98) and place name ('Padua',
1.2.99) in Hortensio's equivalent speech
(1.2.96–9).

108–9 The meaning of this expression,
which has no equivalent in *TS*, is unclear.
Köhler (224) suspects a connection to
Saint Margaret of Antioch who reputedly
escaped alive after being swallowed by
Satan in the shape of a dragon.

110–13 Petruccio's equivalent speech (*TS*,
1.2.100–5) mentions that Katherina's father
'knew [his] deceased father well' (1.2.101).

114 has no equivalent in *TS*.

116 **storm** perhaps another allusion to
Hardman's title 'heir and owner of
Whirlwind Heights' (see 1.3.55, 124, and
List of Roles).

116 **let ... wasps** Grumio advises Hortensio
to 'let [Petruccio] go while the humour
lasts' (*TS*, 1.2.106), i.e., while Petruccio
acts upon a whim. *KK* translates this idea
into, literally, being 'driven by these
crickets' ('wenn jhn diese Grillen
treiben'), i.e. 'foolish and amusing
inventions' (Grimm, 'Grille', 2). This
idiom recalls the beginning of the scene
where Wormfire accuses Hardman of
having hornets buzzing in his brain (see
12–13 and note).

268

soon leave her scolding. If she calls him a rogue once
or ten times, he will interpret it as if she hailed him as   120
a lord. He will take other immodest, peevish words as
the best compliments, and when he's well warmed
up, he'll chase away her impetuous blasts with his
whirlwind. He'll cut such a strange figure in her face
that she'll have no more eyes than a blind cat. He'll   125
treat her so properly that she won't know up from
down, or whether she is in the barn or in the cellar
with him.

HARDMAN I'm only wasting my time by staying here
longer. May God be with you.   130

ALFONS   Brother, wait, I will go with you. My treasure is
also hidden in the house of your future wife. This
occasion allows me to see my heart, Sabina, whom I
hope to conquer as soon as raging Catharina is gone.

WORMFIRE   Raging Catharina, that's a very encomiastic 135
epithet for a maid. She must be a pretty angel who
belongs in the devil's heaven.

119–22 **If ... compliments.** *KK* translates
Grumio's supposition that Katherina 'may
perhaps call [Petruccio] half a score knaves
or so' (*TS*, 1.2.108–9), but adds that
Hardman will understand Catharina's
insults as compliments. Wormfire, unlike
Grumio, thus provides a first glimpse of his
master's taming method of pretending to
understand the reverse of Catharina's words
(see *KK*, 2.1.260–85, and *TS*, 2.1.169–79).

124 **whirlwind** See notes at 1.3.55, 116.

124–5 **He'll ... cat.** *KK* does not reproduce the
English pun on cat/Kate (*TS*, 1.2.114), which
does not work in German, and simply translates the original (1.2.111–14), including
Grumio's anticipation that Petruccio will
'disfigure' (1.2.112) Katherina.

131–4 *KK* considerably condenses Hortensio's
equivalent speech (*TS*, 1.2.115–26), notably
by omitting Baptista's stipulation that his
older daughter must be married before his

younger, which has been explained before
(*KK*, 1.1.1–7; *TS*, 1.1.48–54). Hortensio
describes his 'treasure' as in 'Baptista's
keep' (*TS*, 1.2.116). Alfons, by contrast,
says that his treasure (Sabina) is in 'the
house of your [i.e. Hardman's] future wife',
which takes for granted that Hardman's suit
will be successful and that the inheritance of
the oldest child will become his.

135–6 **encomiastic epithet** ('encomisches
epitheton') translates Grumio's 'of all
titles the worst' (*TS*, 1.2.128), replacing
the untranslatable rhyme ('Curst' / 'worst',
1.2.127–8) with tongue-in-cheek irony.

137 **the devil's** ('Meister Hämmerleins') literally 'Master Small Hammer', a designation for the devil, derived from the
Germanic hammer-wielding god Thor,
who came to be associated with the devil
(Grimm, 'Hämmerlein', 2a). Wormfire
equates Catharina with a fallen angel.

ALFONS [*to Hardman*] But I beg one thing of you,
brother, that you introduce me into Sir Theobald's
house as a musician when the time is right. Since she 140
intends to learn to play the lute, this occasion will
serve to win her favour.

WORMFIRE I believe that when she lends you the belly-
cittern, you'll forget the lute.

ALFONS Well guessed. [*to Hardman*] But do you agree, 145
brother?

HARDMAN You know that our friendship puts me at your
service, and I swear I shall not say a word, since you
are helping me in such a desired affair. So come, we
shall do well.   150

WORMFIRE The young stick together when it comes to
duping the old. The world is full of rascals. But, sir,
who's coming there?

> *Enter* SEBASTIAN [*and* HILARIUS *as*] *Johannes.*
> [*Alfons, Hardman and Wormfire stand aside.*]

ALFONS Hush, Wormfire! He is my rival suitor. He also
strives to win the love of beautiful Sabina.   155

---

140 **musician** compresses Hortensio's
scheme to be 'disguised in sober robes /
. . . as a schoolmaster / Well seen in
music' (*TS*, 1.2.130–2).

140–1 **she . . . lute** Hortensio's equivalent
speech (*TS*, 1.2.129–35) does not provide this information.

143–4 Wormfire, in a speech with no equivalent in *TS*, coins a word, 'belly-cittern'
('Bauchzitter'), with a bawdy reference
to the female genitals, which he may
imagine being fingered like the strings of
the instrument. The word is used by the
same author and with the same innuendo
in *Alamodisch Technologisches Interim*

(1675): 'Ich spielte gestern Abend der
Liese ein wenig auff der Bauchzitter'
(sig. O9v; 'last night I played a bit for
Liz on the belly-cittern', or '. . . on Liz's
belly-cittern'). A cittern is a stringed
instrument that is smaller and easier to
play than the lute. For other sexual puns
on musical instruments, see 2.1.99–104,
3.1.82–4 and notes.

153 SD2 Although *KK* omits the implied SD
in Hortensio's 'Petruccio, stand by
awhile' (*TS*, 1.2.140), it is clear that
Sebastian and Hilarius are unaware of
Alfons, Hardman and Wormfire until the
latter '*step forward*' (185.1).

WORMFIRE   If it's about running a race for her, he's already lost.

SEBASTIAN [*to Hilarius*]   The next thing I want is that you buy for her the best books about love that you can find. These have great power to enflame the fire of 160 love in the hearts of maidens.

WORMFIRE (*aside*)   But not for you.

SEBASTIAN   And they should be bound in the daintiest and prettiest manner. The paper that you use must be well perfumed, for she whom my soul loves is worth 165 more than all exquisite spices. And may I remind you, Johannes, to be as diligent in her service as you can. Your reward from me will exceed even Sir Theobald's generosity.

WORMFIRE [*aside*]   He looks to me as if he would 170 receive his salary from her without your knowledge or will.

SEBASTIAN   But what matters will you treat with her?

HILARIUS   My noble lord, do not trouble yourself with that. Everything that I undertake with her is intended 175 to speak for you as my lord patron, and that just as if

---

156–7 **If ... lost.** In *TS*'s equivalent speech, Grumio comments on the entry of Gremio and Lucentio, '[a] proper stripling, and an amorous' (1.2.141), which could refer to either character. *KK* resolves the ambiguity: Wormfire sarcastically comments on Sebastian's age, which makes it impossible for him to outrun the young suitors.

158–73 This passage corresponds to a single speech by Gremio in *TS* (1.2.142–51) into which *KK* inserts two acerbic asides by Wormfire that have no equivalent in *TS*.

158–60 **The ... find.** *KK* follows *TS* (1.2.142–57) in having the old suitor and the disguised lover enter in conversation. Gremio hands a 'note' (*TS*, 1.2.142) to Lucentio, presumably with a list of the books the latter is using in his instruction

of Bianca, an implied SD that *KK* omits.

160–1 **These ... maidens.** Sebastian's hope of enflaming ('anzublasen', literally 'to blow on') love in the woman he is wooing is implied in the 'books of love' (*TS*, 1.2.144) Gremio wants to be read to Bianca, but only in *KK* is it spelled out.

163–9 *KK* adds Sebastian's encouragement of Hilarius to be 'diligent in her service' (167), unaware of the sexual implications of his words which provoke Wormfire's subsequent innuendo.

174–9 adapts Lucentio's speech (*TS*, 1.2.152–6). By calling him 'a very learned gentleman' (178), Hilarius flatters Sebastian, unlike Lucentio who suggests that Gremio lacks eloquence (*TS*, 1.2.155–6).

271

you were present yourself. Do not doubt my faith,
especially since I do this for a very learned gentleman
such as you.

SEBASTIAN   O, learning, what an excellent piece of work   180
this is!

WORMFIRE   O this old Master Rabbit, what a fool he is!

HARDMAN   Shut your mouth, or I'll bridle you.

ALFONS   Keep your maw shut, Wormfire, don't spoil our
bargain.   185

They step forward.

Good day to you, Sir Sebastian.

SEBASTIAN   My lord, let me thank you heartily. Is this
how we meet?

ALFONS   This time it is. Where are you going?

SEBASTIAN   Where you, my lord, are perhaps not allowed   190
to come for now.

ALFONS   That's too much. I'm sure my feet can do more
than yours. My way leads straight to Sir Theobald's
house.

SEBASTIAN   Hum! I thought such a way was open only to   195
me, as I have found a diligent person experienced
in poetry, music and other sciences to instruct his
beautiful daughter.

---

182 **Master Rabbit** ('Herr Gehasi') 'Gehasi'
is the name of Elisha's dishonest servant
who became leprous as punishment for
his duplicity (see 2 Kings 5.20–7).
Owing to its similarity to 'Hase'
('rabbit'), it is used as a term of abuse for
'fool'. For another 'rabbit' insult, see
1.1.28. See also Köhler, 222–3.

185 SD The SD is implicit in *TS*, or inserted
by modern editors, e.g., '*Coming forward*' (*NOS*, 4.153 SD).

189 **Where . . . going?** *KK* assigns Gremio's
rhetorical question, 'Trow you [i.e., do

you know] wither I am going?' (*TS*,
1.2.163), to Alfons.

190–216 The rivalry between the two suitors
is given greater scope than in the corresponding passage in *TS* (1.2.163–77).
Sebastian, in particular, is more argu-
mentative and distrustful towards the
proposed plan than Gremio.

196–7 **experienced ... sciences** adapts
Gremio's sexual innuendo of the young
tutor possessing 'learning and behaviour
/ Fit for her turn' (*TS*, 1.2.167–8).

WORMFIRE [*aside*]   Men use strange ways of introducing
    themselves nowadays.   200

ALFONS   If that is all it takes to open the door, I also have
    the key in my hands. This nobleman here has promised
    to present me with a very skilful person who is an
    excellent musician. He will instruct the lovely Sabina
    whom I love so ardently.   205

SEBASTIAN   Whom I love so ardently, as you and
    everyone will find out from my deeds.

WORMFIRE (*aside*)   And I believe your purse will find it
    out too.

ALFONS   Sir Sebastian, your heart must be overcome   210
    with passion since you are in such a hurry to put on
    your armour, although there is no war as yet. But this
    is no time to let jealousy overrule us, since we need
    to proceed together in this affair, whether Fortune
    smiles on you or on me. Let us thus set aside our   215
    ancient hate.

WORMFIRE (*aside*)   He means the old hare. How sweetly
    he whistles when he seeks to catch the bird.

SEBASTIAN   I cannot see what should make us stick
    together, but I will willingly hear what you say.   220

ALFONS   By chance this nobleman, my good friend, has
    come to visit me today. He happens to be willing and
    eager to marry Catharina who is rich and noble,
    though too rough and evil for us. Provided, however,
    that he receives her dowry and a few other essentials. 225

201–2 **If ... hands.** has no equivalent in *TS*,
adding another sexual innuendo.

210–11 **Sir ... passion** *KK* adds to *TS*
Alfons' denigration of Sebastian,
alleging he has 'Wust' (dirt, slimy secre-
tion from internal organs; Grimm 1 and
B1a) around the heart.

215–16 **our ... hate** In *TS* there is no evidence of an ancient grudge between
Hortensio and Gremio.

217 **old hare** i.e. Alfons referred to Sebastian.

217–18 **How ... bird.** Wormfire literally
says, 'how sweetly he whistles when the
bird should get into the net' ('Wie süß
pfeiffet man: Wann der Vogel ins Garn
soll'; proverbial, see Wander, 'Garn', 15).

219–32 mostly follows the dialogue in *TS*
(1.2.180–7) but adds Hardman's need for
'a few other essentials' (225), according
to Alfons.

SEBASTIAN   It would be a good thing to do it in this way.
But I fear that even if he were in earnest, he would
soon repent when he realizes her defects, which you
have perhaps not told him about.

HARDMAN   I hear her temper is a little strange, apart from   230
her other qualities, and that she has a nimble tongue,
ready to chide. If that's all, I hear nothing evil of her.

SEBASTIAN   Not a little strange, but as strange as any
creature in the world.

WORMFIRE   [*aside*] That will not alter my lord's resolve.   235
Hard upon hard, speaks the devil and beats the anvil
again.

HARDMAN   Let me worry about that myself if you are too
simple and fearful to marry such a heroical lady, as I
believe you are, given your almost-perished blood.   240

SEBASTIAN   If, my lord, your deeds match your words, I
shall not consider you a swaggerer, but it is hard to
believe. What country are you from?

WORMFIRE   It would be polite to beg leave to ask.

HARDMAN   The old gentleman talks a little too sharply. If   245
you were younger, we would dance the sword dance
together. I think it doesn't matter whether you know

233–48 **Not ... up** Only Sebastian's question about Hardman's origins is based on
TS ('GREMIO ... What countryman?',
1.2.188). The passage adds to the confrontation between Hardman and
Sebastian a sense of barely contained
violence that has no equivalent in *TS*.

236–7 **Hard ... again.** Wormfire suggests
that Catharina and Hardman will match
each other, using a proverb, 'Hart wieder
hart, sagt der Teuffel und schmeiß wieder
einen Ambos', literally 'Hard against
hard, says the devil, and throws another
anvil'. The anvil and, implicitly, the

hammer that strikes on it are equally
hard objects, and will not hurt each other
(see Wander, 'Amboss', 21).

245–9 No reason is provided for Hardman's
(and later Wormfire's, 301–4) evasive-
ness about their origins. Unlike Petruccio
('old Antonio's son. / My father dead'
(*TS*, 1.2.189–90)), Hardman does not
provide the name of his father.

246–7 **dance ... together** Hardman presumably means that they would fight. The
Germanic sword dance referred to in
Tacitus' *Germania* (chapter 24) involves
leaping over bare swords.

my name or not, but I can make you shut up: I am
from Worms. My father is dead.

WORMFIRE *(aside)* It's a marvel he doesn't say 'Thank 250
God'.

HARDMAN I am heir to all his estate, and hope to spend
a long and happy life.

SEBASTIAN I hope, my lord, you have not misunderstood
my words, there was no bad intention in them. If you 255
wish to have such a life, you must not take this lady as
your wife. But if you seek to hang a wild cat about
your neck, I shall be glad to help you.

WORMFIRE He will not be afraid of her scratching like
this old woodcock. Once he's got her in his clutches, 260
he'll romp with her, and make her tame.

HARDMAN I'll soon teach you to speak on my behalf,
and in a way that won't please you. [*to Sebastian*] Sir,
whoever you are, I have come here to marry a rich
woman. If she be rich, I'll have her in despite of the 265

248–53 **I . . . life.** Wormfire's aside is added
to what is otherwise a close adaptation of
Petruccio's speech at *TS*, 1.2.189–91.

249 **Worms** A Free Imperial City of the
Roman Empire, on the Upper Rhine,
about forty miles south of Frankfurt (the
play's likely place of publication, see
Introduction, pp. 147–9). It has several
connotations: it is the capital of the
Nibelungs in the medieval myth of
Siegfried the dragon slayer. It gives
Hardman an urban air like Verona (*TS*,
1.2.189). In the tenth century, Worms was
a seat of the Emperor Charlemagne. In
1521, it hosted the Diet of Worms during
which Luther publicly defended his
reformist thought in the presence of
Emperor Charles V. The city remained
linked to Protestantism in the sixteenth
century, attracting reformers like William
Tyndale. During the Thirty Years' War, it

came under attack several times, most
heavily in 1634.

254–7 **I . . . wife.** *KK* adds Sebastian's
attempt to defuse the situation ('I hope
. . . intention') to a speech which otherwise adapts Gremio's at *TS*, 1.2.192–4.

262–79 *KK*'s version of Petruccio's speech
(*TS*, 2.1.197–209) imitates the structure
of the original but amplifies many of its
elements. For example, *TS* has 'lions
roar' (1.2.199) but *KK* has the 'bellowing, howling and growling of lions'
(269–70). *KK* also adds the colourful
comparison between the pitch of a woman's voice and a fart (275–7).

262–3 **I'll . . . you.** The strained master–
servant relationship is absent from *TS* at
the equivalent point.

263–4 **Sir . . . are** *KK* adds Hardman's implication that, while Sebastian asked for his
identity, he never introduced himself.

devil. She shall be friendly enough, even though
her brawling chops don't speak one good letter, let
alone a word. What do I care for a maid and her
scolding voice? Has the bellowing, howling and
growling of lions, bears and wolves ever startled me?   270
Have I not seen the roaring sea throw its cruel waves
over my head, and open its throat to swallow my
entire body? The cracking and crashing of the fire-
spitting cannon and thunder, that artillery of heaven,
have never frightened me. And should I now fear   275
a woman's voice that makes no greater bang than
wind pressed out from behind, or a nut thrown
into the fire? Go away, and scare boys with bubbles,
not men.

SEBASTIAN   My lord, you have great courage, and, I   280
admit, more than I have.

WORMFIRE   My lord fears no woman, whether she is
born of the devil or hatched by all Margarets of whom
seven banned the devil from hell.

SEBASTIAN   I confess, this brave nobleman has arrived at   285
the right time. I promise him all advancement if he
marries the older and sets the other free.

ALFONS   He'll do it, for although he doesn't need it, his
mind runs on money. That is why I have promised

282–4 Wormfire's speech begins with a version of Grumio's short line ('For he fears
none,' *TS*, 1.2.209) and adds speculations
about Catharina's sinister origins (cf. 137
and note). The origins of the reference to
seven Margarets who banned the devil
from hell ('von allen Margarethen, deren
sieben den Teuffel auß der Hölle
gebannet,   außgebrutet   seyn')   are
unknown. They are mentioned in a book
of comic tales, *Facetiae facetiarum hoc
est joco seriorum fasciculus novus* (1647,

VD17 23:288361L): 'Margaretha . . .
derer sieben den Teuffel die Höllen zu eng
machen' (sig. X9v; in English, literally
'Margretha . . . seven of whom make hell
too narrow for the devil'). The book
seems to have been first published in 1615
(VD17 39:139709Q).

285–7 Sebastian's speech mirrors Gremio's
(*TS*, 1.2.210–12) but adds the insistence
on Hardman's task of setting Sabina free.

288–9 **He'll . . . money.** has no equivalent in
TS.

him that you and I will pay all the expenses he might   290
incur in this affair.

SEBASTIAN   I'm ready to do my part.

WORMFIRE *(aside)*   It will make a hole in your purse,
that's for sure.

SEBASTIAN   I fear he may not take her when he meets her.   295

WORMFIRE   If I received such a dainty dish with such a
pleasant drink as he will take, I'd know how to satisfy
my thirsty throat.

SEBASTIAN   You seem to be an exceedingly good brother.
What country are you from?   300

WORMFIRE   To satisfy my lord's curiosity, I am a
European, and my mother's body is my birthplace. If
my lord means to enter in at the gate, he'll need to go
nose first.

ALFONS   Not too fast, Wormfire.   305

WORMFIRE   Treat every man as he deserves. Truly, this
old sir deserves to be told.

SEBASTIAN   I think this fellow is a bit mad.

WORMFIRE   We served in a regiment under the Dragon at
Bautzen. My lord was hit on the head with a scrap of   310

296–316 This passage is added by *KK* and is humorously concerned with issues of identity similar to those dramatized in relation to Hardman earlier in the scene (241–9).

299–304 Sebastian is as curious about Wormfire's origins as he was about those of Hardman (241–3), and, like Hardman (245–9), Wormfire gives no straightforward answer.

302–5 **my ... Wormfire** The conflation of body and town provokes a sexual innuendo for which Alfons rebukes Wormfire.

306–7 Wormfire defends himself by implying that he speaks in the same vein as he was spoken to (by Sebastian), literally saying that one fries the herring according to the man who eats it; 'Nach dem der Mann ist brätet man jhm einen Häring' (Wander, 'Hering', 55).

309–12 Wormfire wilfully misunderstands Sebastian, who voices doubts about Wormfire's mental sanity, not Hardman's.

309–10 **We ... Bautzen.** Wormfire refers to his and Hardman's alleged military service at Bautzen, a town in east Saxony, which may be intended to recall events from the Thirty Years' War, notably the siege in 1620 and its destruction by fire during occupation by the Catholic imperial army in 1633. Wormfire may also be recalling the now obscure proverb, 'er war vor Bautzen geschossen' (literally 'he was shot before Bautzen'; see Köhler, 225). The present meaning of 'Dragon' ('Lindwurm') is unclear.

277

rabbit fur in such a dangerous encounter that he
almost lost all of his brain.

SEBASTIAN   A man who speaks with fools mustn't expect
wise answers.

WORMFIRE   Then, my over-wise lord, you shouldn't   315
speak with yourself.

Enter FELIX *and* FABIAN.

Goodness me, what have we here, strutting like a
turkey cock?

FELIX   Here are good people who will show me the way.
– Gentlemen, forgive your humble servant if he   320
enquires where Sir Theobald lives.

WORMFIRE [*aside*]   Here's another fellow following the
piper into town. – Do you mean the gentleman with
those two elegant daughters?

SEBASTIAN [*to Felix*]   One word before the answer, my   325
lord. You don't mean her, do you?

FELIX   Perhaps she and him. What business is it of yours?

HARDMAN   The scolding daughter is not your business,
that I advise you.

WORMFIRE   And I too, if you want to save your skin.   330

FELIX   I don't hold with squabbling. – Come, Fabian,
I'm wasting my time here.

316 SD–18 *KK* does not preserve *TS*'s SD of Tranio entering '*brave*', i.e. finely dressed in his disguise as Lucentio (1.2.216 SD). Yet the German play picks up on it by having Wormfire describe Felix as a 'turkey cock' ('Schnautzhan'), a conceited, swaggering person (Grimm, 'Schnauzhahn').

322–3 **Here's ... town.** ('Dem Kerl stehet gewiß auch die Pfeiffe nach dem Dorff,' literally 'the pipe points to the village for this man') This obscure expression also occurs in the same author's *Der Pedanthische Irrthum* (p. 27; see Introduction, p. 144), where it seems to contain a sexual innuendo (Grimm, 'Pfeife', 3b). Wormfire may suspect Felix and the other suitors of being driven by lust in their courtship.

323–4 **Do...daughters?** In *TS* it is Biondello who asks whether Baptista is he 'that has the two fair daughters' (1.2.220). *KK*'s assignment of the speech to Wormfire contributes to his increased disruptive presence towards the end of the act.

323–55 **Do ... Alfons.** *KK* remains close to *TS* (1.2.220–36), but punctuates the dialogue with Wormfire's sarcastic remarks.

FABIAN   I'd rather spend time in the tavern.

WORMFIRE   Well said! We two will be great friends!

HILARIUS   The man plays his part well if it ends as it   335
    started.

ALFONS [*to Felix*]   My lord, a word before you go. Are
    you in love with the maid? Yes or no?

FELIX   That's a brief question. Would it worry you if I
    said yes?   340

SEBASTIAN   No, as long as you go away without another
    word.

FELIX   At your command? It makes me laugh that you
    want to threaten me. Think on your grave rather, and
    leave the world and what's pleasant in it to young folks.   345
    Tell me, is the road not as free for me as it is for you?

SEBASTIAN   Yes, but not the maid.

WORMFIRE (*aside*)   Upon my life, she's not free for you
    either.

FELIX   And for what reason, fine old sir?   350

SEBASTIAN   For this reason: Sir Sebastian has already
    chosen her as his beloved.

WORMFIRE   It takes two to make such a choice.

ALFONS   No. Instead she has been chosen and elected by
    Sir Alfons.   355

FELIX   To this I could and should say: Sir Hilarius of
    Liebenthal wants her to be his. But what's the cause
    of this childish quarrel?

WORMFIRE   It is *vero verius*, truer than truth: where carrion

---

337–8 **Are ... maid?** *KK* replaces
Hortensio's question about whether
Gremio is 'a suitor' (*TS*, 1.2.228) with an
enquiry as to whether he is 'in love'.

346–53 **Tell ... choice.** A passage that is otherwise close to *TS* (1.2.231–5) inserts
two biting comments by Wormfire on
Sebastian's presumptuous wooing of a
much younger woman.

359 *vero verius* Latin (Wormfire goes on to
translate); a short form of the common
Latin tag *vero nihil verius*, nothing truer
than truth.

359–60 **where ... gather.** This proverbial-
sounding phrase imagines Sabina as carrion over which the suitors ('ravens')
fight.

is stinking, there the ravens will gather. I imagine it   360
will be in this affair as it was with the honourable dogs'
wedding: one got the taste of it, and the rest only the
smell. My master comes off the best. Nobody wants to
lodge in his lady's nest or invade his park.

[FELIX]   Gentlemen, hear me if you are truly noble and   365
of sound mind. The maid for whom we doff our hats
is not yet promised to anyone. You are already more
than one sighing for her. Why should you not permit
there to be another, since you cannot refuse it? It is
well known that the mouth waters when one sees a   370
pleasant morsel. Leda's beautiful daughter had a
hundred suitors, so beautiful Sabina may indeed have
one more. I wish to be among them as though Paris
himself came to marry her.

SEBASTIAN   This man means to make us all mute with   375
his prattling.

WORMFIRE   He has a quick tongue; he would make an
excellent mountebank or a wordy lawyer.

360–3 **I ... smell.** Wormfire continues the
conceit that compares his betters to animals, suggesting the courting will lead to
a 'Hunde Hochzeit' ('dogs' wedding'),
which seems to refer to sexual consummation ('the taste') prompted by lust
rather than marriage (Grimm,
'Hundehochzeit').

364 **invade ... park** Wormfire likens
Catharina to a wild animal kept by
Hardman in his park ('Gehäge'). For this
proverbial expression, see Grimm,
'Gehege' 2d.

365 D1 and D2 mistakenly assign the speech
to Fabian.

371 **morsel** For an earlier reference to Sabina
as a tasty morsel, see 1.1.131. Neither

reference has a direct equivalent in *TS*.

371–4 **Leda's ... her.** A close adaptation of
TS, 1.2.243–6. In Greek mythology,
Leda's daughter is Helen of Troy whose
elopement with (or abduction by) Prince
Paris precipitated the Trojan War. That
Felix casts himself in the role of Paris
may indicate that he is an illicit suitor.

378 **wordy lawyer** Wormfire uses the evocative 'Zungendrescher', literally 'tongue
thresher', someone who uses his tongue,
i.e. language, not his hands, to thresh
corn. The word probably refers to
unscrupulous lawyers using their eloquence to justify wrong for personal gain
(see Grimm, 'Zungendrescher'). Perhaps
Wormfire sees through Felix's disguise.

365 SP] *this edn*; Fabian *D1, D2, Köhler*

HILARIUS [*to Sebastian*] My honoured lord, let him try
 his luck a little. His preposterous actions will have a 380
 ridiculous end.

HARDMAN Brother Alfons, why all these vain words?

ALFONS [*to Felix*] With your permission, my lord, I will
 be so bold as to ask you one more question. Have you
 ever seen Sir Theobald's daughters? 385

WORMFIRE (*aside*) Only a fool loves those he doesn't
 know.

FELIX No, but I have learnt from others that he has two:
 one as famous for her rough tongue and manner as
 the other for her virtue and meek modesty. This has 390
 led me to see and woo her if she truly has such noble
 gifts.

HARDMAN Friend, turn your thoughts away from the
 first sister. I seek to win her liking.

SEBASTIAN Yes, yes, my lord, do not fear. We leave this 395
 task to great Hercules.

WORMFIRE My lord has the club ready with which he
 will attack her flesh. It is long and thick enough, and
 covered with good leather.

HARDMAN [*to Felix*] My lord, you should know that the 400
 father will not let go of the younger daughter whom
 you all three think about, before he rids himself of the
 elder who is to be mine.

385 **Sir...daughters** Unlike *TS*'s Hortensio
 (1.2.251), Alfons refers to Theobald's
 daughters in the plural, which explains
 Hardman's touchiness at 393–4.

395–6 *KK* adapts Gremio's speech (*TS*,
 1.2.256–7) but omits his mocking exag-
 geration that Katharine's taming would
 top all of Hercules' labours.

397–9 has no equivalent in *TS*. Wormfire
 builds on Sebastian's comparison of
 Hardman and Hercules to use Hercules'
 club as a phallic image.

400–3 Unlike Petruccio in the equivalent
 passage in *TS* (1.2.259–63), Hardman
 insists that the elder daughter 'is to be
 [his]'.

[FELIX]   Very well, my lord. Because you are the man
who dares to marry the elder sister, I will show you   405
all possible friendship. You are setting the younger
free.

WORMFIRE   But not free from penetration, which is the
lot of womanfolk.

ALFONS   Well now, gentlemen, let us make peace. We   410
can as little ban him from wooing as he can ban us. It
is folly to quarrel and brawl over what's not yet one's
own.

FELIX   I am content with this way of handling it. Come,
gentlemen, let us go in and drink to our fellowship.   415

ALFONS   We are happy to follow.

*[Exeunt Felix, Hardman, Sebastian,
Hilarius and Alfons.]*

WORMFIRE   You and I will thus also get good fellowship.

FABIAN   I'll refuse nothing, except a box on the ears.

WORMFIRE   I heard a delicious word today that tickles

404–7 streamlines the equivalent speech by
Tranio (*TS*, 1.2.264–9).

404 SP D1 and D2 mistakenly assign the
speech to Fabian. This and a number of
other speeches are misassigned to characters whose names start with the same
letter, which may suggest that the manuscript that served as the printer's copy
used abbreviated SPs (see SPs at 4.4.54,
5.2.15, 27, 43, 136, 263 and notes).

408 **But … penetration.** Wormfire suggests
that, even though Sabina might be set
free to be wooed, she is not free from the
penetration of the hymen. The German
word is 'stich frey' (literally 'sting free')
with the common meaning of 'invulner-
able in battle', but, more specifically,
pertaining to women whose hymen does
not break when having sex (Grimm,
'stichfrei', esp. 3).

410–13 Whereas Alfons emphasizes the
suitors' peacemaking, Hortensio's corresponding speech in *TS* (1.2.270–3)
focuses on Tranio's funding of
Petruccio's endeavours.

414–15 condenses the equivalent speech by
Tranio (*TS*, 1.2.274–8).

416 Before Hortensio's equivalent speech
(*TS*, 1.2.280–1) which ends the scene,
Grumio and Biondello speak in unison:
'O excellent motion! Fellows, let's be
gone' (*TS*, 1.2.279). *KK* omits the servants' line, but amplifies its import, the
rough camaraderie and anticipated joys of
drinking, in a subsequent dialogue after
the suitors have left the stage (417–28).

416 SD In *TS*, all the characters exit jointly at
the end of the scene (1.2.281 SD).

419 **word** presumably Felix's reference to
'drink' before his exit.

404 SP] *this edn*; Fabian *D1, D2, Köhler*

my thirsty throat. Be merry, my throat! I know that   420
all the cups that come to my hand will have holes
in them, drink will never stop pouring through.
How beautifully it will flow! But the longer here,
the later there. We are missing out. Let's go, my
friend.   425

FABIAN   Rogues speak like this when they seek to leave.
I follow more than willingly if we go to work this
way. No honest man refuses another's invitation.

Exeunt.

2.[1]   *Enter* CATHARINA *and* SABINA.

CATHARINA   Now I have you alone in my power, you
shall dance to my tune, you spoilt child.

---

421 **holes** Compare the German expression
'saufen wie ein Loch' (literally 'to drink
like a hole'), i.e. to drink like a fish
(Wander, 'saufen', 65).

2.1 No location is specified, but the scene is
presumably set in front of Theobald's
house. The scene falls into five parts:
1–81 (to the entry of the suitors, the
suitors in disguise, and Wormfire),
82–285 (to Catharina's re-entry), 286–
486 (Hardman and Catharina alone),
487–574 (to the exit of Hardman and
Catharina), and 575–670 (the bartering
of Sebastian and Felix). The first part, the
confrontation between the sisters, follows *TS* (2.1.1–38), but adds Veit's innuendos. The second part, the introductions
of the new suitors Hardman and Felix, is
closely adapted from *TS* (2.1.39–179)
but inserts Wormfire's comments and a
brief dialogue between servant and
master on Hardman's taming technique
(235–59). The third part, with Catharina

and Hardman's first encounter, remains
close to *TS* (2.1.180–282) but includes
more banter. The fourth part, dramatizing the conclusion of the match
between Hardman and Theobald, is
equivalent to *TS* (2.1.283–328). The fifth
part, which shows Sebastian and Felix
vying for Sabina's hand, remains close to
TS (2.1.329–414) but adds two vignettes
on the conflict between youth and age
(594–602, 609–20).

1–2 Whereas *TS*'s scene (2.1) begins with
Bianca's plea to her sister (2.1.1–7), *KK*
starts with Catharina's gleeful taunting
of Sabina.

1–2 **Now ... tune** ('nun soltu nach meiner
Pfeiffe tantzen', literally 'now thou wilt
dance according to my whistle') proverbial (Wander, 'Pfeife', 34).

2 **spoilt child** Catharina uses the colourful
expression 'Zartlappe', literally 'tender
morsel', meaning a spoilt child (see
Wander).

2.[1]] *this edn*; Zweyte Handlung. *D1, D2, Köhler*

SABINA   Dearest sister, do not wrong me. I have never
      done you any harm, but you mean to trample me
      under your feet.   5
CATHARINA   Confess here and now, and promptly too,
      which of your suitors is your favourite, for if you
      keep the truth to yourself, I'll not spare you.
SABINA   Believe me as you believe truth itself that
      among all the men I have ever set eyes upon, none has   10
      yet entered my heart.
CATHARINA   A box on the ear is the answer to a lie.

Beats her.

You wild cat, have you not fallen in love with Alfons?
SABINA   Sister, I think it is you who are in love with him.
      If it is so, be content, I'll gladly leave him to you.   15
CATHARINA   O, now I see, that's the way the wind blows!
      Your ambition angles for wealth! You want to elevate
      yourself through marrying the old shitpants, and be
      splendidly kept by him in order to please others! And
      when that one is ridden to death, you will get a new   20
      pot for the old.

3–5 *KK* condenses Bianca's speech (*TS*, 2.1.1–7). For Sabina's weakened presence early in the play, see Introduction, p. 96.

6–8 Instead of Katherina's vague threat, '[s]ee thou dissemble not' (*TS*, 2.1.9), Catharina more menacingly says 'I'll not spare you' ('ich will deines Fells nicht schonen,' literally 'I will not spare your fur').

9   **Believe me** *KK* remains close to the original, but, instead of keeping the affective 'sister' (*TS*, 2.1.10), it has Sabina equate herself proverbially with sober '*truth itself*' ('als wie der Wahrheit selbst'; see Köhler, 227).

12   SD *TS* delays explicit physical violence until line 22 ('*Strikes her.*').

13   **have ... love** Catharina uses a colloquial German expression for 'falling in love', 'hastu dich ... vergaffet' (Grimm, 'vergaffen', 2).

16   **that's ... blows** Catharina uses the proverb 'wo der Hase im Pfeffer lieget' (literally 'where the hare lies in the pepper'). It is based on the idea that 'nobody knows where the hare lies in the pepper [here meaning 'broth'; Grimm, 'Brühe', 2] but he who dressed it' ('keiner aber weiß, wo der haas im pfeffer ligt, als der ihn angericht'; see Grimm, 'Hase', 1).

SABINA   You do me great wrong, as in many things. If it
is for his sake that you are so set against me, put your
mind at rest.

Catharina binds her hands.

But what games are you playing with me? Dear sister,   25
unbind my hands.

CATHARINA   I see, the maid wants to be played with. Just
you wait (*beats her*), if this is play, all else was play
too. I'll whistle for you while you dance.

Enter THEOBALD *and* VEIT.

THEOBALD   What, you raging beast! What's to be done?   30
What wicked mischief is this? Who gave you power
to lord it over this poor child? I reckon you want to be
her very own hangman, you malicious tyrant! [*to
Sabina*] Go in, my child, run away from this dragon.

Sabina weeps.

CATHARINA   O, this darling daughter needs to be flattered,   35
to be greatly spoiled. [*to Sabina*] But I must give you
another punch for the journey.

Moves to beat her again.

THEOBALD   What, in your father's presence? Is there no
respect left in you, you savage beast?

Exit Sabina.

24 **SD** spells out *TS*'s implied stage direction: 'I
prithee, sister Kate, untie my hands' (2.1.21).
27 **played with** Catharina picks up on Sabina's
word 'kurtzweil' ('game') and turns it into a
passive, 'gekurtzweilet', 'played with'.
30 **raging beast!** Baptista, by contrast,
addresses Katherina as 'dame' (*TS*,
2.1.23). Compare her change of epithet
from 'curst Katherine' (*TS*, 1.2.182) to
'raging Catharina' (*KK*, 1.3.134).
34 **Go ... dragon.** In *TS*, it is not clear

whether Baptista's equivalent line, 'Go
ply thy Needle, meddle not with her'
(2.1.25), addresses Katherina or Bianca,
an ambiguity *KK* resolves.
34 **SD** In *TS*, the SD is again implied:
'BAPTISTA ... Poor girl, she weeps'
(2.1.24). Cf. 24 SD.
38–9 **Is ... beast?** replaces Baptista's order
to Bianca ('get thee in', *TS*, 2.1.30) with
Theobald's abuse towards Catharina. Cf.
note at 30.

CATHARINA   Will you prevent my revenge on her? Now I   40
see that you care nothing for me, but this undeserving
thing is the apple of your eye, and not to be touched.
Hang her around your neck or she'll be lost. But no,
she must have a suitor who woos her. She's late
already, and I am even further behind, and may dance   45
barefoot in her honour at the wedding. I will be
scoffed at, and may go lead apes in hell. But before
this happens, I will revenge myself on her thoroughly,
and smash her pretty mouth, that dainty dish of her
suitors.   50

THEOBALD   I am the unhappy father of a disobedient
daughter who tortures virtue itself only to grieve me.

VEIT   My lord, if I may speak, perhaps I know where the
trouble lies. Lady Catharina rants because Lady
Sabina has suitors and she has none, though she is the   55
older and riper.

CATHARINA   Who told you that, you snivelling boy?

VEIT   Dear madam, I know well how it is with virgins:
when they are old enough, they yearn to be burdened
by a man.   60

42 **apple ... eye** transforms Katherina's 'She is your treasure' (*TS*, 2.1.32) into a different metaphor.

44–5 **She's ... behind** Unlike in *TS*, this suggests that both sisters are late in getting married.

47 **may ... hell** faithfully translates the proverbs in *TS* (2.1.33–4). Probably because the second proverb was not known in Germany (Köhler, 227), Catharina clarifies the meaning by adding a further idiom, 'wann mir der Bock, zum Schimpff, geschencket wird', literally 'when I am given the goat for contumely', translated as 'I will be scoffed at'.

47–50 **But ... suitors.** replaces Katherina's admission of passive suffering ('Talk not to me, I will go sit and weep', *TS*, 2.1.35) with a violent threat.

51–2 Baptista's equivalent speech (*TS*, 2.1.37–8) caps the scene's first movement and introduces the next by greeting the approaching suitors.

53–76 has no equivalent in *TS*.

53–4 **where ... lies** ('wo der Has im Kraut sitzet', literally 'where the hare sits in the grass') a version of the earlier hare proverb (see 16 and note).

58–60 Veit literally says 'I know well how it is when virgins can put the thumb into the nose. Then May is burdensome to them' ('ich weiß wohl, wie es ist, wann die Mägdchens den Daumen können in die Nase bringen, dann ist jhnen der May beschwerlich'). Veit picks up on Catharina's nose-related expression, adding a now obscure idiom. But the suggestion of sexual desire and awakening in spring time is clear.

CATHARINA   I'll give you something on the nose.

THEOBALD   Don't be so rude in my presence.

VEIT   If you wish to give me something, madam, I have
a brave young fellow for you. He will please you
when you see him, I know it well. He is tall and   65
strong, has big eyes with a lot of white in them, a big
broad nose, strong, forceful loins and round, firm
calves. His nicely curled hair is blond and red around
the parting like a cock's. You can imagine the rest. I
am sure that when you see him, your heart will open   70
up to him. He will please you and chase away your
silly ideas.

CATHARINA   I'll give you your salary: a bop on the head
instead of a wedding gift! I wish the wooer, with his
bits, were knocked to the dirty ground, since he   75
already lies lowest.   *Exit.*

VEIT   Go on, pretend to be angry. I know your belly is
tickled.

THEOBALD   Hold your peace, rude slave, and get out of
here. – Here come a great group of people, known and   80
unknown.

63–72 Veit elaborately describes a 'brave
young fellow' (his penis) who would
gladly please Catharina.

71–2 **chase … ideas.** Veit literally says his
fellow will 'chase away the crickets'
('wird euch auch die Grillen wohl ver-
treiben'), an idiom for cheering up a mel-
ancholic person imagined as having
crickets in their head, making them rest-
less (Grimm, 'Grille', 5c).

74 **wedding gift!** ('Brautstück') a gift
offered to the servants by the bride
(Köhler, 228).

74–6 **I … lowest.** Catharina understands
that the wooer (Veit) implicitly refers to

his penis, and threatens to knock him
(whether Veit or the penis is left unclear)
down.

77 **belly** For the sexual innuendo, see
'belly-cittern', 1.3.143–4 and note.

80–1 **Here … unknown.** After the added
interlude between Catharina and Veit,
KK reverts to the source text: 'But who
comes here?' (*TS*, 2.1.38).

81 **SD** *TS*'s SD mentions that Lucentio (as
Cambio) enters '*in the habit of a mean
man*', and that Biondello (as Lucentio's
boy) bears '*a lute and books*' (2.1.38.1–2,
4). Unlike Wormfire, Grumio does not
appear onstage in this scene.

287

Enter SEBASTIAN, HARDMAN, FELIX [*as Hilarius*],
[HILARIUS *as*] *Johannes,* [ALFONS *as*] *Musician,*
WORMFIRE *and* FABIAN.

SEBASTIAN   A happy day to you, my lord neighbour.

THEOBALD   Many thanks, my lord Sebastian, welcome
to you and your whole company.

HARDMAN   My lord, let me know without delay if you   85
have a virtuous and dainty daughter called Catharina.

THEOBALD   Yes, I have a daughter of that name.

SEBASTIAN [*to Hardman*]   You speak a bit too bluntly. I
wish you would use more modesty.

HARDMAN   Ha, what do I care, Sir Sebastian? I am no   90
longer beardless.

WORMFIRE [*aside*]   I suspected these thanks would be
remembered.

HARDMAN   I am, to put things briefly, a nobleman from
Worms, and since, my lord, I heard of the beauty,   95
virtue, honour and maidenly modesty of your virgin
daughter Catharina, I could not rest until I came
here to become her suitor. To be more welcome as
the stranger that I am, I offer to you this person

90   **what ... care** Hardman uses an obscure
expression to convey his indifference to
Sebastian ('Ey was küsset mich im
Leibe, Herr Sebastian', literally 'what
kisses me in the body, Sir Sebastian').

90–1   **I am ... beardless.** Hardman refuses
to be patronized by Sebastian by literally
saying 'leave me unshaved' ('lasset mich
unbalbieret'), a beard betokening age
and manhood.

92–223   Wormfire's many asides, all exclusive
to *KK*, constitute the major difference from
the equivalent passage in *TS* (2.1.46–138).

92–3   ('Ich gedachte wohl daß dieser danckhabt auff die Erinnerung kommen
würde') The meaning is obscure. In the
preceding scene, it was Hardman who
accused Sebastian of 'talk[ing] a little
too sharply' (1.3.245), and Wormfire

may have anticipated that Sebastian
would remember that slight; alternatively, Wormfire may simply have anticipated Hardman's objection to Sebastian's
criticism.

94–101   Hardman's introduction is closely
modelled on Petruccio's (*TS*, 2.1.47–53),
moving from his origins (Worms, as
opposed to Petruccio's Verona) to praise
for Catharina (95–8) and to an admission
that he is a stranger.

99–104   **I offer ... arts.** Petruccio specifies
Licio's abilities in 'music and the mathematics' and other 'sciences' (*TS*, 2.1.56–7).
Hardman omits mathematics, and instead
adds that the musician will teach 'the lute',
which prompts an obscure sexual innuendo by Wormfire. For music and sexual
innuendos, see also 3.1.82–4, 112–16.

who will instruct her in music, and especially the 100
lute –

WORMFIRE (*aside*)   On which many hundreds of chords
resound.

HARDMAN   – and who is experienced in other fine arts. I
beg you to accept myself and him most favourably.   105

THEOBALD   Be my guest, dear lord, and this person for
your sake too. But I am sorry you came from so far
away for my daughter.

WORMFIRE [*aside*]   Now we're getting there!

HARDMAN   I see that my person is not acceptable, or she   110
is already taken. God be with you then.

WORMFIRE [*aside*]   Show us the wares, there's a market
in Hanover too.

THEOBALD   No, my lord, do not be so hasty. Understand
me well. I am only very sorry that you will not find   115
such virtues in my daughter as you imagine. Be that
as it may, what is your name, my lord, please?

HARDMAN   My name is Hardman Madfeather. My father,
known throughout the country, has died, and left me
heir of Whirlwind Heights.   120

WORMFIRE [*aside*]   I hear that often enough.

THEOBALD   He was my good friend. I am truly sorry
about his death.

104–5 **I . . . favourably.** *KK* omits Petruccio's
naming of 'Licio, born in Mantua' (*TS*,
2.1.60), in keeping with the play's omission of names and place names elsewhere
(see 3.2.317–19 and note).

106–8 Theobald's speech is close to
Baptista's (*TS*, 2.1.61–3), but adds the
information that Worms is 'far away'
from the unknown setting of the play.

109 The German is obscure, literally saying
'Now the dog is riding on the plug'
('Nun reitet der Hund auff dem Spunde').
See 1.2.62n.

112–13 Wormfire's perhaps idiomatic comment is obscure. Its beginning literally

translates as 'Get the goat around'
('Herum mit der Ziegen'). From 1636 to
1692, Hanover, in northern Germany,
was the capital of the Principality of
Calenberg.

118–20 Unlike Petruccio, Hardman mentions
his family name (see List of Roles), not
his father's first name, Antonio (*TS*,
2.1.68).

120 **Whirlwind Heights** See List of Roles,
HARDMAN.

122–3 Unlike Baptista in the equivalent
speech (*TS*, 2.1.70), Theobald expresses
his condolences, prompting Wormfire's
dry observation (124).

WORMFIRE (*aside*)   But my lord not sorry at all.

THEOBALD   For his sake, my lord, I hope you will be all   125
the more favourable towards me. I am at your service.

WORMFIRE [*aside*]   Now it'll work better than before!
Things will go well from now on. Leipzig surrenders.

SEBASTIAN   Your speeches notwithstanding, Sir Hardman,
I also have some words to address to Sir Theobald. –   130
As I promised you, my lord, I myself have taken pains
to find this young student [*pointing to Hilarius*] who
will be apt –

WORMFIRE (*aside*)   At all times apter than you.

SEBASTIAN   – to instruct your maidenly daughter. I   135
promise his service will satisfy you.

WORMFIRE (*aside*)   But it will satisfy the daughter better
than him if she holds still.

THEOBALD   I will requite it in every possible way.
Meanwhile, I thank you for such great pains. [*to   140
Hilarius*] You shall be kept and paid by me, for
your virtuous character shows that you are of good
breeding.

WORMFIRE [*aside*]   Students generally have good breeding
sano sensu.   145

THEOBALD [*to Felix*]   Good sir, pardon my boldness,
what is your name?

FELIX   My lord, you are permitted to enquire without
pardon after your servant's name which will surely

---

128 **Leipzig surrenders.** Wormfire probably
alludes to the Battle of Breitenfeld
(1642) in the Thirty Years' War in which
Leipzig surrendered to the Swedish
forces (see Forssberg, 109).

131–8 **As … still.** *KK* omits a short hostile
exchange between Gremio and Petruccio
(*TS*, 2.1.71–5). Sebastian introduces the
supposed instructor Johannes (as Gremio
does Cambio, 2.1.76–82), but omits his
name and the qualifications Gremio lists
(2.1.79–82).

145 *sano sensu* Latin, of sound mind.

148–69 *KK* retains Tranio's introduction to
Baptista but departs from it in structure
and wording: Tranio presents himself as
a suitor to Bianca (*TS*, 2.1.89) with gifts
of 'Greek and Latin books' (2.1.99)
before disclosing his origins (2.1.102).
KK turns the passage into a polite dialogue that foregrounds the friendship
between the two families.

be known to you: I am Sir Hilarius of Liebenthal the 150
Younger.

THEOBALD　My heart told me you must be the son of a
good friend. I am most happy to find you in good
health, and I will be pleased to show you my
affectionate friendship.　　155

FABIAN (*aside*)　That goes down well.

THEOBALD　But what brings you here?

FELIX　My father, who sends his humble greetings, –

THEOBALD　Accept my thanks.

FELIX　– has sent me away to gain experience and 160
learning. This has brought me to you, my lord, from
whose wit and famous ability my youth seeks to
profit. I have also come because I have heard of your
maiden daughter's excellent gifts which I would like
to see, and I would be happy if the friendship of the 165
parents could be continued by the children.

THEOBALD　This must have been counselled by the gods.
It will be my greatest concern to keep and continue
such friendship.

SEBASTIAN　[*aside*]　This fellow has got himself 170
straightaway into more favour than all of us.

THEOBALD　Gentlemen, you are all welcome to walk in. I
hope you will do me the honour of accepting what my
humble house can offer. – You, Veit, lead them to the
hall, and tell my people to do them every honourable 175
service.

　　　　　　[*Exeunt Veit, Fabian, Felix, Alfons, Hilarius
　　　　　　　　　　　　　　　　and Sebastian.*]

156 Fabian says, 'Das muß dem Esel krauen', literally 'That scratches the donkey,' a proverb indicating mutual flattery as in the English 'You scratch my back and I'll scratch yours' (Grimm, 'krauen', 2bγ, and Wander, 'Esel', 183).

176 SD D1 and D2 have no exit SD, but it seems likely that only Theobald, Hardman and Wormfire remain onstage.

Sir Hardman, please stay with me a while.

WORMFIRE [*aside*]   The old nag is the first, but wants to
    be the last, or stay at home even, and make good use
    of his tool.   180

HARDMAN   My affairs require my prompt attention. My
    lord, you know I live far from here, and cannot
    journey up and down all the time. I love the maid,
    your daughter. My family and my wealth are known
    to you. If I become your daughter's husband, how   185
    much do you intend to offer as a dowry?

THEOBALD   It is known that I am willing to give 5,000 in
    ready money. After my death, half of my possessions
    are guaranteed.

HARDMAN   I am glad to hear this, and will in return   190
    promise my house, my farm and all my lands if she
    survives me. There is nothing left to do but for you
    to make the customary contract, my lord, so that it
    may be signed by both parties, confirmed and acted
    upon.   195

WORMFIRE [*aside*]   He's forgetting something important.

177–95 The dialogue between Hardman and
Theobald remains close to the original
(*TS*, 2.1.113–26), but omits Petruccio's
specification that he is 'solely heir' and
has 'bettered' his father's bequest
(2.1.116–17).

178 **old nag** ('Krippenbeißer', literally
'trough biter') An imaginative term for a
horse whose teeth scrape the edges of the
trough when drinking, thus scratching the
wood (Grimm, 'Krippenbeißer', 1); a
shrewish person (Grimm, 2). Presumably
an acerbic reference to Theobald.

180 **his tool** ('seinen Lümmel') 'Lümmel' designates a rude person (Grimm, 1), so the
word presumably refers to Hardman here.

For the sexual meaning, see Grimm, 3.

183–4 **I ... daughter.** a comic addition to
Petruccio's equivalent speech (*TS*,
2.1.113–19) given that Hardman has
never met her.

187–8 **5,000 ... money** Given the uneven
monetary situation of the politically
divided German territories, it is hard to
gauge the value of Theobald's offer, but it
is clear that the sum is immense, like
Baptista's 'twenty thousand crowns' (*TS*,
2.1.121).

196 Wormfire uses a proverb, literally saying
'my Master calculates the bill without the
host' ('Mein Herr macht die Rechnung
ohne den Wirt'; Wander, 'Rechnung', 14).

THEOBALD   Good sir, do not be too hasty. One does not
sell the skin unless one has caught the bear.

WORMFIRE (*aside*)   Do not shout 'herring' unless you
have got it by its tail.   200

THEOBALD   This is what worries me: will you be able to
win my daughter's love?

HARDMAN   O, my lord father, you are wide of the mark.
Do not worry. I will speak to her in such a way that it
will be delightful.   205

THEOBALD   You seem to mean it as young folks do, but
her humour is very strange.

HARDMAN   Father, do not make everything so hard. My
humour is well suited to hers. I am as ready to reject
anger and words of scorn as she is ready to promote   210
them. It will be with us as when two strong fires come
together: each feeds on the other's force and thereby
swallows it up. If a small, soft breeze blows, it makes
a fire big and impossible to tame. A storm, however,
disperses it. You can do what you please, thus it will   215
be with us. I am rather rough and wild, and so must
have someone like myself. I never loved tenderlings.

THEOBALD   You are courageous and may make a bold
attempt. It is my heart's desire that you start and end
this joyfully. But first I must warn you: be well armed   220
for peevish words.

WORMFIRE [*aside*]   Such words are his best music when
he is in the vein.

197–8 **One . . . bear.** Our literal translation of
the German expression 'Man verkaufet
die Haut nicht, man habe dann den Bären
gefangen' (Wander, 'Haut', 77), which is
used to warn against overhastiness.

199–200 Wormfire builds on Theobald's previous proverb with an obscure but proverbial-sounding expression: 'rufet nicht

Hering, man ihn dann beim Schwanz',
which we translate literally.

203–17 Petruccio's equivalent speech (*TS*,
2.1.129–36) is slightly expanded and
briefly interrupted by Theobald.

218–27 closely adapts the equivalent speeches
by Baptista and Petruccio (*TS*, 2.1.137–
40), while adding Wormfire's aside.

HARDMAN   I worry as little about those as high stone cliffs worry about furious, blustering winds, even if 225 they are exposed to horrible storms. I am immovable, be it sweet or sour with her.

THEOBALD   Do it your own way. Will you come in with me, or shall I send my daughter to you?

HARDMAN   I think it is advisable that I await her arrival 230 here, so that we have our first little dance alone. Womenfolk are shy, and a little silly, when other people are around.

THEOBALD   As you wish.   [*Exit Theobald.*]

WORMFIRE   I do not think your mistress will be too shy 235 and silly to set the *capitolium* right.

HARDMAN   I was not serious. Just let her come, she will find her man. One honour for another.

WORMFIRE   But I hope I may use my *testiculos* as witnesses for this first meeting, so that I can produce 240 them in case of need.

HARDMAN   Produce a damned gallows for your roguish neck. I need no witnesses nearby.

WORMFIRE   My lord, I expect you are worried that I may witness how worthy you are of your title and the name 245 which you keep reminding me about. But it would not be unlawful to assist you in case of need.

HARDMAN   Fool, shut up now, and go away. I need to think.

228 **Do . . . way.** *KK* here omits a transitional comic passage in *TS*: Hortensio re-enters '*with his head broke*' (2.1.140.1), i.e. injured, and reports how Katherina has hit him with the lute, much to Petruccio's amusement (2.1.141–61).

228–33 **Will . . . around.** The passage follows *TS*, 2.1.165–8, but only Hardman explains why he wants to wait alone. He describes his first meeting with Catharina as a 'little dance' ('Gängelchen', literally 'little walk'). See Grimm, 'Gängchen'.

235–59 has no equivalent in *TS*.

236 *capitolium* figurative for 'head' (see Grimm). Wormfire seems to warn Hardman of Catharina's probable resistance.

239 *testiculos* Wormfire plays with the similar sounds of the Latin word for 'testicles' and 'to bear witness' ('testieren', Grimm, 1).

244–6 **My . . . about.** The German is unclear, but Wormfire probably suggests that Hardman is afraid that his servant will see him having his 'title and name' of shrew-tamer tested.

WORMFIRE   I can well believe you: there will be brave 250
lectiones, you will receive the *contra*. I will go in and
see what kind of maidservant my lord *Signor*'s virgin
lady keeps. If she is pliable and worth the trouble, I
will take pains to introduce my tool into her good
favours. The servant must walk in the footsteps of the 255
master. Meanwhile, my lord, you have my blessing,
and good luck for your work. I will say a solemn
Lord's Prayer for both of you with the maidservant of
your dear lady.   *Exit.*

HARDMAN   The moment is at hand. I am ready, come 260
what may: if she chides and rages according to
her laudable habit, I will praise her grace, and will
prefer her sweet voice to the artificial song of the
nightingale. If she growls and complains, I will praise
her daintiness all the more. If she looks as sour 265
and shrewish as all the furies and the devil's dam
together, I will praise her friendly and clear face
above the bright gleam of the sun. I will compare
her face to lovely roses and lilies, washed clean by
purest dew. If she is mute on purpose and does not 270
honour me with one word, I will scrape eloquence out
of both my pockets, and will glorify her eloquence
above all eloquence. If she bids me a shameful

250–9 Wormfire uses Latin (e.g., '*lectiones*'), Italian ('*Signor*') and a religious register (e.g. the 'Lord's Prayer') to lend a mock formality to his bawdy speech.

250–1 **there ... contra.** Wormfire imagines the first meeting between Hardman and Catharina parallels an educational formula consisting of lessons (*lectiones*), and 'pro et contra' debating, with Catharina resisting Hardman's proposal.

251–6 **I ... master.** Wormfire's first reference to Catharina's maid Sybilla, whom he hopes to seduce.

252 **maidservant** ('Kammerkätzchen', literally 'chamber kitten'). The German word connotes 'lover' (Köhler, 230).

254 **tool** See note at 180.

260–85 *KK* follows Petruccio's soliloquy on his taming technique (*TS*, 2.1.167–79) but amplifies the speech by increasing the number of conditionals from five to six and adding a summary of his strategy ('In short . . . it', 279–83).

266 **furies** See 1.3.282–4n.

266 **devil's dam** See 1.3.87n.

goodbye with abuse, teasing and curses, I will give
obedient thanks, as if she had invited me to the   275
best banquet. If she refuses to honour me with the
slightest favour, I will wish for the day and hour of
our wedding and bedding as if she had set them
herself. In short, I will make such a mixture of sugar
and wormwood that she won't know how to annoy   280
me. This confusion will be to my advantage. A proper
art not known to everyone is how to enter into the
humour of others, and to master it. But here she
comes. The coin is good, and may be accepted for
sterling.   285

[*Enter* CATHARINA.]

Sprightly now: good day, Madame Trina, for they say
this is your name.

CATHARINA   Your fool's head has heard right, although
you are hard of hearing. Sensible people call me
Catharina.   290

HARDMAN   You cut yourself, Lady Trina, with a big
knife. Like Matz, they give you a bad name, like silly

---

280 **wormwood** ('Wermuth') proverbial for
the plant's bitter taste (Grimm, 2a).

284–5 **The ... sterling.** presumably an
approving comment about Catharina on
seeing her approach.

285 SD D1 and D2 provide no entrance SD
for Catharina.

286 **Trina** Petruccio habitually calls
Katherina by the shortened name 'Kate',
while Hardman calls Catharina 'Trina'
('Trine' in German). *KK* may choose
'Trine' over the more common forms
'Käthe' or 'Kätchen' because of Trine's
secondary meaning: silly stupid woman
(Grimm, 'Trine', 4). Unlike Petruccio,
who uses 'Kate' throughout the play,
Hardman calls Catharina 'Trina' only in

this and his next speech. See also 5.1.57n.

288 **fool's head** The German literally means
'hare's head' ('Hasenkopff'). 'Hase'
('hare') was a designation in early
modern German for a foolish person (see
Köhler, 232–3). For other hare insults,
see 1.2.29, 2.1.394–5, 455, 3.1.186–7.

291–304 *KK* preserves much of the shape of
TS (2.1.184–93) but amplifies the hyperbolic praise with further laudatory adjec-
tives, and adds Hardman's (mock) religious point that he has come 'by divine
providence' (303).

292 **Matz** A diminutive of Mathäus
('Matthew'), Matz denotes a common
name (like Jack or Jill) as well as a cow-
ardly man (Grimm, 'Matz', 4).

Trina, and often evil Trina, shrewish Trina. O, you
tenderest example of all Trinas in the world,
you loveliest of all virtuous Trinas, most excellent 295
coy Trina, blessed be all praiseworthy Trinas for
your sake, you never-sufficiently-praised Trina. Your
beauty, meekness, your great maiden bashfulness,
modesty and worthiness, besides other laudable and
fair virtues, are known far and wide. Because I have 300
heard of these (which are merely a shadow compared
with the creature herself), I have been moved to come
here by divine providence to woo you to be my dearest
wife, my flesh and blood.

CATHARINA   You have been moved by your worm- 305
eaten brain to come here. Let the rogue who led
you here lead you away again. I think you are a
movable.

HARDMAN   What kind of animal is that, a movable?

CATHARINA   A chair one can move about.   310

HARDMAN   Well said, come and sit on my lap then.

CATHARINA   That bench is not clean enough for maidens.
Asses like you carry something else.

HARDMAN   Women are made to carry us, and so are you.

CATHARINA   But no such clay-brained rogues as you.   315

HARDMAN   Well, let us cut this short. Dearest Catharina,
I do not want to burden your beautiful body since
I know you are young and tender.

CATHARINA   All too tender to carry so big a swine.

305–79 This passage follows *TS* (2.1.194–243)
mostly speech by speech but occasionally
adds a short sentence (see 312, 316, 327,
340, 364 and 377 and notes), condenses a
few lines (see 320–1 and note) and adds
two short passages (332–8, 369–75).

312 **That . . . maidens.** has no equivalent in
TS.

315 **clay-brained** ('mausköpfische', literally
'mouse-headed') an insult (see Grimm,
'Mäusekopf', 2).

316 **Well . . . short**. has no equivalent in *TS*.

HARDMAN	Buzz not so much, you wasp, you are too angry.	320
CATHARINA	If I'm a wasp, why aren't you wary of my sting?	
HARDMAN	I know a good remedy: it needs pulling.	
CATHARINA	True, if the fool knew where it sits.	325
HARDMAN	Who doesn't know that? In her tail.	
CATHARINA	O, silly boy, that was a little too green. In her tongue.	
HARDMAN	Ha, ha, you speak truth with your tongue.	
CATHARINA	I do, because I am already tired of your boring jokes.	330
HARDMAN	Fairest Catharina, stop joking with your servant. I know you are not serious. Your natural friendliness shines through your performed spite.	
CATHARINA	I am weary of this foolery. Take such useless wind to another place. It bears no fruit here.	335

She starts to leave.

HARDMAN	My dearest lady and heart's darling, you must not speak thus about your love. I am worthy of more honour as a nobleman.	
CATHARINA	I will test your nobility with a slap in the face.	340

[*She strikes him.*]

320–1 condenses *TS*, 2.1.206–10, whose homophonic punning (e.g. 'buzz' and 'buzzard', 2.1.207–8) may have been impossible to adapt into German.

327 **O, ... green** has no equivalent in *TS*.

327 **silly boy** ('O alber[n]er Tropf', literally 'O, silly drop'). 'Tropf' designates an uneducated person as well as a rogue (Grimm, 'Tropf', 3b).

332–8 **Fairest ... love.** While *KK* translates the image of Catharina as wasp from *TS*

(2.1.210–15), it does not continue with the original's sexually suggestive punning on tails and tales (2.1.216–19), presumably owing to the lack of a linguistic equivalent in German. Instead, *KK* adds a brief exchange about wooing and refusal.

335–6 **Take ... place.** ('Wendet solchen unnützen Wind an anderm Orte an.') Proverbial (Wander, 'Wind'. 209).

340 has no equivalent in *TS*.

HARDMAN   You are quick and valiant, but I swear I'll
     slap you back if you dare to do this again.

CATHARINA   You would lose your coat of arms if you
     beat a woman. And with your coat of arms lost, you'd
     be a poor nobleman.   345

HARDMAN   You conclude well, but are an all too pretty
     gaoler. Tenderest Catharina, draw my coat of arms in
     the book of your favours.

CATHARINA   And what is your coat of arms? A coxcomb?

HARDMAN   My dear child, a cock without a fight if the   350
     virtuous Catharina agrees to be my hen.

CATHARINA   O, my good lord, you are no cock for me.
     You crow like an owl.

HARDMAN   No, come, fairest Catharina. Don't sour the
     friendliness of your dear face with frowning.   355

CATHARINA   It's my fashion when I meet an ape.

HARDMAN   What! Well, then you have no occasion, since
     there is no ape here.

CATHARINA   Truly, there is, there is.

HARDMAN   (*Looks around him.*) I am not blind, show   360
     him to me.

CATHARINA   It would be easy if I had a mirror.

HARDMAN   Perhaps it would reflect my face?

CATHARINA   Well guessed. Or did someone tell you?

HARDMAN   By Saint Velten, I am almost too green for you. 365

346–7 **You ... gaoler.** Petruccio describes
    Katherina as a 'herald' (*TS*, 2.1.226), well
    versed in the rules of nobility. Hardman
    spells out his admiration with a pun, liter-
    ally saying to Catharina 'you close well'
    ('Du schliesest wohl'), capitalizing on the
    double meaning of the German 'to close'
    as locking and as concluding, which gives
    rise to his designation of her as 'gaoler'.
353 **owl** a 'craven' in *TS* (2.1.229).
356 **ape** Inspired by Petruccio's imperative not
    to 'look so sour' (*TS*, 2.1.230), Katherina

answers that she does so because she sees
    a 'crab' (2.1.231), alluding to sour crab
    apples, a word play the German cannot
    reproduce. *KK*'s substitute activates the
    idea of imitation (i.e. aping).
364 **Or . . . you?** has no equivalent in *TS*.
365 **Velten** A short form of Valentine, the
    early Christian martyr Valentine of Terni.
    KK replaces *TS*'s 'George' (2.1.238),
    patron saint of England, perhaps owing
    to St Valentine's greater currency on the
    continent. See 4.1.92 and note.

CATHARINA   And yet you pretend to be fantastical.

HARDMAN   Everything I do is meant to amuse you.

CATHARINA   But I don't care for it.

HARDMAN   O, my dearest child, I love you more than anything in the world, so let my heart have a place 370 in yours. Let my body be yours, and yours mine. You will not believe how well I know how to please womenfolk.

CATHARINA   Every fool praises himself. Such praise stinks, and I am against all stench, so farewell.   375

[She starts to leave. He holds her back.]

HARDMAN   No, little Catharina, don't go away like this. Acquit yourself better.

CATHARINA   I'll scratch you if you hold me back one more time. Let me go, in the devil's name.

HARDMAN   If you will act like a cat, then know you have 380 met a true bear. But blessed image, do not go from me yet. I cannot let the soul part from the body thus.

CATHARINA   My soul is much too pure to live on such carrion.

HARDMAN   Such carrion shall feed you with what is 385 daintiest about it, my love.

CATHARINA   Stick such dainties in the mud. You talk like a fool, and you are a fool, and I take you for a fool.

HARDMAN   It is your pleasure to joke with your servant 390

369–75 has no equivalent in *TS*.

370 **place** We translate Köhler's emendation, 'Platz'; D1 and D2 read 'Plag' (i.e. 'nuisance').

377 **Acquit ... better.** has no equivalent in *TS*.

370 place] *Köhler* (Platz); *D1, D2* Plag

380–95 **If ... perfection.** *KK* adds this short passage on Catharina's refusal to accept his advances, and Hardman's insistence on offering them.

in all friendliness. I know well that my poor self does
not deserve such great praise.

CATHARINA   Indeed, I shall have to bring the *ABC
of Fools* and talk you through the *praedicamenta
hasionis*.   395

[HARDMAN]   A learned maid is truly a delightful piece of
work. What a pity the skilful Catharina does not
travel, but she shall do so now, with me. It gladdens
my flesh, bones and marrow that I shall live in such a
gifted body. I discern its highest perfection. You, my 400
heart's love, were depicted as blacker to me than our
Lord God's ape, yet I see you are whiter than his best
likeness. I was told you were shrewish, choleric,
blustering and sullen. Yet I see you are bathed in
grace, pickled with courtesy and spiced with modest 405
chastity. I will put you on the spit of my constancy,
and roast you so well in my hot love as will do
you good in body and soul. You are as sweet
and agreeable as the most delicious claret, and an
exquisite woodcock bathed in her own gravy. It 410

393–4 *ABC of Fools* (Gecken A.B.C.) The
reference to the Fools' Alphabet is
obscure. Köhler suggests that there may
have been an alphabetical list of characteristics of a fool (232).

394–5 *praedicamenta hasionis* combines the
scholastic *praedicamenta*, or categories,
which apply to objects of human appre-
hension, with mock Latin for 'Hase'
('hare'). Catharina insults Hardman by
suggesting that he is a fool. For hare jokes
and insults, see 2.1.288, 455, 3.1.186–7.

396 SP D1 and D2 mistakenly assign the
speech to Catharina.

396–400 **A . . . perfection.** has no equivalent
in *TS*. The beginning of Hardman's
speech about Catherina's learning seems
to be prompted by her use of Latin.

399–400 **live ... body** presumably by
having sex with her.

402 **Lord God's ape** ('Herr Gotts Affe') proverbial for the devil (Köhler, 234).

403–4 **shrewish . . . sullen.** *TS* has three adjec-
tives at the equivalent moment ('rough
and coy and sullen', 2.1.245). *KK* adds a
fourth, explicitly referring to Catharina's
fame as 'shrewish' ('eyterbüssig', literally
'pus-biting'); see Prologue, 3.

406–10 **I ... gravy.** The vivid image for
Hardman's comically ambiguous praise of
Catharina has no direct equivalent in *TS*.

410 **gravy** The German literally reads 'spiced
in thy own dirt' ('in deinem eigenen
Dreck gewürtzet'), referring to the
remains of butter in a pan after melting
(Grimm, 'Dreck', 9).

396 SP] *Köhler*; Catharina *D1, D2*

is impossible for you to look sour unless you have
drunk vinegar. You cannot show a resentful face to
anyone, nor bite your coral lips, nor twist the rose red
of your ruby mouth, nor make wrinkles on the lily
of your fair forehead as evil wives do. You receive   415
those who love you with virtuous politeness, and you
entertain them with graceful conversation. A modest
blush adorns your face whenever you hear a wicked
or unnecessary word. Your bright sparkling eyes
hide themselves when something immodest strikes   420
them. Why then does the unjust world say virtuous
Catharina is filled with vices? O, vicious topsy-turvy
world! Catharina is as upright and strong as a well-
grown hazel bush, and as brown and smooth as the
shell of a ripe hazelnut, though so much sweeter than   425
the dainty kernel inside.

CATHARINA   Dirty flatterer, be careful not to bite open
such a nut, as it shits into the mouth.

HARDMAN   There is no danger. That only happens with
those nuts that are worm-eaten, but Catharina is far   430
from being so. With your inestimable permission,
I would like to ask you to walk to and fro before me.
I know you do not limp.

CATHARINA   Go away, fantastico! Go, it is time you went
to the gallows or wherever you have come from.   435

HARDMAN   Dearest Catharina, you mean the knee-
gallows. You are right, my child, yours shall be for
me, it is perfectly shaped for me.

427–33 *KK* inserts a scatological exchange
before its adaptation of the last line of
Petruccio's equivalent speech (*TS*,
2.1.258) about Catharina's regular gait.
434 **fantastico** (Fantast) See 1.1.97n.
436–49 **Dearest ... over-adorable.** *KK*
inserts a brief passage with no equivalent

in *TS* containing sexual innuendoes and
more false praise by Hardman.
436–7 **knee-gallows** a euphemism for 'vagina'
(Grimm, 'Kniegalgen'), probably owing
to its shaft-like shape to which Hardman
alludes. 'Knee' was used to refer to the
genitals (Grimm, 'Knie', II.1.i).

CATHARINA   Nothing else is. You may present yourself, but at the right time.   440

HARDMAN   I will not miss this time. The sooner, the better.

CATHARINA   Do not sell yourself before the time.

HARDMAN   There is no hurry. The solemnities have already been agreed upon, and are witnessed between us. But what sense Catharina speaks as if she borrowed   445 from the sayings of the wisest. She is a true oracle whose voice is pure reason. Praised be the excellent host who lives in such a beautiful house. Her reason is more than admirable, her body over-adorable. Has beautiful Diana ever illuminated the woods with   450 her loveliness more than Catharina brings light to this place with her singular form? O sweet Catharina, you be Diana, and let Diana be Catharina. May that Catharina be coy and chaste, and that Diana cheerful.

CATHARINA   Astonishing inventions! From where did   455 you borrow all these wise speeches?

HARDMAN   They flow to me extempore, without study, from my natural mother, reason.

CATHARINA   A foolish son for such a sage mother.

HARDMAN   Am I not exceedingly wise, my reason-rich   460 Catharina?

446 **sayings ... wisest** ('Sprüchwörtern der weisesten') probably a reference to the Old Testament Book of Proverbs (Buch der Sprichwörter), whose central theme is wisdom.

447–9 **Praised ... over-adorable.** The body/house metaphor has a long history in the Judeo-Christian tradition. Compare Sebastian's reference to Catharina as 'a fine house' with 'an evil owner' (1.1.142–3).

449–86 **Has ... wife.** This passage adapts *TS* (2.1.260–82) speech by speech, with the exception of a short passage added by *KK* (466–70).

449–52 **Has ... form?** In the equivalent passage in *TS*, Katherina is compared to Diana, the Roman goddess of hunting and chastity, because of her 'princely gait' (2.1.261).

455 **Astonishing inventions!** Catharina literally says 'hare inventions worthy-of-astonishment' ('Verwunderns würdige Hasen Einfälle'). For other comic references to hares, see 2.1.288, 394–5, 3.1.186–7.

CATHARINA   Yes, and so beware of excess.

HARDMAN   You speak well according to your good
fashion. I will do what you say, when I lie in your soft
bed and warm lap.   465

CATHARINA   Be as keen as you like. One does not burden
the cradle with an ass.

HARDMAN   That would not be worthwhile. For now I
only wish to take care of your bed, lovely Catharina.
The cradle will follow when the time is right. I will   470
also hold back all other words for now, and tell you
my suit in plain German: your father has wholly
agreed that you shall be my wife. We are of one mind
concerning the dowry. I will have your hand this very
moment, whether you like it or not; whether you look   475
sweet or sour, I must and will have you, I and no
other. By this clear light by which I see your shining
beauty, I swear that you please me mightily, and that
I do not and cannot love any other in the world, and
that you must not trust any other but myself. Dearest   480
Catharina, I have been born to do you honour and to
tame you with friendliness, in order to turn a wild cat
into a Catharina as virtuous as all other virtuous
Catharinas. Here comes your father. Do not refuse, it
cannot be otherwise. I can, will and must have you as   485
my dear wife.

462 **beware ... excess** In the German text,
Hardman's reference to himself as 'weiß'
(wise) is deliberately misunderstood by
Catharina as meaning *white* (also 'weiß'
in German), an indication, Catharina
implies, that he may have caught cold,
whence her mock advice to him to keep
warm ('haltet euch nur warm'). Given the
impossibility of preserving the German
wordplay in translation, we substitute for
it the pun on 'exceedingly' and 'excess'.
466–70 **Be ... right.** has no equivalent in *TS*.
Catharina's second sentence ('Man leget

keinen Esel in die Wiege.') is probably
proverbial (Köhler, 235), prompting
Hardman's reference to their future offspring.
468–86 mostly a close rendering of Petruccio's
equivalent speech (*TS*, 2.1.269–82), with
two additions in which Hardman affirms
their mutual exclusivity: 'I and no other'
(476–7) and 'I do not and cannot love any
other in the world' (479).
486 SD Baptista enters with Gremio and
Tranio (as Lucentio) (*TS*, 2.1.277 SD),
Veit having no equivalent in *TS*.

Enter THEOBALD, SEBASTIAN, FELIX
[*as Hilarius*] *and* VEIT.

THEOBALD   Well, Sir Hardman, how is it with you? How
is fortune dealing with you both?

HARDMAN   Very well, very well, father. How could I be
unfortunate with such a dear favourite of fortune?   490

THEOBALD   But why so sad and sullen, my daughter?

CATHARINA   Can you still call me daughter? You have
proved unfatherly to me and given me to such a
madman without my knowledge or consent, a raging,
bloodthirsty fellow, a swearing and blaspheming   495
fantastico who intends to outwit me with all sorts of
evil and foolish wiles. Is this the work of a well-
meaning father?

HARDMAN   You are rightly angry, dearest heart. [*to
Theobald*] It is true, father. It offends her that you and   500
all the world have done her such injustice by painting
her as evil, raging, stubborn, sullen, roaring, choleric
and I don't know what else. From now on I will not
permit anyone to do so again, and will defend her
name with my life. Indeed, though she is a little mad,   505
she is so for her own reasons, that is, in order to
protect her modesty and honour from deceptive
seducers. I know this angelic image is as modest and

487–574 This passage is mostly a close adaptation of *TS* (2.1.278–328), with some
short additions (see 497–8, 516–17, 519–
24, 528–9, 530–1, 560, 569–70) and one
that is slightly longer (544–52). The most
significant omissions are two short
speeches by Tranio (*TS*, 2.1.305, 324);
Felix remains silent in this passage.

493 **proved unfatherly** Katherina, by contrast, uses sarcasm: 'showed a tender
fatherly regard' (*TS*, 2.1.289).

496 **outwit** ('überteufeln', literally 'out-
devil')

497–8 **Is . . . father?** *KK* adds the last sentence
to *TS*'s equivalent speech (2.1.288–92).

499–515 Hardman's speech is close to
Petruccio's but adds the first sentence,
addressed to Catharina, with the feigned
acknowledgement that she is 'rightly
angry', and inserts the pledge to defend
Catharina's name against slander ('From
. . . life', 503–5).

507–8 **from . . . seducers** ('für vernaschten
Vögeln', literally 'from nibbling birds')
See Grimm, 'vernaschen', 2, and
'Vogel', 14.

meek as a turtle-dove, with no gall or choler. She is as
moderate as the dawn in summer time. Her great   510
patience makes me believe she is another Griselda
who endures every injury. Her chastity makes her into
another Lucrece. In short, because she pleases me,
and I please her too, we have concluded between us
that we want next Sunday to be our wedding day.   515

CATHARINA   Deny it, deny it, you rogue! I'd rather see
you hanged on Sunday!

SEBASTIAN   Do you hear what she says, Sir Hardman?

HARDMAN   Shut your mouth. You try to poke your nose
in everything, don't you? I took her as mine, and she   520
took me as hers. If we are content, what has it to do
with you and others? Who would speak against our
marriage? What are these rogues who desire to sow
discord between the betrothed? We are of one heart.
Our cause is right, and we have decided between us to   525
speak indirectly. There are certain necessary reasons
why I allow her to be shrewish when we are in the

---

511 **Griselda** (Chrysilla) The context and the
equivalent name in *TS* ('Grissell',
2.1.298) make clear that 'Chrysilla' is a
variant of 'Griselda', the model of wifely
patience known from Boccaccio,
Chaucer and elsewhere. The German
text praises the patience of Griselda by
using a probably proverbial but now
obscure expression, literally saying that
'mice have nested in her body' ('welcher
auch gar die Mäuse in den Leib gen-
istet'). See Köhler, 237.

513 **Lucrece** Roman model of wifely chastity who killed herself after being raped
by Tarquin. Cf. 'Roman Lucrece' (*TS*,
2.1.299).

516–17 *KK* adds the forceful first sentence to
TS's equivalent speech (2.1.302).

519–58 adapts Petruccio's speech at *TS*,
2.1.306–21, by adding several short passages and inserting a short dialogue with
Catharina ('Your . . . her', 542–55).

519–24 **Shut ... betrothed?** The degree of
Hardman's (pretended) irritability has no
equivalent in *TS*, where Petruccio simply
says, 'Be patient, gentlemen', and asks,
'If she and I be pleased, what's that to
you?' (2.1.306–7).

522–3 **Who ... marriage?** ('Es heisset mit
euch nun verbott die Kaute.') The
German is obscure, but Hardman's
objection to any opposition to the marriage is clear.

525–6 **to ... indirectly** ('so verblümet zu
reden', literally 'to speak with such
flowers') See Grimm, 'verblümen', 2.

company of fools. When we are alone, the business
is quite different. She loves me as fervently and
whole-heartedly as I love her. I dare anyone who lays   530
a finger on her! She is the friendliest Catharina that
ever was born. The dear child fell upon my neck, and
wound herself around me as ivy circles around a
tree. She gave me one kiss after the other. O, you
gentlemen are mere novices in the world: you do not   535
know how the world runs. You will not believe how
graciously she behaves when we are *solus cum sola*.
But since my cause is well advanced, I must travel to
Frankfurt now, and buy the most gorgeous robes and
jewels. My dearest must make her beauty yet more   540
beautiful with beautiful gems. She shall not lack
ornaments whatever the price. – Your little hand on
this, my heart's darling.

He extends his hand to her.

CATHARINA   A hand is not to be thrown away like that.

528–9 **When ... different.** has no equivalent in *TS*.

530–1 **I dare ... her!** ('Trotz dem der jhr ein
Haar krümmet', literally 'Beware he
who bends one hair of her hairs'). For
this proverb, see Grimm, 'Haar', 17g,
and Wander, 'Haar', 128. The sentence
has no equivalent in *TS*.

533–4 **wound ... tree** *KK* substitutes this
vivid image for *TS*'s 'hung about my
neck' (2.1.312).

535–6 **you ... runs** ('Ihr wisset noch nicht,
wo Barthel den Most holet', literally 'you
do not know yet where Barthel gets the
must', i.e. the freshly-pressed grape juice)
a proverb, referring to someone who is
worldly wise and concludes well (Grimm,
'Barthel').

537 *solus cum sola* Latin, a man alone with a
woman.

539 **Frankfurt** a Free Imperial City of the
Holy Roman Empire in which trade
flourished; presumably the play's
place of publication (see Introduction,
pp. 147–9). See also 'Worms' at 1.3.249
and note.

542–7 SD **Your ... his.** *KK* repositions
Petruccio's order, 'Give me thy hand,
Kate' (*TS*, 2.1.318), adds a SD in which
he extends his hand to her (543 SD) and
only later grabs her hand for a forced
consent (547 SD). For the clarification of
action through *KK*'s SDs that is not
spelled out in *TS*, see Introduction,
pp. 121–4.

544–52 **A ... ourselves.** *KK* inserts this brief
exchange into the adaptation of
Petruccio's speech (*TS*, 2.1.306–21),
making Catharina articulate her
resistance.

HARDMAN Be not ashamed, my heart. All these 545
people present are our friends. Come, give me your
hand.

He takes her hand and presses it into his.

CATHARINA I believe this rogue is not only a magician
but also stark mad.

HARDMAN You speak well, fairest Catharina. I, Hardman, 550
have bewitched you, and you me through the poison
of love. We will help ourselves. – Indeed, father,
you have raised the good child too simply: she is
ashamed and blushes when someone so much as
looks at her. There is nothing more to do now but 555
arrange the wedding festivities and invite merry
guests. This coming Sunday we will stand in church;
today I must leave.

THEOBALD I am so confused by this thing, I hardly know
what to say. I am signing a pact with the devil. 560

HARDMAN Pardon me, father, do you wish to go back on
your word? How is it with you?

THEOBALD If the match is ordained by the Highest,
so may it be. May your hearts be like your hands,
indissolubly locked together. May God give you 565
joy.

SEBASTIAN We all join in that wish from the bottom of
our hearts.

---

547 SD The violent action contrasts with *TS*,
where Baptista politely asks for both their
hands in order to join them (2.1.322).

560 **I . . . devil.** Theobald literally says 'now
I am holding the wolf by the ears' ('Ich
halte jetzt recht den Wolff bey den
Ohren'), expressing his concern that his
daughter has vocally resisted the match.
The proverb refers to someone in a com-

plicated situation in which they can neither advance nor return. For its Latin
origins, see Köhler, 238. See also
Wander, 'Wolf', 580. The passage has no
equivalent in *TS*.

567–8 Gremio and Tranio jointly say they
'will be witnesses' (*TS*, 2.1.324) to the
match. *KK* assigns the speech to
Sebastian alone.

VEIT [*aside*]   Hit the virgin mark, that will not be hard.
Remember my wedding gift.   570

HARDMAN   We two lovers wish you the same, and now
adieu, gentlemen, until we meet again. – Come, my
dearest darling, we shall take loving leave of each
other inside.

[*Exeunt Catharina and Hardman.*]

SEBASTIAN   This iron is oiled quickly. I have never seen   575
a marriage concluded so swiftly.

THEOBALD   May God on High bless this marriage. I have
played the adventurous merchant and pawned my
goods at great risk.

SEBASTIAN   Venture often wins. I have no doubt about   580
its success and wish it wholeheartedly. But my lord,
what about your resolution concerning your younger
daughter? I am your neighbour and was the first to
court her. I have the oldest letters.

VEIT (*aside*)   But they were ill-received.   585

FELIX   And I am the one who loves and deserves this
beautiful lady most.

SEBASTIAN   My young lord, you could not love as
faithfully and steadily as I do.

FELIX   Old frost-beard, your love is as frozen as your   590
powers.

569–70 Veit's bawdy aside is added by *KK*.
For the 'wedding gift' ('Brautstück'), see
74 and note.
573–4 **we ... inside** in marked contrast to
Petruccio's 'And kiss me, Kate' (*TS*, 2.1.328).
575 **This ... quickly.** ('Dieses Eysen ist
bald, und hurtig geschmieret.') added by
KK, perhaps proverbial.
577–84 **May ... her.** *KK* remains close to *TS*
(2.1.330–7), but omits Tranio's continuation of Baptista's conceit, imagining
Katherina as a commodity (2.1.332–3),
and its conclusion in a couplet shared by

Baptista and Gremio (2.1.334–5).
584–5 **I ... ill-received.** *KK* adds the vivid
detail of Sebastian's 'oldest letters' and
its subversion in Veit's aside.
586–602 This passage at first follows *TS*
closely (586–91; 2.1.339–42) but then
replaces a brief tit for tat on Tranio's
youth and Gremio's age (2.1.343–4) by a
longer version, including the extended
horse-riding conceit, with a suggestive
comment by Tranio that Sabina is a
'young jade' who needs to be ridden by a
vigorous 'horseman' like Felix.

SEBASTIAN   I trust I am more able-bodied than you,
    milksop.

FELIX   What do you want, old man? Your spirit is
    willing, but your flesh is weak. You are much too   595
    stiff to mount a fresh young jade, and to manage it
    like a good horseman.

SEBASTIAN   Young fellow, you are too light, and would
    soon be unsaddled.

FELIX   And you, old schoolboy, have lost your spurs.   600
    Your whip is much too limp. When others dance, you
    must hold the lights.

THEOBALD   It is not seemly that you gentlemen should
    quarrel like boys. Sir Hilarius, I wish to talk with
    you in private for a while before I inform you of my   605
    decision.

They go to the side.

SEBASTIAN   This doesn't please me at all. Such great
    confidence between them, O me.

VEIT [*aside*]   I fear you will come second. Our maid
    likes the young man more than the old.   610

SEBASTIAN   It's a shame that people who lack
    understanding have small respect for honourable old
    age. *Magna fuit capitis quondam reverentia cani.*

VEIT [*aside*]   Even if you gather all the maxims from

---

592   **you** From this point in their confrontation
   (592–602), Sebastian and Felix use the
   familiar (and here impolite) second-person
   singular pronoun, 'du', to address each other.

593   **milksop** (Milch-Maul) See 1.1.102 and
   note.

594–5   **Your ... weak.** proverbial, derived
   from Matthew 26.41 / Mark 14.38.

594   **old man** The German literally says 'turnip
   robber' ('Rübendieb'). Not in Grimm.

601–2   **When ... lights.** proverbial (Wander,
   'tanzen'. 110). Felix charges Sebastian with
   the inability to engage in (sexual) action.

604–20   **Sir ... alive.** Whereas in *TS*,

Baptista directly goes on to ask the two
suitors about the dowry, *KK* inserts a private talk between Theobald and Felix
during which Sebastian complains to
Veit about disrespect for old age.

613   *Magna ... cani.* Latin, reverence
   towards the white head used to be great
   in the past. From Ovid's *Fasti* (V, 57).

614   **maxims** ('Sprüche', literally 'sayings')
   Veit mocks Sebastian's pompous Latin
   quotation by referring to the humanist ped-
   agogical practice of commonplacing, i.e.
   collecting quotations from classical authors
   in order to use them at opportune moments.

Cicero and Seneca, you will not convince a pretty 615
maid that you are more suitable for her than a fresh
young gentleman. I would not recommend our maid
to you; she has too much fire and would melt your
remaining strength. You would sink into your grave
alive.   *Exit.* 620

THEOBALD   Gentlemen, because it is my fatherly task
to do the best for my daughter, I have taken the
decision that he who can and will keep his promises
towards her, and who receives her consent, he shall
have her.   625

SEBASTIAN   My wealth is well known to you, my lord.
My house is filled with many beautiful wares for use
and ornament. My coffers hold many coins and other
valuables. My estates outside town have oxen, horses,
cattle, sheep and enough of everything else. My acres 630
are well tilled. I myself am somewhat old, but if I pay
my debt to nature tomorrow, my love will inherit
everything.

FELIX   The last sounds best, the first least. I can set three
houses against his, the least of them better than his by 635
far. Everyone knows that they are abundantly and
most nobly furnished. The rent of my estates adds up
to at least 2,000 thaler a year, not counting the sale of
the harvest. Have I tickled you with that, sir?

621–5 *KK* stays close to *TS* (2.1.345–8) but
has Theobald add that the suitors need to
'receive [Sabina's] consent' (624).

626–33 *KK* follows *TS* (2.1.350–66) but condenses Gremio's lavish description of his
wealth, notably by collapsing exotic
luxuries like 'Tyrian tapestry' and
'Turkey cushions' (2.1.353–7) into general 'ornament'.

634–9 *KK* follows Tranio's bragging
response (*TS*, 2.1.367–75), but omits the

place names ('Pisa', 'Padua', *TS*,
2.1.371–2), as elsewhere (see 3.2.317–19
and note).

634 **The . . . least.** 'The last' probably refers
to Sebastian's death; 'the first' presumably to his wealth.

638 **thaler** ('Reichsthaler') a silver coin that
was widely in use in the Holy Roman
Empire from the sixteenth to the nineteenth century. Cf. Tranio's 'two thousand ducats' (*TS*, 2.1.373).

SEBASTIAN　If this is true, you outstrip me. Yet I still　640
have 20,000 ducats *in banco*. This concludes my case,
will you accept it?

FELIX　Say no more. My father has a ton of gold in
exchange, discounting what is here and there in other
goods. I will assure this beautiful lady of what I have　645
said here, and ten times more than you. Besides I am
a fresh young man who will please her in everything
else.

SEBASTIAN　I must not promise more than I have.

FELIX　Then the bride is mine according to my lord.　650

THEOBALD　Yes, as long as your father gives his consent
and assurance. Should you die before Lord Sebastian,
my daughter would be in a delicate position given
your promise.

FELIX　O, have no fear on that account. He is old, I am　655
young.

SEBASTIAN　Can young people not die? Fine reasoning!

FELIX　According to the ordinary course of nature, I
mean, if Sir Know-It-All can understand that.

640–2　**Yet . . . it?** *KK* replaces Gremio's offer
of riches bound up in merchandise (*TS*,
2.1.378–80) by money 'in banco', and
eliminates all references to argosies,
galleys and other sea vessels (*TS*,
2.1.380–3), perhaps because the locations mentioned in the play are all distant
from the sea.

641　**This . . . case** The German uses a metaphor that literally says, 'this will close
the door' ('dis wird die Thür zuthun').

645–8　**I will . . . else.** Tranio offers 'twice as
much whate'er' Gremio proposes' (*TS*,
2.1.384). The last sentence of this passage has no equivalent in Tranio's corresponding speech (*TS*, 2.1.381–4).

649–59　*KK* follows *TS* speech by speech
(2.1.385–95), except that it adds the last
one, allowing Felix to have the last word
in his confrontation with Sebastian.

649　*KK* omits Gremio's promised gift of all
his possessions including himself ('me
and mine', *TS*, 2.1.387).

659　**Sir Know-It-All** ('eure nasenweisheit',
literally 'your nose-whiteness') with a
pun on 'Weisheit' and 'Weissheit'
(wisdom and whiteness). See Grimm,
'nasenweis', 3.

THEOBALD   It remains as I've said: if your father does   660
    not consent to the conditions, Sir Sebastian still has
    hope. Meanwhile, please step inside with me.
                    Exeunt [Theobald and Sebastian].
FELIX   An ill hope it is for him. I served my master well
    in this first bout. Now, I must think about further
    schemes: I think we need another player for the game.   665
    The unlawful son needs an unlawful father. I must
    look for one. All is topsy-turvy: usually parents
    produce children; now I must produce a father. But
    there's no harm in that; I hope my work will be
    handsomely rewarded.   *Exit.*   670

[2.2]   *Enter* WORMFIRE.

WORMFIRE   What the devil, not a soul here? Has the devil
    already taken my lord? Or is he hiding inside his lady?
    There's a mad wasp in the hornets' nest! May fortune
    smile on him. But he will not lose himself. What
    belongs to the gallows doesn't drown in the bath. I   5

660–2 **It ... hope.** *KK* omits Baptista's
reminder that 'Katherine is to be married' (*TS*, 2.1.397) on Sunday, followed
by Bianca a week later, which increases
the urgency of the disguise schemes in
TS. If Lucentio fails to meet Baptista's
ultimatum, Gremio is to marry Bianca
(*TS*, 2.1.400), a certainty which *KK*
dilutes by merely allowing Sebastian to
'still have hope'.

662 SD Theobald and Sebastian exit together,
while Gremio lingers after Baptista's exit
in order to taunt Tranio with his increased
chances of success (*TS*, 2.1.402–6).

663–70 *KK* stays close to *TS* (2.1.407–14),
but transforms Tranio's reference to
gambling ('I have faced it with a card of

ten', 2.1.408) into the newly arisen
necessity to seek 'another player for the
game' (665) of winning Sabina.

2.2 Wormfire's soliloquy has no equivalent
in *TS*. For the soliloquies added to *KK*,
see Introduction, pp. 104–9.

1   **What...devil** ('Wie nun zum Hencker',
literally 'What the hangman'). A
common expression for surprise or discontent in which 'Henker' is a euphemism for 'devil' (Grimm, 'Henker', 3).

3   **There's ... nest!** For the use of hornets
and wasps to figure madness, see 1.3.12–
13, 116 and notes.

4–5 **What ... bath.** ('Was an den Galgen
gehöret, ersäuffet nicht im Bade.') proverbial (Wander, 'Galgen', 34).

313

have set up my cause well. She is ready on certain
conditions. If my lord says yes, and her lady yes, the
whore will be mine. I thought my tool would have it
my way, but not this time. Such an honourable tree
will not fall with one stroke. I think she must be *harum*   10
bonarum and one of our kind, since her sign shows
that the host is a mad wag. Well, the more the merrier.
I will become an honourable cuckold from now on,
and cry cuckoo to my brothers. No matter, it's the
fashion now. I have many high and noble brothers in   15
the order, and doubtless some among you here, good
gentlemen, since I see your wives are laughing. The
whore pretends to be honourable towards my chaste
person. One is allowed to finger her a little, but to
pluck the cittern properly, that is not allowed. Patience,   20

6   **She** Sybilla, Catharina's maid (see
2.1.251–6).
7–8   **the whore** ('die Hure') Köhler bowdlerizes the text here and at line 18 by substituting 'sie' (i.e. 'she').
8   **tool** (Lümmel) See note at 2.1.180.
9–10   **Such ... stroke.** ('Ein solcher ehrbarer
Baum fällt nicht von einem Streiche.')
proverbial (Wander, 'Baum', 109).
10–11   **harum bonarum** Latin, of these good
ones. The reference is obscure, but
Wormfire presumably means that Sybilla
is among those women who are easily
persuaded to have a sexual relationship.
11   **one ... kind** ('unsers Volcks', literally
'of our people') here, those who are sexually available.
11–12   **her ... wag** ('der Schild [i.e. heraldic
sign] zeiget bey jhr an, daß der Wirth ein
Schalck sey') proverbial (Wander,
'Schild', II.3).
12   **the ... merrier** Wormfire literally says,
'many brothers-in-law, many friends'

('viel   Schwäger,   viel   Freunde').
Wormfire happily embraces his suggestion that Sybilla has promiscuous relationships with several men as long as he
is among them.
13–14   **I ... brothers.** Wormfire alludes to
the cuckoo's habit of laying its eggs in
other birds' nests, which accounts for the
term 'cuckolding'.
17–18   **The whore** See 7–8 and note.
19–23   **One ... better.** The first of four passages Köhler omitted in his edition
because he considered them 'besonders
schmutzig' (xxxviii), i.e. particularly
dirty (see Introduction, p. 158). See also
5.2.110–39, 146–54, 345–93 and notes.
19–20   **pluck ... cittern** a sexual metaphor.
See 1.3.143–4 and note.
20–1   **Patience ... farting** ('Was hilffts
patience ein par Fürtze') The German
text is unclear. Wormfire may jokingly
consider farting as a way to while the
time away.

2.2.7–8 the whore] *D1, D2* (die Hure); sie *Köhler*   17–18 The whore] *D1, D2* (Die Hure); Sie
Köhler   19–23 One ... better.] *not in Köhler*

patience, a bit of farting, one stays *in atrio* the first
time. But if the opportunity comes around again, the
wind shall swell my sails better. I will drift into the
Netherlands, though I aimed for England. It is good to
walk on a paved road, and the rider on a trained horse   25
doesn't stumble so easily. I must find my lord now to
see how it fares with his love, and to find something
wet. The heat of wooing has dried up my throat.

Exit.

3.[1]   *Enter* SABINA, [HILARIUS *as*] *Johannes,
and* [ALFONS *as*] *Musician* [*with a lute*].

HILARIUS   I tell you, dallier, put your pipe away, or blow a
milder note. Or else I'll set your mouthpiece straight
and show you a fingering that shall make your face fall.

21   *in atrio* Latin, in the entrance hall.

23–4   **I ... England.** The German uses 'Holland' for 'the Netherlands', suggestively punning on its similar sound to 'hollow' ('hohl'). Wormfire seeks the 'hollow land' of Sybilla's genitals which he also describes as 'England' ('Engeland', literally 'tight land').

3.1   No location is specified, but the scene is presumably set inside Sir Theobald's house. The scene falls into four parts: 1–105 (Hilarius' poetry lesson), 105–42 (Alfons' music lesson), 143–78 (Alfons' song) and 179–249 (to Alfons' concluding soliloquy). The first part closely follows *TS* (3.1.1–54), but replaces Lucentio's Latin lesson by dactylic composition in German. The second preserves the frame of *TS*'s music lesson (3.1.54–79), but delays the indirect discovery of the suitor's name to the third part, Alfons' song, for which there is no precedent in the English. The last part adds a brief discussion of the song between Sabina and Hilarius (179–91)

before it returns to equivalence with *TS* in having the servant call the daughter away from the teachers (*TS*, 3.1.80–4). *KK* inserts a short dialogue between Veit and Alfons, speculating on Hilarius' identity (203–23), followed by Alfons' reflections on his rival and Sabina's relationship to him, equivalent to *TS* (3.1.85–90) though greatly elaborated.

1   **dallier** Although both Hortensio and Alfons carry a lute, both plays use a term of general abuse for a bad musician regardless of the instrument in question. *TS* uses '[f]iddler' (3.1.1), *KK* the lyre, literally saying 'lyre Matz' ('Leyermatzen', see Grimm).

1–3   **or ... fall.** In the equivalent passage in *TS* (3.1.1–3), Lucentio menacingly reminds Hortensio of 'the entertainment' with which Katherina 'welcomed' him when he attempted to give her a music lesson (that is, hitting him on the head). *KK* realizes the threatened violence, portraying a more aggressive Hilarius who '*starts to beat*' (18.1) Alfons.

3.[1]]   *this edn*; Dritte Handlung. *D1, D2, Köhler*

ALFONS   You quarrelsome peevish pedantic school fox,
don't you know that noble music takes precedence,   5
and so do we her kindred. So be kind and give me
precedence, so that I may instruct this beauty for the
space of an hour. You then have the remaining time to
purvey your tittle-tattling drudgery.

HILARIUS   You brainless flog-worthy stockfish, you don't   10
have enough reason to understand that music is just a
parergon to refresh the mind when the higher *studia*
tire it. So stand back, and let me instruct her first, or I
will teach you to sing the *la mi*.

ALFONS   You are truly a brute. Beware or I'll explain the   15
syntax to you so well that the grammar hits your head.

HILARIUS   *Melius praevenire, quam praeveniri* is what I
learnt at school.

He starts to beat him.

SABINA   Hold, my lord. It's strange that you should
quarrel about what lies in my choice alone. I am not a   20

---

4   SP Here and throughout this scene, the
SP for Alfons in D1 and D2 is 'Musicus',
i.e. musician. For the same convention
regarding Hilarius, see 1.2.0 SD and
note. Our edition standardizes the SPs.

4   **school fox** ('Schulfuchs') *KK*'s adaptation of *TS*'s 'pedant' (3.1.4), referring to
petty pretentious teachers who were said
to wear cheap fox-furred coats (Grimm,
3).

8–9 **to . . . drudgery** *KK* replaces *TS*'s neutral 'lecture' (3.1.8) with an insult.

10–16 *KK* stays close to *TS* (3.1.9–15) but
has the suitors compete by adding
learned words (see notes at 14 and 16).

10   **flog-worthy stockfish** ('blauenswür-
diger Stockfisch') 'Stockfisch' was used
as an insult, particularly in relation to
beating someone up (Köhler, 240).
'[B]lauenswürdig' literally means 'worthy

to be made blue' with bruises (Grimm 1,
'bleuen').

12   *parergon* Latin, accessory.

14   **the *la mi*** The names of notes from tonic
solfa (see note at 1.3.18). 'Auf ein lami
ausgehen' (literally, 'ending on a lami')
also designated a pitiful ending, stem-
ming from the melodic movement from
la to mi which gives a plaintive close to
certain tunes (Grimm, 'Lami').

16   **the grammar** Alfons literally says he
will hit Hilarius with 'the Donat', a
common school grammar of Latin whose
title was inspired by the popularity of the
works of Aelius Donatus, a fourth-century Roman teacher of grammar and
rhetoric (Grimm, 'Donat').

17   *Melius . . . praeveniri* Latin, better to
forestall than to be forstalled. Unattributed
Latin proverb (see Philippi, 1.245).

schoolboy to whom you can give orders, and I do not
want to be bound to any lessons of yours, but to take
what pleases me. [*to Alfons*] There, go and tune your
instrument. In the meantime, I will hear something
from this gentleman.   25

ALFONS   And turn to me when I have tuned?

HILARIUS   Time will tell. As it is, the intrument does not
please; go and tune.

ALFONS [*aside*]   There is something strange behind this
preference. I must watch.   30

HILARIUS   My most beautiful lady, please be seated.

SABINA   How far did we get?

HILARIUS   Dearest, not yet as far as I would wish. I have
explained the necessary rules of poetry and shown
you the manner of the short long, namely when two   35
long hang from one short. But I notice that you do not
like it.

SABINA   I admit it seems a little boring. Show me another
manner.

HILARIUS   The best manner is the reverse, namely when   40
two short hang from one long. This manner is very
graceful and is called the *dactylic* manner, because
the *dactylis* shows its pleasant leaping fashion in its
own name: one longer syllable from which two

29–30 *KK* inserts Alfons' suspicions much
earlier than *TS* does (3.1.87–9), which
may suggest Sabina's greater forwardness in comparison to Bianca.

33–60 *KK* preserves the idea of *TS*, showing
the teacher express his interest in the
pupil through poetry, but departs substantially from the original by having
Hilarius treat native versification rather
than Latin translation (see Introduction,
pp. 118–19).

35–6 **the ... short** Hilarius describes the
seldom-used bacchius, a verse foot con-

sisting of an unstressed and two stressed
syllables: da-DUM-DUM.

40–50 Unlike Lucentio (*TS*, 3.1.31–6),
Hilarius does not reveal his true identity in
the course of his teaching (but has presumably done so earlier). Instead, he makes an
elaborate sexual allusion to the dactyl as
his penis ('one longer syllable', 44) from
which hang his testicles ('two shorter syllables', 44–5), before reciting a dactylic
quatrain about their love, including their
physical union. For the origins of the
dactyl as a figure for the penis, see Wollin.

shorter syllables hang in the most elegant fashion. 45
Listen to this example:

> **Love** me, my **dar**ling, my **love** will be **on**ly
> For **you**, the dear **love**ly one, **cher**ished for**ev**er,
> **So** that not **on**ly our **souls**, but our **bod**ies
> May **lov**ingly **move** and with **love** come to**geth**er. 50

SABINA I admit this manner is very delightful and
pleasant. But I find it is a little difficult and therefore
hard to learn.

HILARIUS My dearest, one simply needs to understand
well the qualities of the *dactyli*, and what kind of 55
nature and force lie in the three parts. Do not imagine
the thing to be more difficult than it is. Although it
may appear to you a little sour the first time, afterwards
it will seem so sweet that your appetite will not be
stilled. 60

ALFONS Honoured lady, my instrument is tuned.

SABINA Let's hear. Bah, how it jars!

HILARIUS Fellow, spit into the hole. The peg is not right.
Pull it higher. [*to Sabina*] Now try how the verse
works for you. 65

SABINA Well, I will try:

> **Lov**ing is **not** what has **been** my past **prac**tice,
> So **should** I choose **now** as the **mom**ent to **start**?

47–50 Our translation seeks to replicate the
German's dactylic quatrain with cross-
rhymes and four stresses to each line,
here displayed in bold.

51–60 Sabina and Hilarius jointly extend his
conceit, equating the loss of virginity and
sexual intercourse with the composition
of dactylic poetry.

61–81 After replacing *TS*'s Latin with a class
on native poetry, *KK* returns to *TS* (*KK*
61–6; *TS* 3.1.37–40) only then to diverge
again, substituting Sabina's dactylic
attempt for Bianca's supposed Latin
translation (*KK* 67–81; *TS* 3.1.40–3), in

which the women neither dismiss nor
encourage their suitor.

63–4 **Fellow ... higher.** Pegs of a lute
tended to slip out of place, but could be
made to stick by spitting into the peg
hole.

67–81 Sabina's dactylic composition
answers Hilarius' in kind, delaying her
answer to his suit (67–70). *KK* then
transforms Bianca's distrust (coupled
with the quiet encouragement expressed
by her translation (*TS*, 3.1.40–3)) into a
brief added dialogue between Sabina and
Hilarius (71–81).

    Taking their **time** is how **maids** please to **pon**der
    Unless there's some **fool**ish mis**take** on my **part**.   70

HILARIUS   You will improve in this form of poetry, but
    you need to choose better words. These are a little too
    rough and hard.

SABINA   Be content. The beginning is hard. It will
    improve.   75

HILARIUS   Indeed, I desire it, my love.

SABINA   Your wish will become true the sooner if I can
    trust your art. Mistrust sometimes weighs heavily on
    us women.

[HILARIUS]   I hope my heart's love shall yet find faith in   80
    me, because I will surely prove what I have spoken.

ALFONS   My instrument has a good tone now, Madam.

HILARIUS *[aside]*   But an ill one for me if your tuning has
    determined it.

[Hilarius and Sabina speak aside]

    I have little trust in this cord-twanger, he looks quite   85
    fiery.

SABINA   Perhaps the tuning warmed him up.

HILARIUS   I judge this fire differently and half believe

---

80 SP We follow Köhler in assigning the speech to Hilarius. D1 and D2 mistakenly ascribe it to Sabina.

82–106 *KK* loosely corresponds to and expands upon the equivalent moment in *TS* (3.1.44–54), flagging up the distrust between the two teachers, as well as between teachers and pupil.

82–4 *KK* converts *TS*'s musical joke into a more explicitly sexual one: Hortensio interrupts the lovers, saying that his instrument is 'now in tune' (3.1.44), to which Lucentio's reply ('All but the bass,' 3.1.44) plays on 'bass' (the lowest voice in a song) and 'base' (of low character). Alfons literally says 'my instrument now stands in a good tone' ('Mein Instrument stehet nunmehr im rechten Thon'), potentially with phallic insinuations. Hilarius picks these up, playing on the German 'Stimmung' ('tuning'), which could also mean 'mood'.

84 SD D1 and D2 have no SD here, nor at 98 SD and 178 SD. It seems clear, however, that the dialogue between Hilarius and Sabina at 85–96, 99–106 and 179–91 is spoken aside, unheard by Alfons.

80 SP] *Köhler* (Johannes); Sabina *D1, D2*

that you have lit it in his liver, my dearest. A lover
always wears the spectacles of jealousy on his ears. I   90
think I must put these on my nose now.

SABINA   You have nothing to fear.

HILARIUS   My dearest, do not hold it against me that I
keep some watch over him. Distrust is an effect of
love.   95

SABINA   Do not doubt me.

ALFONS   Lady, would you like to hear me too now?

SABINA   Sir, you hurry as if you were dying.

[Hilarius and Sabina speak aside]

HILARIUS   My highly honoured Sir Fiddle Artist has an
appetite that is much too keen. I bet my life the rogue   100
loves what I love. I have great reason to keep watch.

SABINA   Don't wrong me with this distrust.

HILARIUS   Trusting him and trusting you are two different
things, my lovely heart.

SABINA   The end will tell. *[to Alfons]* So come here, sir,   105
and let me hear your instrument.

ALFONS   Most honoured lady, I will not treat the matter
superficially with you, as we *musici* usually do, but
will deal with it quite deeply so as to impress the
science upon you.   110

HILARIUS *(aside)*   The devil take that pressing.

ALFONS   Here is the *scala* which I have devised in a
perfect new manner. Women usually conceive better

---

89   **you . . . liver** Love was believed to start
in the liver (see Grimm, 'Leber', 3).

99–100   **has . . . keen** Hilarius literally says
that Alfons 'is keen on the dear bread'
('ist gar eyfrig auff das liebe Brod'),
equating Sabina with the most basic sustenance.

107–16   KK follows *TS* (3.1.62–8) in having
Alfons introduce his lesson by presenting

his particular method of gamut teaching
(107–10), but adds Hilarius' jealous aside
and elaborates the sexual musical joke (*KK*,
111–16; *TS*, 3.1.62–3). Alfons' new '*scala*'
(i.e. scale, 112), a euphemism for his penis,
depends on his innuendo on the German for
b flat major ('dur', Latin for 'hard'), a
rising series of notes (*ascendendo*) followed by a falling series (*descendendo*).

of *b flat major* than *b flat minor*, so I will first instruct
you in the *ascendendo*, and then in the *descendendo* 115
which teaches itself.

SABINA   I already know much of this and wish to know
nothing further from you. There is no need to teach it
again.

ALFONS   But, Madam, here is a new manner. I do not 120
show it to everyone, but I will not be guilty of keeping
it from you.

SABINA   Sir, I am not so curious, so stick with the old
manner.

ALFONS   Will you take a lesson on the lute then?   125

SABINA   I am not in the mood now, nor ready to be
attentive enough.

ALFONS   Hear only one song which I composed yesterday
in honour of your favourite whom you know very
well.   130

SABINA   You must be mistaken, as I have not yet chosen
anyone as my favourite.

ALFONS   Your amusing politeness is well known. Do you
not know Sir Alfons of Nistlingen?

SABINA   Not more than I know you, nor do I love him 135
more.

ALFONS   As he is my great friend, I entreat you to listen
kindly to my composition, and to bless him with your
well-disposed favour.

SABINA   This   last   requires   some   time   and   ample 140

117–19 *KK* translates Bianca's rebarbative
rejection of the gamut (*TS*, 3.1.69),
adding that she is not desirous to learn
more about it through Alfons ('from
you', 118).

120–4 *KK* faithfully renders Hortensio's

offer and Bianca's rejection of the lesson
(*TS*, 3.1.70 and 3.1.77–8), but omits the
'gamut of Hortensio' (3.1.70–6). Instead,
KK adds a brief dialogue between the
two (125–42) in which Alfons' identity is
decoded.

consideration. If your song is fit for a maiden's ear, I shan't forbid you to play, since I love a good invention.

ALFONS *sits down a little apart, and sings the following song to the lute. To the melody of 'Is there anyone still living like me', &c.*

How oft has mighty Jove,
Lord of the heavens above,
Disguised himself to win   145
Some nymph that he has seen,
Her body made for play
To pass the time away.

Once he became a bull
Upon the beautiful   150
Europa strand, so named
For that sweet maid who came
Into his arms. O see
How lovely that can be!

---

142 SD ***To ... &c.*** ('*Lebt jemand noch wie ich &c.*') The text of the song to whose tune Alfons performs his composition was printed in a contemporary song book, *Tugendhaffter Jungfrauen und Jungengesellen Zeit-Vertreiber* (place of publication unknown, *c.* 1670; VD17 1:739188Q), by Hilarius Lustig von Freuden-Thal (Song 109, sigs G6v–G7r); see Scheitler, 1.1053–4. Hilarius Lustig von Freuden-Thal appears to be a pseudonym that may have inspired the name of 'Hilarius von Liebenthal' in *KK*.

143–78 Alfons reveals his identity to Sabina through a song telling how Jove seduced mortal women by transforming himself into various animals. Alfons' analogy between Jove and himself is unintentionally comic. The German song consists of rhymed iambic trimeter couplets, six stanzas of six lines each, as in our translation. Additionally, in the German version the second couplet in each stanza has feminine endings, the other couplets masculine ones.

143–66 The myth of Jove's transformations is told, most famously, in Ovid's *Metamorphoses*, a hugely popular work in early modern Europe (see Keith and Rupp).

149–54 For Jove's transformation into a white bull and his ravishing of the princess Europa, see *Metamorphoses*, 2.833–75, 6.103–7.

When he became a swan   155
The same old game went on.
With warm white legs wrapped round,
He was not fully bound,
For wandering at ease,
His beak went where it pleased.   160

A cuckoo in the nest
Was what he tried out next,
Leaving behind a pair
Of eggs to show how there
He was love's lucky one,   165
Like all who have such fun.

What Jove found easy then
Is much too hard for men;
We mortals must devise
Some less extreme disguise.   170
A man remains a man
Whatever he puts on.

He who now pines for you
With all his heart, he too
Has put on this disguise   175
To come before your eyes.
Ah! take him, grant relief
Lest he should die of grief.

155–66 Ovid merely alludes to Leda and the
swan as one in a list of Jupiter's affairs
(*Metamorphoses*, 6.109), suggesting that
the myth was well known by his time. Leda
gave birth to two eggs, one of them containing Helen. See also 2.2.13–14 and note.

157 The German literally says that her 'warm
white legs enclosed his' ('Die warmen
weisen Beine / Umschlossen ja die
seine'), perhaps suggesting Leda's (and
by extension Sabina's) willing surrender.

[Hilarius and Sabina speak aside]

HILARIUS   What comfort or wisdom do you draw from
      this song, my heart?   180
SABINA   It is too high for my low wit.
HILARIUS   It seems to me he has either presented my
      person in it, or is not who he pretends to be. I hardly
      know what to say or think.
SABINA   I know this bird from his song, although he   185
      covers himself in other's feathers. But he should not
      believe he can get away with his trick.
HILARIUS   I'd rather cut his throat.
SABINA   Don't be angry. If your words are true and I may
      trust them, then trust me likewise.   190
HILARIUS   These are golden words from a ruby-red mouth.

Enter VEIT.

VEIT   Madam, for some reason your father asks you to
      leave the books and tidy your chamber as best you can.
SABINA   What is going on?
VEIT   I don't know, but I think pelt-mongers have arrived.   195
      They'll want to work on fur if the maid gives them
      something to do.

179–91 Like Alfons' song, the short dialogue
between Hilarius and Sabina, in which
they reflect on the song's meaning and
Alfons' disguise, has no equivalent in *TS*.
185–6 **although ... feathers** ('ob er sich
schon mit andern Federn behencket')
proverbial (see Wander, 'Feder', 133).
Sabina refers back to Alfons' song about
Jove's disguise, and alludes to Alfons'
own disguise as a musician.
186–7 **But ... trick.** Sabina literally says,
'may he not believe that he will be able
to fix his hare-eggs here' ('aber er glaube
nur nicht / daß er seine Hasen-Eyer
anbringen werde'), mocking Alfons'
song by referring to the 'foul play' sug-

gested by the cuckoo eggs, which she
intends to prevent. For other hare jokes
and insults, see 2.1.288, 394–5, 455.
188 For Hilarius' anger and aggressiveness,
see 1–3 and note.
192–9 *KK* inserts this brief exchange between
Sabina and Veit, with a characteristic
sexual innuendo by the latter, 'fur' (196),
presumably alluding to Sabina's pubic hair.
192–3 *KK* returns to *TS*, assigning to Veit the
lines of a servant who reports Baptista's
request to end her lesson (*TS*, 3.1.80–2).
While the servant reminds Bianca to
'dress [her] sister's chamber up', since
'tomorrow is the wedding day', *KK*
avoids all temporal markers.

SABINA   O, you and your foolery. But I think I must go.
[*to Hilarius*] Farewell, sir.   *Exit.*

HILARIUS   I have nothing left to do here. Shadow follows   200
light.   *Exit.*

VEIT   Go forth with the blessing of the Lord.

ALFONS   This ink-eater follows her as if he were
something other than a servant. Honest Veit, what do
you think of your maid's fine Sir *Praeceptor*, will he   205
instruct her well?

VEIT   Between you and me, I almost think that he
instructs her as do other *Praeceptores* to whom noble
virgins are entrusted. They take them for their
underlings. He is a fresh young man named Johannes.   210
Perhaps he seeks to prepare the way to qualify our
maid according to the current mode, because he heard
it is no longer the fashion to enter the wedding bed as
a virgin. I cannot hold it against him. If I had the
means or the permission to do it, for all my sins, I   215
would. A saddled horse rides well.

ALFONS   Did you not observe their behaviour? Are they
very friendly together when they are alone?

VEIT   If I had seen that they bit into each other's mouths
in an over-trusting fashion, and rubbed against each   220

202–23 *KK* adds an exchange between Veit and Alfons which anticipates the latter's doubts about Sabina's chastity repeated at 224–49, in accordance with *TS* (3.1.87–9).

203 **ink-eater** ('Dintenfresser') Scribbler (see Grimm).

205 *Praeceptor* Latin, teacher.

205–6 **will . . . well?** As earlier in the scene, instruction implies ambiguously humanist teaching and sexual initiation.

207 **Between . . . me** The German reads '*sub rosa*', Latin for 'under the rose', meaning 'in secret'. According to legend, roses decked the ceilings of political meetings in ancient Rome, so that everything that was

said 'sub rosa' ('under the rose') remained in the room, i.e., was confidential.

211–12 **qualify . . . mode** Veit implies that the current mode is not to be a virgin, and so the qualification he has in mind is sex.

216 **A . . . well.** Veit suggests that sleeping with a sexually experienced woman is more pleasurable than with a virgin. Compare Wormfire's comment at 2.2.23–4.

217 **their behaviour** The German allows for the possibility that Alfons refers to 'her behaviour' ('jhr thu[n]'), rather than theirs, which would suggest Sabina's forwardness.

219 **they . . . mouths** i.e. they kiss.

other, I would not have permission to say so plainly. I
must go now. There is work inside, and I come away
empty-handed.   [*Exit.*]

ALFONS   It tortures me. I noticed it at once. I don't know
what to make or say of my fine colleague. I see   225
familiarity between them. Her friendliness to him is
too great. What loving looks she gave him when they
parted, while she hardly granted me one at all! It is
impossible she should not know me in this disguise
since I make myself known quite clearly. Does she   230
prefer a miserable tutoring fool, a lousy knave, a scurvy
school fox like him to a nobleman like me? Who knows
if this Veit is complicit with this tutor? Let the hangman
swear to it! But who is he? Nobody knows who he is,
although his character and brave appearance show   235
something noble. Yet it is the custom of noblemen to
sow seed in common earth. Many a brave lad has no

222–3 **I . . . empty-handed.** The German literally says 'it's up to me to wipe my
maw' ('Mein Maul wischen gilt mit'), as
if Veit had nothing to eat and could only
wipe away his saliva.

224–49 *KK* broadly follows *TS* (3.1.85–90) in
conveying Alfons' suspicions and thoughts
of revenge, but greatly amplifies his brooding
by adding insult upon insult (e.g. 230–2) and
sketching out his suspicions about Hilarius'
identity (234–6). Unlike *TS*, *KK* has Alfons
dwell on Sabina's guilt in 'prefer[ring] a miserable tutoring fool' (231) to a nobleman like
himself, and accuses her of giving him
'loving looks' (227). While Hortensio ends
his brief soliloquy on a rhymed promise to
'quit' Bianca by 'changing' his favour (*TS*,
3.1.90), i.e. courting another woman, should
she prefer the supposed lowly poetry teacher,
Alfons plans to expose Sabina by revealing
her liaison to Felix, the supposed 'Monsieur
of Liebenthal' (244–7).

231 **miserable . . . fool** The German literally
says 'a miserable labour shitter' ('einen
elenden Plackscheisser'), meaning a poor
teacher (see Grimm, 'Blackscheißer').

232 **school fox** See note at 4.

233 **complicit . . . tutor** ('unter dieser
Pedantendecke ist') Alfons draws on the
expression 'mit jemandem unter einer
Decke stecken' (Wander, 'Decke', 22),
literally to stick with someone under one
cover, i.e. to be complicit with him or
her. For 'Pedant', see 1.2.20n.

233, 238 **hangman** For other invocations of
the hangman, see 1.1.122, 1.3.31, 38,
2.1.33, 3.2.19 and 3.3.139.

236–7 **Yet . . . earth.** This proverbial
sounding expression means that
noblemen often have illegitimate children with common women, and the subsequent sentence indicates that Alfons
suspects Hilarius of being of such illegitimate origins.

bad parents. But whoever he is, I wish the hangman
would break his neck. He is just too forward. He may
be a rogue who tempts her and shames her reputation 240
through his fraud and mischief. Who knows what he
has done to her or given her to drink. It is impossible
that so noble a lady should be attracted to such a poor
lowly servant. I will observe a little longer. If I learn
something for certain, I will revenge myself on them 245
most grievously, and I will inform Monsieur of
Liebenthal how things are with her. As a virtuous
gentleman, he will leave her to public shame, and this
double-dealer will get his just punishment.   *Exit.*

239 **He . . . forward.** Alfons literally says 'he plays bad tricks for my taste' ('Er macht mir schlechte Possen'). 'Possen' could refer to tricks, pranks or jokes (Grimm, 2), but also specifically to farcical plays with Pickelherring, the itinerant players' fool figure (Grimm, 2b).

[3.2]   *Enter* CATHARINA.

[CATHARINA]   Now it is as I feared. I am put to shame. O,
    had I never been born! If only my father had died
    before he created me! I am a fine bride who is
    supposed to hold her wedding dance today. My heart
    warned me that this mad devil would torture me – me,   5
    who have tortured many, tit for tat. Now evil Catharina
    will become scorned Catharina. Dogs will pass by me
    and lift their leg. O, shame beyond shame! If this
    monster returns, I will give him the kindest words,

3.2 There is no specified location, but the
scene is presumably set in front of
Theobald's house. It falls into five parts:
1–85 (to Wormfire and Hardman's
entrance), 86–147 (to Theobald and
Wormfire's exit to the wedding), 148–232
(to the re-entry of the wedding group),
233–348 (to the exit of Theobald, Sabina
and Felix) and 349–98 (the dialogues
between Sebastian and Hilarius, and Veit
and Fabian). The first part, in which
Catharina and her father anxiously wait
for the groom, follows *TS* (3.2.1–83), but
adds Catharina's soliloquy at 1–12, and
shortens Biondello's report on the strange
clothing of bridegroom and servant (*TS*,
3.2.43–61 and *KK*, 72–80). The second
part, the arrival of Hardman and
Wormfire, fantastically dressed, remains
close to *TS* (3.2.84–126) but inserts
Wormfire's humorous comments. The
third part has Hilarius and Felix update
each other on their disguise scheme, and
Sebastian report on the wedding ceremony. It follows *TS* (3.2.127–82) but
elaborates on the shocking and amusing
descriptions of the wedding and adds
Fabian's caustic observations on service
and money (164–76). The fourth part,
which includes the re-entry of the company after the ceremony and Hardman's
insistence on leaving abruptly, is closely

adapted from *TS* (3.2.183–253), but adds
Wormfire's comments and augments the
fast-paced exchange between Catharina
and Hardman (258–312), while omitting
most of Petruccio's speech claiming
Katherina as his property (3.2.228–40).
The last part has no equivalent in *TS*. It
includes Sebastian and Hilarius talking
about the suit to Sabina (349–67), and
Veit and Fabian trying to make sense of
recent events (368–98).

1–12 Before adapting *TS*'s beginning of the
scene (11), *KK* adds a brief soliloquy by
Catharina in which she expresses her
fear of acquiring the reputation of
scorned bride, and promises to improve
her behaviour towards Hardman upon
his return (see Introduction, pp. 105–6).

1   SP In D1 and D2, the SP is implied in the
entrance SD.

1   **I am ... shame** Catharina literally says
'I sit in the jeer' ('Ich sitze im Schimpf');
see Grimm, 'Schimpf', 2.

4   **wedding dance** Catharina refers to the
communal festivities that she thinks will
be denied her, but she may also allude to
the wedding night (Wander, 'Tanz', 77).

6   **tit for tat** Catharina literally says 'sausage
for sausage' ('Wurst wieder Wurst'), a
proverb that reflects the custom of offering
one's neighbours fresh sausage when a pig
is slaughtered (Wander, 'Wurst', 67).

and force myself to be friendly even though it is   10
against my nature. Here comes the man who has
caused all this evil.

Enter THEOBALD *and* FELIX *[as Hilarius]*.

THEOBALD   Now I greatly desire news from the lad.
Today is the appointed wedding-day. Everything is
ready, but nobody has had any news from the groom.   15

Enter VEIT.

VEIT   My lord, I asked at Sir Hardman's usual lodgings
and all other sorts of places in search of news, but
could not discover the least trace of him or when he
will arrive. I reckon the hangman has broken his mad
neck.   20

CATHARINA   I would to God you were a prophet.

THEOBALD   I do not know what to do. This insult is too
great for my noble degree; with others it would seem
a farce. What will they say, those scornful people to
whom the high status of nobility is always a thorn in   25
the side? O, that I must endure such mockery!

11–12 **the ... evil** Compare Catharina's accusations against Sir Theobald in her speech at 27–41.

12 SD In *TS*, Baptista and Tranio enter with Katherina, Bianca, Gremio '*and others, Attendants*' (3.2.0.3), including presumably Lucentio. In *KK*, Catharina is already onstage, while Sabina, Sebastian and Hilarius do not enter until later, at lines 232, 176 and 152 respectively.

13–26 *KK* adapts Baptista's speech (*TS*, 3.2.1–7) but interrupts it with speeches by Veit and Catharina, added by *KK*, that heighten the suspense about Hardman's arrival.

22–6 *KK* preserves Baptista's fear of mockery (*TS*, 3.2.4) but adds the humorously self-reflective statement that the

situation would seem like a scene from a farce ('Posse') if only others experienced it too.

24–6 **What ... side?** Theobald literally asks, 'what verdicts will the splinter-judges render who are constantly stung in the eye by nobility's preference' ('Was für urtheilen werden die Splitter-Richter führen / welche doch des Adels Fürzug stäts in die Augen sticht'). Those harshly judging the petty foibles of others were called 'splinter judges' (Grimm, 'Splitterrichter'), a term derived from Christ's Sermon on the Mount: 'why beholdest thou the mote [i.e. splinter] that is in thy brother's eye, but considerest not the beam that is in thine own eye?' (Matthew 7.3).

CATHARINA   You should keep quiet, for who bears the
shame, father, except for me who am innocent?
Against my will I must submit to the desire of this
raging madcap. I must be promised to a rough rogue   30
who has no intention of keeping his word. I must be
forced to offer my faith to one who is faithless. That
kind of faithless man who would swear a hundred
oaths and then play his tricks. Here is your bride, now
marry her. O, that this should happen even to wisdom   35
like yours, yet even old hens lay in nettles sometimes.
But I am the one who has to suffer most, I mean the
jeering voice of the people. They will laugh enough at
mad Hardman and his bride, and make a song about
them. They will point their fingers at me, O, what a   40
shame!

FELIX   Peace, madam. Sir Hardman is not so thoughtless
as to expose Sir Theobald to shame and leave you to
the mockery of the people. Who knows what has
prevented his journey? Such things are common with   45
travellers. He will not fail us.

CATHARINA   If only I had never seen him! I wish him the
gallows or the wheel for his faithfulness! But none of
this does me any good.   *Exit.*

27–41 Catharina's speech remains reasonably close to *TS* (3.2.8–20) but shows a
more independent Catharina, pitching
her 'will' (29) against Theobald's, while
Katherina is 'forced / To give [her] hand
opposed against [her] heart' (3.2.8–9).

36 **even … sometimes.** Proverbial
(Wander, 'Huhn', 158).

37–8 **the jeering … people** Catharina literally says 'the people's fairy-tale voice'
('der Leute Mährlein Stimm'), linking
the oral and fictive quality of these popular stories to the way news of her slight
will spread.

38–40 **They … them.** *KK* adds the idea of
the slanderous song, concluding it with a
rhyme ('Die des tollen Hartmans und
seiner Braut genug lachen, ein Liedlein
von jhnen machen').

42–6 *KK* stays close to *TS*, but omits Tranio's
supposed acquaintance with Petruccio
('I know him passing wise', 3.2.24) and
offers instead a commonsensical explanation for Hardman's absence, adding
that '[h]e will not fail *us*', a reference to
his status as Sabina's supposed husband-
to-be.

49 SD In *TS*, Katherina exits at the equivalent moment, and she does so '*weeping*'
(3.2.26.1).

330

VEIT   He could do her good. I take it our lady has   50
  understood that there's something good about him.

THEOBALD   The poor child has cause enough to grieve
  and grumble. It would make a patient lamb impatient,
  let alone an angry cat.

Enter FABIAN.

FABIAN   Sir, sir, *mirabilia nova, mirabiliorum novissima*   55
  mirabilissima. Strange news of old stories the like of
  which you've never heard before, nor never will as
  long as the newsforgers fool men with lies.

FELIX   You speak merrily. Is it new and old at the same
  time?   60

FABIAN   The thing is merry indeed. It is Sir Hardman's
  arrival.

THEOBALD   How is he coming?

FABIAN   I do not say he is coming, but his horse is.

THEOBALD   Did he meet with some mishap on the way?   65

FABIAN   I have no report of that. The horse brings him on
  its back.

FELIX   You are indeed a fool. So he must be coming as
  well, since they are one.

FABIAN   Far off the mark: a horse and its man are two.   70

50–4 *KK* preserves Baptista's speech, substituting 'lamb' for 'saint', and 'angry cat' for
'shrew' (*TS*, 3.2.28–9), but inserts Veit's
sexually suggestive remark before it.

55–8 *KK* adapts Biondello's excitement (*TS*,
3.2.30–1), adding the Latin *mirabilia
nova, mirabiliorum novissima mirabilissima* ('new wonders, newest most wonderful of all wonders'), perhaps alluding to
the satiric anti-Catholic pamphlet *Nova
Mirabilia oder Neue Zeitung aus dem
Fegefeuer* (Nova Mirabilia or News from
Purgatory) by the pseudonymous
Theophilum Antipapium, which went
through a number of editions in 1668 and
1669 (see VD17 3:318763B, 12:154610G,
3:653749G, 14:678664E and 12:107853P).

59–70 *KK* assigns two speeches by Baptista to
Felix (*TS*, 3.2.32 and 3.2.78; *KK*, 59–60
and 68–9), transposes *TS*'s later conceit of
the horse and its rider (3.2.76–83) and omits
the somewhat obscure reference to 'Saint
Jamy' (3.2.79). *KK* also omits the brief dialogue between Baptista and Biondello
about whether Petruccio has 'come' or 'is
coming' (3.2.35 and 38), a grammatical
play that cannot be reproduced in German.

70 **Far ... mark** Proverbial, referring to
hitting the mark in archery (Wander,
'fehlen', 41).

FELIX   Well, what is your old and your new news?

FABIAN   He comes very honourably dressed with a new hat and old garments. He goes about in such Shrove-tide honours, and is surrounded by much *comitat.*

THEOBALD   Who is coming with him?   75

FABIAN   My lord brother, the lord's servant, decked out the same way. They both present themselves in such a peculiar way that you could take their garments for monsters and them for fools without hurting your conscience.   80

THEOBALD   I am glad he is here, let him be dressed as he pleases. It would be a good thing if the man could be as easily changed as the garment.

FABIAN *[aside]*   My vice-lord was fortunate in that, but hush, *pudeat te talia protulere.*   85

Enter HARDMAN *and* WORMFIRE, *strangely dressed.*

WORMFIRE   Ha, courage, in the name of all the saints, we have returned to German ground. Lord of a thousand

---

72–4 *KK* adapts Biondello's first words ('Why, Petruccio is coming in a new hat and an old jerkin', *TS*, 3.2.43–4), but radically condenses his lengthy description of Petruccio's outlandish dress (3.2.43–61).

73–4 **Shrove-tide** See 1.2.43n.

74 *comitat* Latin, retinue, companions.

75–80 *KK* faithfully translates Baptista's question (*TS*, 3.2.62) but compresses Biondello's description of Grumio's clothes (3.2.63–8).

81–3 *KK* translates Baptista's concession that he is 'glad' Petruccio has come 'howsoe'er he comes' (*TS*, 3.2.71), but adds Theobald's proverbial second sentence (see Wander, 'Kleid', 28).

84 **My ... that** presumably a reference to Felix and his disguise as Hilarius.

85 *pudeat ... protulere* Latin, you should

be ashamed to say such things. The speech has no equivalent in *TS*.

85 SD *strangely dressed* Not mentioned in *TS*'s equivalent SD (3.2.83 SD).

86–147 While Grumio is present in the equivalent passage in *TS* (3.2.84–122), he does not speak. Wormfire's four speeches (86–90, 117, 124–5, 138–9) strengthen his comical presence. See also 246–331 and note.

87 **returned ... ground** Presumably a foolish comment by Wormfire rather than an indication that he and Hardman have gone on foreign travels. In 2.1, Hardman affirmed that he 'must travel to Frankfurt' (538–9) to make purchases for the wedding.

87–8 **Lord ... years** ('Tausend guter Jahr Herr') probably a reference to Christ's thousand-year reign announced in the Book of Revelation (20.1–4).

good years, how nicely we shall be welcomed by our
flesh and blood, what affectionate rubbing there will
be, how it tickles me! 90

HARDMAN   Shut up, you babbling rogue, or I'll give you
a clout. But ye gods and little fishes! Greetings, father,
and greetings to you, gentlemen! Why do you stand
here with gaping mouths?

THEOBALD   Welcome, my lord. 95

HARDMAN   Yet I see I have not come well.

FELIX   We are pleased to see you but would rather see
you in more pleasing clothes.

HARDMAN   You don't understand, so please spare me
your further wisdom. If I were dressed even more 100
strangely, it would please me well. Why am I wasting
my time with fools here? Where is my dearest
Catharina? My sense and inclination are for her.
Where is my heart's beloved? How are you, father?
You gentlemen all gape at me as if you had never seen 105

88–9 **our ... blood** The German literally
says 'the opposites of our belly' ('unsers
Bauchs Gegentheilen'), i.e. the female
genitals (see Grimm, 'Bauch', 3).

92 **ye ... fishes** Our translation of Hardman's
blasphemous interjection, 'potz hundert
tausend Sack voll enten' (literally, 'a hundred thousand bags full of ducks'), which
collapses 'sacerment' (sacrament) into
'Sack' (bag) and 'Ente' (duck). The word
'potz' is derived from 'Gottes' ('God's').

94 **gaping mouths** Hardman literally says
'you stand here and sell maw apes'
('Stehet jhr hier und haltet Maulaffen
veil'). 'Maw apes' is a corruption of
'Maul offen' ('maw open'), which probably originates in the custom of selling
earthen pots in the shape of heads with
open mouths into which people would
stick kindling.

95–8 *KK* adapts *TS*'s pun on 'welcome' and
'come not well' (3.2.86–7), i.e. well
dressed, by means of 'willkommen' (welcome) and 'nicht wohl nach jhrem Willen
kommen' (not come according to your
will). *KK* omits Baptista's continuation
of the word play (*TS*, 3.2.88) and instead
inserts a punning speech by Felix.

99–107 *KK* closely adapts Petruccio's speech
(*TS*, 3.2.90–5), but adds Hardman's sarcastic comments about his interlocutors'
'wisdom' (100) and their inability to
'understand' (107).

105–6 **You ... man.** Hardman literally says,
'you lords gape at me like the goose at a
new gate' ('Ihr Herren gaffet mich alle
an wie die Gans ein neues Thor'), referring to a proverbial conception of geese
as being easily puzzled by commonplace
objects (Grimm, 'Gans', 2a γ).

a man. Am I a demi-beast? It's a wretched situation
when inexperienced people fail to understand things.

THEOBALD   This appearance will seem strange to every
reasonable person. You know that today is your day
of honour, and yet you come thus unready. A little   110
while ago we were disappointed about your absence,
now we are dismayed by your appearance in such an
unfitting fashion. Come, take off these foolish clothes!
It is shameful for you and for us.

FELIX *[to Hardman]*   Speak, sir, what held you up so   115
long?

WORMFIRE *[aside]*   That which does not press us down.

HARDMAN   It would be annoying for me to tell you at this
busy time, and still more boring for you to hear. Why
do you care? It is enough that I am here to deliver   120
myself up to my dearest lady and to fill her arms.
That's why I must go. Time flies, and I haven't
finished anything yet.

WORMFIRE *[aside]*   Damn it, time is getting long for me
and my appendage too.   125

FELIX   Wait, don't go in like that. Please, go to my
chamber and put on more suitable clothes first.

HARDMAN   Let me be hit by lightning if my love does not

---

106 **Am ... demi-beast?** *KK* transforms
TS's cosmic marvels ('Some comet or
unusual prodigy', 3.2.95) into, literally, a
'wonder-animal' ('Wunder-Thier'), that
is, a monster or a creature half-human,
half-animal (Grimm, 'Wundertier', 1a).

108–14   Theobald's speech remains close
to Baptista's in *TS* (3.2.96–100) except
that *KK* adds Theobald's first sentence.

115–16 Felix's question is a condensed version of Tranio's (*TS*, 3.2.101–3), but
Wormfire's aside, with its play on prepo-
sitions – 'held you up' ('aufhalten') and

'press us down' ('niederdrücken') – has
no equivalent in *TS*.

118–23 *KK* stays close to *TS* (3.2.104–10)
but omits Petruccio's hint at excusable
reasons for his late arrival (3.2.106–8).

124–5 *KK* adds Wormfire's aside about his
appendage (i.e. penis), as eager for
Sybilla as Hardman is for Catharina.

126–32 *KK* remains close to *TS* (3.2.111–14)
except that it turns Petruccio's straightforward 'Not I, believe me; thus I'll visit
her' (3.2.113) into a more emphatic
rejection of Felix's suggestion.

receive me in this outfit! A whole consistory of the
holiest people will not prevent me. My will is my   130
compass.

THEOBALD   But I hope you will not marry her like this.

HARDMAN   Exactly like this, or else may I drop dead! It
is me she marries, and not my garments. Why do I
need to argue? I have no need for a steward. I'm   135
wasting my time with these foolish antics. I will go in
and greet my bride with a lovely kiss.   *Exit.*

WORMFIRE   I will not be absent from there either. *A Dieu,
mon frère*, we'll drink to health and happiness today!

FABIAN   I am *pro* and *contra* to dispute this matter.   140

FELIX *[aside to Fabian and Wormfire]*   You are two fine
gentlemen.

FABIAN   Indeed, in fine drinking health!

THEOBALD   I must follow to be present at the reception.
If he doesn't take off these fool's robes, I think it   145

129 **consistory** (*'Consistorium'*) a high-level
ecclesiastical court.

130–1 **My … compass.** Hardman literally
says, 'mein Will ist meine Richtschnur'
('my will is my plumb line'), referring to
the device used to gauge the straightness
of surfaces (Grimm, 'Richtschnur', 2).

133–7 *KK* closely adapts Petruccio's equivalent soliloquy (*TS*, 3.2.115–22) except
that it omits the middle sentence
(3.2.117–19) about what 'Kate' will
'wear' in him, i.e. possess and enjoy,
including sexually.

137 SD–43 Modern editors of *TS* assume that
Grumio leaves with Petruccio (3.2.122
SD), but *KK* inserts a short exchange
between the servants and has Wormfire
exit a bit later.

138–9 *A … frère* French, farewell, my
brother. Wormfire takes leave of Fabian.

139–40 **we'll … matter** Wormfire literally
says 'today, drink shall set the cheers on
top of the toast' ('heut soll noch ein
Trunck das *prosit* auff *salus* setzen').
Wormfire's use of student Latin provokes Felix's subsequent allusion to the
manner of university disputations.

141–2 Felix sarcastically describes Wormfire
and Fabian as, literally, 'modest' ('be-
scheidene') gentlemen. Fabian puns on
the word by using an expression that
refers to pledging when being toasted
('Bescheid thun', Grimm, 'Bescheid', 8).

144–52 *KK* inverts the order of the corresponding speeches in *TS*, where Tranio
speaks before Baptista (3.2.123–6).

144–7 *KK* closely adapts Baptista's short
speech (*TS*, 3.2.126) before adding
Theobald's anxious plan to hide the wedding party to avoid public scandal.

would be wise to invite you all to my home. I would
rather not be scorned by the people.

                                    Exit [with Wormfire].

FELIX   I think that would be for the best. He will no
doubt play some other tricks. I believe his own
reasons have brought him to this. His good sense   150
shines through his mad and foolish behaviour. The
fool's cap covers many a shrewd mind.

                Enter [HILARIUS as] Johannes.

Here comes my master just at the right moment! –
How is it going with your own affairs? What you
have entrusted to me will soon be brought to a happy   155
end.

HILARIUS   Indeed I like the sound of this, since my
business looks pretty fair, too. Only one thing plagues
me, and it is no small problem: I have a fellow suitor
who doesn't seem to be the man he pretends to be. I   160
believe he is known to my lady, but so far I have
learned nothing from her, although I see her heart
belongs to nobody but me. But – (*They go to the side.*)

---

147 SD *KK* does not mention Wormfire's
exit, but as he has announced it (138–9)
and does not speak before he re-enters at
232 SD, we assume that he leaves the
stage with Theobald. Modern editors
assume that Biondello exits with Baptista
(*TS*, 3.2.126 SD), but Fabian remains
onstage, witnessing and then commenting on the conversation between
Hilarius and Felix (148–76). The other
character whom modern editors assume
exits at the equivalent moment is Gremio,
who is mentioned in the entrance SD at
the beginning of the scene (*TS*, 3.2.0.1)
but has remained silent. In *KK*, by contrast, Sebastian is offstage at this point
and does not enter until 176 SD.
148–52 Felix's speech expands on Tranio's
line, 'He [i.e. Petruccio] hath some

meaning in his mad attire' (*TS*, 3.2.123).
151–2 **The ... mind.** ('Die Narren-Kappe
decket manchen klugen Kopff.') proverbial (Wander, 'Narrenkappe', 4).
152 SD Most editors of *TS* since Rowe
assume that Lucentio has been onstage
since the beginning of the scene; in *KK*,
Hilarius only enters here. Oxf begins a
new scene at this point, whereas in *KK* it
is clear that Felix remains onstage when
Theobald and Wormfire exit, and does
not leave the stage until Hilarius arrives.
153–63 Whereas in *TS* (3.2.127–47), Tranio
and Lucentio discuss the need to find a
fake father and float the possibility of
abducting Bianca 'to steal our marriage'
(3.2.139), *KK* has Hilarius speculate
about Alfons' identity and talk aside with
Felix.

FABIAN   He'll sting her soon. I take it she's still to be
stung. I thought there was something else behind it. 165
What rogues there are in the world! One can rise
through such tricks. I could have helped my lord to
trick the people as much as this upstart does, strutting
around in such gorgeous clothes, and spending the
time feasting and guzzling. It plagues my blood when 170
I have to serve him. But when we're among people
who have nothing to do with my lord's business, I'll
happily let others do it. But what help is there? I must
bear it. *Spes lucri* is a pretty thing. If it were not for
that and my master, we would start a fight to change 175
places in this masquerade.

Enter SEBASTIAN *laughing.*

[*aside*] What's the matter with this old flatterer?
Laughter looks as pretty on him as on an ape that
wrinkles its nose when emptying its behind. O, blind
world, that this old, incapable man desires to venture 180
into someone young.

SEBASTIAN   I cannot breathe for laughter! But what's
the meaning of this, my go-between with my fellow
suitor?

164–76 *TS* has no equivalent to Fabian's
soliloquy about the dishonour of serving
a fellow-servant (see Introduction, pp.
104–5).

164 **sting** take her virginity.

173–4 **I . . . it.** Fabian literally says 'I have to
bite it away', that is, 'swallow it' ('ich
muß es so verbeissen') (see Grimm,
'verbeißen'. 2d).

174 *Spes lucri* Latin, in the hope of reward.

175–6 **we . . . places** Fabian literally says 'we
would start a movement of caps' ('wir
wolten ein Kappenrückens anfangen'),
that is, a fight symbolized by the disloca-
tion of caps when pushing each other (see
Grimm, 'Kappenrücken', 2).

176 SD *laughing* not mentioned in *TS*'s
equivalent SD (3.2.147 SD).

177–81 As in the preceding SD, the insistence on Sebastian's laughter has no
equivalent in *TS*.

177 **this . . . flatterer** Fabian mocks
Sebastian by literally calling him a 'soft
treader' ('Leisetreter'), an insult that presumably stems from the care with which
flatterers need to move in the presence of
a patron (see Grimm).

182 **I . . . laughter!** Sebastian literally says 'I
have nearly laughed myself into having a
bloated belly' ('Ich habe mich fast
bauchblässig gelachet'), i.e. he has been
struggling to breathe.

182–6 **But . . . news.** Sebastian's suspicion
and Felix's reassurance have no equivalent in *TS*.

FELIX   Your servant, Sir Sebastian. I recognized my   185
          countryman, and asked for the news. Where have you
          just come from?

SEBASTIAN   You ask where; well, from Sir Theobald's
          lodgings, where I attended an amusing *copulation.*

FELIX   Of what sort, my lord?   190

SEBASTIAN   And you ask? I see it is I rather than you
          who have been given the honour of being witness to
          this business. Sir Hardman is bound to Lady Catharina.
          There's a couple that is mad beyond all measure. But
          he is past compare. He's a true devil.   195

FELIX   And she is a fury among the devil's lovers.

SEBASTIAN   She's not to be compared to him. She's a
          patient lamb with a raging wolf, a meek dove with an
          angry hawk. Not even the devil can resemble his
          extraordinary nature. He cares for neither heaven   200
          nor hell.

FELIX   But what did he do inside?

SEBASTIAN   The priest had to hurry there, and then
          Hardman ordered him abruptly to couple them in
          God's name. The priest begged to be excused, pleading 205
          a lack of preparation. When he said he did not even
          have the book with him, Hardman threw a calendar
          into his hands and threatened him, ordering him not to

188–95 **You ... compare.** *KK* loosely adapts
the beginning of Gremio's account of the
wedding and Tranio's questions (*TS*,
3.2.149–53).

188–9 **Sir ... lodgings** In *TS*, Gremio has
come 'from the church' (3.2.148).

189 *copulation* (*copulation*) a joining; more
specifically, a wedding. In German it was
not until later that the generative act
became the dominant meaning.

195–9 **He's ... hawk.** This closely adapts
the exchange between Gremio and
Tranio (*TS*, 3.2.154–6) but adds the
'raging wolf' and 'angry hawk' to
Sebastian's characterization of Hardman.

197–202 *KK* adds to the equivalent passage
in *TS* both the hyperbolic conclusion to
Sebastian's description of Hardman and
Felix's subsequent question.

203–17 Sebastian's account begins with a
passage that has no equivalent in *TS*:
Hardman's roughness with the priest
(203–10), who is forced to perform the
ceremony with a calendar. The second
half of the speech, by contrast, closely
follows Gremio's (*TS*, 3.2.157–63).

208–9 **not ... fuss** Sebastian literally says
Hardman ordered the priest not 'to make
too much equipment' ('viel Geschirr zu
machen'); see Grimm, 'Geschirr', 20 g β.

make so much fuss. In sheer terror, the priest performed
his office as swiftly as possible. When he came to ask 210
the bride whether she wished to be Hardman's wife,
Hardman shouted a loud yes, and swore so abominably
that the good father dropped his fine book of
ceremonies for fear, and, as he stooped to pick it up
again, a cold sweat broke from the fat man who was 215
so amazed that the raging bridegroom gave him a
blow that knocked the book to the ground again.

FELIX   What did she say to this? Did she take no part in
all this raging?

SEBASTIAN   She trembled and shook like a leaf. When 220
Hardman saw that, he growled and thundered with a
violence that made all his previous oaths seem tame,
and he behaved without sense as if we wished to take
away his bride. When all was done, he seized his
bride by the neck and pressed her so hard against him 225
that she almost shit herself and turned blue in the
face. Then he kissed her loudly, which sent an echo
through the hall, and I ran out –

FABIAN [*aside*]   – as fast as I could.

SEBASTIAN   – because I could no longer stay or watch for 230
laughing. Nothing like this has ever happened before or
will ever happen again. But here comes the madcap.

---

215 **the fat man** the priest.

218–32 *KK* places Felix's question at the same
moment as Tranio's in *TS* (3.2.165) and
preserves some specific features of
Gremio's speech (*TS*, 3.2.166–82) in
Sebastian's, notably Katherina's reaction
('Trembled and shook', 3.2.166) and
Petruccio's 'clamorous smack' (3.2.177).
The rest of the speech is more loosely
adapted, and *KK* adds Fabian's aside at 229.

226 **shit herself** Sebastian literally says

Hardman pressed Catharina so hard she
had almost 'let marrow' ('Marck
lassen'), a euphemism for defecating
(see Wander, 'Mark', 13).

232 SD In *TS*, unlike in *KK*, '*Music plays*'
(3.2.181 SD) as the newly-weds and the
wedding guests enter. Alfons is not
among the characters who enter, whereas
Hortensio (as Licio) is (*TS*, 3.2.182 SD),
although he remains silent for the rest of
the scene.

Enter HARDMAN, CATHARINA, THEOBALD, SABINA,
WORMFIRE *and* VEIT.

HARDMAN   It's no use pleading with me. I have no choice
but to go away even if the table were more richly set
or there were even greater friends present. I am not   235
a man who acts against his nature on account of
entertainment and company. My affairs are absolutely
essential. Thus, be it sour or sweet, the moment of
parting has come.

THEOBALD   Do you really want to leave tonight?   240

HARDMAN   Tonight? Today, this hour and moment! If
you knew my business, father, you would hurry me
on my way. So, gentlemen, may God be with you. Be
merry, feast and drink as if you were mad. Drink to
both our healths, drink whole cups and half ones!   245

WORMFIRE   Master, shall I stay and see that they drink
everything up?

HARDMAN   A rope round your neck!

WORMFIRE   That would hardly suit me. A cup of
Bacherach wine would be better.   250

FELIX [*to Hardman*]   Brother, relent and stay here.

WORMFIRE   Yes, my lord, I would dearly like to stay here.

HARDMAN   It cannot be.

SEBASTIAN   Sir, shall I beg you?

WORMFIRE   O, yes please, beg for me too.   255

HARDMAN [*to Sebastian*]   You are the right person to
move me.

233–45 *KK* paraphrases *TS*, but omits
Petruccio's assertion that he gave himself away to Katherina (*TS*, 3.2.193–4),
which alludes to his usurpation of the
priest's authority during the ceremony.

246–331 As in the scenic movement before the
wedding (see note at 86–147), Wormfire's
comical presence is much greater than in
TS (3.2.183–240), where Grumio has only
one short speech (3.2.206–7).

250 **Bacherach wine** Wormfire literally says a
cup of 'Bacheracher', a wine from the
famous wine-growing region of Bacherach
in the Rhine-Palatinate (see Köhler, 246).

251–69 *KK* follows *TS* speech by speech
except for Wormfire's added interjections.

256–7 Compare Hardman's scoffing rejection of Sebastian with Petruccio's simple
dismissal of Gremio ('It cannot be', *TS*,
3.2.200).

CATHARINA   And if I asked, my darling?

HARDMAN   With that I would be content.

CATHARINA   I love to hear that you are content to stay.   260

WORMFIRE   And I even more so.

HARDMAN   I am content that you ask me, but not that you ask me to stay.

WORMFIRE [*aside*]   Alas, that sounds bad.

CATHARINA   Well, if you love me, stay. This is my first   265
request to you.

HARDMAN   Wormfire, are my horses ready?

WORMFIRE   Yes, my lord. The horses have eaten the oats by now, but I still haven't said goodbye to my lady.

HARDMAN   I'll write such shit on your back with my club   270
that it will make you break into a cold sweat! Away, away!

CATHARINA   Well then, do what you have to do.

HARDMAN   You do well to bend to my will, my dearest darling. I love you all the more for it.   275

CATHARINA   Go then, I shan't go away today, nor tomorrow either.

WORMFIRE [*aside*]   That's music to my ears. I shan't go at all.

CATHARINA   I'll go when it pleases me.   280

WORMFIRE [*aside*]   I wish I could say the same.

HARDMAN   That's right, Catharina, you will leave when it pleases me. That is how it must be.

---

260 *KK* replaces Katherina's careful question ('Are you content to stay?', *TS*, 3.2.202) with an affirmation.

265–6 *KK* translates Katherina's 'if you love me, stay' (*TS*, 3.2.205), but adds the remark that this is her 'first request' to her new husband.

268–9 *KK* translates Grumio's nonsense about the oats eating the horses (*TS*, 3.2.206–7) and adds the phrase about

taking leave of his lady, i.e. Sybilla, who has no equivalent in *TS*.

270–2 has no equivalent in *TS*. For the fact that Hardman's violence and abuse exceed Petruccio's, see 3.3.104 SD and note.

273–89 *KK* closely adapts Katherina's speech (*TS*, 3.2.208–15), but splits it into several parts by having it interrupted by Hardman and Wormfire.

CATHARINA   The door is open to you, and you know the
        way. Dance while your feet are itching. As for me,   285
        I won't.

HARDMAN   What's this tune now? I do not like it.

CATHARINA   Nor I yours. You'll be an evil cock if you
        crow so strangely so early.

HARDMAN   Sweetest Catharina, I crow and scratch the   290
        ground for your own good, so be a good and patient
        hen, not an ill-tempered and angry one.

CATHARINA   I will be angry. – Gentlemen, pay no
        attention to his behaviour.

SEBASTIAN   Now the dragon starts to stir.   295

HARDMAN   Gentlemen, mind your own business, and
        don't mind my darling.

CATHARINA   A pretty darling you are.

HARDMAN   And your favourite darling, I know that for
        sure.   300

CATHARINA   This would make a fool out of a woman if
        she didn't have the spirit to resist. – Gentlemen, let's
        go in to the bridal feast.

HARDMAN   That's right, fairest, they ought to go as you
        command. – Away, gentlemen, obey the bride, feast   305
        and lord it like God's children. Be merry and mad, or
        go and hang yourselves from despair. But my dearest

---

285 **Dance ... itching.** *KK* translates *TS*'s
    proverb ('be jogging whiles your boots
    are green', 3.2.212) with an equivalent,
    proverbial-sounding sentence.

288–92 *KK* transforms Katherina's expres-
    sion of discontent towards her 'surly
    groom' (*TS*, 3.2.214) into a conceit that
    makes Hardman 'an evil cock', which he
    develops by asking her to be 'a good and
    patient hen', whereas Petruccio simply
    asks, 'O Kate, content thee; prithee be
    not angry' (*TS*, 3.2.216).

293–303 *KK* adapts Katherina's two speeches
    and Gremio's glee at witnessing the

impending power struggle between her
and Petruccio (*TS*, 3.2.217–22), but adds
Hardman's intervention and his 'darling'
exchange with Catharina.

304–28 The passage corresponds to a single
    speech by Petruccio at the end of which
    he, Katherina and Grumio exit (*TS*,
    3.2.223–40). *KK* interrupts the speech
    with Catharina's and Theobald's peti-
    tions to leave her there, and two comic
    interjections by Wormfire.

304–8 **That's ... me.** A close adaptation of
    the first part of Petruccio's equivalent
    speech (*TS*, 3.2.223–8).

Catharina shall come with me. I cannot leave my
dearest earthly possession behind.

He takes her by the hand.

CATHARINA Leave me, and go away if you wish. 310

HARDMAN Don't be angry, my heart's child, nobody will
do you any harm when you're with me.

THEOBALD Then leave her here, sir.

HARDMAN Why do you seek to steal away my heart? –
You, pretty soul. (*He kisses her.*) You are my all, my 315
nothing, my life and death depend on you. – Here my
treasure stands. Woe to him who is bold enough to
touch her. I will protect her against you all, and all the
world, yes, the devil himself will not take her from me.
What, you rogues! Wormfire, out with your pistol! 320

WORMFIRE My lord, my warm beer has frozen in this
heat.

HARDMAN I see, we are beset by rogues and thieves who
want to block our way. Help, save your lady, my
faithful servant, if you have a heart in your stomach! 325

---

309 SD There is no SD at the equivalent
moment in *TS* (3.2.228).

310–13 Theobald's petition echoes
Catharina's and shows him taking her
part. Baptista, in contrast, remains silent,
and the next that is heard from him, after
his daughter and son-in-law have left, is
'Nay, let them go – a couple of quiet
ones' (*TS*, 3.2.241).

315–16 **You . . . you.** *KK* adds Hardman's
address to Catharina and his kiss. The
equivalent passage in Petruccio's speech
is addressed not to Katherina but to the
wedding guests he is about to leave (*TS*,
3.2.231–3). Whereas Petruccio reduces
Katherina to one of his possessions
amongst other 'goods' (3.2.231), Hardman
calls Catharina his 'all' and 'nothing' on
whom his 'life and death depend'.

317–19 **Woe . . . me.** *KK* has no equivalent
for Petruccio's mention of 'Padua' in the
equivalent passage (*TS*, 3.2.236), in
keeping with the play's omission of
place names elsewhere (see 1.3.106–7,
2.1.104–5, 634–9 and notes).

320 **you rogues** Hardman literally says 'you
mice heads' ('ihr Mausköpfe'), referring
to thievish dishonourable people (see
Grimm, 'Mäusekopf', 2).

320–8 **Wormfire . . . protection.** *KK* closely
adapts the equivalent portion of
Petruccio's speech in *TS* (3.2.236–40)
and adds Wormfire's interjections.

321 **warm beer** ('Warmbier') Wormfire
plays on the word 'warm beer', referring
to both a firearm and a rich drink with
beer, eggs and spices (see Grimm).

343

WORMFIRE   That's not much.

HARDMAN   Have no fear, my dearest child. Not a soul
shall harm you, you are under my protection.

He carries her out in his arms.

WORMFIRE   May the devil thank my lord that he is
holding such a drunken wedding. Let the gallows host   330
him, as long as he leaves me behind.   *Exit.*

SABINA   What a merry company! But it is wrong not to
keep the bride at least until the wedding feast. It
would be good to keep her here awhile.

FELIX   I don't think it's good that his stubborn head   335
could not be tamed to stay.

THEOBALD   We must let them leave together. God grant
that they tame each other.

HILARIUS   What does my most beautiful lady think of
her sister?   340

SABINA   I think she is mad herself, and now has a mad
husband who suits her perfectly.

THEOBALD   Gentlemen, please step inside. Sir Hilarius
of Liebenthal will replace the groom, and my daughter
will keep him company.   345

FELIX   Thus the groom's place is filled. A good prelude.

---

328 SD While the equivalent SD in *TS* is a
simple '*Exeunt*' (3.2.240.1), *KK*'s spells
out how they do so.

331 SD The early editions of *TS* have no exit
SD for Grumio, but editors since Capell
usually assume that he exits at the same
time as Petruccio and Katherina (3.2.240
SD).

332–6 There is no equivalent in *TS* to
Sabina's and Felix's disapproving comments on Hardman's behaviour.

337–8 *KK* transforms Baptista's ironic
description of Petruccio and Katherina as

'quiet ones' (*TS*, 2.3.241) into a prayer
that they will tame each other or, literally, make each other cease raging ('sich
wohl vertoben').

339–42 *KK* closely adapts Lucentio's question and Bianca's answer about her sister
(*TS*, 3.2.244–5), but omits Gremio's and
Tranio's comments on the comical nature
of the situation (*TS*, 3.2.242–3, 246).

343–5 Theobald, like Baptista, determines to
make the younger sister and her suitor
substitutes for the newly-weds at the
wedding feast (*TS*, 3.2.247–51).

HILARIUS   I wish she would do this with her dearest love.

SABINA   I hope both our wishes will be granted.

> *Exeunt Theobald, Sabina and Felix.*

SEBASTIAN   I will follow the gentlemen soon. Sir Johannes, stay awhile.   350

HILARIUS   I am bound and desirous to obey my lord.

SEBASTIAN   I must tell you about my sorrows for a little while. This Liebenthal has received her father's consent under certain circumstances. I am out of the race, unless you have something to comfort me with.   355

HILARIUS   I am sorry to hear this, since I already have the maid quite on my side.

SEBASTIAN   That fills me with joy. But is there hope?

HILARIUS   Yes, if I still have time, for as you can imagine, my lord, I cannot bring her to requite my love fully in   360 such a short time.

SEBASTIAN   I will be ready *communicato consilio* to help in every way with what is to be done next. Let us go in now. In there, I shall easily get to her myself and continue what you have begun.   *Exit.*   365

HILARIUS [*aside*]   Just go inside, your continuation will be of no avail.   *Exit.*

FABIAN   Who's this black-coat? He's all too friendly with your lady.

347–8 Whereas *TS* has Baptista conclude the scene ('Come gentlemen, let's go', 3.2.253), *KK* ends the scenic movement with a brief exchange between Sabina and Hilarius; here she reciprocates his love.

349–98 *KK* adds two dialogues after the end of the equivalent scene in *TS*, one between Sebastian and Hilarius on the success of the latter's love suit, suppos-

edly in the name of the former (349–67), and one between the two servants Fabian and Veit, who forthrightly comment on the sexual mores of their social superiors (368–98).

362 *communicato consilio* Latin, when the plan has been imparted.

368 black-coat ('Schwartzmantel') a cloak worn by students, particularly those studying theology (see Grimm).

VEIT   He is her *praeceptor*, though I think he teaches her   370
        too much. I bet if your master knew it, he'd give him
        bad wages for that information.

FABIAN   It is the fashion now, noblemen make children
        for the peasants, and the peasants are thankful for it.
        One honour for another.   375

VEIT   That's a fine thing. But I wonder how the blood
        will be changed, though it is none of our concern. If
        we're needed, we'll offer help without thinking twice
        about it. I wonder why our lady is so friendly with this
        rogue; she cared little for men before. She has surely   380
        seen something good in him.

FABIAN   Don't you know what rascals these students are?

VEIT   I once waited on one, and he was bad enough.

FABIAN   Those who desire grafting, let them go to the
        students, I say. I know many noble maids who desire   385
        to be near a university. Our master's wife has often
        mentioned how full of pleasure those academies are.
        You may guess why. But do you think this student
        cloak covers a bad core?

VEIT   I don't know.   390

FABIAN   If you can keep your mouth shut, I might tell
        you something in confidence.

370 *praeceptor* Latin, teacher.
373–5 For the same idea, see Alfons at
   3.1.236–8.
376–7 **how ... changed** Veit refers to the
   idea of the pure blood of the nobility
   which the non-noble mistress threatens
   to dilute (see Kautsky, 205–10).
378–9 **without ... it** Veit literally says
   'without worrying a hair about it'
   ('bekümmern uns nicht ein Haar
   darum'), referring to the insignificance
   of a hair (see Grimm, 'Haar', 17).
380 **rogue** The German is 'Mauser', describing
   someone who stealthily preys on others,

like a cat hunting mice (see Grimm).
384 **grafting** ('propfreiser') The German
   word designates grafts or scions and, as
   in English, was also used figuratively.
387 **academies** Academies along the classical
   models of intellectual societies concerned
   with language or science flourished in
   Renaissance Europe (see Moran).
388–9 **this ... cloak** ('dieses Penal
   Mäntelchen') 'Penal' refers to a box
   with writing feathers and was used as a
   condescending designation for students
   (see Grimm, Pennal, *m.*); also, a penis
   (see Grimm, Pennal, *n.* 2).

VEIT   You know well that what is unknown to me is safe
        with me.

FABIAN   I'll tell you in your ear.   395

        [*Fabian whispers in Veit's ear.*]

VEIT   I would never have believed this! Well, fortune be
        my guide.

FABIAN   But brother, we tarry too long, *i prae sequar*.

                                                    Exeunt.

[3.3]   *Enter* WORMFIRE.

WORMFIRE   Ugh, disgusting! The devil take all tired
        horses, all mad masters and all shitty paths! I'm so
        knackered! Cold, rain and mud have thoroughly
        drenched and covered me inside and out, and yet I
        must act the quartermaster and am sent to order a fire,   5
        so that those behind me may shake off the cold. If I
        were not a small fast-boiling pot, my lips would have
        frozen to my teeth, my tongue to the roof of my mouth
        and my heart to my breast before I came by a fire. I
        marvel how our women have fared, since they are   10
        open and cannot easily defend themselves against the
        cold. In short, the weather is cold, and a man as big as

---

395 SD Fabian presumably tells Veit about
     the disguise of Hilarius and Felix.
398 *i prae sequar* Latin, go before, I follow.
3.3 The scene is set in Hardman's house. It
     falls into two parts: the dialogue between
     Matz and Wormfire (1–95), and
     Hardman's anger towards his servants
     (96–186). The first part showing
     Wormfire's arrival and his exchange with
     Matz stays close to *TS* (4.1.1–105), but
     has an additional short passage about
     Sybilla (27–32) and omits a hearty
     welcome of Grumio by the household
     (4.1.95–101). The second part includes
     Hardman's irate refusal to wash or eat.

KK loosely follows *TS* (4.1.106–67) but
rearranges and transforms the source passage, in particular adding short passages
that demonstrate Hardman's roughness
and Catharina's attempts at peacemaking.
1–14 *KK* follows *TS* (4.1.1–10).
1   **Ugh, disgusting!** The German literally says
      'Fie, illness' ('Pfuy kränckheit'). For the
      word as expletive, see Grimm, 'krankt', 2b.
5   **quartermaster** ('*Fourier*') a military
      officer responsible for food provision
      and other supplies.
9–12 **I . . . cold.** There is no direct equivalent
      in *TS* for this reference to the female
      genitals.

347

I am is easily robbed of warmth by the violence of the
frost. Holla holla, Matz Trumper!

Enter MATZ.

MATZ   Who calls with such a cold voice?   15
WORMFIRE   A mere block of ice. If you doubt it, run a
      sleigh down my shoulders to the heels, you'll find ice
      all the way. O, Matz, a good fire now.
MATZ   Does my master come with his wife?
WORMFIRE   Yes, yes, he comes, and so throw wood on   20
      the fire, and cast no water, Matz. Fire and wood!
MATZ   Is she as angry and shrewish as she is said to be?
WORMFIRE   She was half-half, good Matz, before this
      frost. But your reason well knows that winter tames
      men and women, yes, all evil animals, and it has done   25
      so with my old evil master, my angry mistress and
      my new fellow servant and faithful owner of my
      enamoured heart.
MATZ   Are you in love?
WORMFIRE   What's that to you in any case? Yes, she has   30
      tamed me, my honest Matz, so that everything about
      us is limp except for what's stiff from the cold. Just
      kindle the fire, Matz, or shall I hand my mad master a
      libel to complain of your disobedience? I know you
      shall feel his hands soon enough, and rightly so for   35
      your cold comfort, since you are slow in your warm
      office.

15–28 Almost a verbatim translation of *TS*
(4.1.11–28), except that *KK* replaces a
short passage about Grumio and his size
('myself . . . least'; *TS*, 4.1.21–5) with a
passage about Sybilla and Wormfire's
love for her ('my new . . . cold', 27–32).
23   **half-half** Whereas Grumio merely confirms that Katherina was as bad as her
reputation ('She was', *TS*, 4.1.19),

Wormfire's answer is more nuanced.
31–2 **everything ... cold** with a salacious
joke on the state of his penis.
33–4 **shall   ...   disobedience** Whereas
Grumio's threat is to tell 'our mistress'
(*TS*, 4.1.26), Wormfire's is to complain
to Hardman, perhaps in keeping with
KK's increasing of the male protagonist's
roughness.

MATZ　Tell me, my honest man –

WORMFIRE　– ho, careful, that's yet to be proved.

MATZ　– how does the world go?　　　　　　　　　　40

WORMFIRE　O, the world is very cold, Matz, in all offices except yours. So, kindle the fire, do your Vulcanic office and feed your warm element. My master and mistress will soon be frozen to dirt.

MATZ　The fire is ready, so tell me something new from　45
the old world, Wormfire.

WORMFIRE　That term suits you well. But where's the cook? Is supper ready? The house swept and polished? Are the servants dressed in their best robes? Are the maids wearing their feast-day ornaments? Is　50
everything in order?

MATZ　It is all ready. So, say, my good man, what news?

WORMFIRE　*Pro primus*, an old woman laid a new egg.

MATZ　That's old news.

WORMFIRE　Indeed, then take it to you while it is still　55
warm. Moreover, my horse is very tired, I am

39　**that's ... proved** Wormfire jokingly calls into doubt his own honesty.

40–6　*KK* closely follows *TS* (4.1.29–35), but adds Wormfire's evocative command to Matz to do his 'Vulcanic office' (42–3), from Vulcan, the Roman god of fire.

43　**feed ... element** presumably by adding wood to the fire.

44　**dirt** *KK* replaces Grumio's 'frozen to death' (*TS*, 4.1.33) with 'frozen to dirt', which becomes understandable a little later when Wormfire mentions Hardman and Catharina's fall 'into the mud' (57–8).

45–7　**tell ... well** In asking Wormfire to tell him some news, Matz uses the Latinate word 'narrire', which here alludes to the German for 'fool' ('Narr'), an insult that Wormfire returns to Matz himself.

47–51　Before adapting Grumio's series of

inquiries about the household preparations (*TS*, 4.1.40–5), *KK* omits a brief exchange between the two servants on the news (*TS*, 4.1.36–40), possibly owing to its intricate puns and allusions.

53　*Pro primus* Latin, first of all.

53–6　*Pro ... warm. KK* inserts a joke on fanciful fake news before returning to *TS*.

55–6　**while ... warm** presumably referring to the newly laid egg.

56–8　**Moreover, .. it.** Wormfire's speech is close to Grumio's (*TS*, 4.1.47–8) but adds the description of his exhaustion as 'checkmated', in German 'schachmatt' (D1), the word 'matt' referring to feeling weak. D2 drives home the point by reading 'schwach mat', literally 'weak weary', punning on the phonic similarity to 'schachmatt'.

checkmated, and my mistress and master fell into the
mud. There you have it.

MATZ   You speak too briefly, tell me more.

WORMFIRE   Now I'll start. First, we slowly rode down a   60
foul mountain, my master behind my mistress.

MATZ   Both on one horse?

WORMFIRE   What's it got to do with you?

MATZ   I ask whether they both rode on one horse.

WORMFIRE   Make a song of your story if you want to   65
become an absolute fool. If you hadn't interrupted me
and disturbed my invention, you would have known
how our mistress fell from the jade into the mud, how
soiled she was, how her skirt fell over her head, and
what I saw there. How my master hit me because she   70
fell and because of what I saw there. How my master
hit me because she fell and I looked there. How he
cursed, how she prayed who had never prayed before,
how the maid scraped the mud off her, and I the shit,
how I shouted and my own lady wailed. How my   75
horse ran away, and my lord's bridle broke, with
many other things worth eternal remembrance for
posterity's sake which will now die and rot in oblivion,
and you, like all others, shall crawl uninstructed to
your grave.   80

MATZ   It appears from what you say that our lord is more
evil than she after all.

59–80 *KK* stays close to *TS* (4.1.59–75) but
inserts the detail of Catharina's skirt
falling over her head and Wormfire
looking at what is revealed there (69–72).

61   **foul mountain** 'foul hill' in *TS* (4.1.59). In
the German text, 'faulen Berg' (literally
'lazy mountain') seems to result from a

misunderstanding of the meaning of 'foul'.

65–6 **Make ... fool.** Wormfire literally says
'tell the news until you become a total
fool' ('Narrire du die Zeitung, biß du
zum gantzen Narren wirst'). He teases
Matz through the same pun on fool
('Narr') as at 45–7 (see note).

3.3.57 checkmated] *D1* (schach matt); schwach mat *D2*

WORMFIRE Indeed, and experience will perhaps teach
you that when he comes home. But why do I linger
here, where are Lazypaunch, Alwayswet, Noosehalter   85
and the others? Did they prepare themselves to make
a good *révérence avec baise les mains* and a fine
compliment to our ruling lady? Order them for the
sake of our lord, *meo nomine*, not to touch my master's
horse's tail before they have kissed our noble lady's   90
hand. Are they ready?

MATZ They are. Out, boys! You must greet your master
and mistress. Are they far off?

WORMFIRE They are nearby. Peace now! He's coming
with a great hubbub. I can hear him.   95

Enter HARDMAN, CATHARINA *and* SYBILLA.

HARDMAN Where are these lazy rogues? May a hundred
thousand pounds of lead strike them dead! What?
Why do I keep these fellows? Nobody by the door to

83–91 *KK* stays close to *TS* (4.1.77–84), but
reduces the number of named servants
from six to three and omits Grumio's
insistence on their tidy appearance (4.1.80–
2). It also replaces his suggestion that they
'curtsy with their left legs' (4.1.82) with a
polite greeting expressed in French.

84–5 **But ... here** Wormfire literally says
'but I uselessly blow the wind into the
world here' ('Aber blase ich hier verge-
bens den Wind in die Welt'), suggesting
a vain effort. For the proverb, see
Wander, 'Wind', 413.

85 **Lazypaunch ... Noosehalter** See the
List of Roles.

87 *révérence ... mains* French, curtsy with
a kiss of the hands.

88 **compliment** a tribute of courtesy.

89 *meo nomine* Latin, on my behalf.

92–3 *KK* translates Curtis' call to the servants (*TS*, 4.1.87–8), but omits the subsequent joke (4.1.89–102) prompted by his

use of the word 'to countenance' for 'to
greet', perhaps owing to the lack of
German equivalent.

95 SD In *TS*, Petruccio and Katherina
appear onstage (*TS*, 4.1.105 SD) after the
entrance of '*four or five* Servants' (*TS*,
4.1.93 SD). *KK* delays their entrance and
omits their welcome to Grumio (4.1.94–
103). Sybilla has no equivalent in *TS* (see
pp. 107–9). She remains silent until her
exit with Wormfire (113 SD).

96–113 a fairly close adaptation of *TS*,
4.1.106–24, that occasionally condenses
passages.

96–100 Hardman's speech corresponds to
Petruccio's (*TS*, 4.1.106–8), but Hardman
replaces the servants' names with a
generic insult ('these lazy rogues').

98 **fellows** Hardman describes the servants
as, literally, 'birds' ('Vögel'), an image
of carelessness also used as an insult
(Grimm, Vogel, 14).

hold my stirrup, or to take my lady's horse and mine?
Where are you, you gallows-birds?   100

Enter three SERVANTS.

[SERVANTS]   Here!

HARDMAN   Here, here, here. You block-headed slaves
and lazy dogs! May your legs become lame! Is there
no respect and dutiful attendance anymore?

He strikes them.

Where is the foolish thief I sent ahead? May lice   105
choke him!

WORMFIRE   Here, my lord. As foolish as I was before.

HARDMAN   You galley-slave! You beast, didn't I order
you to come and meet me for the honour of my love
and to bring these cursed thieves with you?   110

WORMFIRE   My lord, Alwayswet's frock was not ready,
and Noosehalter lost his thievish hat, and Lazypaunch
couldn't find his rapier.

Exit with Sybilla [and Matz].

---

100 SD In *TS*, the servants enter before the
couple's arrival and heartily greet
Grumio (4.1.95–100).

101 In D1 and D2, the servants' call is
implied in the preceding SD which reads,
'Drey Diener gehen ein, ruffen alle hier'
('Three servants enter, all call here').

104 SD The first of several SDs indicating
Hardman's physical violence towards his
servants (see also 127 SD and 133 SD);
there is no unambiguous equivalent in *TS*
(see Ard³, 248). For Hardman's extra violence when compared to Petruccio, see also
1.3.233–48, 3.2.270–2, 3.5.15–25 and notes.

108–13 *KK* remains close to *TS* (4.1.115–
24), but condenses Grumio's speech
about the servants' failure to arrive.

108 **galley-slave** ('Galeywürdiger *esclave*') a
strong term of abuse (see Grimm, 'galei-
würdig', i.e. deserving the galley). From
the late Middle Ages, slaves were

increasingly employed as rowers.

110 **cursed thieves** Hardman literally calls the
servants 'cursed halters' ('verfluchte
Galgenschwengel'), metonymically referring to the criminals hanging from them.
'Galgenschwengel' evokes the gallows
('Galgen') and swinging ('schwengen')
(see Grimm, 'Galgenschwengel').

112 **thievish hat** *KK* literally says 'thief's
lid' ('Diebs-Deckel'), in reference to the
clothes thieves need in order to hide (see
Grimm, 'Diebsdeckel').

113 SD The German text provides no exit SD
for Matz in this scene. He may well leave at
this point with Wormfire and Sybilla,
although he could also do so with an
unnamed servant at 113 SD or with the servants and Wormfire at 164 SD. Most modern
editors leave it unclear when Grumio exits
in the equivalent scene; in Ard³, he does so
considerably later (4.1.156 SD).

HARDMAN   You are useless cowards and lazy dogs. I
have been away from home for a short while, and 115
what has happened to my authority? Where is the life
that I led before? Is there no awe anymore? I will put
some order into you birds. Is there no slave ready to
bring my love a chair? – Be welcome, dearest darling.

He kisses her, while she stands still.

Don't be upset by this disorder, I will put everything 120
in order for you.
CATHARINA   O, the order is good.
HARDMAN   You do well, my love, to praise what I have
done. [*to the Servants*] Why are you standing around,
you gallows-birds? Bring in the food.   125
                                        [*Exit First Servant.*]
Sit down, my heart's love. – You, rogue, take off my
boots.

He strikes the [Second] Servant.

114–21 Following the servants' exit, Petruccio immediately shouts for supper, asks Katherina to sit down, demands his boots be removed and sings snatches of ballads (*TS*, 4.1.125–32); Hardman instead complains about his loss of authority, requests a chair for Catharina, kisses her and comments on the disorder, all actions with no immediate equivalent in *TS*.

116–17 **Where ... before?** *KK* preserves Petruccio's quotation of the first line of a popular ballad ('Where is the life that late I led,' *TS*, 4.1.126), but there is no indication that the translator or adaptor was aware that this was a musical reference.

118 **birds** (Vögel) See note at 98.

119 SD Another kiss by Hardman with no equivalent in *TS* (see above, 3.2.315–16 and note).

122 Catharina objects to the mistreatment of the household earlier than Katherina does (*TS*, 4.1.142).

123–41 Like Petruccio (*TS*, 4.1.125–40), Hardman alternates between making irascible commands to his servants and seemingly supplying good-natured invitations to his wife. While some elements are the same or similar in the two versions ('supper . . . be merry . . . boots . . . water', *TS*, 4.1.125–40), others are specific to *TS* (the domestic 'Where's my spaniel Troilus? . . . Where are my slippers?', 4.1.136–9) or to *KK* (e.g., Hardman's request for a 'towel' and 'clean water', 135–7).

125 **gallows-birds** ('Galgenschwengel') literally 'halter'; see note at 110.

126 **rogue** ('Schinder') literally 'hangman' (see Grimm).

127 SD Most modern editors since Rowe have understood Petruccio's 'Take that' (*TS*, 4.1.134) to be an implied SD and assumed that he strikes the servant. In *KK*, the stage action is spelled out. See note at 104 SD.

You slave, do you want to tear off my foot? – How are
you, my lady? You look sad. – Will you dull dogs not
bring water for us to wash our hands? – Be merry, my   130
child, it will soon be better.

[The Second and Third Servants] bring water.

You, stupid brute, did someone shit on your fists? Are
you spilling the water?

He strikes [a servant].

Dearest Catharina, wash yourself and be glad. –
Rotten wretch, can't you bring a towel? What kind of   135
water is this? Dish-water?

He strikes [a servant] down with the bowl.

I'll show you clean water, may the devil take you. –
Come to the table, dearest heart.

Enter WORMFIRE.

Where did the hangman hide you? You're always
warming your whore's nest. Get out, and fetch Master   140
Rich-With-Joy to keep my love company.

WORMFIRE   That's the company she needs.

Enter [FIRST] SERVANT *with food.*

HARDMAN   What do you say, whoreson villain?

---

133 SD Modern editors of *TS* often insert a
SD at the equivalent point (4.1.141) – e.g.
Thompson: '*He strikes the Servant.*' –
though Ard³ does not. See note at 104 SD.

138 SD–44 Unlike Grumio (who may have
exited or remains onstage silently; see
note at 113 SD), Wormfire re-enters,
makes a (probably sarcastic) comment
on the character of Master Freudenreich
and receives Hardman's insult.

139–40 **You're ... nest.** Hardman suggests
Wormfire is not on duty because he is in
Sybilla's bed.

140–1 **Master   Rich-With-Joy** ('Herr
Freudenreich'); the only mention of this
shadowy figure who never appears, like
the equivalent 'cousin Ferdinand' in *TS*
(4.1.137).

WORMFIRE   Nothing, my lord, I obey your every order.
HARDMAN   What, you rogue, will you spill the broth on   145
my lady's lap?

He beats him.

CATHARINA   It was an unwilling fault, my love.
HARDMAN   He is a fool-born, stupid animal. Be content,
dearest Catharina, I must keep order in my own home
the way I see fit. – What food is this? How dare you   150
welcome my love with this? Is there nothing better?
WORMFIRE   I will return it, God willing.
HARDMAN   Let us sit now. My darling, will you say
grace, or shall I? – Where is the rascal cook? Is this
baked? Is this roasted? It's all burnt up and fried!   155
Catch the boar-pig and bind him to the trough. Whip
him till his blood spills out.
CATHARINA   My dearest, really, the food is very good.
HARDMAN   You are too polite, my darling, to put up with
things for the sake of such an incompetent fellow. The   160
dirty dog has spoiled everything, and it offends me
that you will think it is always like this in my house.
CATHARINA   Have no fear of that. I like it very well.
HARDMAN   Now I see you are being politic and only
speak to flatter me. The food is all burnt, fried and   165

145–8 **What ... animal.** *KK* closely adapts
Petruccio's anger and Katherina's plea
for indulgence (*TS*, 4.1.141–3).

146 SD literally, 'It rains cuffs' ('Es regnet
stösse').

150–2 **What ... willing.** *KK* retains
Petruccio's question ('What's this', *TS*,
4.1.146), but has Hardman stress his
domestic authority, and replaces the
unnamed servant in *TS* by Wormfire. In
terms of staging, it is not clear whether
Hardman addresses the first servant or
Wormfire, who replies perhaps for himself, perhaps for the servant (152).

153–62 **Where ... house.** *KK* corresponds
to *TS* (4.1.150–6), but Hardman's anger
focuses on the cook, not the servants.

154 **Where ... cook?** ('wo ist der Saumage
der Koch') literally, 'where is the sow's
stomach of a cook'. As a pig's stomach
takes a lot of filling, the term came to be
used as an insult to a gluttonous, unclean
person (Grimm, 'Saumagen', 3).

163–9 **Have... victim.** *KK* closely adapts the
equivalent passage in *TS* (4.1.157–64),
but adds Hardman's observation about
Catharina's 'politic' navigation (164) of
the power dynamics in her new home.

dried up. The juice and power are gone. Only the
burnt bones are left, and these my doctor expressly
forbids me to eat, because it increases gall and choler
to which we are both victim. – There, you dogs, feed
and may it choke you. (*He throws it to them.*) With 170
what shall I treat my love?

CATHARINA   I would be well-contented with these foods.

HARDMAN   I praise your good cheer, my darling, but you
must be treated to better food, or nothing at all. [*to
Wormfire*] Villain, serve us better tomorrow, and take 175
that to the cook. (*He strikes him.*)

WORMFIRE   Lord, you may save your labour. I have a
good memory.

HARDMAN   Away, you beasts.

Exeunt [Servants and Wormfire].

Dearest darling, it's not my fault, and it pains my soul 180
that you have been so poorly welcomed and served. I
would offer my blood for your sake. But comfort
yourself that the fault was not mine because I was
absent. I will make up for everything. Today's fasting
will be broken tomorrow. Come, my darling, I will 185
lead you to bed, you shall be served better there.

Exeunt.

167 **bones** ('Schindknochen ') literally,
'hangman's bones'.
169–79 **There ... beasts.** Between a rendition of Petruccio's speech on his choleric
humour (164–9; *TS*, 4.1.159–64) and his
promise to Katherina to mend her welcome the next day (180–6; *TS*, 4.1.165–
7), *KK* inserts another version of
the scene's theme, that is, Hardman's
studied anger and Catharina's attempt to
defuse it.
170 SD *KK*'s SD and the preceding sentence

have no equivalent in *TS*. In *A Shrew*, a
SD reads, '*Manent servingmen and eat
up all the meat*' (Miller, 6.32.2).
176 SD There is no equivalent SD in *TS*. See
note at 104 SD.
180–6 Unlike in *TS*, Hardman and Catharina
are alone onstage for his last speech of
this scene, corresponding to *TS*,
4.1.165–7. Hardman stresses his devo-
tion to his new wife more so than
Petruccio, suggestively adding that she
will be 'served better' in bed (186).

[3.4]   *Enter* MATZ *Trumper and* WORMFIRE.

WORMFIRE   Monsieur Matz, what do you think of this
fine wedding day? Has anything like this ever
happened to you? No food and no drink, hey? The
devil take such weddings!

MATZ   I don't believe such a wedding has been recorded   5
in the chronicles since the destruction of Troy.

WORMFIRE   You talk well given your fire-stoker's wit.

MATZ   I could not have believed that there would ever be
such a holiday. It's as though Poverty were to marry
Necessity, and would invite Hunger and Thirst to the   10
wedding. But where is he?

WORMFIRE   He is with her in the bridal chamber, and
continues making his speech on unhealthy food which
he firmly denigrates with curses and complaints in a
true litany of sayings.   15

MATZ   But what does she do?

3.4   The scene is set in Hardman's house and
corresponds to a brief passage in *TS*
(4.1.168–76) that consists of a brief
exchange between four servants
(Nathaniel, Peter, Grumio and Curtis)
who comment on Petruccio's shocking
taming techniques. *KK* substitutes a dialogue between Matz and Wormfire in
which they deplore the lack of wedding
celebrations and Wormfire reports on the
goings-on in the bridal chamber.

2–3   **Has … drink** Wormfire literally says,
'did the like ever happen to you, that the
teeth were saved and the throat had a
holiday?' ('Ist dir dergleichen wohl
fürkommen / daran man die Zähne
gesparet / und der Hals einen Feyrtag
gehabt'), humorously pointing towards
the neglect of providing the customary
food and drink at a wedding.

6   **destruction … Troy** by the Greeks in
the Trojan war, as recounted in Homer's
Iliad.

7   **fire-stoker's** ('stubenheitzerischen')
Wormfire's condescending reference to
Matz's occupation. 'Stubenheizer' is a
term recorded from the sixteenth to the
eighteenth century for an indoors firekeeper (Grimm).

9–11   **Poverty … wedding.** Matz imagines a
wedding with allegorical personifica-
tions. Compare Wormfire's personified
'Patience' at 17.

11   **where … he?** In *TS*, this question is
asked by Grumio (4.1.170).

12–24   *KK* adapts Curtis' speech (*TS*,
4.1.171–6) but divides it into three parts,
signalled by Matz's brief interruptions at
lines 16 and 20.

WORMFIRE   She sits in her chamber like holy Patience,
her face as dark as if she had woken from some sad
dream, and did not know where she was.

MATZ   He will kill her with such inhuman treatment.   20

WORMFIRE   It seems as though she doesn't know whether
she's standing or walking, or what she ought to do.
One devil has met another. I think I hear him. Let's
go, or he'll dismiss us.   *Exeunt.*

[3.5]   *Enter* HARDMAN.

HARDMAN   Thus it must be. I have begun my reign most
politically. With my friendliness mingled with angry
rage, I have given her such doubts that she cannot
altogether trust my professed love, nor complain
about my pretended anger, which looks like affection.   5
I am now like the rowers that turn their backs on the
way they seek to go. A Scythian shoots while fleeing.
I confess I love her dearly. In order to make her all the
worthier of my love, I must perform the moral tutor

---

17   **holy Patience** Wormfire refers to the
proverbial patience of saints (Wander,
'Geduld', 178). Compare Matz's per-
sonifications at 9–11.

23   **One ... another** Wormfire literally says,
'one devil above another' ('ein Teuffel
über den andern Teufel'). See Wander,
'Teufel', 538.

24   **dismiss us** *KK* adds Wormfire's suggestion that Hardman may dismiss the men
from his service.

3.5 The scene, presumably set in Hardman's
house, corresponds to Petruccio's soliloquy at *TS*, 4.1.177–200. It closely adapts
the original but inserts a reflection on the
paradoxical effect of Hardman's taming
technique (2–7) and the necessity to play-
act (8–12). For another version of this

speech, see *A Shrew* (Miller, 6.37–47).

1–2   **Thus ... politically.** Petruccio's soliloquy begins similarly: 'Thus have I
politicly begun my reign' (*TS*, 4.1.177).

6–7   **rowers ... go** Hardman means he needs
to do the opposite of what might seem
necessary in order to succeed. For the
proverb, see Wander, 'Rudersmann'.

7   **A ... fleeing.** Reiterating the idea of the
previous proverb, Hardman alludes to the
classical myth that warriors from Scythia,
a people in Central Asia famed for horsemanship, hit their target by riding past it
and turning around to shoot their arrows.

9   **moral tutor** (Sitten-Lehrer) The same
German word is used in Patient Job's reference to 'the teacher of morals who will
now appear' (Prologue, 19–20).

under the guise of *Jean Potage*, and play several 10
persons. Not every fool can do this since it is the
office of the master. I have already achieved wonders.
My falcon is sharp and hungry now, and will not be
fed until it humbles itself. I must therefore adopt the
manner in which wild animals are tamed. She hasn't 15
eaten the whole day, and she had little yesterday, and
shall not eat tonight. She had no rest last night, and
shall be allowed to rest even less tonight. I will find
fault with the bed as I did with the food. The maids'
backs will bear the brunt of my rage. I will throw the 20
pillows around and stamp on the linen and pull up the
bed to make the feathers fly. Little of the curtains and
bedframe will be kept whole, and the straw shall be
made to cover the chamber ground. Additionally I
shall curse and rage till the beams tremble. But in the 25
midst of this madness I will cuddle with her and swear
it happens out of great affection to her. I will continue
this the whole night, turning from one to the other so
that she will be unable to close an eye or rest her head.
It is the right way: make a bad wife good through 30
friendliness, or kill her. Her heated stubbornness

10 **under ... *Potage*** Hardman literally
describes himself as having to 'act under
the hat and coat of Jean Potage' ('unter
Jean Potage seinem Hut und Mantel
agiren'), alluding to the French clown
figure (see Asper).

13–15 **My ... tamed.** *KK* continues its close
rendition of *TS*, translating the first four
lines of Petruccio's falconry metaphor
(4.1.179–82), but replacing the subsequent more technical elaboration
(4.1.183–5) by a generic summary that
he must 'adopt the manner in which wild
animals are tamed'.

15–25 **She ... tremble.** *KK* translates the
uproar Petruccio creates (*TS*, 4.1.186–

91), but makes Hardman more gratui-
tously violent by adding that he will beat
the maids for the supposed untidiness of
the beds. See also 3.3.104 SD and note.

20 **bear the brunt** Hardman literally says
that 'the maids' hump backs will have to
atone' ('der Mägde Buckel werden
büssen müssen').

30–1 **It ... her.** In adapting *TS*'s proverbial
'[t]his is a way to kill a wife with kindness'
(4.1.197), *KK* provides the two options of
making her 'good through friendliness' or
killing her in the process. The sentence
incorporates part of the play's title. *TS*
alludes to its title slightly later in the corresponding speech (4.1.199).

will cool when a stronger one overcomes her. If
she changes her tune, I will strike a milder chord
afterwards. He who knows a better way than mine, let
him come forward. We shall see who prevails.   35

Exit.

4.[1]   *Enter* FELIX [*as Hilarius*] *and*
                      [ALFONS *as*] *Musician.*

FELIX   I can hardly believe what you tell me, good sir.
ALFONS   My lord Hilarius of Liebenthal, rest assured
     that it is nothing other than the bare truth. Let us hide
     a little here to discover it better. Her lesson is taking
     place now. By witnessing the charming instruction   5
     she receives, you will see in action what I have
     disclosed to you in words.

34–5 **He ... prevails.** Like Petruccio at the
     equivalent moment (*TS*, 4.1.199–200),
     Hardman addresses the audience.

35 **We ... prevails.** Hardman literally says
     'let us pull for being the master' ('Wir
     wollen uns um den Meister ziehen'),
     proposing a tug of war (see Köhler, 249).

4.1 There is no specification of location, but
     the scene is presumably set in Sir
     Theobald's house and roughly corre-
     sponds to *TS*, 4.2.1–72. It falls into two
     parts: the first shows Alfons and Felix
     witnessing the love scene between
     Sabina and Hilarius (1–85, *TS*, 4.2.1–
     59); the second shows the scheme of
     finding someone to impersonate Hilarius'
     father (86–105, *TS*, 4.2.60–72). *KK* has

an added soliloquy by Sabina, expressing
her strong love for Hilarius, and it elaborates upon the subsequent exchange
between the lovers (9–40). It omits the
entire dialogue between Tranio and the
Merchant (*TS*, 4.2.73–122), compressing
the scheme's description into a brief
explanation by Fabian (90–7).

1–7 *KK* largely follows the original (*TS*,
     4.2.1–5), but while *TS* reveals Bianca's
     and Lucentio's affair straight away
     through Tranio's mock surprise, *KK* has
     Alfons merely suggest the dishonour of
     Sabina's 'instruction' (5), increasing the
     impact of the subsequent passage which
     dramatizes the love between the young
     couple.

4.[1]] *this edn*; Die vierdte Handlung. *D1, D2, Köhler*

FELIX   I obey your will.

> *They go to the side.*
> *Enter* SABINA *and sits down at a table on the inner stage.*

SABINA   Happy hour which will bring my soul to my
body. O love, never tried by me before, how great is   10
your sweetness! Everything else in the world is stale
and miserable in comparison! True joy and pleasure
lie in you alone, pervading all my senses, body and
soul. Many things can be found to entertain the body,
but the soul cannot find pleasure and contentment   15
except through another soul, united in sweet love. But
where is the comfort that I long for so much? Does his
mind not feel the same yearning desire as mine?

> *Enter* [HILARIUS *as*] *Johannes.*

But why do I complain? The light of my sun rises
bright and clear. My dearest, be welcome.   20

> *She kisses him.*

HILARIUS   My beautiful lady, to receive such lovely
words, accompanied by such pretty works, makes me

---

8   SD1–8 SD2 *KK* adds careful stage directions, suggestive of the spatial organiza-
tion of the early modern German stage. An
inner stage ('innere Scene' as in *KK*, or
'innerer Schauplatz') is mentioned in various other German plays of the mid to late
seventeenth century, for instance,
Christian Weise's *Baurischer
Machiavellus* (Dresden, 1679; VD17
23:290747H), sig. A3v, and Johannes Rist,
Das Friedewünschende Teutschland (n.p.,
1647; VD17 23:249118M), sig. F3r. See
also Willi Flemming, *Andreas Gryphius
und die Bühne* (Halle a. S., 1921), 424.

9–20 SD Before adapting *TS*'s dialogue
between the lovers, *KK* inserts a soliloquy
by Sabina which is notable for its frank
expressions of intense love and female
desire, in keeping with her initiative in
kissing Hilarius later in the scene (20 SD
and 84 SD). See Introduction, pp. 106–7.

21–40 SD In the equivalent passage in *TS*
(4.2.6–10), Lucentio and Bianca flirt by
referring to an actual book he claims to
be reading, Ovid's *Ars Amatoria* ('*The
Art to Love*', 4.2.8). *KK* replaces the
learned courting with the explicit affirmations of love by Sabina and Hilarius.
It gently mocks the original's literary
games by having the couple describe
how they have put away actual books
(see 24–6), and adds an elaborate conceit
in which 'book' stands for each character's heart.

your happy servant. I hope to find in them the
constancy I look for. But, my darling, are you here
without any books at all?   25

SABINA   I wish to have no other book than your heart,
and in that my name, just as your name is indelibly
written in mine; and this I hope is assured through the
faith of your mouth and your eyes.

HILARIUS   My soul pledges to assure you of this. I am   30
glad to have accomplished my instruction fully by
teaching you to feel love for me, my dear heart's
heart. I do not wish to study in any other library but to
leaf through your beautiful book for ever. My mind
will read in it as long as it has a brain. Are you content   35
with that, my lovely angel?

SABINA   I do not know what your quips mean. But my
love, you know I am wholly yours.

HILARIUS   And I yours, my heart's child, as long as there
is breath in my body.   40

They embrace and kiss.

ALFONS   Are my words now confirmed by the action? Or
do they need more proofs?

FELIX   I believe this, and much else. But Monsieur lute-
player, who would have thought so?

ALFONS   I no longer wish to be mocked in this guise. I   45
am not a lute-player, but a nobleman well-known to
you: Alfons of Nistlingen. I will no longer be a suitor
to this unworthy person, but will give my love where

41–4 *KK* stays close to *TS* (4.2.11–15) but,
rather than translating Tranio's pretended railing against 'unconstant wom-
ankind', it adds Felix's mocking of
Alfons as 'Monsieur lute-player'.

45–60 *KK* reconfigures the dialogue between
Tranio and Hortensio (*TS*, 4.2.16–43),

omitting Tranio's indictment of Bianca's
supposed 'lightness' (4.2.24) and
Hortensio's promise to abandon the pursuit of 'beautous looks' (4.2.41) in
women, and adding the two men's
expression of supposed solidarity.

47   **Alfons...Nistlingen** See the List of Roles.

my offer is returned. I swear never more to honour
her in this way. I will reciprocate the friendliness 50
and desire of a young rich widow, and will link my
life to hers. You, sir, do as you wish, and suffer what
you can.

FELIX   Alfons, to please you I swear to withdraw my suit
to her. May you prosper in all your further endeavours. 55

ALFONS   I dutifully thank you, both for your good
decision to leave this light lady and for your good
wishes which I offer in return. May we be eternally
linked in constant friendship.

FELIX   Rest assured that I will be yours for ever. 60

Exit Alfons.

Felix goes towards Sabina and Hilarius.

Now you may help yourselves to each other. Surely
Master Tutor's lessons are very delightful, as the
student proves so good.

HILARIUS   Such lovely students can give orders to the
tutor. 65

SABINA   And such worthy tutors have the heart of the
student in their hand.

FELIX   This union is the reason why I and Sir Alfons
forswear you. I may not aim so high in any case, nor
want to, but he wishes to link himself to a widow, and 70
will take pains to make her tame and pious.

---

51   **young ... widow** 'a wealthy widow' in
TS (4.2.37), with no indication of her
age. She is called 'Eulalia' in *KK* in 5.2,
the only scene in which she appears. See
also the List of Roles.

60   SD2 *TS* has no equivalent SD.

61–7   **Surely ... hand.** *TS* has no equivalent
to Felix's tongue-in-cheek comment on
the student–tutor fiction of Hilarius and
Sabina.

68–70   **This ... widow** *KK* condenses

Tranio's news of Bianca's freedom from
suitors and Alfons' intention to marry a
widow, and omits the response to it (*TS*,
4.2.46–52), while adding the assurance
that he had never had the intention to
marry his social superior.

71–9   **take ... tongue.** follows speech-by-
speech Tranio and Bianca's exchange
about 'the taming school' to which
Hortensio is said to have gone (*TS*,
4.2.53–9, 55).

SABINA   How presumptuously he flatters himself! That's
not how the world runs.

FELIX   He believes he has understood the art of the
taming-school.   75

SABINA   Is there such a place?

FELIX   Yes, and Sir Hardman is its tutor. He teaches how
to make eleven and twenty be even: how to tame a
bad wife, and heal her shrewish tongue.

SABINA   That's a hard thing. But my lesson is over. My   80
darling, take care.

HILARIUS   A goodbye without a kiss?

SABINA   (*laughing*) I had almost forgotten the most
delightful thing.

She kisses him and exits.

HILARIUS   My heart, farewell.   85

Enter FABIAN.

But who comes here?

FELIX   Well, Fabian? I hope you have found an
honourable father for me. How does our business
stand?

77–8 **He ... even** In *TS*, Petruccio, according
to Tranio, 'teacheth eleven-and-twenty
long / To tame a shrew' (4.2.58–9). The
numbers in *KK* and *TS* are the same, but
Felix's point differs from Tranio's: while
Felix comments on the impossibility of
the taming task, Tranio's reference to the
card game Thirty-one, in which the goal
is to get a hand which has thirty-one
points, implies that Petruccio's teaching
is just right. The author of *KK* may well

have failed to understand the reference to
the card game.

79 **heal ... tongue** Similarly, the effect of
Petruccio's teaching is said to be to
'charm her chattering tongue' (*TS*, 4.2.59).

80–5 The leave-taking between Sabina and
Hilarius has no equivalent in *TS* where
Bianca remains onstage and so becomes
complicit in the scheme of the fake
father.

84   SD **She ... him** See note at 9–20 SD.

FABIAN   Pretty well, thanks to my great effort. I am dog-   90
tired from searching for a grave gentleman. He looks
as honourable as Saint Valentine, is filled to the brim
with imagined wisdom, and when it comes to natural
philosophy, thinks he is the biggest pig in the sty. In
sum, he agrees to your business, although he is not   95
the man he thinks he is. That aside, he is willing to do
anything for gain.

FELIX   It is good to have him. I will train him to become
an apt sub-father.

HILARIUS   It will be good to rely on a trick this time. A   100
little one can do no harm.

FABIAN   My comrade is apt enough for that. But *vel
quasi*, my lord, won't you come? He waits for you in
our lodging.

FELIX   Immediately. Let us neglect nothing.   [*Exeunt.*]   105

90–105 This passage corresponds to *TS*'s
introduction of the fake father (4.2.60–
72), but substantially departs in its treatment of the scheme: Tranio refrains from
revealing his strategy of duping the
Merchant, which is dramatized after
Bianca and Lucentio have left the stage
at 4.2.72. *KK* omits the passage in which
Tranio tricks the Merchant into agreeing
to the disguise (4.2.73–122), which is
rendered irrelevant by *KK*'s emphasis on
the business transaction between the
schemers and the 'grave gentleman' (91)
who is 'willing to do anything for gain'
(96–7).

90–1 **I ... searching** *KK* literally says 'I

have become dog-tired over this' ('ich
bin aber Hund müde darüber worden'),
echoing the English 'dog-weary' (*TS*,
4.2.61). The proverb probably comes
from hunting dogs tiring themselves out
(Wander, 'Hund', 12).

92   **Saint Valentine** The patron saint of travellers and lovers was often referred to on
the early modern German stage (see note
at 2.1.365).

100–1 While Lucentio seems uninvolved in
Tranio's doings (see *TS*, 4.2.67), Hilarius
explicitly approves of the proceedings.

102–3 *vel quasi* Latin, or as if / or almost.
The meaning in the present context is
unclear.

[4.2]   *Enter* WORMFIRE *and* SYBILLA *with a*
               cup of wine and cold roast.

WORMFIRE   Now, you dear container of my appendage,
come here. I know it will taste good tonight. He who
works is worthy of his food, *exemplum gratia* the
threshing ox. But shall we first perform a courtly
cochleation or charitably fill our guts with the   5
ingredients?

SYBILLA   I prefer to fill our gaping mouths.

               She feeds eagerly.

4.2 There is no specified location, but the scene is presumably set in Hardman's house. It corresponds to Act 4, Scene 3 in *TS*, and falls into four parts: part one to the arrival of Hardman and Alfons (1–104), part two to the arrival of Fritz the tailor (105–138), part three to Fritz's dismissal (139–297), and part four, Hardman's plans to visit his father-in-law (298–326). The first part, in which Wormfire and Sybilla tease the hungry Catharina, stays close to *TS* (4.3.1–35) but adds two short dialogues between the two servants on their affair (1–25), and between the two women about Hardman's behaviour (73–104). Part two corresponds to *TS* 4.3.36–62 in Hardman's starvation of Catharina, but adds Hardman's anger with the tailor for coming at meal time (131–8). Part three, the confrontation with the tailor, adapts *TS*, 4.3.63–167 and comically elaborates the description of the fine clothes (238–68). The sequence of events is slightly changed and there is some addition to the dialogue between Catharina and Hardman (180–205). The last part stays particularly close to *TS* (4.3.168–95).

1–25 Wormfire and Sybilla's dialogue, for which there is no equivalent in *TS*, contributes to a mini-subplot through which the servants' love throws light on that of their social betters. For *KK*'s addition of Sybilla, see Introduction pp. 107–9.

1   **appendage** ('Anhang') penis, see note at 3.2.124–5 and note.

2–3 **He ... food** ('wer arbeitet ist der Nahrung wert') an adaptation of Luke 10.7: 'the labourer is worthy of his hire' ('ein Arbeiter ist seines Lohnes wert').

3   *exemplum gratia* Latin, for example; Wormfire's first of several learned foreign-language terms in this passage (1–72), which contrast with the down-to-earth subject matter.

4   **threshing ox** The implicit reference is to 1 Corinthians 9.9: 'For it is written in the law of Moses, thou shalt not muzzle the mouth of the ox that treadeth out the corn.'

5   *cochleation* Latin, from *cochlear*, spoon. Wormfire may play on the German word the Latin translates, 'löffeln', which means both to behave like a fool (Grimm, 1) and to court (Grimm, 2). See Köhler, 250.

WORMFIRE   Above or below? Or both? But no, mine counts as well. You think perhaps that man and woman are one body. But it doesn't work in this case.   10

SYBILLA   A man and his wife? It's a bit too soon.

WORMFIRE   But not too soon for us to crawl into each other.

SYBILLA   Yes. In a way that conforms to *courtoisie*.

WORMFIRE   If the thing finds a jolly outbreak before its   15 time, we shall have to make spiritual amends for our courtesy, and sing the *poenitere* aloud in front of an honourable congregation. Well, the heart has its reasons.

SYBILLA   There's no harm, it's the fashion. We shall not   20 be the first nor the last. As long as the baptism doesn't come before the wedding.

WORMFIRE   The parson counsels so. But much talk fills few maws. Fill the cup!

SYBILLA   May God bless us. What will be, will be.   25

They feed eagerly.
Enter CATHARINA.

8–9 **Above ... well.** Wormfire's suggestive remarks refer to various bodily orifices.

9–11 **You ... soon.** Wormfire alludes to the religious teaching that man and woman in marriage become one flesh (see, for example, Mark 10.6–8). The German 'Mann und Weib' can be translated as both 'man and woman' (9–10) and '[a] man and his wife' (11; i.e. husband and wife). Sybilla reminds Wormfire that man and woman are said to become one flesh (or body) in marriage, and that they are not (yet) married.

12–13 **crawl ... other** have sex.

14 **conforms ... *courtoisie*** Sybilla seems to suggest that by having sex outside marriage, they are conforming to courtly manners.

15–18 **If ... congregation.** Wormfire suggests that if a pregnancy results from their affair, they will atone by marrying, imagined as singing their repentance (*the poenitere*). Public penitence for sexual sins was fairly common in Protestant countries.

24 **Fill the cup!** ('Es gilt / Hänschens im Keller') Wormfire alludes to a certain kind of cup, literally called 'little John in the cellar', that contains a figurine that rises from the base (the 'cellar') to the top when it is filled. The process of filling the empty vessel and the resulting emergence of the little man suggest insemination and conception, or birth. Such cups were used for drinking toasts to women who wished to conceive, or were about to give birth (Wander, 'Hänschen', 1).

CATHARINA   Well, the two of you know how to take care
of yourselves.

WORMFIRE   Yes, that's right. Thank you for saying so. It
is such fitting weather tonight.

SYBILLA   My lady, you have arrived a little late. But   30
you would not have accepted our company anyway,
I think.

CATHARINA   I would not have rejected it this time. But do
you know if the cook still has something cold in the
pantry?   35

SYBILLA   I believe not. He refuses to give out anything.
We managed to get our food in special ways.

WORMFIRE   Will my lady take a piece of this mustard-
flavoured ox rump? And a Paderborn beer?

[CATHARINA]   It sounds very good if it is to hand.   40

WORMFIRE   I am afraid the mustard is too choleric. It will
be *contraire* to your humour. But how good would a
cloth taste that had purged the hind of a cow, with a
delicate broth from raisins spiced with *Citrocynamo-*

26–37 In the equivalent passage in *TS*,
Grumio and Katherina enter the stage in
mid-conversation: Katherina has begged
Grumio for food in vain and laments
Petruccio's treatment of her (4.3.1–16).
KK replaces this passage with a dialogue
between the starving Catharina and the
two servants finishing their dinner.

38–58 The succession of offers and answers
roughly corresponds to that in the equivalent dialogue in *TS* (4.3.17–35).
Wormfire's descriptions of the kind of
food he would offer his mistress are
more elaborate, however, and add unsa-
voury culinary details, like capers being
'farted from a goat's fundament' (53–4),
a humorous element absent from *TS*.

39   **Paderborn beer?** Wormfire literally says
'a drink of man-poem from Paderborn'
('einen Tunck Paderbornisch Menschen

Gedicht'), referring to beer from the town
of Paderborn in north Rhine-Westphalia
(Wander, 'Menschengedicht', 2).

40   SP D1 and D2 assign the speech (and that
from line 57) to Sybilla, probably the result
of a printer's error or other textual corruption.

44–5   *Citrocynamo-Cariophyllικᾶς* This
inventive compound of Greek words is
obscure but could pertain to prawns
(*Cario* from 'karis') stuffed in wine
leaves (*phyllικᾶς* from 'phyllikos'
meaning 'leaf-like'), and seasoned with
lemon (*Citro*) and cinnamon (*cynamo*
from 'kinnamomon'). This exotic dish
stands in stark contrast to Wormfire's
previous references which are to rustic
food. A possible source for this exchange
could be Athenaeus' *Deipnosophistae*, a
fictive account of a series of philosoph-
ical banquets from the third century AD.

4.2.40 SP] *Köhler*; Sibylla *D1, D2*

Cariophyllikãç, especially with an *arrière-garde* that 45
contains a Bacheracher, Hochheymer or Necker nectar?

CATHARINA It would be even better if there were some.

WORMFIRE Sweetness increases choler too much,
particularly when mingled with the heat of grape
juice. What do you say to a dish of morels prepared 50
with the best wild pears, qualified with an onionish
garlic-broth? Or a nice dish of Westphalian field-
beans with sour milk and capers farted from a goat's
fundament, excellently spiced, hey! Alongside that a
good claret of the kind that the Marburgers name after 55
your own rigour.

[CATHARINA] Keep these dishes for your own hoggish
maw, you fool! Go away, or I'll make you clear off.

WORMFIRE There's no need for that job, for right now I
am busy preparing to make my fine companion 60
another set of feet. But I must go in now. My lord has
commanded me to go to the top chef today. Thus,
honoured lady, rejoice that you have an appetite.
There will be a fine dinner, the whole kitchen is
polished, the servants are turning the roast like fools, 65
the cook goes around the kitchen like a madman, the
pots, kettles and pans boil, fry and foam on the fire
most nonsensically. The cake pans and pastries in the

---

45 *arrière-garde* French, rearguard.
46 **Baccharacher ... Necker** Wormfire
mentions three wine regions in south-
west Germany.
52 **Westphalian** from the region of
Westphalia in north-western Germany.
53–4 **farted ... hey!** Wormfire puns on
'farted' ('gefürzet') and 'spiced'
('gewürtzet').
56 **your ... rigour.** Wormfire addresses
Catharina as 'Ihr Strengheit' ('your

rigour'), a title for nobility (see Grimm,
'Gestrenge'). Köhler (251) suggests that
the wine may have been called
Catharinenclaret, prompting Wormfire's
allusion.
57 SP See note at 40.
59–72 *KK* adds Wormfire's vivid description
of the busy kitchen in order to tease the
hungry Catharina.
60–1 **preparing ... feet** i.e. getting Sybilla
pregnant.

4.2.57 SP] *Köhler*; Siylla *D1*; Sibylla *D2*

oven are about to give birth and all the fine baking
stuff looks delicious. In sum, Bacchus will honour   70
Ceres, and she will refresh him with many delicacies.
Today shall be better than yesterday.   *Exit.*

CATHARINA   If it were otherwise, to the devil with today!
It is as though he wanted to kill me with hunger out of
love: the beggers that came to my father's house did   75
better.

SYBILLA   Madam, perhaps your night was better than
your day?

CATHARINA   May God have pity on me, so that I don't
experience such another. I did not close an eye. More   80
such nights would soon kill me.

SYBILLA   But surely he did not handle you roughly,
madam. Sensible grooms do not show too much to
their brides on the first night.

CATHARINA   You need not address me as a married   85
woman. He has left me all too pure so far. He did not
once seem to think there was something womanly
in me.

SYBILLA   That's strange, he otherwise seemed to have
good inclinations.   90

CATHARINA   I do not doubt his goodness in this thing at
all, I have noticed it enough. I don't know why he
keeps to himself like this.

70–1 **Bacchus ... Ceres** Bacchus is the
Roman god of wine and drinking, Ceres
the Roman goddess of wheat and agri-
culture.

73–6 *KK* transposes three lines from
Katherina's otherwise completely
supressed complaint to Grumio at the
beginning of the scene (*TS*, 4.3.2–16,
4–6). See note at 26–37.

77–104 *KK* adds this exchange between

Catharina and her maid about the newly-
weds' first night, Catharina's continuing
virginity, and her admission that she has
been 'bewitched' by Hardman and 'have
to be gentle to him almost against [her]
will' (103–4). See Introduction, pp. 102–3.

91   **goodness ... thing** interest in, or ability
to perform, sex. The German 'stücke',
like the English 'thing' with which we
translate it, may contain a phallic pun.

SYBILLA Who knows what his thoughts are in this
matter. I hope and wish most heartily that his mad   95
manner would change to a better one, since there is
much pretended method in it. I wish to God you could
bend your mind to his. He will surely stop his raving
soon, and you will have the best of husbands.

CATHARINA I think I am bent already, but only my heart   100
knows just how bitter I am, and those who are
acquainted with the mind of women. I believe this
man has bewitched me, because I have to be gentle to
him almost against my will.

Enter ALFONS *and* HARDMAN, *both bearing
food,* [*and enter a Servant*].

HARDMAN Are you here, my heart's darling? See, how I   105
take pains for your sake? And do you like it? Are you
silent? – There, young friend, take the stuff away
again. My love does not like it.

CATHARINA Wait, I like it! Leave it!

HARDMAN Even a boy would repay a small service with   110
thanks. Shall my lady spurn mine?

He bears the bowls away.

[*Exit.*]

Alfons gives his to the Servant.

[*Exit Servant.*]

---

104 SD In *TS*, Petruccio and Hortensio enter
'*with meat*' (4.3.35.1). No servant is
onstage in the equivalent passage in *TS*.

105–11 *KK* remains relatively close to the
equivalent passage in *TS* (4.3.36–48),
but omits Hortensio's 'Mistress, what
cheer?' (4.3.37) and Katherina's remark
that she is 'cold' (4.3.38).

107 **the stuff** the food.

111 SD–24 *He bears ... hurry.* In *TS*

(4.3.49–54), Petruccio is immediately
pacified by Katherina's thanks, remains
onstage and invites her and Hortensio to
eat. *KK* complicates the passage by
having Hardman and the servant bear the
food away, offering Catharina and
Alfons a moment to speak amongst
themselves, before Hardman re-enters,
pacified, and invites Catharina and
Alfons to 'come in for the meal' (123–4).

CATHARINA   Indeed, I am thankful, my darling. It's just
  that you don't know my way of showing it.

ALFONS   My dearest lady, reconcile yourself a little to
  his stormy manner. I assure you he loves you heartily.   115
  If you offer him friendliness, you will be able to live
  with him very pleasantly.

CATHARINA   It's much too difficult for a stubborn woman
  to change so swiftly; the transformation would have
  to be complete.   120

ALFONS   If you are reasonable enough, you will be able
  to turn this transformation to your advantage.

Enter HARDMAN.

HARDMAN   Well, my darling, and brother Alfons, come
  in for the meal, we have to hurry. I have much to
  do before our journey to your lord father's house   125
  tomorrow. I must acquire some jewels for you today,
  and many other costly things for both of us, to enable
  the people to see that we are not of mean rank. We will
  walk around in our magnificence, so that they will talk
  of nobody but us. So, come in. Dinner is getting cold.   130

Enter WORMFIRE.

WORMFIRE   My lord, the tailor is waiting outside, all
  laden with his stuff.

123–30 In the equivalent speech in *TS*
  (4.3.52–62), Petruccio revels in imagining the extravagant clothes the couple
  will wear upon returning to Katherina's
  father, an elaborate rhetorical flight
  reduced in *KK* to the plain information
  that they will have 'costly things' (127).
126 **tomorrow** Hardman's intention to leave
  the next day, which has no equivalent in
  TS, is contradicted by his later wish to
  'be gone today' (310).

128 **we ... rank** *KK* literally reads 'that a
  donkey did not bring us to the market'
  ('daß uns kein Esel auffs Marckt
  gebracht'). This obscure, perhaps proverbial expression alludes to market days
  when sellers would show off their wares.
131–8 *KK* adds this short passage to the
  equivalent scene in *TS*, where the tailor
  simply enters (4.3.62 SD).

HARDMAN   Must this fool come at mealtime? Tell the
rogue, if he has fed himself, he must grant me and my
love time for a meal too.   135

CATHARINA   He can come after the meal.

HARDMAN   Tell him to go away at once! But, wait, let the
fool come in. I can jest with him during the meal.

[*Enter* FRITZ.]

WORMFIRE   [*to Fritz*]   Move your bones inside, my
thread-wise and needle-sage lord.   140

FRITZ   A blessed day to you, gentlemen, health and long
prosperity.

HARDMAN   Let's see what pretty stuff you have made to
grace the beautiful form of my lady. What's this?

FRITZ   Your honour, a shirt made according to the   145
fashion, as your honour ordered.

HARDMAN   A carnival cap, a jester's blanket around
rabbit fur! Will you make fools of us? Will you dress
children, and decorate dolls? Away, cover a post with
your things and put it up amidst pea stalks. My love   150
must not wear such clothes as are made by fools.
Such children's stuff is not seemly.

CATHARINA   The camisole is good, both the material and
the work.

---

138 SD–42 *TS* has a haberdasher and a tailor,
two unnamed figures, present their
wares: the tailor enters first and is
greeted by Petruccio (4.3.63), but only
speaks after the haberdasher, who has
entered immediately after him (4.3.64),
has been dismissed (4.3.88 SD). *KK* simplifies the sequence by conflating the two
roles into one, the tailor Fritz Thimble of
Scratch-hill (see the List of Roles).

145–52 *KK* remains close to the equivalent
passage in *TS* (4.3.65–70), but has Fritz

offer a shirt rather than the haberdasher's
'cap' (4.3.65).

147 **jester's blanket** ('Narrendecke') This
rare word is also used by the same author
in *Der Pedanthische Irrthum*, 133 (see
Introduction, p. 144).

150 **put ... stalks** Hardman suggests the
shirt be worn by a scarecrow to protect
peas from birds.

153–7 *KK* interpolates Catharina's defence
of the dress and Hardman's argument
against it.

HARDMAN   My heart, the material is good, I have chosen   155
it myself for you, but this sloppy apprentice has
utterly spoilt it with his work.

CATHARINA   It is well done, the way gentlefolk wear
things nowadays.

HARDMAN   We must not look to become gentlefolk   160
through garments. – What ape's ware have you there?
What can this be?

FRITZ   Your honour can surely see that it is a well-made
piece.

HARDMAN   A well-made piece! A piece for a fool! An   165
ass! Is this frippery to be worn in Tom Thumb's place?
What have you done with the sleeves, you witless
block?

FRITZ   It is done the way it should be. I would like to see
a tailor who can show me better work whether he had   170
been in France or all over Europe. I know my craft as
a tailor *de façon* should do.

CATHARINA   You talk well, Master. It is well made, and I
see the dress will fit like a glove.

ALFONS [*aside*]   She's getting warm. There'll be blows   175
soon.

158–61 **It . . . garments.** *KK* corresponds to
the equivalent passage in *TS* (4.3.71–7),
but has Catharina replace Katherina's
remark on 'gentlewomen' (4.3.72) by
'gentlefolk' ('Edelleute'), leading to
Hardman's comment on gentility and
clothes. Petruccio picks up on Katherina's
'gentlewomen' by applying the adjective
'gentle' to Katherina ('When you are
gentle you shall have one too' (4.3.73),
i.e. a cap), playing on the polysemy of
'gentle' as 'noble' and 'mild'. This pun is
impossible in German.

161–83 This sequence of Hardman's
humorous debasing of Fritz's work, and

Fritz's and Catharina's defence of it has
no equivalent in the corresponding passage in *TS*.

166 **frippery** ('Firlefantz') The German
word's roots are obscure but originally
refer to an outlandishly dressed fool
figure performing strange dances (see
Grimm, 'Firlfanz').

166 **Tom . . . place** ('an statt eines
Däumlings') Tom Thumb (in the German
version, 'ein Däumling') is a little man
the size of a thumb, popular in European
folklore.

172 **tailor *de façon*** a proper tailor, from
French, *de façon*, i.e. in the (right) manner.

HARDMAN [*to Fritz*]   You know your craft like a fool *de façon*, and you would make my love a fool. I'll crush your brains before that happens.

CATHARINA   I see you take me for a stupid child. You   180
intend to cloud my reason with your strange antics. I see you have little respect for me. Your pretended love is a mere semblance.

HARDMAN   What are you saying, dearest?

CATHARINA   I hope I am not denied words.   185

HARDMAN   My love is free to do as she likes. [*to Fritz*] But what else do you have, you cheating rogue? Is this the skirt? Dear me, this beautiful stuff is spoilt by your thievery! You have stolen half of it. I'd rather have paid you double than have a thing spoilt like this.   190

CATHARINA   I do not know what to say. Are you mad, or are we? I say the tailor has made no fault in anything.

FRITZ   I confirm this. Sir, you're mistaken. I have made everything according to your order that was delivered to me by Wormfire.   195

WORMFIRE   The villain wants to make me guilty of the spoilt stuff! He lies if he says I gave him orders rather than material for the garments.

HARDMAN [*to Fritz*]   You old goat, don't abuse my patience, or I'll rain blows. You have worked like an   200
apprentice.

---

185 *KK* radically reduces Katherina's outburst against Petruccio's patronizing (*TS*, 4.3.75–82), and condenses her eloquent claim to verbal self-expression into a single line. For a similar implosion of Katherina's eloquence, see *KK*, 5.2.340–1 and note.

186–90 Hardman's renewed rejection of the tailor's work follows Petruccio's at *TS*, 4.3.88–94.

188 **Dear me** The German literally says 'sorrow and damage' ('Jammer und Schad'). For the formulae, see Grimm, 'Jammer', 7.

193–201 *KK* follows the equivalent passage of *TS* (4.3.96–102) but inserts the tailor's accusation against Wormfire and Wormfire's response to it (193–8), transposed from a later point of *TS* (4.3.117–20).

196–7 **guilty … stuff!** Wormfire literally says that Fritz wants to 'pour the spoilt stuff into his shoes' ('die verdorbene sache in die Schue schütten'), drawing on a proverb about incriminating somebody else for one's actions (Wander, 'Schuh', 185).

CATHARINA   I say he has worked well. You want to make a rogue of him, and a fool of me.

HARDMAN   You speak right. It's the rogue who wants to make a fool of you.   205

FRITZ   She says, my lord, it is you who wants to make a fool of her.

HARDMAN   O, great presumption by the shadow of a man in my own house! You lie, you lie, you thread, you Tom Thumb, you needle tip, you flaky-headed clod of   210 earth, you! I'll soon measure your mangy back with your mete-yard and make you remember it all your life. You've wasted everything that's been put into your hands.

FRITZ   May I die this very moment if all is not made as your   215 honour ordered it through the man who stands here.

WORMFIRE   I told you to make it with thread and needle.

FRITZ   But it needs to be cut first.

WORMFIRE   A rogue told you to cut it, now stop lying and flattering yourself, or you'll be sorry for it.   220

HARDMAN   Whichever of you two birds is wrong has to pay the bill.

FRITZ   I am right, and the lady is well pleased with my work, let this fool say what he will.

WORMFIRE   What, you miserable skeleton of a tired old   225 goat, you quintessence of all that is mangy, you home of lice and fleas, you needle-noble and thread-honour,

---

202–18 *KK* closely follows the original (*TS*, 4.3.103–23).

203–7 **fool ... fool** The threefold use of the same term corresponds to *TS*, but *TS*'s characters say 'puppet' (4.3.105–7) instead of 'fool' ('Närrin').

210 **Tom Thumb** See 166n.

210–11 **flaky-headed ... earth** The German uses 'Grindschulpe', an obscure word that we have not found elsewhere. It may derive from (or be a corruption of) 'Grindschüppel', a rare term of abuse

recorded by Grimm, composed of 'Grind' (a term for 'head') and 'Schüppel' (from 'Schuppe', 'dandruff').

219–20 *KK* reduces the increasingly heated exchange between Grumio and the Tailor (*TS*, 4.3.124–9) to Wormfire's threat.

221–33 **Whichever ... quarrelling?** A passage with no equivalent in *TS*.

227–8 **needle-noble ... clout-commissary** Wormfire insults Fritz by relating terms of social respectability to simple objects from tailoring.

you clippers-commandant and clout-commissary whom I respect as much as a fart, do you address my reason thus? If I didn't respect my lordship, I'd chase 230 you out of the world.

FRITZ I'd serve you well. But what good is there in quarrelling? [*holds out the paper to Wormfire*] Here is your own paper. That will show the instructions.

WORMFIRE What paper? You are lying through your teeth! 235

HARDMAN Come, read it.

WORMFIRE But truthfully, without lies.

FRITZ 'Extracted small memorial from the great instruction given regarding our dear and gracious lady: how the slender shaft of her noble body is to be 240 divided, encompassed and elaborated in the nicest manner, and be concentrated in the narrowest part *memoriae juvandae.*'

ALFONS The rubric is apt.

WORMFIRE My lord, it is my own invention. 245

ALFONS The work shows that clearly enough.

HARDMAN [*to Wormfire*] Shut up, fool – and you, read on.

FRITZ '*Pro primus*, a conjugated fishbone breast armour

232–89 This passage with Wormfire's written instructions, read out by Fritz and commented upon by Hardman, Wormfire and Alfons, rearranges and expands the corresponding passage in *TS* (4.3.130–51). In *TS*, the 'loose-bodied gown', a particularly contentious item, is mentioned first (4.3.133–4), whereas in *KK* there is a considerable build-up towards it, with items Wormfire grants he commissioned, before its mention in line 271. Whereas the 'note' (4.3.130) in *TS* consists of no more than a short list of items, the 'paper' (234) in *KK* is considerably more elaborate (238–43, 248–51, 256–9, 262–8, etc.). The note's suggestive language (e.g., 'the slender shaft of her

noble body is to be divided', 240–1), pompous diction (e.g., 'small memorial from the great instruction', 238–9), repeated use of Latin and French, convoluted syntax and elaborate sartorial descriptions all add to the comedy of the passage.

232 **I'd ... well** a threat to retaliate if Wormfire tried to 'chase [him] out of the world' (230–1).

243 *memoriae juvandae* Latin, of pleasant memory.

244 **rubric** (Rubric) i.e. the instructions.

248 *Pro primus* Latin, first of all.

248 **conjugated ... armour** a corset stiffened with boning, i.e. the rigid parts that form its frame.

in linen with trunk sleeves *à la mode*, and *euphonia gratia* covered with silk which we call a ladies' gown   250
in our German mother tongue.'

WORMFIRE   I confess, a lady's doublet with two sleeves.

FRITZ   Confess what you will, here is the letter.

WORMFIRE   The letter, too, can be by a lying thieving villain like you. Shut your prating mouth.   255

FRITZ   'A black silken coat with bobbinlace mingled with silk embroidered according to the craft, and an added train with a long long untapering stick, as pleases women, belonging to the bodice instead of a tunic.'

WORMFIRE   I let all of this pass if only the tail of my   260
gracious lady be well placed.

FRITZ   'And another cape of linen hangings, covering the lower cupboard with a cloth of mixed silver and gold threads, prepared and *à la mode*, from German money acquired *à la française*, also the sun and moon entwined   265
together in curious fabric, daintily covered and decorated. *Explicatius*, an undergarment with pieces of gold and silver and lace of such like material.'

WORMFIRE   I grant all this. It'll come to an end now, I hope, for fear makes time seem long.   270

FRITZ   'Further, a loose-bodied gown.'

---

249 *à la mode* French, fashionable.

249–50 *euphonia gratia* Latin, for the sake of euphony. The words may indicate that the silk should give the gown a pleasantly rustling sound.

256 **coat** ('Windfang') literally a windscreen (Grimm A.1.c).

258–9 **train … bodice** another passage in which the sartorial description offers occasion for sexual innuendo (see 232–89 and note).

263 **lower cupboard** a periphrasis for 'female genitalia'.

264 *à la mode* See note at 249.

265 *à la française* French, in the French manner; the meaning of the phrase in the present context is unclear.

265 **sun and moon** a proleptic allusion to the 'sun and moon' passage (see 4.4.11–27).

265–6 **entwined together** ('spinnenmässig elaborirtem Gewebe') literally, spider-like elaborated fabric

267 *Explicatius* Latin, completed.

269–70 **It'll … long.** This sentence may be spoken as an aside.

271–89 *KK* remains close to the equivalent passages in *TS* (4.3.133–7 and 4.3.142–51).

HARDMAN   What folly is this?

WORMFIRE   Master, if I said loose-bodied, sew me into
the gown and beat me as dead as a doornail with a
whole spool of blue thread. I said a proper and modest   275
gown.

HARDMAN [*to Fritz*]   Fool, read on.

FRITZ   'With a pleated body, the sleeves prettily cut.'

HARDMAN   Rogue, do you think I am a fool?

WORMFIRE   My lord, a mistake, an error in the paper, the   280
witless thief has not understood me well. I told him to
cut the sleeves and then sew them. [*to Fritz*] I will
defend myself against you, you wasteful fly-catcher,
even if all your fingers are armed.

FRITZ   What! I say it is true! And if I met you in another   285
place, we'd have a little dance.

WORMFIRE   To the tailor's song. But ho, come now, give
me the mete-yard, you take the paper, and we'll fence
for the honour.

HARDMAN   I told you just now, Master Mex, you have   290
spoilt everything, and shall pay me damages. My love
should not wear such worthless stuff on her precious
body.

He beckons Alfons to come nearer.

Get out of my sight.

---

274 **dead ... doornail** Wormfire literally says
'mouse-dead' ('Mäuse tod'), that is, as easily
killed as a mouse (Grimm, 'mausetotd').

283–4 **wasteful ... armed.** Wormfire insults
Fritz by debasing his profession, mockingly referring to thimbles as armour, and
calling him, literally, a 'light fly catcher'
('leichten Fliegenfänger'), someone who
is content with small exploits (Grimm,
'Fliegenfänger').

286 **little dance** i.e. they would fight.

290 **Mex** a derisory term for tailors, origi-
nating in a now obscure connection to
goats and the sound the animals were
thought to produce (Wander, 'Mex').

293 SD In *TS*, Petruccio, in an aside, asks
Hortensio, 'say thou wilt see the tailor
paid' (4.3.163), an action that is implied
in *KK* in the present SD. Hortensio, in
the subsequent speech, promises the
tailor payment (4.3.165–7), just as
Alfons does (*KK*, 295–6).

ALFONS   Good master Fritz, keep the things for me. I 295
will pay you tomorrow.

FRITZ   My lord, I am content.   *Exit.*

HARDMAN   We must travel to your people in rags, dearest
Catharina. Does the covering matter if the man is
good? It is better to be able to pay for costly goods 300
than to hang them around us. Our purses shall be rich
with gold; ourselves in poor clothes. Add virtue to
this: the best garment to grace us both.

WORMFIRE (*aside*)   But it's invisible.

HARDMAN   Is the hoopoe better than the lark because his 305
feathers are more beautiful, or the snake than the
eel because he is decorated with such gleaming
colours? So do not be unwilling, dearest heart. It is
not shameful for us to wear this mean array. If it is,
blame me, I will stand for it. Let us be gone today. 310
Brother Alfons travels with us. It is now around seven
o'clock.

WORMFIRE   The hand of the clock is surely ruled by a
fool.

HARDMAN   We can go some of the way before noon until 315
we find good lodgings.

CATHARINA   Seven o'clock? It is midday. What are you
saying?

298–323 *KK* remains close to *TS* (4.3.168–95), but omits Petruccio's mention of their means of transportation (4.3.183–5) and punctuates Hardman's grandiloquent moralizing speech by inserting Wormfire's deflating comments (304 and 313–14).

305 **hoopoe ... lark** ('Wiedehopff ... Lerche') 'the jay' and 'the lark' in the corresponding passage in *TS* (4.3.174). The hoopoe and the jay are both colourful birds.

306–7 **snake ... eel** ('Schlange ... Aal') 'the adder' and 'the eel' in *TS* (4.3.176). The visually striking zigzag pattern on the adder's back means that the passage may work better in the English original than in the German adaptation.

317 **midday** 'almost two' according to Katherina in *TS* (4.3.188). Petruccio's reference to 'seven o'clock' (4.3.186), by contrast, is faithfully preserved by *KK* (317).

HARDMAN   What are you saying, dearest Catharina? Always against me? I think my love for you deserves 320 more. We will not go from here until the clock says what I say it says. Come what may. *Exit.*

ALFONS   Commanding the sun, that's something new.
    Exeunt [Alfons, Catharina and Sybilla].

WORMFIRE   Not for my honourable master. I thank God it is over with Master Scratch-hill. My back was ready 325 to be hurt. *Exit.*

[4.3]   *Enter* FELIX *[as Hilarius] and* BLASIUS.

BLASIUS   I will take care of everything and settle the business to my lord's liking. I have acted in a comedy before now.

FELIX   You must study to acquire an unstudied freedom of manner. 5

323 Hortensio's equivalent speech (*TS*, 4.3.195), which occurs when Petruccio is still onstage, is sometimes assumed by editors to be an aside (e.g. Oxf, Thompson).

323 SD *Sybilla* D1 and D2 do not specify when Sybilla exits the stage. Although she never speaks after line 99, it makes sense for her to remain onstage in order to attend to her mistress. She might, however, exit at another point, for instance after line 104, leaving Catharina alone onstage to meet Hardman and Alfons, or with Wormfire at the very end of the scene.

323–6 *TS* concludes the scene with Hortensio's comment, 'Why so, this gallant will command the sun' (4.3.195), adapted in Alfons' speech, to which *KK* adds Wormfire's humorous reflection on the escalating situation with 'Master Scratch-hill' (325), a reference to Fritz, the tailor.

4.3 No location is specified, but the scene is presumably set in front of Hilarius' lodgings. It corresponds to a brief dialogue in *TS* between Lucentio's servants and the false father (4.4.1–18). *KK* omits the subsequent passage in *TS* in which Baptista and the Merchant meet, verbally conclude the marriage contract, and leave for Baptista's house in order to sign the documents in private (4.4.19–71). It also leaves out Biondello's report of their success to Lucentio, and his advice to take Bianca to church for a secret marriage (4.4.72–106). By omitting much of the corresponding scene in *TS*, *KK* thus asks its audience to accept as given the wedding between Hilarius and Sabina. The effect of the omissions is that *KK* focuses *TS*'s several strands of interweaving action into a single line pointing to the resolution in 5.1.

1–5 The exchange between Felix and Blasius adapts the brief dialogue between Tranio and the Merchant (*TS*, 4.4.1–7). In both plays, the men are rehearsing how to convince as Hilarius' / Lucentio's father. While *TS*'s Merchant is already in his role as Lucentio's father, Blasius metatheatrically thinks of his future performance as a 'comedy' (2).

Enter FABIAN.

So, what's the answer?

FABIAN   Sir Theobald has instructed me to offer his
regards, and will shortly pay my lord a visit.

FELIX   This respect is too great an honour for us, but
since it is his wish, we must obey. Swiftly, Fabian,   10
clean your chamber. Let's go inside to welcome him
in the best possible way.   *Exeunt.*

[4.4]   *Enter* ADRIAN.

[ADRIAN]   Fatherly love as well as care have brought me
here. My son left me some time ago, and I have no
news of his fortune either from him or from anyone
else. I almost fear that something bad has happened
to him. His nature always tended towards virtue, so I   5

6–12 The passage corresponds to Biondello's
return from his errand to Baptista (*TS*,
4.4.14–18). While Fabian announces
Theobald's imminent visit before they
'go inside' (11) in preparation for it, *TS*'s
characters remain onstage where they are
joined by Baptista and Lucentio (4.4.18
SD).

4.4 The location is not specified, but the
scene is presumably set on the street
(1–88) and in front of Hilarius' lodgings
(89–205). It corresponds to two successive scenes in *TS*, Act 4, Scene 5 and Act
5, Scene 1. It falls into three parts: one,
Hardman's deliberate confusion of the
sun and the moon and the party's
encounter with Adrian (1–98, *TS*, 4.5.1–
77); two, the confrontation between the
real and the fake father of Hilarius (99–
175, *TS*, 5.1.1–99); and, three, the conciliatory dialogue between Hardman and
Catharina (176–205, *TS*, 5.1.132–41). In
its adaptation of *TS*, *KK* shows signifi-

cant independence in the second part,
and omits the presence of Katherina,
Petruccio and Baptista at the confrontation. It replaces the increasingly violent
conflict between the real and the fake
Vincentio (*TS*, 5.1.57–99) with Adrian's
loss of consciousness (149–70), and
delays the resolution of the plot through
the entry of Bianca and Lucentio (*TS*,
5.1.100–31) by moving the announcement of the marriage of Hilarius and
Sabina to the next act (5.1). *KK* rounds
off the scene with Sybilla's reflections on
the conciliatory power of sex and marriage (196–205).

1–9 The first appearance of Hilarius' father.
Unlike his equivalent in *TS*, Vincentio (who
first enters at 4.5.26 SD), Adrian is given a
short soliloquy in which he expresses his
worries about the lack of news from his son
(see Introduction, p. 105).

1   SP In D1 and D2, the SP is implied in the
entrance SD.

4.4.1 SP] *Köhler*; no SP *D1, D2*

hope bad company has not seduced him into a dishonest life. The message I received from him is strange, and I need to know what is going on. But who are these people here?

       Enter ALFONS, HARDMAN, CATHARINA,
            WORMFIRE *and* SYBILLA.

HARDMAN   Now let us bravely ambush old Sir Theobald.   10
How bright the moon is shining: it must be a full moon.

CATHARINA   The moon? Why, darling, it's the sun.

HARDMAN   What sun? So now I can't see straight?
Wormfire, get the horses from the inn. We must go   15
home in this moonlight which shines as certainly as my father's son wears my own trousers.

ALFONS *[to Catharina]*   Tell him what he wants, you know his meaning.

CATHARINA *[to Hardman]*   Well, then, stay here in this   20
moonlight.

HARDMAN   I say it over again, it's the moon.

CATHARINA   Now I see, it is nothing else.

HARDMAN   Now you are mistaken after all, it is the
blessed sun.   25

CATHARINA   Good Lord, then let it be the sun. I am
content, be it a wax light, star, torch or what you wish.

ALFONS   My brother may now gently lay his weapons
down: the field is won.

HARDMAN   That's how the river should flow. But what's   30
this? *[to Adrian]* Good day, fairest maid. Why are you walking alone?

10–17 *KK* stays close to *TS* (4.5.1–10) but omits Petruccio's wilful threat that '[i]t shall be moon or star or what [he] list[s]' (4.5.7).

18–32 *KK* closely follows the equivalent passage in *TS* (4.5.11–28), except that it omits a short passage (4.5.20–3) and transposes the equivalent of Katherina's exasperated admission of any name for the sun (4.5.13–15) to Catharina's last speech in this passage (26–7).

ALFONS   I do not understand, my lord.

HARDMAN   Tell me, dearest Catharina, have you ever
seen such a beautiful maid in all your life?   35

WORMFIRE   And you, Sybilla, are you also transformed?

SYBILLA   Yes, you have made a boy of me by attaching
something of yours to me.

HARDMAN   My darling, go and greet this fair maid with a
kiss.   40

CATHARINA   I see no one maidenly.

HARDMAN   What, do you resist me in everything?

CATHARINA   My darling, calm yourself. I believe the
ancient sire is a beautiful maid. [*to Adrian*] Therefore,
fairest maid, take this kiss from an unknown friend.   45

[*She kisses Adrian.*]

ALFONS   Brother, leave off this joking.

HARDMAN [*to Catharina*]   I do not know if I am the fool
or you. This is an old gentleman whom you think a
maid, dearest darling.

CATHARINA   I see now. [*to Adrian*] My lord, pardon my   50
error. The rays of the moon-changed sun have so
bedazzled my face that I can no longer tell black from
white.

34–8 *KK* follows the beginning and end of
Petruccio's equivalent address to
Katherina, asking her to greet Vincentio
as a young maid (*TS*, 4.5.29–35), but
omits Petruccio's commonplace praise
of the supposed maid's beauty (4.5.31–3)
and inserts the brief exchange between
Wormfire and Sybilla.

37–8 Sybilla's allusion to her copulation with
Wormfire constitutes another addition in
KK to the equivalent material in *TS*. The
servants provide a comic reflection of the
behaviour of their social superiors (see

3.2.349–98, 4.2.1–25, 5.2.345–93 and
notes). Sybilla's supposed transformation
has an Ovidian flavour and is reminiscent
of the third quatrain of Shakespeare's
Sonnet 20.

41   Catharina's last moment of resistence to
Hardman has no counterpart in the
equivalent passage in *TS*.

42–53 *KK* stays close to the equivalent
moment in *TS* (4.5.38–50), but inserts
Alfons' objection (46) and omits
Katherina's second polite excuse to
Vincentio (4.5.49–50).

[ADRIAN]   I gladly pardon you, my merry lady. I do not
know how to understand your comic behaviour and   55
speech, but it has made me laugh.

CATHARINA   Do not resent my behaviour. My love has
infected me with his merry manner.

WORMFIRE (*aside*)   That will show in three quarters of a
year.   60

CATHARINA   To avoid further confusion, I will go in and
announce the arrival of my dearest.

Exit with Sybilla.

HARDMAN   I will follow soon. – My lord, pardon me, I
beg to know your name.

ADRIAN   I am the older Liebenthal, and have come here   65
to visit my son.

HARDMAN   It gladdens my heart to bid you welcome,
good sir, the more so because you come on time to
attend a wedding.

ADRIAN   I don't understand what you are saying, my lord.   70

HARDMAN   I am the first to inform you that your son is a
bridegroom, and will hold his wedding feast soon.

54–62 *KK* preserves the father's good-
humoured excuse of the prank in *TS*
(4.5.54–5), but omits Petruccio's invitation to Vincentio to accompany them on
their way (4.5.51–3) and adds Wormfire's
bawdy aside (59–60). While Katherina
remains onstage, *KK* has Catharina exit
with Sybilla in order to go and announce
their arrival (61–2).

54   SP D1 and D2 mistakenly assign the
speech to Alfons; Köhler emends the SP.
See also 1.3.404 SP and note.

59–60 Wormfire bawdily suggests that Hardman
has 'infected' (58) Catharina with a baby, to
be born in 'three quarters of a year'.

65–82 *KK* adapts the equivalent passage in

TS (4.5.56–68), notably by inserting into
it Adrian's expressions of incredulity and
outrage (70 and 73–4). It also adds
Hardman's attempt to appease Adrian by
letting him know that his son's bride is
the daughter of Sir Theobald, who happens to be Adrian's good friend (75–9;
see also 155 and note). Petruccio simply
tells Vincentio that his daughter-in-law is
'wealthy, and of worthy birth' (4.5.66).

65   **Liebenthal** See the List of Roles.

68–9 **you … wedding** In *TS*, by contrast,
Petruccio informs Vincentio that his 'son
by this hath married' (4.5.64). For the
two plays' different treatments of the
wedding, see the headnote to 4.3.

54   SP] *Köhler*; Alfons *D1, D2*

ADRIAN   This is madness! I sent my son abroad to study, not to get married!

HARDMAN   My lord, don't be surprised. The lady he   75
takes is my darling's sister, rich with gifts of both body and mind. She is blessed by fortune. Her friendship and family cannot seem unfitting to you, given that she is the daughter of Sir Theobald.

ADRIAN   Your last words give me some comfort, and will   80
assure my son forgiveness for his fault as he is linking two intimate friends.

HARDMAN   I wish to be included in this band of friendship. Sir, I beg you to be like a father to me.

ADRIAN   I will assist you in all your desires. But, my   85
lord, can you not tell me where my son is staying? I wish to surprise him without warning and to shock him most horribly.

HARDMAN   He may be where I am going right now. Here are his lodgings. I will accompany you, my lord, if   90
you would like me to.

ADRIAN   I beg to see him privately first. We will speak afterwards. Meanwhile, send fair greetings to Sir Theobald.

HARDMAN   Thank you, I am at your service. – Brother   95
Alfons, come, let's see what is to be done within.

WORMFIRE   And I shall see what business the cup can give to my throat.

Exeunt [all but Adrian].

83–98 *KK* considerably departs from *TS* by adding Adrian's wish to surprise his son alone, as a result of which Adrian is left onstage alone. In *TS*, Vincentio accepts Petruccio's proposal to proceed jointly to go and 'see [his] honest son' (4.5.70), after which all the characters exit (4.5.77 SD), the last being Hortensio, who, in a short concluding soliloquy, decides to go to his widow and tame her if need be (4.5.78–80).

89–90 **Here ... lodgings.** Whereas *TS*'s Vincentio does not meet his fake alter ego until the next scene after travelling onward with Petruccio, *KK*'s scene directly continues to Adrian's encounter with Blasius, so that the scene's location, at least from this point, must be outside Hilarius' lodgings.

ADRIAN   Now I shall see whether my arrival brings joy
   or fear. Ho, ho!   100

Knocks on the door.
[*Enter* BLASIUS *above as Adrian of Liebenthal.*]

BLASIUS (*from the window*)   Who is knocking so loudly?
ADRIAN   Someone who wishes to speak to Monsieur of
   Liebenthal.
BLASIUS   He cannot receive any stranger at present; he is
   going about his business.   105
ADRIAN   Hum! And if someone came with a bag of gold
   for him? What then?
BLASIUS   He expects nothing like that, because I have
   already lined his bag.
ADRIAN   You? And who are you to shower money on   110
   him?
BLASIUS   I take it a father will not deny his son anything.
ADRIAN   You, his father?
BLASIUS   Yes, I am. But who are you?
ADRIAN [*aside*]   What devilment is this? First I am taken 115
   for a maid. Then another man pretends to be me. I
   hope to God there is nothing evil behind this.

Enter FABIAN.

99–100 SD By the time Vincentio knocks on the
   door at his son's lodgings (*TS*, 5.1.12 SD),
   Lucentio and Bianca have hurried to church
   to get married (5.1.1–5) and Vincentio has
   re-entered in the company of Petruccio,
   Katherina and Grumio (5.1.6 SD).
101–17 *KK* remains close to *TS* (5.1.15–36) but

omits Petruccio's interventions (5.1.23–7,
   33–4), Hardman having previously left the
   stage. The Merchant's threat to '[l]ay hands
   on' Vincentio (*TS*, 5.1.35) is replaced by
   Adrian's puzzled aside (115–17).
101 SD Similarly, the Merchant in *TS* '*looks
   out of the window*' (5.1.14.1).

[FABIAN]   What, do I see ghosts?

ADRIAN   You monkey, where do you come from?

FABIAN   Monkey? What Anabaptist are you?   120

ADRIAN   Listen. What's happening in your master's house? Rascals are dwelling in there.

FABIAN   What, rascals? That word will cost you dear. My master's father does not belong to such a guild.

ADRIAN   But who is this honest father? Do you not   125
recognize me?

FABIAN   I have never even dreamt of you. I swear I've never seen you in my life.

ADRIAN   A curse on you, do you still know my hands at least, you mad bird?   130

He beats him.

FABIAN   Help, ho, help! The man is mad!

118–31 *KK* roughly corresponds to the equivalent passage in *TS* (5.1.41–53), climaxing in Adrian/Vincentio beating Fabian/Biondello (130 SD / 5.1.51 SD). *KK* retains the gist of the misunderstanding in *TS* while verbally departing from it. The passage contains no trace of Biondello's report of having 'seen [Bianca and Lucentio] in the church together' (*TS*, 5.1.37–8), and of his realization that their scheme will be discovered when he recognizes his old master (5.1.38–40).

118 SP] *Köhler*; no SP *D1, D2*

118 SP In D1 and D2, the SP is implied in the preceding entrance SD.

119 **monkey** ('Meerkatze') A more common term of abuse than *TS*'s 'crackhemp' (5.1.41), although it was generally applied to women (Grimm, 'Meerkatze', 2).

120 **Anabaptist** ('Wiedertäuffer') The Anabaptists, members of a radical Protestant movement, were often persecuted in various parts of sixteenth- and seventeenth-century Europe.

388

BLASIUS (*runs out*)   What! Treating my servant thus?

ADRIAN   Who are you, slave, to bewitch this rogue in order to impersonate me?

BLASIUS   What? Addressing a gentleman like this? If 135 you're mad, you rogue, you should be bound in chains.

ADRIAN   Thus honest people are insulted abroad. You'll regret these words, and my son will regret consorting with such guests and playing such tricks.

FABIAN (*aside*)   I fear this business will have a bad end. 140

ADRIAN   Where is this honest son?

Enter FELIX [*as Hilarius*].

BLASIUS   There you have him.

FELIX (*all aghast*)   O, I wish I were far from here!

ADRIAN (*shocked*)   This one may be your son if you are a brush-maker. But these garments are not suitable 145 for him.

132–70 *KK* considerably transforms and shortens the equivalent passage in *TS* (5.1.57–131). In *TS*, the Merchant appears on the main stage in the company of Baptista and Tranio (as Lucentio) (5.1.56 SD), and the conflict over who is Lucentio's real father intensifies until an officer arrives who is charged by Tranio and Baptista to take Vincentio to jail (5.1.57–97). The entrance of the newly-married Lucentio and Bianca (5.1.97 SD) results in the flight of Biondello, Tranio and the Merchant '*as fast as may be*' (5.1.101.1) and clears up the misunderstanding regarding Vincentio's identity. In *KK*, the conflict between Lucentio's real and his fake father, Adrian and Blasius (131–41), is cut short when the arrival of Felix as Hilarius (141 SD) makes Adrian suspect that his son has been killed (149–50), so that he swoons (150 SD1). Fabian,

Felix and Blasius exit (150 SD2), like their equivalent characters in *TS*, but the arrival of Hilarius and Sabina is postponed until the next scene. Instead, Theobald and Hardman arrive (150 SD3) and help Adrian recover (151–70).

132 SD '*Läufft heraus*' in the German text, which suggests that he comes to the main stage in a horizontal, not in a vertical, movement. Blasius has been speaking '*from the window*' ('*Aus dem Fenster*') since 4.4.101 SD. Shakespeare's editors usually assume that the Merchant, when he '*looks out of the window*' (*TS*, 5.1.14.1), finds himself above, and that he later re-enters '*below*' (*TS*, 5.1.56.1). What exact movement is involved when Blasius '*runs out*' remains unclear, but it should not be taken for granted that a space above from which he descends is involved.

389

BLASIUS   What, a brush-maker? Neither the elder nor the
    younger Liebenthal will tolerate this!

ADRIAN   O Justice, unsheathe your sword! These knaves
    must have strangled my poor son and now –   150

> *He falls in a swoon.*
> *Exeunt Blasius, Felix and Fabian.*

> *Enter* THEOBALD *and* HARDMAN.

HARDMAN   Father, what's this? What has happened to
    this honourable old man? Why do these rogues run
    for their lives?

THEOBALD   These things are killing me!

> *They shake [Adrian].*

My bosom friend! My other self! And do you give me   155
grief, though I come to rejoice with you? O, it is true,
he's dead and gone. O, how this fair day is darkened!
How joy turns to sorrow!

> *They rub him with balm. He recovers a little.*

HARDMAN   Father, there is no need to grieve. Life is still
    in him.   160

ADRIAN   O, my son! My only comfort!

> *He sinks down again.*

THEOBALD   O, my brother! My dear close friend! How
    painful to lose you!

HARDMAN   Father, do not mourn for those who are still
    alive as if they were dead. – [*to Adrian*] I will call the   165

---

155 **My bosom ... self!** Whereas Baptista in
TS is taken in by the Merchant (4.4.19–
71) and considers Vincentio a madman
whom he wants taken to jail (5.1.57–97),

Theobald happens to be a good friend of
Adrian's, as we found out earlier in the
scene (see 77–82).

servants so that you can be carried inside where you
will be better looked after. – Ho! Servants, boys,
come out here!

Enter Servants.

THEOBALD   Take up this honourable old man, and carry
    him gently inside.   170
                Exit with [Adrian and the servants].
HARDMAN   This is a mad thing. What could be behind
    this? I will see what is the matter at my brother-in-
    law's lodgings.   *Exit.*

       [HARDMAN] *re-enters shortly after.*

The nest is completely empty, and the birds flown.
Something is the matter.   175

     Enter CATHARINA *and* SYBILLA.

Now the hen follows the rooster. This is a fine thing.
Where are you going, my darling, where?
CATHARINA   Where but to you.
HARDMAN   Then come and kiss me heartily.
CATHARINA   What, in front of all these people?   180
HARDMAN   Are you ashamed of me? I don't deserve that.
    – Sybilla, call my servant.

171–5 Whereas the newly-married Lucentio and Bianca have appeared onstage by the equivalent point in *TS* (5.1.97), Hilarius and Sabina have not been onstage since 4.1 and will not reappear, newly married, until the next scene. The present passage reminds us of their prolonged absence and creates a certain suspense.

176–95 *KK* adapts the equivalent passage in *TS* (5.1.132–41). Notably, *KK* expands Petruccio's couplet which ends the scene – 'Is not this well? Come, my sweet Kate. / Better once than never, for never too late' (5.1.140–1) – into a fuller passage about Hardman and Catharina's reformation and newly-found peace.

180 **all … people** Only Sybilla is onstage with Catharina and Hardman, so Catharina may be gesturing to the audience.

CATHARINA   How strange. I am not ashamed of you,
except in front of these people. But let shame be put
away.   185

She kisses him.

HARDMAN   Do you see now, my love, that this is much
better than when we are at odds? So let us put away
all tricks and stubbornness, and live in peace and
pleasure after wearing down our horns. I will chase
away the mad Hardman, and you must chase away the 190
bad Catharina. Thus we shall be an honourable couple
renowned in all the world.
CATHARINA   I am content with you if you are content
with me.
HARDMAN   Amen.   *Exeunt [Hardman and Catharina].* 195
SYBILLA   Well, I take it she is content with him now. She
has had better nights than the first. I've heard the
instrumentum pacis is a pretty thing. But I do wish to
be bound to my man as well, even though this obstacle
doesn't hinder us. It doesn't hinder me much for I live 200
more safely than when I lacked a man to cover me,
but we must be honourably conjoined. Our guests
shall feast at young Sabina's wedding banquet, and
my dear fiancé will not lust after the bride because I
shall already have said yes to him.   *Exit.* 205

196–205 Sybilla's humorous soliloquy on
marital and pre-marital sex has no equivalent in *TS*.

198 *instrumentum pacis* Latin, the instrument
of peace, i.e., the male member.

5.[1]   *Enter* ADRIAN *and* THEOBALD, *sad.*

THEOBALD   I am so shocked and truly sorry, I do not
    know what to say.

ADRIAN   O, I am sad indeed, that at my age, expecting
    extreme gladness, I must exchange it now for deadly
    sorrow.   5

THEOBALD   I do not know what hope still sustains me.

ADRIAN   O miserable hope.

THEOBALD   Let hope not leave us before we capture the
    deceitful birds. They shall not slip through our fingers
    with unplucked feathers. O, how timely that this fraud   10
    was discovered before my daughter was given to a
    brush-maker's son, an eternal insult to nobility.

ADRIAN   My bosom friend, at least you can console
    yourself. I cannot do the same since I have lost all;
    you nothing.   15

THEOBALD   I lose as much as you do in losing a dear son.

ADRIAN   O, pity, pity, pity.

Enter HILARIUS *and* SABINA, *both well dressed, and
accompanied by* HARDMAN *and* CATHARINA.

5.1 No location is specified, but the scene is presumably in front of Sir Theobald's house, and corresponds to *TS*, 5.1.102–31. It falls into three short parts: in part one, Theobald and Adrian comfort each other for the supposed death of Hilarius (1–17); part two includes the revelation of Hilarius' disguise scheme and his marriage to Sabina (18–56); and in part three, Catharina and Hardman make a pact of peaceful communication (57–70). *KK* adapts some of part two from *TS* (5.1.102–31) but adds parts one and three, and inserts a dialogue into part two on the happy union between the two families (37–56) in a general move-

ment towards reconciliation and acceptance that is absent from *TS*.

1–17 Before returning to *TS* for the resolution of the plot, *KK* adds a dialogue between Theobald and the revived Adrian about the supposed murder of Hilarius (see 4.4.149–50), whom they had hoped to see as Bianca's husband (see line 16).

12 **brush-maker's son** i.e. Felix (see 4.4.141–8).

17 SD The entrance of the two sisters and their spouses, with the newly-weds 'well dressed', creates an image of balance and harmony, a 'pageant' (18) which strikes the onlookers with wonder.

5.[1]] *this edn*; Die fünffte Handlung. *D1, D2, Köhler*

393

THEOBALD   What is this pageant?

ADRIAN   What! What do I see? The ghost of my son?

HILARIUS [*kneeling*]   Not the ghost, but the true living   20
son who hopes to receive forgiveness for his
mistake.

SABINA   Having been in all else an obedient daughter, I
also beg for this.

ADRIAN   Stand, my son. I know of no fault.   25

[*Hilarius rises.*]

THEOBALD [*to Sabina*]   How could my daughter have
angered me?

SABINA   I know of no reason, but that I turned this
honourable gentleman into a tutor. But he has now
reverted to his former standing.   30

THEOBALD   Is this not the man we thought was Johannes?

HILARIUS   I am all you wish to make me, father.

SABINA   Love has provided him with an object, my
father with a worthy son, and my lord Adrian with an
obedient daughter, as I shall call myself with my   35
father's permission.

18–56 *KK* transposes the revelation of the
disguise scheme from its original context
in *TS* (where it occurs as the conflict over
the fake and the real father of Lucentio
comes to a head; 5.1.102–31) to a separate, subsequent scene. This has allowed
the two fathers to meet and discuss the
seemingly shattered union between their
children. The recovery of seemingly lost
children, typical of the romance genre,
results in paternal appeasement and harmony, whereas *TS*'s fathers storm offstage 'to be revenged for this villainy'
and 'sound the depth of this knavery'
(5.1.126–7), and Gremio leaves in frustration (5.1.130–1).

18–25 In the equivalent passage in *TS*,
Lucentio and Bianca simply ask their
respective fathers for '[p]ardon' (5.1.102,
104).

20 SD Whereas the Folio spells out the fact
that Lucentio kneels, the same action is
implied here by Adrian's 'Stand, my son'
(25).

28–30 In *TS*, Lucentio, not Bianca, answers
Baptista's question (5.1.106–8) and dis-
pels the confusion over the disguises.

28–9 **this . . . gentleman** i.e. Hilarius.

29 **tutor** (Pedanten) See 1.2.20n.

31 *KK* preserves a version of Baptista's
question, 'is not this my Cambio?' (*TS*,
5.1.112), but omits Lucentio's explanations about his disguise scheme with
Tranio (5.1.114–20).

ADRIAN   I love most dearly my lovely daughter who
gives me my son again, and my son who brings me
such a daughter.

THEOBALD   And I must approve of my daughter's   40
otherwise culpable behaviour for the sake of such a
dear son, and am glad about these events. But why
was the need for such disguises?

HILARIUS   Father, you will hear this with amusement. I
must now also beg forgiveness for all those who   45
have acted in this, for my sake, as others than
themselves.

ADRIAN   They should at least be frightened, especially
that fool who wanted to make me mad.

HARDMAN   This day is a day of joy. We should mingle   50
nothing upsetting or grievous with it.

ADRIAN   Then they should undergo an amusing kind of
punishment, and all for their own good.

THEOBALD   I add my voice to this, because my house
ought to be a place of pleasure and gladness. So bring   55
them all in, please.

> *Exeunt* [*all but Catharina and Hardman*].

HARDMAN   Come here, my lovely little Trina. We two
fare best in the end, because we have proceeded in the
best way. The beginning was rough and hard, but it
has improved in the very fairest manner. Let us   60
continue in this vein.

CATHARINA   And let us not think about the past, and
inflict punishments because of it, or do the same when
we disagree.

37–56 In *TS*, both fathers continue to be shocked at the disobedience of their children and servants (5.1.121–9). *KK* turns their barely suppressed violence into forgiveness and joy.

57–70 *KK* adds a dialogue between Hardman and Catharina which enlarges the scene's themes of peace, forgiveness and cooperation.

57   **little Trina** ('Trinchen') the diminutive of the shortened form of Catharina's name Hardman used at 2.1.286–97. See 2.1.286n.

HARDMAN   If I do so, I won't sleep with you. If you do   65
   so, you shall lie alone.
CATHARINA   I am content. But I will take heed of what
   you say, since I am no longer used to sleeping alone.
HARDMAN   Me neither. This is how it is when both know
   what they have in each other.   *Exeunt.*   70

[5.2]   *Enter* ADRIAN, THEOBALD, SEBASTIAN, ALFONS,
          EULALIA, HARDMAN, CATHARINA, HILARIUS
                and SABINA. *They sit.*

                    Enter VEIT.

THEOBALD   Gentlemen, if it is your pleasure, let us view
   the criminals and give them their sentence.
ADRIAN   It will please everybody.
THEOBALD   You, Veit, order them to appear.
VEIT   I leave to obey my master's order.   5

                Exits and re-enters.

Here they come.

            Enter BLASIUS, FELIX, FABIAN *and*
            WORMFIRE, *who acts as bailiff.*

THEOBALD   [*to Blasius, Felix and Fabian*]   You three,
   your crime is so great that it must not go unpunished.

5.2   No location is specified, but the scene is
   presumably set in Sir Theobald's house,
   and adapts *TS*, 5.2. The scene falls into
   five parts: the mock trial (1–193), the
   confrontation between Catharina and the
   widow (194–216), Felix's hunting song
   (217–66), the wager about which wife is
   most obedient (267–344), and a final
   sequence with the four servants,
   including Fabian's song (345–93). The
   first, third and fifth parts have no equivalent in *TS*. The second and fourth parts

are fairly close adaptations of *TS* (5.2.1–
49, 64–141), although *KK* strikingly
replaces Katherina's long and eloquent
speech on wifely obedience (5.2.142–
85) with a brief statement (340–1).

0   SD EULALIA The first appearance of the
   'widow' mentioned earlier by Alfons
   (see 4.1.51 and note). See also the List of
   Roles.

1–193 The mock trial and the betrothal of
   Wormfire and Sybilla have no equivalent
   in *TS*.

As justice requires, hear this judgment, and bear your
punishment.   10

WORMFIRE   Be merry, there are still things to be done!

THEOBALD   Sir Sebastian, read the judgment, loud and
clear.

WORMFIRE   But without glasses.

[SEBASTIAN]   The three accused are present, namely   15
Master Blasius Nosewhite and Felix Muchwind, who,
having credited themselves, contrary to all laws, with
the honour and character of nobility, the last-named
meeting his master face to face, have severely
transgressed against holy justice and their superiors   20
and lords. They will therefore be stripped of their
honours as punishment and as an example to others.
Master Blasius Nosewhite and Felix are condemned
to sweat out the nobility they wrongfully assumed in
a hot bath house for three days. Fabian will wait upon   25
them and serve them food, but no drink.

[FELIX]   I'd rather die! O, O! No drink! Brother Wormfire,
beg for me!

WORMFIRE   It is not my current duty. – But, O, gentlemen,
the poor devil cannot bear it. Condemn him rather to   30
sit in a wine tub, and make me the gaoler.

BLASIUS   I hope, setting aside all strict justice, that the
power of mercy will do some good. I will therefore

---

14 **glasses** ('Brill') perhaps an implied SD
(Sebastian may look for his glasses).

15 SP D1 and D2 mistakenly assign the
speech to Sabina; Köhler assigns it to
Sebastian. See also 1.3.404 SP and note.

25 **hot ... house** ('Badstube') a public bath
with hot steam, a sauna.

27 SP D1, D2 and Köhler assign the speech

to Fabian, but since he does not suffer
from the judgement, it makes more sense
to attribute it to Felix. See also 1.3.404
SP and note.

27 **I'd ... die!** ('Lieber Tod!') The German
is ambiguous and, literally translated,
could mean either 'dear death!' or 'rather
death!'.

5.2.15 SP] *Köhler*; Sabina *D1, D2*   27 SP] *this edn*; Fabian *D1, D2, Köhler*

ask the old gentleman whom I have insulted to
intercede for me. 35

FELIX   My master, for whose service I did it all, will
speak for me.

FABIAN   My comrade has already presented my dearest
desire.

THEOBALD   Today shall be a day of joy, so let the 40
punishment to the accused not be grievous; instead
turn mercy into merriment.

[SEBASTIAN]   Gracious Mercy has seen that strict justice
has committed some *errorem calculi* in the conferring
of this punishment and has not applied its legal rule 45
well. Taking this into consideration, she has corrected
correction, and turned its rough side inwards and its
soft side outwards. Here follows her judgment to the
effect that rather than three days in a hot bath house,
Master Blasius shall join Ceres and Bacchus, and 50
make friends with them for eight days and longer in
Sir Theobald's lodgings in tolerable temperatures. To
repair and augment his little honour, he shall act as
quasi-marshal at Sir Hilarius' wedding, grace the
office with his usual dexterity, and introduce Sir 55
Gelasium in his pleasant manner. Felix will hear an
acceptably merciful judgment from his own master,

43–68 Imitating legal language, the speech is
full of Latinate terms and intricate grammatical turns that make it at times hard to
understand.

43   SP D1 and D2 mistakenly assign the
speech to Sabina. Sebastian continues to
'read the judgment' (12). See also
1.3.404 SP and note.

44   *errorem calculi* Latin, error in calculation.

50   **Ceres and Bacchus** See note at 4.2.70–1.

54   **quasi-marshal** ('quasi Marschalck')
The German term 'Marschalck', like its
English equivalent, can refer to the
person responsible for the arrangement
at ceremonies.

55–6   **Sir Gelasium** It is unclear to whom this
name refers. Church history knows of
two popes called 'Gelasius', one from
the late fifth and one from the early
twelfth century.

43   SP] *Köhler*; Sabina *D1, D2*

and will behave like a modest guest. Fabian, on the
other hand, will be handed over to Wormfire for his
excesses, who will put him into the pillory, and run   60
wine through him until he falls to the ground
powerless, having done his duty to justice. When he
has recovered his modest standing, he shall be made
an inspector over the law of the jug. He shall diligently
pour the cups overfull. They will be drunk to the   65
bottom, and he shall not forget himself in his duty. He
may remain in further expectation of what will be
done to him.

BLASIUS   Thanks be to holy justice for this mercy.

FELIX   I would never have expected anything else from   70
my lordship.

FABIAN [*to Wormfire*]   Brother, do your office.

WORMFIRE   It shall not lack through any fault of mine.
But holy law has not yet closed justice's case, and
so I have to *praemissis praemittendis, et vel quasi*   75
prettily *omnibus solennibus requisitis introducendibus
introductis.* And I must confer another more or
less dirty thing to the *Sacro-Sanctae Justitiae* in

60   **put ... pillory** literally 'put him into the
Bacheracher neck-iron' ('Er jhn erstlich
an das Bacheracher Hals-Eisen stelle').
The 'neck-iron' was an iron chain that
attached the neck of criminals to the pillory for public shaming (Grimm 1,
'Halseisen'). 'Bacheracher' was a wine
(see 3.2.250n). Sebastian says that Fabian
will be punished by being made drunk.

61   **wine** The German literally reads 'a
Roman from Heilbronn' ('Heylbronner
Römern'), a kind of wine (Grimm,
'Römer', 2), here from the city
Heilbronn, a Roman settlement in the
south-west of Germany.

64   **law ... jug** ('Kannen-Recht') literally,
jug-law. The word may pun on 'jus
canonicum', canon law.

73–87 Wormfire struggles to be clear about

Sybilla's pre-marital pregnancy and hides
his embarrassment in confusing syntax, diction and Latin, with the result that Hardman,
like the audience, fails at first to understand.

75   ***praemissis ... quasi.*** Latin, the things
that are requiring to be sent out in
advance having been sent out in advance,
or the like. Here and in what follows,
Wormfire's pseudo-learned language is
meant to impress but often fails to make
good sense and is not properly integrated
into the text in English.

76–7 ***omnibus ... introductis*** Latin, all
solemn requirements having been introduced that are requiring to be introduced.

77–8 **another ... thing** an oblique reference
to Sybilla's pre-marital pregnancy.

78   ***Sacro-Sanctae Justitiae*** Latin, sacro-
sanct Justice.

order to wash the chambermaid. The *dominationibus
permission* to effect the like I have lately acquired.   80

HARDMAN   What is it you say, fool?

WORMFIRE   Nothing much understandable. But now to
the wisest and foolishest in the world: it concerns a
lawful thing. Another interested lady is required, so I
request permission once again to introduce such a   85
one, and to propose my pretty thing, to acquire orally
a benevolent rescript.

THEOBALD   You have pleasant permission. All must be
entertained today.   *Exit Wormfire.*
Something fine may be afoot.   90

Enter WORMFIRE *with* SYBILLA.

WORMFIRE   Here comes one *membrum* of my plaint, I
am the other. *Salvis salvandis Titulisque titillandis.*
Honourable gentlemen, through seduction of that
cursed rogue, the old Adam, of my own flesh and of
the lusty world, my maid here, I mean my lady   95
comrade, for one must not lie at a trial, and my flesh

79 **wash ... chambermaid** i.e. to regularize
Sybilla's situation through marriage?

79–80 **dominationibus permission** garbled
Latin (*'permissio'* would be Latin but
'permission' is not), the permission of
the powers, of those who hold power.

80 **to ... like** ('solches zu effectuiren')
Wormfire rephrases his plan to regularize
Sybilla's situation in stilted language.

83 **wisest ... world** presumably a reference
to Wormfire himself ('the wisest') and to
Sybilla (the 'foolishest').

84 **lawful thing** marriage (see Wormfire's
subsequent speech).

86 **pretty thing** presumably a reference to
Sybilla.

86–7 **to ... rescript** presumably an oblique
reference to his and Sybilla's lawful
marriage by a priest (see Wormfire's

subsequent speech).

88 **pleasant permission** ('Vergnügünsti-
gung') Theobald puns on 'permission'
('Vergünstigung') and 'amusement'
('Vergnügen') by conflating the two
words.

91 *membrum* Latin, part, limb.

92 *Salvis ... titillandis* Latin, those things
being safe that are required to be safe and
titles requiring to be tickled. The exact
meaning of Wormfire's Latin is again
obscure.

93–5 **through ... world** Wormfire seems to
explain Sybilla's pre-marital pregnancy
as a result of original sin, of his own lust
and, more generally, of lust in the world.

95–6 **my maid ... trial** Wormfire means that
it would be a lie to claim that Sybilla is
still a 'maid' (i.e. virgin).

and blood have come together, which has produced a
conjunction that will separate itself in three quarters of
a year from my modest companion. In order that this
conjunction may not part from honour, and because it   100
originated in the unchaste marriage bed, we both pray
that priestly glue may agglutinate and conjugate us
so that thereafter no error may separate us. We pray,
expecting what is right from the helpful *officio Judicis*,
being the viceroy of holy *Astraea* herself.   105

THEOBALD   This is a matter of the highest importance
which concerns the women. We will therefore hear
their voices through what the youngest has to say, and
draw our conclusions from that.

SABINA   I think they ought to be put into the hole for a   110
time, and they can be together afterwards.

WORMFIRE *(aside)*   The former happened a long while
ago, and I will continue it.

HILARIUS   I think they ought not be permitted to be
bedfellows after this wedding.   115

WORMFIRE   O, please! No, I pray you!

SYBILLA   And I pray you even more. [*to Sabina*] O, dear
lady, mercy, mercy!

WORMFIRE   O, merciful lord, mercy!

CATHARINA   What can you do with whores and knaves?   120
Have them married.

SYBILLA   Great thanks for this judgment.

---

101 **unchaste . . . bed** before wedlock.

104 *officio Judicis* Latin, the office of the
judge.

105 *Astraea* A goddess symbolizing innocence and just judgement.

110–39 This passage was omitted in Köhler's
edition; see 2.2.19–23n.

110–13 Sabina uses 'hole' to refer to the
prison (Grimm, 'Loch', 4), while
Wormfire thinks of the physical orifice in
Sybilla's body.

115 **wedding** (copulation) See 3.2.189n.

110–39] *not in Köhler*

HARDMAN   I am of my Cathy's opinion concerning the coupling. But after that, give the honest groom a fine strong purgation, good food and drink aplenty. The   125 chaste bride must keep him in her lap the whole night without getting up once.

WORMFIRE   Sir, sir, the purgation and the food are good.

EULALIA   I will be merciful to them and deliver them to the priest.   130

ALFONS   I will not gainsay my dearest, and Sir Wormfire is my good friend.

SEBASTIAN   I think it would be advisable to cater for the groom with bread and water after the coupling.

WORMFIRE *(aside)*   He's an old thief.   135

[SEBASTIAN]   And to rub the bride's ticklish flesh with nettles.

SYBILLA *(aside)*   And to clean your mouth with them afterwards, you old shitter.

[THEOBALD]   After hearing everyone's voices, Sir Adrian   140 and I will pronounce the sentence.

WORMFIRE   O merciful, wise lord, if you have reason, pronounce the best.

SYBILLA   I also humbly beg for this.

THEOBALD   It will be what is just.   145

---

123 **Cathy's** ('Käthen') The only occurrence of this form of Catharina's name in the play (cf. 206). Elsewhere, Hardman calls her 'Trina' ('Trine'; see 2.1.286n) or 'little Trina' ('Trinchen', 5.1.57n), although he most commonly uses her full name. See also the List of Roles.

136 SP D1 and D2 assign this speech to Sabina, but Sebastian seems to continue his judgement begun at 133–4, and Sybilla is unlikely to call her former mis-

tress an 'old shitter' (139). See also 1.3.404 SP and note.

140 SP As at 136, the speech is mistakenly assigned to Sabina in D1 and D2. Wormfire's response to the 'wise lord' (142) makes better sense if addressed to Theobald, who pronounces the sentence from line 161. Köhler assigns the speech to Sabina but correctly mentions in the notes (256) that the words are no doubt spoken by Theobald.

136 SP] *this edn*; Sabina *D1, D2*   140 SP] *this edn*; Sabina *D1, D2, Köhler*

WORMFIRE   Sybilla, did you not notice whether the good tease us more than the bad?

SYBILLA   Who can tell me that? As long as there are no nettles. O, how I would like to shit into the beard of this old fantastico.   150

WORMFIRE   My darling, think of drinking water for three days. If you wish, keep remembering his words, for the purgation could also mean good food for us.

SYBILLA   Let us ask the old fantastico to be our guest.

BLASIUS   *Silentium, silentium.*   155

WORMFIRE   That's school-boy Latin. Listen diligently, Sybilla, in case something good is coming.

THEOBALD   Because we are more mindful of joy than sadness these days –

WORMFIRE   That's a good start.   160

THEOBALD   Ludolf Wormfire and Sybilla Fleafur will be coupled with each other, and handed over to the priest. Furthermore, these two will not bring together their maidenheads in the wedding bed, but will be burdened with having to act as honourable spouses   165 and shall lead the dance. For this, Wormfire will borrow the short frock and the ruff. When his helper is lightened of her load, this whole company shall serve as godparents.

146–54 This passage was omitted in Köhler's edition; see 2.2.19–23n. Wormfire and Sybilla are likely to talk aside, unheard by the other characters.

149 **shit** Sybilla uses the word 'hofieren', which originally connoted 'to woo' but had evolved into 'to shit' (Grimm, 'hofieren', 9).

150, 154 **fantastico** ('Fantasten') See 1.1.97n.

152 **keep ... words** Wormfire literally says 'don't forget his maw' ('Drum vergiß jhm / meinetwegen / deß Mauls nicht').

155 *Silentium* Latin, silence.

160 Wormfire literally says 'that sounds well *pro primus*' (i.e., first of all), in German 'Das lautet *pro primus* wohl'.

167 **ruff** Theobald says that Wormfire can borrow the 'paper lapel' ('papiernen Kragen'), referring to the expensive fashion accessory of the higher classes.

167–8 **When ... load** when Sybilla will have given birth.

146–54] *not in Köhler*

WORMFIRE   Not couple in bed? Is this a good decree?   170

SYBILLA   I think it is. Go, and thank them.

WORMFIRE   Dear Lord Justices and assistants of this
tribunal, which is hard as a bone and painful, you are
by diamond chains insurmountably linked to dear
Justice. *Quantas, quam solidas, solidiores, solidissimas,*   175
maximas, debitissimas agam gratiarum gratiosè
gratias gratus, nescio. Hum! Latin suddenly sticks in
my throat at the moment when too much of it wants to
get out. I'll say the rest in German. My mistress, *à la*
française, and I are extremely content with the   180
sentence, particularly concerning point one. There is
no need for point two, for we have already done it. In
order to fulfil point three, we would like to assume the
title *Juris de Edendo*, and add that of *de Bibendo*, both
of which we will illustrate most prettily. We will   185
dutifully exercise point four with the agility of our
joints and it will be decorated with fitting ornaments.
For the last and fifth point, you recommend to us what
the wisdom of our brain has already concluded,
because *est, interest regit dativum:* we thus thank you   190

170–1 Wormfire and Sybilla are again con-
versing aside, unheard by the other characters (see 146–54).

170 **Is ... decree?** In the German text,
Wormfire says '*Secret*' (i.e. privy or
excrement; Grimm, 'Sekret', 3) before
correcting himself: 'holla *decret*' (i.e.
'no, decree'), a slip of the tongue that
allows Wormfire to indicate what he
thinks of the 'decree'.

172–5 **Dear ... Justice.** The beginning of
Wormfire's speech is excessively convoluted and unintelligible, perhaps a mock
imitation of legal language.

175–7 ***Quantas ... nescio.*** Latin, how great,
how genuine, more genuine, most gen-
uine, greatest, owed thanks I will give

being gratefully grateful, I do not know.
Wormfire's Latin is again more designed
to impress than to make sense.

179–80 *à la française* French, in the French
manner. The meaning in the present context is unclear.

181–2 **There ... it.** Wormfire is saying that
Sybilla and he have already brought
'together their maidenheads' (163–4).

183 **point three** i.e. 'act[ing] as honourable
spouses' (165).

184 ***Juris de Edendo*** Latin, the Judge of
Eating.

184 ***de Bibendo*** Latin, of Drinking.

190 ***est ... dativum*** Latin, 'est' and 'interest'
take the dative case. Wormfire's Latin
phrase seems another *non sequitur* here.

most prettily, and rest obliged and dutifully bound to
our masters in all similar cases. *Dixi.*

THEOBALD   Now all is joyful, and will be amicable.

ALFONS [*to Hardman*]   That would be a pretty word,
would it not, brother?   195

HARDMAN   I think you are afraid of your wife.

EULALIA   He whose head is dizzy thinks the whole world
is going round.

CATHARINA   What do you mean by this?

EULALIA   Your darling understands me well enough.   200

CATHARINA   And I not a bit more clearly.

EULALIA   He thinks that because he has received
something bad, my husband has done so too.

CATHARINA   That would be a simple opinion and utterly
groundless.   205

HARDMAN   To her, dear Cath!

ALFONS   To her, defend yourself, my dear!

EULALIA   I do not want to be your fool any longer. *Exit.*

CATHARINA   I must find out what's the matter with her.

Exit swiftly.

---

192 **Dixi** Latin, I have spoken.

193–216 While the previous material in this
scene has no equivalent in *TS*, the confrontation between Catharina and the
widow adapts *TS* (5.2.1–49).

193 In *TS*, it is Lucentio who announces the
happy resolution and invites the company to his house (5.2.1–11).

194–6 *KK* remains close to the equivalent
exchange between Hortensio and
Petruccio (*TS*, 5.2.15–16).

194 **word** As in the equivalent passage in *TS*
(PETRUCCIO Padua affords nothing but
what is kind. / HORTENSIO For both our
sakes I would that word were true.',
5.2.14–15), 'word' ('Wort') seems to
refer not to a single word but to the preceding utterance more generally.

197–209 *KK* adapts the confrontation

between Katherina and the Widow fairly
closely (see *TS*, 5.2.17–35), but omits
word play on 'conceive' (i.e. having
ideas as well as getting pregnant; see
5.2.23–5) that fails to work in German.

206 **Cath** ('Cathrinchen') The only occurrence of this form of Catharina's name in
the play. See 123 and note.

206–9 After Petruccio's 'To her, Kate!' and
Hortensio's 'To her, widow!' (*TS*, 5.2.34–
5), Katherina and the Widow have no
scripted reaction. 'Katherine may chase the
Widow . . . or otherwise physically intimi-
date her' (*NOS*), but there is no exit SD,
and editors since Nicholas Rowe usually
assume that they do not depart until later,
with Bianca (*TS*, 5.2.49 SD). Eulalia and
Catharina, however, leave earlier and separately, after their respective short speeches.

HARDMAN   But without help. I know she'll put her down. 210
ALFONS   That's usually my duty. [*to Sabina*] But my
    lady bride, why so quiet? You are surely tired.
HARDMAN   She is also somewhat hit. The little bird must
    not go home alone.
SABINA   If I were a bird, I would fly to a bush so that you 215
    could not hit me.   *Exit.*
FELIX   In order to show my penitence, I have composed
    a little wedding wish in prison. Please observe my
    good intentions, not the bad words.
HILARIUS   I thank you most amicably, and know that 220
    your heart and words are good. Rest assured of my
    eternal favour towards you. But now, read us your
    invention.
[FELIX]   The tale that I must tell you is a story of the
    chase
    In which three gallant huntsmen set out upon the
    trace   225

---

210 **put ... down** ('leget sie nieder') The ambiguity of the phrase – carried over from Petruccio's 'my Kate does put her down' (*TS*, 5.2.36) – as meaning either 'winning an argument' or 'dominating during sex' equally works in German. Alfons activates the second meaning in his response.

213–16 The passage adapts the exchange between Petruccio and Bianca at *TS*, 5.2.45–8.

217–66 The passage with Felix's song replaces suggestive banter between Petruccio, Hortensio, Lucentio and Tranio (*TS*, 5.2.50–63).

224–55 The German song consists of fairly rough octameter couplets, with a caesura dividing each octameter into two tetrameter half-lines. Our English translation approximates this form by using fourteeners (with occasional variation in the syllable count), with the aim of providing the impression of a fairly rudimentary

verse technique. The fourteeners usually fall into two half-lines, the first with four stresses or feet and the second with three. End-rhymes in the German original are usually full, but are translated here by a mixture of full and half-rhyme.

224–45 The main part of Felix's song uses a transparent hunting conceit to summarize the plot: a 'hind' (226; Sabina) was hunted by 'three ... huntsmen' (225), 'one [who] was old' (227; Sebastian) and two 'youths' (228; Hilarius and Alfons), of whom one (Hilarius), who had 'a helper' (232; Felix), won 'the prize' (238). The 'second' (239; Alfons) also 'found a prey', though less 'lovely' (242; Eulalia, the widow), yet still better than 'the wild beast' (243; Catharina) found by 'the stern huntsman' (243; Hardman).

224 SP D1 and D2 have no SP prior to the song, but the context makes clear that it is delivered by Felix.

224 SP] *Köhler*; no SP *D1, D2*

Of a fair hind untamed and free, a prey they prized
    the most,
But one was old already, and his hunting skills were
    lost.
The other two, however, were lusty youths and
    strong,
And when they shot an arrow it never went far
    wrong.
Yet one surpassed the other in hunting of this kind,   230
Choosing to stalk the deer himself and leave the dog
    behind.
He also left a helper, whom he trusted with the
    work
To stop all rival huntsmen from intruding in the
    park,
If thus he should desire; and his wishes were
    obeyed
By that same second huntsman who was ready with
    his aid.   235
As for the old companion with his white and feeble
    staff,
The faithful helper soon arranged for him to be
    sent off.
It was the first best huntsman who won the prize he
    sought;
His efforts were rewarded. The second too had thought
To catch the deer but failed because his strategy was
    wrong,   240
For he was too impatient and could not wait so long.
Yet he, too, found a prey, though not so lovely as
    the hind
Nor yet as bad as the wild beast that the stern
    huntsman found
Deep in the bush and firmly bound. Now they all
    have their part;

Except for one who was too fast and another slow to
    start.   245

But still the fast one made a catch and he is well
    content,

Because through him his master gained the prize for
    which he spent

So many drops of burning sweat that streaked his
    frozen skin.

Thus he who sends down wagon loads of all good
    things throws in

A goodly dose of what's called luck, and the man
    that has that name   250

Hopes that he'll be remembered then and that he will
    remain

Fixed in his master's favour and never be betrayed.

By him to whom his loyal vows of endless faith
    were made;

And if such trust is so rewarded and his hopes
    fulfilled,

Then will he always follow him and be his servant
    still.   255

But now, you other hunters:

Follow your hounds while they are fresh and while
    the woods are green

Range through the flowering forest, and let it not
    be seen

That when you shoot an arrow your strong stiff bow
    goes soft:

To get your fill of pleasure prepare another shaft.   260

---

245 **one ... start** Felix and Fabian.

246–55 This part of Felix's song is a plea to Hilarius for continued patronage and employment.

249–50 **luck ... name** The name 'Felix', a common cognomen since Roman times, means 'happy' or 'fortunate'.

256–60 Felix's song concludes with advice to other 'hunters' (256; i.e. men) for successful wooing, with suggestive phallic puns on 'arrow', 'stiff', 'soft' and 'shaft' (259–60). The passage may well be an address to the audience.

HILARIUS   The invention is good.

HARDMAN   Only that it's a little too like doggerel.

[SEBASTIAN]   Everyone has their fortune expressed in it,
    and I most of all, because I have not caught anything.
    But I prefer this to getting something I'd be frightened   265
    of.

THEOBALD [*to Hardman*]   Son, that's a reference to you,
    since I believe you have obtained the worst thing.

HARDMAN   I do not believe so, and let us prove it. Let
    every man send for his wife, and we shall see which   270
    comes most obediently.

HILARIUS   Here, I bet twenty ducats that I win.

ALFONS   I bet as many.

HARDMAN   What, twenty, I bet as many on my whippet.
    A hundred is not enough.   275

HILARIUS   Content, here is my hand. – Fabian, go and
    tell my love to come to me.

FABIAN   I go, my lord.   *Exit.*

THEOBALD   I'll bet half with you, good son, she'll come
    at once.   280

HILARIUS   I do not seek halves. A whole, or none.

[*Enter* FABIAN.]

---

262 **doggerel** ('hündisch') The German word
was generally used in reference to the
abject qualities of dogs (Grimm, 2), not,
like the English 'doggerel', specifically
in the context of verse.

263 SP D1 and D2 assign the speech to
Sabina, but it makes better sense when
given to Sebastian, who has 'not caught
anything' (264), i.e., has no wife, unlike
Hardman, Hilarius and Alfons. See also
1.3.404 SP and note.

267–308 With few exceptions, the wager

passage follows *TS* (5.2.64–112) speech
by speech and often word for word: *KK*
slightly rearranges and condenses the
negotiations of the terms of the wager
(269–76; *TS*, 5.2.67–76), but has no
equivalent for Baptista's interjection
when Katherina enters ('Now, by my
halidom, here comes Katherina',
5.2.105), and adds Wormfire's words at
297 and Catharina's confident assertion
that she will 'know how to tame them'
(307), i.e. Sabina and Eulalia.

263 SP] *Köhler*; Sabina *D1, D2*

FABIAN   My lord, she sends word she is busy and cannot come.

HARDMAN   What, she is busy and cannot come? Is this an answer?   285

SEBASTIAN   Yes, and a kind one. How will yours be?

HARDMAN   Sir Sebastian always tries to fool us. Wait for the end.

ALFONS   Go, and tell my wife I entreat her to come.

[Exit Fabian.]

HARDMAN   I entreat her to come, O, O!   290

ALFONS   Yours will surely not come upon any entreaty.

[Enter FABIAN.]

Well, where is she?

FABIAN   She says you must be jesting and bids you come to her.

HARDMAN   Graver than grave! You, Wormfire, go tell my   295 wife to come to me at once.

WORMFIRE   Incontinently, swift as the wind.

[Exit Wormfire.]

ALFONS   I know her answer. She'll not come.

HARDMAN   Then no one wins the bet. But she'll come with another answer.   300

Enter CATHARINA.

CATHARINA   What is your will, my darling?

HARDMAN   Where is your sister, and the wife of brother Alfons?

CATHARINA   They are sitting outside clattering away.

HARDMAN   Fetch them in. Should they resist, carry those   305 disobedient women here.

---

297 **Incontinently** The German text has '*Incontinent*', from Latin 'incontinenter', i.e. instantly.

304 **clattering away** ('bey der Klappermühle') literally, at the clappermill (see Grimm, 'klappern', II.2).

CATHARINA I know how to tame them.

[*Exit Catharina.*]

HILARIUS If we must talk of miracles, here is one.

THEOBALD My son, your effort must be rewarded.
Another daughter, another dowry. I add 5,000 ducats 310
to the previous one. Look, how she brings them in
like prisoners!

[*Enter* CATHARINA *with* SABINA *and* EULALIA.]

SABINA I don't know if she is mad or not.

HILARIUS I wish we were mad. Your wisdom costs me
too much. 315

ALFONS [*to Eulalia*] You could have saved me a hundred
ducats; I have bet and lost because of you.

EULALIA Why are you such a fool then to put such trust
in me?

ALFONS I admit I feared what I had nothing to worry 320
about, and by trusting one I have been cheated by
both.

[SEBASTIAN] I thank God that the goat I made gardener

309–12 Theobald's speech adapts that of
Baptista (*TS*, 5.2.117–21), who promises
'twenty thousand crowns' (5.2.119). *KK*
omits *TS*'s preceding speech, Petruccio's
rhapsody on married life with a tamed
wife (5.2.114–16), as well as his slightly
later request for Katherina to trample on
her cap, eliciting scorn in Bianca and the
Widow (5.2.127–31).

311–12 **Look ... prisoners!** In *TS*, the
equivalent announcement is made by
Petruccio: 'See where she comes, and
brings your froward wives / As prisoners
to her womanly persuasion' (5.2.125–6).

313–19 closely adapts *TS* (5.2.131–5) but
assigns part of the hostile exchange
between Lucentio and Bianca
(5.2.133–5) to Alfons and Eulalia.

320–2 Alfons' slightly cryptic sentence

seems to acknowledge that he has been
wrong about both Catharina and Eulalia,
leading to his loss of the wager.

320–34 ALFONS ... **that.** This passage seems
to have no equivalent in *TS*.

323 SP D1 and D2 mistakenly assign the
speech to Sabina. Köhler (259) rightly
observes that the SP does not fit the
speech but unconvincingly suggests that
the speaker may be Theobald. See also
1.3.404 SP and note.

323 **the ... gardener** ('der Bock / den ich
zum Gärtner gesetzet') refers to Hilarius
through whose proxy Sebastian sought
to woo Sabina. Sebastian may allude to a
proverb according to which goats make
for poor gardeners since they eat the
plants instead of caring for them
(Wander, 'Bock', 14, 67).

323 SP] *this edn*; Sabina *D1, D2, Köhler*; Theobald *Köhler (conj.)*

411

has become the master. My horns would otherwise
have been far too weak.   325

ADRIAN   It may be true that all maids are pious.

HARDMAN   Then their husbands would need to make
them bad afterwards. But it is not so.

HILARIUS   That one had as his symbol *Non cernuntur et
adsunt.*   330

THEOBALD   I am overjoyed by my new daughter.

CATHARINA   I hope I will be doubly obedient towards my
father because I sinned before.

THEOBALD   You will renew my old age through that. O,
what an excellent thing it is when children are   335
obedient.

HILARIUS   But it is very gross when wives are stubborn.

HARDMAN   My dear Catharina, give these shrewish
women a lesson.

CATHARINA   Let me put it briefly. You men, love your   340
wives. And you women, obey your husbands.

THEOBALD   You make a good conclusion, daughter. So
let us now make a good beginning to our joy.
Gentlemen, you are warmly invited inside.
Exeunt [all but Wormfire, Sybilla, Fabian and Felix.]

327–8 The implication, to which Hardman
objects, is that married women are no
longer pious.

329 **That one** It is not quite clear to whom
Hilarius refers: to himself, present but
not seen because of his disguise?

229–30 **Non ... adsunt.** Latin, they are not
seen, and yet they are present.

334–7 **O,...stubborn.** In *TS*, the equivalent
passage occurs after Katherina's long
speech, and the first statement is made by
Vincentio, not by Baptista (5.2.188–9).

338–9 This speech adapts Petruccio's request to
Katherina to give the 'headstrong women' a
lesson in wifely obedience (*TS*, 5.2.136–7).

340–1 *KK* compresses Katherina's elaborate
and multi-layered defence of female obedience in marriage (*TS*, 5.2.142–85) into

a brief and sober speech. Its content and
balanced grammatical structure are
indebted to St Paul's Letter to the
Ephesians: 'Husbands, love your wives
...' (5.25); 'Wives, submit yourselves
unto your own husbands ...' (5.22).

342–4 *KK* replaces a dialogue between the
three husbands about their respective
marital success (*TS*, 5.2.186–95) with a
more peaceful conclusion by Theobald.

344 SD Among the characters who exit are
Hardman and Catharina. According to
the early editions of *TS*, Petruccio leaves
separately (5.2.193 SD), before the other
characters (5.2.195 SD), although editors
since Rowe have usually emended the
text to give Petruccio and Katherina a
joint exit (see Ard³, 306–8).

WORMFIRE   The sequence is now ours.   345

FABIAN   Ho, brother; first you must see my learned
  invention. Felix should not think he is the only one
  who has sucked up wisdom. I can do something, too.

WORMFIRE   Well then, let us hear what little learning you
  have to offer. I wonder how the horse of *Bacchus*   350
  inspired the lustfulness of your folly.

FABIAN   You're mad, my brother Worm-
  fire, yes, mad as a storm,
  With horns on head so high
  They almost touch the sky.   355
  This was your finest sport,
  To climb into the fort-
  ress. O then you were warm
  When your vigorous third arm
  Pushed hard into the press;   360
  And though it felt the stress,
  It chose to make no stay
  Until it forced its way
  Along the secret ditch,
  The watery passage which   365

345–93 *KK* adds a concluding sequence with four of the play's servants. For the play's interest in the servants as foils and comic mirrors of their social betters, see 4.4.37–8n. The passage was omitted in Köhler's edition; see 2.2.19–23n.

345 **sequence** (sequens) a musical term, originally designating a chant that followed (Latin, *sequi*) the Alleluia in the liturgy of the Eucharist.

350–1 **I wonder ... folly.** Wormfire encourages Fabian so that, literally, 'Pegasus of Bacchus makes your Venus' folly flow' ('wie das *Bacchi Pegasus* die *Venam* deiner Würmerey in den Fluß gebracht'). Wormfire seems to suggest that the com-

position was shaped by Fabian's drinking and lust. For Wormfire's other references to Bacchus, see 4.2.70–1n and 5.2.50n.

352–79 Fabian's poem, addressed to Wormfire, deals with Sybilla's possible marital infidelity. Its fairly stumbling trimeter couplets have been translated here into lines of the same length, with the exception of the final couplet which has an extra foot.

354 **horns** ('Hörner') The traditional cuckold's horns introduce the poem's themes of marital infidelity and cuckoldry.

356–68 The barely disguised conceit is that of Wormfire's sexual penetration of Sybilla.

345–93] *not in Köhler*

413

Is where it caught the hare,
Fresh, young and sitting there,
Fool, croaking in the reed.
Your hen now croaks indeed,
So cry as cuckolds do,   370
Get down to work anew,
Run after those bold men
Who are ahead, and lend
You cuckoo's eggs. I too
Found your dove and played cuckoo   375
So merrily that after
She almost burst with laughter.
So take your turn and have your due
As I, and all kind cousins do.

WORMFIRE   I admit it is prettily elaborated, and well   380
worth pricking, I mean, printing. [*to Sybilla*] But now,
my darling, come inside, our shameful wedding day
has arrived. I hope nobody will raise verbally what
they secretly have in mind. I doubt I lack cousins.

SYBILLA   When a man seeks to be happy, he must not   385
believe this or think about it.

WORMFIRE   Well, it comes without our bidding. But who

369–77 Fabian claims to be one of the men who
have cuckolded Wormfire with Sybilla.

379 **all ... do** ('nach Schwagers Brauch')
'Schwager' could mean brother-in-law
as well as, more generally, any relative
acquired through marriage; here the
'cousins' stand for Wormfire's sexual
rivals. See also 384–7n.

380–1 **well ... printing.** Wormfire literally
says that the song is 'well worth giving
over to the dirt (*inquam* [i.e., I mean]
printing)' ('wohl werth daß es in den
Dreck (*inquam* Druck) gegeben werde').
The pun relies on phonetic similarity
between 'Dreck ('dirt') and 'Druck'

('printing'). For a similar slip of the
tongue by Wormfire, see 170.

382 **shameful ... day** ('schändlicher
Ehren-Tag') 'Ehren-Tag', literally 'day
of honour', designated the wedding day
(Grimm), resulting in an oxymoron, a
shameful (given Sybilla's pregnancy)
day of honour.

384–7 **I doubt ... bidding.** Wormfire seems
to fear being cuckolded by Sybilla who
tries but fails to reassure him. According
to D1 and D2, he does *not* doubt he lacks
cousins (i.e. sexual rivals), but the passage makes better sense without the
negation (see also 379n).

384 doubt] *this edn*; nicht zweifele *D1, D2, Köhler*

amongst the two of us will lift the shirt tonight?
SYBILLA   I think whoever comes first.
FABIAN   I would gladly be of service.   390
WORMFIRE   Yes, at the halter of a gallows' bell. But it is
altum tempus, claudite jam rivos pueri sat prata
biberunt, et plaudite.   *Exeunt.*

---

388 **lift ... shirt** ('das Hembd auffheben')
presumably a suggestive allusion to
sexual activity.
391 **gallows' bell** ('Galgen Glocke') The
exact meaning is obscure, but Wormfire
clearly rejects Fabian's bawdy offer to be
'of service' during the wedding night.
392–3 *altum ... plaudite.* Latin, it is high

time; close up the streams, boys, the
fields have drunk enough, and applause.
Wormfire quotes from Virgil's *Eclogues*
(3.111).
393 *plaudite* a conventional appeal for
applause at the end of a play or, conceiv-
ably, a statement of applause, relating to
readers what happened in performance.

APPENDIX

Doubling charts for Tito Andronico
and Kunst über alle Künste,
ein bös Weib gut zu machen

The following doubling charts rely on the assumption that the plays were performed with as few actors as possible. Like Scott McMillin, we 'never count immediately juxtaposed roles as fit for doubling' (185), and we follow William A. Ringler in assuming that 'a plural for mute "attendants", "soldiers", etc., should usually be interpreted as no more than two' (115).

SYMBOLS

-	enters after the scene begins
-	exits before the scene ends
?	presence on stage uncertain

female
male
mute

417

TITO ANDRONICO

Tito Andronico may be staged by a minimum of ten actors, who would perform the three female parts (Aetiopissa, Andronica and the Midwife), the eleven male speaking parts (Tito, Vespasianus, Victoriades, the Emperor, Morian, Saphonus, Helicates, Andronica's Husband, Tito's Messenger in Act 5, Tito's Messenger in 8.1, and the Soldier who arrests Morian in 7.1), the 'Romans' who acclaim the new Emperor in 1.1, and the three mute parts (the attendant in 5.2 and the two soldiers in 7.3).[1] The scene with the greatest number of actors on stage is the first one, and it is noticeable that Victoriades (unlike Marcus in *TA*) is absent from the scene, perhaps because the actor was needed to double as a Roman citizen. The same actor may have performed the attendant in 5.2. In 6.1 the Midwife may have been doubled by the actor playing Andronica (though not by Aetiopissa, who is onstage at the end of Act 5).[2] In the final scene the servants preparing the banquet who bring out the pies may be doubled by the actors performing Helicates and Saphonus (who were killed in 7.3), with the added irony that the pies contain some of the brothers' remains.

Abbreviations

A	Actor	Mor	Morian
Aet	Aetiopissa	Rom	Roman
And	Andronica	Sap	Saphonus
Att	Attendant	Ser	Servant
Emp	Emperor	Sol	Soldier
Hel	Helicates	Tit	Tito
Hus	Andronica's Husband	Ves	Vespasianus
Mes	Messenger	Vic	Victoriades

---

[1] Shakespeare's play requires a considerably larger cast: 'thirteen adults, three boys, [and] at least four extras' (*NOS CRE*, 1.143).

[2] As a rule, 'British troupes on the continent had no actresses before the 1650s' (Katritzky, 'English', 38).

Scene	1.1	2.1	3.1	3.2	3.3	4.1	4.2	4.3	5.1	5.2	6.1	7.1	7.2	7.3	8.1	8.2
A 1	Ves-					Ves		Ves	-Ves-			Ves				Ves
A 2	Emp-	Emp-	Emp							Emp			Emp		Emp	Emp
A 3	Tit-		Tit	Tit		Tit		Tit	Tit					-Tit		Tit
A 4	*And-*				*And-*		*And*	*-And*	*And*		*Mid*					*And*
A 5	*Aet-*	*Aet-*	*Aet*		*Aet*					*Aet*				*Aet-*	*Aet*	*Aet*
A 6	Mor	Mor			-Mor	-Mor		Mor-			-Mor	-Mor				
A 7	Hel-	Hel			-Hel-		Hel-				-Hel-			Hel		Ser
A 8	Sap-	Sap			-Sap-		Sap-				-Sap-			Sap		Ser
A 9	Rom-					Vic	-Vic	-Vic	Vic	-Att		-Sol		-Sol		Vic
A 10	Rom-				Hus				-Mes	-Mes				-Sol	-Mes-	

KUNST ÜBER ALLE KÜNSTE

Kunst über alle Künste can be performed with fifteen actors, four of them female.[1] Act 5, Scene 2 is the scene with the largest number of actors onstage at the same time. There are various doubling options. For instance, Patient Job can be doubled by Hardman; the servants in Act 3, Scene 3 by Theobald, Sebastian and Hilarius, and Matz by Felix in Act 3, Scene 3 and Act 3, Scene 4; Fritz can be doubled by Veit and the servant by Sebastian in Act 4, Scene 2; the servants in Act 4, Scene 4 can be doubled by Veit and Sebastian.

Abbreviations

A	Actor	Fri	Fritz	Se1	Servant 1
Adr	Adrian	Har	Hardman	Se2	Servant 2
Alf	Alfons	Hil	Hilarius	Se3	Servant 3
Bla	Blasius	Job	Patient Job	Syb	Sybilla
Cat	Catharina	Mat	Matz	The	Theobald
Eul	Eulalia	Sab	Sabina	Vei	Veit
Fab	Fabian	Seb	Sebastian	Wor	Wormfire
Fel	Felix	Ser	Servant		

---

[1]   Performances of *The Taming of the Shrew* probably required a cast of at least fifteen (see the Appendix on 'Casting' in Ard3 *TS*, 399–402).

Sc.	Pro	1.1	1.2	1.3	2.1	2.2	3.1	3.2	3.3	3.4	3.5	4.1	4.2	4.3	4.4	5.1	5.2
A 1	Job			Har-	-Har-			-Har-	-Har		Har		-Har-		-Har-	-Har	Har-
A 2		The-			-The-			-The-	-Se1-						-The-	The-	The-
A 3		*Cat-*			*Cat-*			*Cat-*	*-Cat*				*-Cat-*		*-Cat-*	*-Cat*	*Cat-*
A 4		Seb		-Seb-	-Seb-			-Seb-	-Se2-				-Ser-		-Se1-		Seb-
A 5		Alf		-Alf-	-Alf-		Alf					Alf-	-Alf-		-Alf-		Alf-
A 6		Vei-			-Vei-		-Vei-	-Vei					-Fri-		-Se2-		-Vei-
A 7			Fel	-Fel-	-Fel			-Fel-	-Mat-	Mat		Fel		Fel	-Fel-		-Fel
A 8			Hil-	-Hil-	-Hil-		Hil-	-Hil-	-Se3-			-Hil				-Hil-	Hil-
A 9			-Fab	-Fab	-Fab-			-Fab				-Fab		-Fab	-Fab-		-Fab
A 10				Wor	-Wor-	Wor		-Wor-	-Wor-	Wor			Wor		-Wor-		-Wor
A 11					*Sab-*		Sab-	-Sab-				-Sab-				-Sab-	*Sab-*
A 12									*-Syb-*				*Syb*		-Syb		*-Syb*
A 13														Bla	-Bla-		-Bla-
A 14															Adr-	Adr-	Adr-
A 15																	*Eul-*

ABBREVIATIONS AND REFERENCES

Quotations from and references to works by Shakespeare are from The Arden Shakespeare Third Series.

ABBREVIATIONS

ABBREVIATIONS USED IN NOTES

app.	appendix
conj.	conjecture
edn	edition
Fig.	figure
fn.	footnote
l., ll.	line, lines
MS	manuscript
SD	stage direction
sig., sigs	signature, signatures
SP	speech prefix

WORKS BY AND PARTLY BY SHAKESPEARE

Ham	*Hamlet*
Lear	*King Lear*
Mac	*Macbeth*
Oth	*Othello*
RJ	*Romeo and Juliet*
TA	*Titus Andronicus*
TS	*The Taming of the Shrew*

REFERENCES

EDITIONS OF *TITO ANDRONICO*

In German:

Brauneck — Manfred Brauneck and Alfred Noe (eds), *Spieltexte der Wanderbühne*, 7 vols (Berlin, 1970–2007), vol. 1 (1970), 461–522

Genée	Rudolph Genée, *Geschichte der Shakespeare'schen Dramen in Deutschland* (Leipzig, 1870), 369–82
Cohn	Albert Cohn, *Shakespeare in Germany in the Sixteenth and Seventeenth Centuries: An Account of English Actors in Germany and the Netherlands and of the Plays Performed by them during the Same Period* (London, 1865; repr. 1971), 156–236
Creizenach	Wilhelm Creizenach (ed.), *Die Schauspiele der Englischen Komödianten* (Berlin, 1888, Darmstadt, 1967)
Marti	Markus Marti (trans. and ed.), *William Shakespeare: Titus Andronicus* (Tubingen, 2008), 360–95
Tieck	Ludwig Tieck, *Deutsches Theater*, 2 vols (Berlin, 1817), vol. 1, 369–407
1620	*Eine sehr klägliche Tragœdia von Tito Andronico vnd der hoffertigen Käyserin, darinnen denckwürdige actiones zubefinden*, in *Engelische Comedien vnd Tragedien* (Leipzig, 1620), sigs 2N4v–2S4r
1624	*Eine sehr klägliche Tragœdia von Tito Andronico vnd der hoffertigen, Käyserin, darinnen denckwürdige actiones zu befinden*, in *Engelische Comedien vnd Tragedien* (Leipzig, 1624), sigs 2N4v–2S4r
In English:	
Brennecke	Ernest Brennecke and Henry Brennecke, *Shakespeare in Germany 1590–1700: With Translations of Five Early Plays* (Chicago, 1964), 18–51
Cohn	Albert Cohn, *Shakespeare in Germany in the Sixteenth and Seventeenth Centuries: An Account of English Actors in Germany and the Netherlands and of the Plays Performed by them during the Same Period* (London, 1865, New York, 1971). English translation by Moritz Lippner, 157–236

OTHER EARLY *TITUS* TEXTS

Ballad	'The Lamentable and Tragical History of Titus Andronicus', Bullough, 6.44–8
Buitendijk	Jan Vos, *Aran en Titus, of Wraak en Weerwraak*, in *Jan Vos: Toneelwerken*, ed. Wim J. C. Buitendijk (Assen, 1975), 47–210

Chapbook	'The Tragical History of Titus Andronicus', in Bullough, 6.35–44
Cohn, 'Breslau'	Anon., Tragoedia gennant Raache gegen Raache Oder der Streitbare Römer *Titus Andronicus* ([Linz], 1699), in Albert Cohn, 'König Lear 1692, and Titus Andronicus 1699 in Breslau aufgeführt', *Jahrbuch der Deutschen Shakespeare-Gesellschaft*, 23 (1888), 266–81 (277–81)
Thomasius	Hieronymus Thomasius, *Titus und Tomyris. Oder Traur-Spiel, Beygenahmt Die Rachbegierige Eyfersucht* (Giessen, 1661)
1656 programme	Anon., *Aran und Titus, Oder Tragödia von Raach und Gegen Raach* ([Schwäbisch Hall], 1656)
1658 playbill	Anon., *Rach und Gegen-Rach* ([Augsburg, 1658])

EDITIONS OF *KUNST ÜBER ALLE KÜNSTE*

In German:

Köhler	Reinhold Köhler (ed.), *Kunst über alle Künste Ein bös Weib gut zu machen: Eine deutsche Bearbeitung von Shakespeare's The Taming of the Shrew aus dem Jahr 1672* (Berlin, 1864)
D1	*Kunst über alle Künste Ein bös Weib gut zu machen* (Rappersweyl: Bey Henning Lieblern, 1672)
D2	*Kunst über alle Künste Ein bös Weib gut zu machen* (Rappersweyl: Bey Henning Lieblern, 1672)

OTHER EARLY CONTINENTAL *SHREW* TEXTS

Sybant	Abraham Sybant, *De Dolle Bruyloft* (Amsterdam, 1654)
Weise	*Comoedie von der bösen Catharine*, in *Schauspiele III*, eds Hans-Gert Roloff and Susanne Kura, in *Christian Weise, Sämtliche Werke*, gen. ed., Roloff, vol. 16 (Berlin, 2002), 1–272
1678 programme	*Der meist aus dem Frantzösischen Herrn Corneille ins Teutsch gebrachte, und vormals in offentlichem Trauer-Spiel zu Leipzig von Herrn Kormarten vorgestellete Polyeuctus, oder Christliche Märtyrer: Welchen mit E. E. E.*

Hochweisen Raths Einwilligung, nebst der Wunderbahren Heyrath Petruvio mit der bösen Katharinen, auff offentlicher Schau-Bühne zu einer nützlichen und erbaulichen Schul-Ubung Die bey der Görlitzischen Ober-Schule Studierende Jugend im October des MDCLXXVIII Jahrs, so Gott will, auffzuführen gewillet. (Görlitz, 1678)

OTHER WORKS CITED

Adams	Joseph Quincy Adams (ed.), *Shakespeare's Titus Andronicus: The First Quarto, 1594* (New York, 1936)
Akademie	*Die deutsche Akademie des 17. Jahrhunderts: Fruchtbringende Gesellschaft*, http://www.die-fruchtbringende-gesellschaft.de/
Åkerman	Susanna Åkerman, *Queen Christina of Sweden and her Circle: The Transformation of a Seventeenth-Century Philosophical Libertine* (Leiden, 1991)
Alamodisch	*Alamodisch Technologisches Interim* ('Rappersweil', 1675), VD17 23:235914D
Alexander	John Alexander, 'Will Kemp, Thomas Sacheville and Pickelhering: A Consanguinity and Confluence of Three Early Modern Clown Personas', *Daphnis*, 36 (2007), 463–86
Arber	Edward Arber, *A transcript of the registers of the Company of stationers of London. 1554–1640 A.D.*, 5 vols (London, 1875–77), vol. 2
Ard² *TA*	J. C. Maxwell (ed.), *Titus Andronicus*, The Arden Shakespeare (1953)
Ard³ *TA* 1995	Jonathan Bate (ed.), *Titus Andronicus*, The Arden Shakespeare (1995)
Ard³ *TA*	Jonathan Bate (ed.), *Titus Andronicus*, The Arden Shakespeare, revised edn (2018)
Ard³ *TS*	Barbara Hodgdon (ed.), *The Taming of the Shrew*, The Arden Shakespeare (2010)
Asper	Helmut G. Asper, *Hanswurst: Studien zum Lustigmacher auf der Berufsschauspielerbühne in Deutschland im 17. und 18. Jahrhundert* (Emsdetten, 1980)

Baesecke	Anna Baesecke, *Das Schauspiel der Englischen Komödianten in Deutschland: Seine dramatische Form und seine Entwicklung* (Halle an der Saale, 1935)
Ball	Gabriele Ball, 'Alles zu Nutzen: The Fruchtbringende Gesellschaft (1617–1680) as a German Renaissance Academy', in *The Reach of the Republic of Letters: Literary and Learned Societies in Late Medieval and Early Modern Europe*, eds Arjan van Dixhoorn and Susie Speakman Sutch, 2 vols (Leiden, 2008), 2.389–422
Bartels, 'Making'	Emily C. Bartels, 'Making More of the Moor: Aaron, Othello, and Renaissance Refashionings of Race', *Shakespeare Quarterly,* 41.4 (1990), 433–54
Bartels, *Speaking*	Emily C. Bartels, *Speaking of the Moor: From Alcazar to Othello* (Philadelphia, 2008)
Barthelemy	Anthony Gerard Barthelemy, *Black Face, Maligned Race: The Representation of Blacks in English Drama from Shakespeare to Southerne* (Baton Rouge, 1999)
Barton	Anne Barton, 'Parks and Ardens', *Proceedings of the British Academy*, 80 (1993), 49–71
Baskervill	Charles Read Baskervill, *The Elizabethan Jig and Related Song Drama* (Chicago, 1929)
Bate and Massai	Jonathan Bate and Sonia Massai, 'Adaptation as Edition', in *The Margins of the Text*, ed. D. C. Greetham (Ann Arbor, 1997), 129–51
Benzing	Josef Benzing, 'Die deutschen Verleger des 16. und 17. Jahrhunderts: eine Neubearbeitung', *Archiv für Geschichte des Buchwesens*, 18 (1977), 1078–322
Berry	Herbert Berry, 'The Date on the "Peacham" Manuscript', *Shakespeare Bulletin*, 17 (1999), 5–6
Beyer and Penman	Jürgen Beyer and Leigh T. I. Penman, 'Printed Autobibliographies from the Sixteenth and Seventeenth Centuries', in *Documenting the Early Modern Book World: Inventories and Catalogues in Manuscript and Print*, eds Malcolm Walsby and Natasha Constantinidou (Leiden, 2013), 161–86
Bindman and Gates	David Bindman and Henry Louis Gates, Jr. (eds), *The Image of the Black in Western Art*, 5 vols (Cambridge, MA, 2010–14)

427

Birken	*Die Tagebücher des Sigmund von Birken*, ed. Joachim Kröll, 2 vols (Würzburg, 1971–4), vol. 1
Blinn and Schmidt	Hansjürgen Blinn and Wolf Gerhard Schmidt, *Shakespeare – deutsch: Bibliographie der Übersetzungen und Bearbeitungen* (Berlin, 2003)
Bolte, '*Kunst*'	Johannes Bolte, 'Zur *Kunst über alle Künste*', *Archiv für Litteraturgeschichte*, 15 (1887), 446
Bolte, 'Schulkomödie'	Johannes Bolte, '*Der Widerspenstigen Zähmung* als Görlitzer Schulkomödie (1678)', *Shakespeare Jahrbuch*, 27 (1892), 124–9
Bolte, *Singspiele*	Johannes Bolte, *Die Singspiele der englischen Komödianten und ihrer Nachfolger in Deutschland, Holland und Skandinavien* (Hamburg, 1893)
Bosman	Anston Bosman, 'Renaissance Intertheater and the Staging of Nobody', *English Literary History*, 71 (2004), 559–85
Braekman	W. Braekman, 'The Relationship of Shakespeare's *Titus Andronicus* to the German Play of 1620 and to Jan Vos's *Aran en Titus*', *Studia Germanica Gandensia*, 9 (1967), 9–117, and 10 (1968), 9–65
Brandt and Hogendoorn	George W. Brandt and Wiebe Hogendoorn (eds), *German and Dutch Theatre, 1600–1848. Theatre in Europe: A Documentary History* (Cambridge, 1993)
Brauer	Adalbert Brauer, 'Grosse, Henning', *Neue Deutsche Biographie*, 7 (1966), 147–8
Brauneck and Noe	Manfred Brauneck and Alfred Noe (eds), *Spieltexte der Wanderbühne*, 7 vols (Berlin, 1970–2007)
Bullough	Geoffrey Bullough (ed.), *Narrative and Dramatic Sources of Shakespeare*, 8 vols (London, 1957–73)
Bürger	Thomas Bürger, *Deutsche Drucke des Barock 1600–1720: Katalog der Herzog August Bibliothek Wolfenbüttel Begründet von Martin Bircher: Register der Verleger, Drucker und Orte* (Munich, 1996)
Cam	*Works*, ed. W. G. Clark and W. A. Wright, The Cambridge Shakespeare, 9 vols (Cambridge, 1863–6)
Catalogus Autumn 1671	*Catalogus Universalis. Hoc est: Designatio omnium Librorum, qui hisce Nundinis Autumnalibus Francofurtensibus & Lipsiensibus* (Leipzig, 1671), VD17 23:269482K

Catalogus Spring 1671   *Catalogus Universalis. Hoc est: Designatio omnium Librorum, qui hisce Nundinis Vernalibus Francofurtensibus & Lipsiensibus* (Leipzig, 1671), VD17 1:067773P

Chambers, *Elizabethan*   E. K. Chambers, *The Elizabethan Stage*, 4 vols (Oxford, 1923)

Chambers, 'Review'   E. K. Chambers, 'Review: The King's Office of the Revels, 1610–1622 by Frank Marcham', *RES*, 1.4 (1925), 479–84

Chambers, *William Shakespeare*   E. K. Chambers, *William Shakespeare: A Study of Facts and Problems*, 2 vols (Oxford, 1930)

Clark   Eleanor Grace Clark, 'Titus and Vespasian', *Modern Language Notes*, 41.8 (1926), 523–7

Clegg and Skeaping   Roger Clegg and Lucie Skeaping, *Singing Simpkin and Other Bawdy Jigs: Musical Comedy on the Shakespearean Stage: Scripts, Music and Context* (Exeter, 2014)

'Complaint'   Anon., 'Titus Andronicus' Complaint', in Richard Johnson, *Golden Garland of Princely Pleasures and Delicate Delights* (1620, STC 14647)

Creizenach   Wilhelm Creizenach (ed.), *Die Schauspiele der Englischen Komödianten* (1888, Darmstadt, 1967)

Dahlberg   Torsten Dahlberg, 'Friedrich Menius und die "englischen" Komödiantenspiele: Sprachliche und text-geschichtliche Beiträge zur Diskussion über zwei Dramensammlungen aus dem 17. Jahrhundert', in *Aspekte der Germanistik: Festschrift für Hans-Friedrich Rosenfeld zum 90. Geburtstag*, ed. Walter Tauber (Göppingen, 1989), 323–37

Deneke   Gertie Deneke, 'Johann Hoffmann (1629–1698)', *Archiv für Geschichte des Buchwesens*, 1 (1958), 337–64

Dent   Robert W. Dent, *Shakespeare's Proverbial Language: An Index* (Berkeley, CA, 1981)

de Sousa   Geraldo U. de Sousa, *Shakespeare's Cross-Cultural Encounters* (New York, 1999)

Dessen and Thomson   Alan C. Dessen and Leslie Thomson, *A Dictionary of Stage Directions in English Drama, 1580–1642* (Cambridge, 1999)

Donecker, 'Arbeiten'   Stefan Donecker, 'Arbeiten und Projekte des Dorpater Professors Friedrich Menius in den

1630er Jahren', *Forschungen zur Baltischen Geschichte*, 6 (2011), 31–60

Donecker, *Origines* — Stefan Donecker, *Origines Livonorum: Frühneuzeitliche Hypothesen zur Herkunft der Esten und Letten* (Cologne, 2017)

Donum nundinale — *Donum nundinale oder Mess-Gaabe; allerhand merkwürdige Lähren, Fragen u. scharfsinnige Beantwortungen wider die Melancholey* ('Rapperschweyl', 1673), VD17 1:642505G

Ellinger — Georg Ellinger, 'Die Dramen des Verfassers der *Kunst über alle Künste*: Ein Beitrag zur Geschichte des deutschen Schauspiels im 17. Jahrhundert', *Archiv für das Studium der neueren Sprachen und Litteraturen*, 88 (1892), 267–86

Eschenburg — Johann Joachim Eschenburg (trans.), *William Shakespear's Schauspiele*, vol. 4 (Zurich, 1775)

Exorcist — *Der viesierliche Exorcist* (1675), appended to *Alamodisch*, sigs 2B7r–2E4v

F — *Mr William Shakespeares Comedies, Histories and Tragedies*, First Folio (1623)

Fassel — Horst Fassel, 'Franz Rheter und das siebenbürgisch-sächsische Schauspiel des 17. Jahrhunderts', in *Migrationen/Standortwechsel: Deutsches Theater in Polen*, eds Artur Pełka, Karolina Prykowska-Michalak, Horst Fassel and Paul S. Ulrich (Łódź and Tübingen, 2007), 180–97

Fiedler — Leslie A. Fiedler, 'The Stranger in Shakespeare: Aaron', in *Titus Andronicus: Critical Essays*, ed. Philip C. Kolin (New York, 1995), 157–62

Flemming — Willi Flemming, *Das Schauspiel der Wanderbühne: Barockdrama*, vol. 3 (Leipzig, 1931)

Flood — John L. Flood, *Poets Laureate in the Holy Roman Empire: A Bio-bibliographical Handbook* (Berlin, 2006)

Foakes, *Diary* — R. A. Foakes (ed.), *Henslowe's Diary*, 2nd edn (Cambridge, 2002)

Foakes, *Illustrations* — R. A. Foakes, *Illustrations of the English Stage, 1580–1642* (Stanford, CA, 1985)

Forssberg — Anna Maria Forssberg, *The Story of War: Church and Propaganda in France and Sweden 1610–1710* (Lund, 2016)

Fredén, 'L'auteur' — Gustaf Fredén, 'A propos du théâtre anglais en Allemagne: l'auteur inconnu des "Comédies et

430

	Tragédies anglaises" de 1620', *Revue de littérature comparée*, 8 (1928), 420–32
Fredén, *Friedrich*	Gustaf Fredén, *Friedrich Menius und das Repertoire der englischen Komödianten in Deutschland* (Stockholm, 1939)
Freeman and Freeman	Arthur Freeman and Janet Ing Freeman, *John Payne Collier: Scholarship and Forgery in the Nineteenth Century*, 2 vols (New Haven, CT, 2004).
Fulda	Ludwig Fulda (ed.), *Die Gegner der zweiten schlesischen Schule, Part 2*, in *Deutsche National-Litteratur*, gen. ed. Joseph Kürchner, vol. 39 (Berlin, 1884)
Fuller	Harold DeW. Fuller, 'The Sources of *Titus Andronicus*', *PMLA*, 16.1 (1901), 1–65
Fürstenau	Moritz Fürstenau, *Zur Geschichte der Musik und des Theaters am Hofe zu Dresden: nach archivalischen Quellen*, vol. 1 (Dresden, 1861)
Gadebusch	Friederich Conrad Gadebusch, *Liefländische Bibliothek nach Alphabetischer Ordnung*, 3 vols (Riga, 1777)
Gärtner	Theodor Gärtner, *Quellenbuch zur Geschichte des Gymnasiums zu Zittau: 1. Heft: Bis zum Tode des Rektors Christian Weise (1708)* (Leipzig, 1905)
Gottsched	Johann Christoph Gottsched, *Nöthiger Vorrath zur Geschichte der deutschen dramatischen Kunst*, 2 vols (Leipzig, 1757–65)
Green	Leslie C. Green, *The Contemporary Law of Armed Conflict*, 3rd edn (Manchester, 2008)
Greer	David Greer, 'Dowland, Robert (c.1591–1641), musician', *ODNB*
Greg, *Diary*	W. W. Greg (ed.), *Henslowe's Diary*, 2 vols (London, 1904–7), vol. 2 (1907)
Greg, *Papers*	W. W. Greg (ed.), *Henslowe Papers: Being Documents Supplementary to Henslowe's Diary* (London, 1907)
Grimm	Jacob and Wilhelm Grimm, *Deutsches Wörterbuch*, 16 vols (1854–1961), http://woerterbuchnetz.de/DWB/
Gstach	Ruth Gstach, Die Liebes Verzweiffelung *des Laurentius von Schnüffis: Eine Bisher unbekannte Tragikomödie der frühen Wanderbühne, mit einem*

	Verzeichnis der erhaltenen Spieltexte (Berlin, 2017)
Gurr	Andrew Gurr, 'Baubles on the Water: Sea Travel in Shakespeare's Time', *SEDERI*, 20 (2010), 57–70
Haekel	Ralf Haekel, *Die englischen Komödianten in Deutschland: Eine Einführung in die Ursprünge des deutschen Berufsschauspiels* (Heidelberg, 2004)
Hall	Kim F. Hall, *Things of Darkness: Economies of Race and Gender in Early Modern England* (Ithaca, NY, 1995)
Halliwell-Phillips	J. O. Halliwell-Phillipps, in *Memoranda on* All's Well that Ends Well, The Two Gentlemen of Verona, Much Ado about Nothing, *and on* Titus Andronicus (Brighton, 1879)
Hart	Alfred Hart, 'The Number of Lines in Shakespeare's Plays', *Review of English Studies*, 8 (1932), 19–28
Hauthal	Günter Hauthal, *400 Jahre Geschichte der Druckerei zu Altenburg, 1594–1994* (Altenburg, 1994)
Hay	David L. Hay (ed.), *Nobody and Somebody* (New York, 1980)
Hayn	Hugo Hayn, *Bibliotheca Germanorum erotica*, 2nd edn (Leipzig, 1885)
Hejnic and Záloha	Josef Hejnic and Jiří Záloha, 'Český Krumlov und die Theatertradition', in *Teatralia Zámecké Knihovny v Českém Krumlově*, 1 (1976), 37–63
Helmers	Helmer J. Helmers, 'Unknown Shrews: Three Transformations of The/A Shrew', in *Gender and Power in Shrew-Taming Narratives, 1500–1700*, eds David Wootton and Graham Holderness (Basingstoke, 2010), 123–44
Hillman and Mazzio	David Hillman and Carla Mazzio (eds), *The Body in Parts: Fantasies of Corporeality in Early Modern Europe* (New York, 1997)
Hilton	Julian K. Hilton, *The 'Englische Komoedianten' in German-speaking States, 1592–1620: A Generation of Touring Performers as Mediators Between English and German Cultures* (DPhil thesis, University of Oxford, 1984)

History	*The History of Titus Andronicus, the Renowned Roman General, Newly Translated from the Italian Copy Printed at Rome* (n.d. [*c.* 1736–64], ESTC N33327)
Hoenselaars	Ton Hoenselaars, 'The Seventeenth-Century Reception of English Renaissance Drama in Europe', *SEDERI*, 10 (1999), 69–87
Hoenselaars and van Dijkhuizen	Ton Hoenselaars and Jan Frans van Dijkhuizen, 'Abraham Sybant tames *The Taming of the Shrew* for the Amsterdam Stage (1654)', *Ilha do Desterro*, 36 (1999), 53–70
Hughes	Alan Hughes (ed.), *Titus Andronicus*, updated edn, New Cambridge Shakespeare (Cambridge, (2006)
Hulfeld and Mansky	Stefan Hulfeld and Matthias Mansky (eds), *Spieltexte der Comœdianten: Teil 1: Deutsches 'Internationaltheater' aus dem Kodex Ia 38.589 der Wienbibliothek* (Göttingen, 2020)
Irace	Kathleen O. Irace, *Reforming the 'Bad' Quartos: Performance and Provenance of Six Shakespearean First Editions* (Newark, NJ, 1994)
Irrthum	*Der Pedantische Irrthum* ('Rapperswell', 1673), VD17 23:252481T
Iyengar	Sujata Iyengar, *Shades of Difference: Mythologies of Skin Color in Early Modern England* (Philadelphia, 2005)
Jaanson	Ene-Lille Jaanson, *Tartu Ülikooli trükikoda 1632–1710: Ajalugu ja trükiste bibliograafia* (Tartu, 2000)
Jantz	Harold Jantz, 'Introduction', *German Baroque Literature, Harold Jantz Collection*, https://www.galesupport.com/psm/2025000
Jones	Eldred Jones, *Othello's Countrymen: The African in English Renaissance Drama* (Oxford, 1965)
Junkers	Herbert Junkers, *Niederländische Schauspieler und niederländisches Schauspiel im 17. und 18. Jahrhundert in Deutschland* (The Hague, 1936)
Katritzky, 'Paintings'	M. A. Katritzky, '"Some tymes J have a shillinge aday, and some tymes nothinge, so that J leve in great poverty": British Actors in the Paintings of Frans Hals', in *Others and Outcasts in Early Modern Europe: Picturing the Social Margins*, ed. Tom Nichols (Aldershot, 2007), 197–214

Katritzky, 'Pickelhering' M. A. Katritzky, 'Pickelhering and Hamlet in Dutch Art: The English Comedians of Robert Browne, John Green, and Robert Reynolds', *Shakespeare Yearbook*, 15 (2005), 113–40

Katritzky, 'Troupes' M. A. Katritzky, 'English Troupes in Early Modern Germany: The Women', in *Transnational Exchange in Early Modern Theater*, eds Robert Henke and Eric Nicholson (Aldershot, 2008), 35–48

Kautsky John H. Kautsky, *The Politics of Aristocratic Empires* (Chapel Hill, NC, 1982)

Keenan Siobhan Keenan, *Travelling Players in Shakespeare's England* (Basingstoke, 2002)

Keith and Rupp Alison Keith and Stephen Rupp (eds), *Metamorphosis: The Changing Face of Ovid in Medieval and Early Modern Europe* (Toronto, 2007)

Keller et al. Andreas Keller, Susanne Kura, Brigitta Lizinski, Markus Mollitor, Hans-Gert Roloff, Benedikt Sommer and Volkhard Wels, 'Beiträge zur Christian-Weise-Bibliographie I', *Daphnis*, 24 (1995), 645–708

Klein Karl Kurt Klein, 'Shakespeare in Siebenbürgen', *Siebenbürgische Vierteljahrsschrift*, 61 (1938), 233–8

Klöker Martin Klöker, 'Ein Dichter kommt in die Stadt: Flemmings literarische Kontaktaufnahme in Riga', in *Was ein Poëte kan! Studien zum Werk von Paul Fleming (1609–1640)*, eds Stefanie Arend and Claudius Sittig (Berlin, 2012), 297–316

Knack Anon., *A Knacke to Knowe a Knave* (1594, STC 15027)

Knutson Roslyn L. Knutson, '*Henslowe's Diary* and the Economics of Play Revision for Revival, 1592–1603', *Theatre Research*, 10.1 (1985), 1–18

Königes Sohne *Eine schöne lustig triumphirende Comœdia von eines Königes Sohne auß Engellandt vnd des Königes Tochter auß Schottlandt*, in *Engelische Comedien vnd Tragedien* (Leipzig, 1620), sigs R6v–Y3v

Korhonen Anu Korhonen, 'Washing the Ethiopian White: Conceptualising Black Skin in Renaissance

England', *Black Africans in Renaissance Europe*, eds T. F. Earle and K. J. P. Lowe (Cambridge, 2005), 94–112

Kröll   Joachim Kröll (ed.), *Die Tagebücher des Sigmund von Birken*, 2 vols (Würzburg, 1971–4)

Kühlmann   Wilhelm Kühlmann et al. (eds), *Killy Literaturlexikon: Autoren und Werke des deutschsprachigen Kulturraums*, 2nd edn, vol. 6 (Berlin, 2009)

Levin   Richard Louis Levin, 'The Longleat Manuscript and *Titus Andronicus*', *Shakespeare Quarterly*, 53.3 (2002), 323–40

Limon   Jerzy Limon, *Gentlemen of a Company: English Players in Central and Eastern Europe 1590–1660* (Cambridge, 1985)

Loomba   Ania Loomba, *Shakespeare, Race, and Colonialism* (Oxford, 2002)

Lost Plays Database   Lost Plays Database, https://lostplays.folger.edu

Lowe, 'Representing'   Kate Lowe, '"Representing" Africa: Ambassadors and Princes from Christian Africa to Renaissance Italy and Portugal, 1402–1608', *Transactions of the Royal Historical Society*, 17 (2007), 101–28

Lowe, 'Stereotyping'   Kate Lowe, 'The Stereotyping of Black Africans in Renaissance Europe', in *Black Africans in Renaissance Europe*, eds T. F. Earle and K. J. P. Lowe (Cambridge, 2005), 17–47

Malone-Boswell   *Variorum: The Plays and Poems of William Shakespeare, with the corrections and illustrations of various commentators, comprehending a life of the poet and an enlarged history of the stage, by the late Edmond Malone, with a new glossarial index*, ed. James Boswell, 21 vols (1821)

Marcus   Leah. S. Marcus, *Unediting the Renaissance: Shakespeare, Marlowe, Milton* (London, 1996)

Markus   Paul Markus (ed.), 'Der neugeborne Jesus, den Hirten und Weisen offenbaret. Von Mag. Christian Keimann', *Neues Lausitzisches Magazin*, 112 (1936), 21–75

Marlow   Richard Marlow, 'Farnaby, Giles (d. 1640), composer', *ODNB*

Maurer   Margaret Maurer, 'Constering Bianca: *The Taming of the Shrew* and *The Woman's Prize, or The Tamer*

	Tamed, *Medieval and Renaissance Drama in England*, 14 (2001), 186–206
McCarthy and Schlueter	Dennis McCarthy and June Schlueter, 'A Shakespeare/North Collaboration: *Titus Andronicus* and *Titus and Vespasian*', *Shakespeare Survey*, 67 (2014), 85–101
Metamorphosis	*Die seltzame Metamorphosis, der Sutorischen in eine Magistrale, Person* (1673), appended to *Pedantische Irrthum*, sigs L11r–N12v
Metz, '*History*'	G. Harold Metz, '*The History of Titus Andronicus* and Shakespeare's Play', *N&Q*, n.s. 22.4 (1975), 163–6
Metz, *Studies*	G. Harold Metz, *Shakespeare's Earliest Tragedy: Studies in* Titus Andronicus (Madison, 1996)
Metz, 'Versions'	G. Harold Metz, 'Titus Andronicus: Three Versions of the Story', *N&Q*, n.s. 35.4 (1988), 451–5
Meurer	Susanne Meurer, '"In Verlegung des Autoris": Joachim von Sandrart and the Seventeenth-Century Book Market', *The Library*, 7.4 (2006), 419–49
Meyer	C. F. Meyer, 'Englische Komödianten am Hofe des Herzogs Philipp Julius von Pommern-Wolgast', *Shakespeare Jahrbuch*, 38 (1902), 196–211
Miller	Stephen Roy Miller (ed.), *The Taming of a Shrew: The 1594 Quarto*, The New Cambridge Shakespeare: The Early Quartos (Cambridge, 1998)
Moran	Bruce T. Moran, 'Courts and Academies', in *The Cambridge History of Science: Volume 3: Early Modern Science*, eds Katharine Park and Lorraine Daston (Cambridge, 2006), 251–71
Morgan	Oliver Morgan, *Turn-Taking in Shakespeare* (Oxford, 2019)
Munro	John Munro, '*Titus Andronicus*', *Times Literary Supplement* (10 June 1949), 385
Nassau-Sarolea	Annie van Nassau-Sarolea, 'Abraham Sybant, Strolling Player and First Dutch Shakespeare Translator', *Theatre Research / Recherches Théâtrales*, 13.1 (1973), 38–59
Ndiaye, 'Aaron's Roots'	Noémie Ndiaye, 'Aaron's Roots: Spaniards, Englishmen, and Blackamoors in *Titus Andronicus*', *Early Theatre*, 19.2 (2016), 59–80

Ndiaye, 'Everyone'   Noémie Ndiaye, '"Everyone Breeds in His Own Image": Staging the *Aethiopica* across the Channel', *Renaissance Drama*, 44.2 (2016), 157–85

Nicklas   Thomas Nicklas, *Macht oder Recht: Frühneuzeitliche Politik im Obersächsischen Reichskreis* (Stuttgart, 2002)

Nordström, 'Editor'   Johan Nordström, 'The Editor of "Englische Comoedien und Tragoedien" discovered', Universitätsbibliothek Uppsala, Nachlass Johan Nordström 31

Nordström, 'Friedrich'   Johan Nordström, 'Friedrich Menius: En äventyrlig Dorpatprofessor och hans glömda insats i det engelska komediantdramats historia', *Samlaren*, 2 (1921), 42–91

NOS   *The New Oxford Shakespeare: The Complete Works: Modern Critical Edition*, gen. eds Gary Taylor, John Jowett, Terri Bourus and Gabriel Egan (Oxford, 2016)

NOS CRE   *The New Oxford Shakespeare: The Complete Works: Critical Reference Edition*, 2 vols, eds Gary Taylor, John Jowett, Terri Bourus and Gabriel Egan (Oxford, 2017)

ODNB   *Oxford Dictionary of National Biography* (Oxford, 2004), www.oxforddnb.com

OED   *Oxford English Dictionary*, 3rd edn (Oxford, 2006), www.oed.com

Oxf   *William Shakespeare: The Complete Works*, eds Stanley Wells and Gary Taylor, with John Jowett and William Montgomery (Oxford, 1986)

Paisey   David L. Paisey, 'German Printers, Booksellers and Publishers of the Seventeenth Century: Some Amendments and Additions to Benzing', *Gutenberg-Jahrbuch*, 64 (1989), 165–79

Paré   Ambroise Paré, *The workes of that famous chirurgion Ambrose Parey translated out of Latine and compared with the French*, trans. Thomas Johnson (1634, STC 19189)

Peacham, *Gentleman*   Henry Peacham, *The Compleat Gentleman* (1622, STC 19502)

Peacham, *Minerva*   Henry Peacham, *Minerva Britanna* (1612, STC 19511)

Pescheck   Christian Adolf Pescheck, *Handbuch der Geschichte von Zittau*, vol. 2 (Zittau, 1834)

Philippi	Karl Ferdinand Philippi, *Kleines lateinisches Conversationslexicon*, 2 vols (Dresden, 1825)
Possenspiel	*Singendes Possenspiel Die doppelt betrogene Eyfersucht vorstellend*, appended to *Kunst*, sigs K1r–11r
Price	Lawrence Marsden Price, *English Literature in Germany* (Berkeley, CA, 1953)
Q1 *TA*	the First Quarto of *Titus Andronicus* (1594)
Q1 *TS*	the First Quarto of *The Taming of the Shrew* (1631)
Q2 *TA*	the Second Quarto of *Titus Andronicus* (1600)
Q3 *TA*	the Third Quarto of *Titus Andronicus* (1611)
Quellen	*Quellen zur Geschichte der Stadt Kronstadt in Siebenbürgen* (Kronstadt, 1915), vol. 6
Ravenscroft	Edward Ravenscroft, *Titus Andronicus, or the Rape of Lavinia. Acted at the Theatre Royall, A Tragedy. Alter'd from Mr Shakespears Works* (1687)
Richter	Werner Richter, *Liebeskampf 1630 und Schaubühne 1670: Ein Beitrag zur deutschen Theatergeschichte des siebzehnten Jahrhunderts*, Palestra 78 (Berlin, 1910)
Ricquier	Kirsten Ricquier, 'The Early Modern Transmission of the Ancient Greek Romances: A Bibliographic Survey', *Ancient Narrative*, 15 (2019), 1–34
Roloff and Kura	Hans-Gert Roloff and Susanne Kura (eds), *Comoedie von der bösen Catharine*, in *Schauspiele III*, in *Christian Weise, Sämtliche Werke*, gen. ed. Hans-Gert Roloff, vol. 16 (Berlin, 2002), 1–272
Royster	Francesca T. Royster, 'White-limed Walls: Whiteness and Gothic Extremism in Shakespeare's *Titus Andronicus*', *Shakespeare Quarterly*, 51.4 (2000), 432–55
Rudin, 'Textbibliothek'	Bärbel Rudin, 'Die Textbibliothek der eggenbergischen Hofkomödianten in Ceský Krumlov/Böhmisch Krumau (1676–1691). Eine kulturgeografische Zeitreise', in *Sammeln, Lesen, Übersetzen als höfische Praxis der Frühen Neuzeit: Die böhmische Bibliothek der Fürsten Eggenberg im Kontext der Fürsten- and Fürstinnenbibliotheken der Zeit*, eds Jill Bepler and Helga Meise, Wolfenbütteler Forschungen 126 (Wiesbaden, 2010), 73–106

Rudin, '"Zwei Mal"'   Bärbel Rudin, '"Zwei Mal in der Wochen Komödie": Das erste deutsche Hoftheater in Heidelberg: Zur ortsfesten Subventionierung professioneller Schauspielkunst seit 1656', *Daphnis*, 46 (2018), 467–503

Salvadore   Matteo Salvadore, *The African Prester John and the Birth of Ethiopian–European Relations, 1402–1555* (2017)

Sanford   James Sanford, *The Amorous and Tragicall Tales of Plutarch Wherevnto is Annexed the Hystorie of Cariclea & Theagenes* (1567, STC 20072)

Sargent   Ralph M. Sargent, 'The Source of *Titus Andronicus*', *Studies in Philology*, 46.2 (1949), 167–83

Scheitler   Irmgard Scheitler, *Schauspielmusik: Funktion und Ästhetik im deutschsprachigen Drama der Frühen Neuzeit*, 2 vols (Tutzing, 2013)

Schindler   Otto G. Schindler, '*Romeo und Julia* auf Schloß Krumau, der *Basilisco* von Kolin und das Armenspital in Kukus: Über böhmische Theaterhandschriften in Wiener Bibliotheken und das Wasserzeichen in Wissenschaft und Praxis', *Biblos*, 44.1 (1995), 81–103

Schlueter, 'Across'   June Schlueter, 'Across the Narrow Sea: The 1620 Leipzig Volume of English Plays', in *The Text, the Play, and the Globe: Essays on Literary Influence in Shakespeare's World and his Work in Honor of Charles R. Forker*, ed. Joseph Candido (Lanham, MD, 2016), 231–50

Schlueter, '*Fortunati*'   June Schlueter, 'New Light on Dekker's *Fortunati*', *Medieval and Renaissance Drama in England*, 26 (2013), 120–35

Schlueter, 'Longleat'   June Schlueter, 'New Light on the Longleat Manuscript', unpublished typescript, 28 pp.

Schlueter, 'Rereading'   June Schlueter, 'Rereading the Peacham Drawing', *Shakespeare Quarterly*, 50.2 (1999), 171–84

Schrickx, *Foreign*   Willem Schrickx, *Foreign Envoys and Travelling Players in the Age of Shakespeare and Jonson* (Wetteren, 1986)

Schrickx, '"Pickleherring"'   Willem Schrickx, '"Pickleherring" and English Actors in Germany', *Shakespeare Survey*, 36 (1983), 135–47

Schuster	David Schuster, *Mahomets und Türcken Grewel* (Frankfurt, 1664)
Seelig	Lorenz Seelig, 'Christoph Jamnitzer's "Moor's Head": A Late Renaissance Drinking Vessel', in *Black Africans in Renaissance Europe*, eds T. F. Earle and K. J. P. Lowe (Cambridge, 2005), 181–209
Seelmann	W. Seelmann, 'Rollenhagen, Gabriel', *Allgemeine Deutsche Biographie*, 29 (1889), 84–7
Smith	Ian Smith, 'The Textile Black Body: Race and "Shadowed Livery" in *The Merchant of Venice*', in *The Oxford Handbook of Shakespeare and Embodiment: Gender, Sexuality, and Race*, ed. Valerie Traub (Oxford, 2016), 170–85
Spicer	Joaneath Spicer, 'Heliodorus's *An Ethiopian Story* in Seventeenth Century European Art', in *The Image of the Black in Western Art*, eds David Bindman and Henry Louis Gates (Cambridge, MA, 2010), vol. 3, part 1, 307–35
Streete	Adrian Streete, 'Nashe, Shakespeare, and the Bishops' Bible', *Notes and Queries*, n.s. 41.7 (2000), 56–8
Taylor and Loughnane	Gary Taylor and Rory Loughnane, 'The Canon and Chronology of Shakespeare's Works', in *The New Oxford Shakespeare Authorship Companion*, eds Gary Taylor and Gabriel Egan (Oxford, 2017), 417–602
Thiede	Friedrich Thiede, *Pomerania: Geschichte und Beschreibung des Pommernlandes*, 2 vols (Stettin, 1844)
Thompson	Ann Thompson (ed.), *The Taming of the Shrew*, New Cambridge Shakespeare (Cambridge, 1984)
Tobin	J. J. M. Tobin, 'Nomenclature and the Dating of *Titus Andronicus*', *Notes and Queries*, n.s. 31.2 (1984), 186–7
van Ingen	Ferdinand van Ingen (ed.), *Philipp von Zesen: Sämtliche Werke*, vol. 12 (Berlin, 1985)
Vaughan	Virginia Mason Vaughan, *Performing Blackness on English Stages, 1500–1800* (Cambridge, 2005)
Vaughan and Vaughan	Alden T. Vaughan and Virginia Mason Vaughan, 'Before *Othello*: Elizabethan Representations of Sub-Saharan Africa', *William and Mary Quarterly*, 54.1 (1997), 19–44

VD16	*Verzeichnis der im deutschen Sprachbereich erschienenen Drucke des 16. Jahrhunderts*, http://www.vd16.de/
VD17	*Verzeichnis der im deutschen Sprachraum erschienenen Drucke des 17. Jahrhunderts*, http://www.vd17.de/
Vickers	Brian Vickers, *Shakespeare, Co-Author: A Historical Study of Five Collaborative Plays* (Oxford, 2002)
von Blow and Powell	Gottfried von Blow and Wilfred Powell, 'Diary of the Journey of Philip Julius, Duke of Stettin-Pomerania, through England in the year 1602', *Transactions of the Royal Historical Society*, 6 (1892), 1–67
Waith	Eugene M. Waith (ed.), *Titus Andronicus* (Oxford, 1984)
Wander	Karl Friedrich Wilhelm Wander, *Deutsches Sprichwörter-Lexicon*, 5 vols (Leipzig, 1866–80), https://www.woerterbuchnetz.de/Wander
Watanabe-O'Kelly, *Court Culture*	Helen Watanabe-O'Kelly, *Court Culture in Dresden: From Renaissance to Baroque* (Basingstoke, 2002)
Watanabe-O'Kelly, 'Early Modern'	Helen Watanabe-O'Kelly, 'The Early Modern Period (1450–1720)', in *The Cambridge History of German Literature*, ed. Helen Watanabe-O'Kelly (Cambridge, 1997), 92–146
Weller	Emil Weller, *Die falschen und fingierten Druckorte: Repertorium der seit Erfindung der Buchdruckerkunst unter falscher Firma erschienenen deutschen, lateinischen und französischen Schriften* (Leipzig, 1858)
Wiggins	Martin Wiggins, with Catherine Richardson, *British Drama 1533–1642: A Catalogue*, 9 vols published (Oxford, 2011–), vol 2: *1567–89* (2012), vol. 3: *1590–1597* (2013), vol. 4: *1598–1602* (2014)
Williams	Kelsey Jackson Williams, 'Canon before Canon, Literature before Literature: Thomas Pope Blount and the Scope of Early Modern Learning', *Huntington Library Quarterly*, 77 (2014), 177–99
Wilson	John Dover Wilson, '*Titus Andronicus* on the Stage in 1595', *Shakespeare Survey*, 1 (1948), 17–22

Wollin   Carsten Wollin, 'Der erotische Daktylus', *Archivum Latinitatis Medii Aevi (Bulletin Du Cange)*, 70 (2012), 147–61

Worp   J. A. Worp, *De Invloed van Seneca's Treurspelen op ons Tooneel* (Amsterdam, 1892)

Záloha, 'Divadelní'   Jiří Záloha, 'Divadelní Život na Českokrumlovském Zámku v 2. Polovině 17. Století', *Acta Musei Nationalis Prague*, 40.2 (1986), 53–79

Záloha, 'Eggenbergischen'   Jiří Záloha, 'Zu den Anfängen der "Eggenbergischen Hofkomödianten" in Böhmisch Krumau', in *Maske und Kothurn*, 48 (2002), 265–70

INDEX

Milton Keynes UK
Ingram Content Group UK Ltd.
UKHW020349070823
426434UK00009B/225

9 781350 262430